Communications in Computer and Information Science 2337

Series Editors

Gang Li ⓘ, *School of Information Technology, Deakin University, Burwood, VIC, Australia*
Joaquim Filipe ⓘ, *Polytechnic Institute of Setúbal, Setúbal, Portugal*
Zhiwei Xu, *Chinese Academy of Sciences, Beijing, China*

Rationale

The CCIS series is devoted to the publication of proceedings of computer science conferences. Its aim is to efficiently disseminate original research results in informatics in printed and electronic form. While the focus is on publication of peer-reviewed full papers presenting mature work, inclusion of reviewed short papers reporting on work in progress is welcome, too. Besides globally relevant meetings with internationally representative program committees guaranteeing a strict peer-reviewing and paper selection process, conferences run by societies or of high regional or national relevance are also considered for publication.

Topics

The topical scope of CCIS spans the entire spectrum of informatics ranging from foundational topics in the theory of computing to information and communications science and technology and a broad variety of interdisciplinary application fields.

Information for Volume Editors and Authors

Publication in CCIS is free of charge. No royalties are paid, however, we offer registered conference participants temporary free access to the online version of the conference proceedings on SpringerLink (http://link.springer.com) by means of an http referrer from the conference website and/or a number of complimentary printed copies, as specified in the official acceptance email of the event.

CCIS proceedings can be published in time for distribution at conferences or as post-proceedings, and delivered in the form of printed books and/or electronically as USBs and/or e-content licenses for accessing proceedings at SpringerLink. Furthermore, CCIS proceedings are included in the CCIS electronic book series hosted in the SpringerLink digital library at http://link.springer.com/bookseries/7899. Conferences publishing in CCIS are allowed to use Online Conference Service (OCS) for managing the whole proceedings lifecycle (from submission and reviewing to preparing for publication) free of charge.

Publication process

The language of publication is exclusively English. Authors publishing in CCIS have to sign the Springer CCIS copyright transfer form, however, they are free to use their material published in CCIS for substantially changed, more elaborate subsequent publications elsewhere. For the preparation of the camera-ready papers/files, authors have to strictly adhere to the Springer CCIS Authors' Instructions and are strongly encouraged to use the CCIS LaTeX style files or templates.

Abstracting/Indexing

CCIS is abstracted/indexed in DBLP, Google Scholar, EI-Compendex, Mathematical Reviews, SCImago, Scopus. CCIS volumes are also submitted for the inclusion in ISI Proceedings.

How to start

To start the evaluation of your proposal for inclusion in the CCIS series, please send an e-mail to ccis@springer.com.

Nimmi Rangaswamy · Gavin Robert Sim ·
Pranjal Protim Borah
Editors

Human-Computer Interaction

Design and Research

15th Indian Conference, IndiaHCI 2024
Mumbai, India, November 7–9, 2024
Proceedings, Part I

 Springer

Editors
Nimmi Rangaswamy
IIIT Hyderabad
Hyderabad, Telangana, India

Gavin Robert Sim
University of Central Lancashire
Preston, UK

Pranjal Protim Borah (iD)
IIT Jodhpur
Jodhpur, Rajasthan, India

ISSN 1865-0929   ISSN 1865-0937 (electronic)
Communications in Computer and Information Science
ISBN 978-3-031-80828-9   ISBN 978-3-031-80829-6 (eBook)
https://doi.org/10.1007/978-3-031-80829-6

This Springer imprint is published by the registered company Springer Nature Switzerland AG
The registered company address is: Gewerbestrasse 11, 6330 Cham, Switzerland

If disposing of this product, please recycle the paper.

Preface

The IndiaHCI conference series is a premier platform for Human-Computer Interaction (HCI) in India. First organized in 2004, it has been held annually since 2010. Initially, groups of volunteers managed the conferences. HCI Professionals Association of India was formed as a not-for-profit organization in 2013, and it has since taken over the financial responsibility for the conference. Previous conferences were held in different cities in India, namely Mumbai, Bangalore, Pune, Delhi, Guwahati and Hyderabad.

IndiaHCI 2024 was the 15th edition of the conference. This year's conference featured multiple tracks, each undergoing a rigorous review process, as outlined below.

(I)Track - Papers:

The **Papers Track** offered a platform for researchers to showcase their work across diverse areas of HCI and design. It offered an opportunity to share pioneering and cutting-edge research, engage in meaningful scholarly discussions, and contribute to advancing these fields.

Each paper underwent a rigorous review process overseen by the two Paper Chairs (Program Committee Chairs). Each submission was assigned two Associate Chairs and two external reviewers, all of whom were experts in the field of HCI. The second Associate Chair (2AC) and the external reviewers provided blind reviews, while the first Associate Chair (1AC) contributed a meta-review. Each reviewer was tasked with evaluating approximately 3 to 4 papers. Authors of selected papers received the initial reviews and were given the opportunity to submit a 500-word rebuttal to address questions or clarify any misunderstandings raised by the reviewers. The final decision on whether to accept or reject a paper was made during a virtual Program Committee (PC) meeting, where the Paper Chairs, 1AC and 2AC discussed each submission, managing any conflicts. High-quality papers were accepted directly, while promising papers requiring revisions were shepherded and accepted only if the shepherd approved the changes.

All acceptances were conditional, contingent on potential changes suggested by the Papers Committee for the final camera-ready draft. The primary author of each accepted paper received detailed instructions on how to submit a final, publication-ready version of the paper. Formal acceptance into IndiaHCI was granted once authors revised their submissions and submitted a final draft for approval by the Program Committee.

There were 84 submissions for the Papers Track, of which 15 were accepted as full papers.

(2) Other Tracks - Game Design, Student Research Consortium, Posters and Demo, Artworks and Installations:

In addition to the Papers Track, the conference included other tracks such as Game Design, Student Research Consortium, Posters and Demos, and Artworks and Installations.

- The **Game Design Track** provided a platform for individuals passionate about games, game design, applied games, gamification, play and related areas to engage in the conference. This Track offered opportunities for participants to share insights, explore emerging trends and contribute to the evolving field of game design and play.

- The **Student Research Consortium Track** offered undergraduate, postgraduate and doctoral students unique opportunities to present their research efforts. This Track facilitated connections with peers, helped expand professional networks and provided valuable feedback and guidance from experts, supporting students in refining their research.
- The **Posters and Demos Track** provided students and professionals from diverse disciplines a platform to collaborate in advancing HCI for positive social impact. It offered an opportunity to present innovative ideas, connect with peers, expand networks and gain insights from domain experts, fostering cross-disciplinary engagement.
- The **Artworks and Installations Track** offered a space for artists and researchers exploring the intersection of art, design, technology and HCI. This Track aimed to build a community of creative professionals and researchers, encouraging exploration of how these fields converge and inspiring thought-provoking discussions on the role of art and technology in shaping human experiences.

The Game Design Track featured two categories: short papers and demos. The review process for short papers followed a double-blind format, while demos underwent a single-blind review. Each submission in both categories received three reviews—two individual reviews and one meta-review—by domain experts.

The Student Research Consortium and Posters and Demos Tracks followed a double-blind review process. Each submission received three reviews (two individual reviews and one meta-review) from domain experts. For the Student Research Consortium, the chairs also ensured that selected papers were shepherded, with final acceptance granted only upon the shepherd's approval.

Submissions for the Artworks and Installations Track were reviewed by the Track Chairs and a panel of domain experts through a single-blind peer-review process. Each paper in this track received three reviews—two individual reviews and one meta-review.

The final decision on accepting or rejecting papers in all these tracks was made during a virtual meeting where the track chairs discussed each submission. All acceptances were conditional, pending revisions suggested by the reviewers. The primary authors of accepted papers were provided with detailed instructions on submitting a final, camera-ready version. Formal acceptance into IndiaHCI was confirmed after authors revised their submissions and received approval from the track chairs.

- There were 48 submissions in the Game Design Track, of which three were accepted as full-length papers and six as short papers.
- There were 54 submissions in the Student Research Consortium (SRC) Track, of which seven were accepted as full-length papers and one as a short paper.
- There were 36 submissions in the Posters and Demos Track, of which four were accepted as full-length papers and two as short papers.
- There were 13 submissions in the Artworks and Installations Track, of which three were accepted as short papers.

October 2024

Nimmi Rangaswamy
Gavin Robert Sim
Pranjal Protim Borah

Organization

General Chairs

Pallavi Rao Gadahad   IIT Bombay, India
Bhakti Khandekar   eQ Technologic, India

Program Chairs

Khyati Priya   IIT Bombay, India
Pallavi Rao Gadahad   IIT Bombay, India

Paper Chairs

Gavin Sim   University of Central Lancashire, UK
Nimmi Rangaswamy   IIIT Hyderabad, India

Associate Chairs

Aakash Johry   IIT Delhi, India
Abhishek Shrivastava   IIT Guwahati, India
Anirudha Joshi   IIT Bombay, India
Ayushi Tandon   Mahindra University, India
Devanuj Balkrishan   JK Lakshmipat University, India
Dipanjan Chakraborty   BITS Pilani, India
Gautami Tripathi   Jamia Hamdard, India
Girish Dalvi   IIT Bombay, India
Jyoti Kumar   IIT Delhi, India
Khyati Priya   IIT Bombay, India
Malay Dhamelia   IIT Bombay, India
Mamata Rao   NID Ahmedabad, India
Manjiri Joshi   Swansea University, UK
Manohar Swaminathan   Microsoft Research, India
Naveen Bagalkot   Srishti Manipal Institute, India
Pallavi Rao   IIT Bombay, India
Pradipta Biswas   Indian Institute of Science, India

Pranjal Borah	IIT Jodhpur, India
Pratiti Sarkar	Paytm, India
Pushpendra Singh	IIIT Delhi, India
Ravi Mahamuni	TCS Research, India
Sandeep Athavale	TCS Research, India
Saurabh Tewari	IIT Delhi, India
Sayan Sarcar	Birmingham City University, UK
Seema Krishnakumar	IIT Hyderabad, India
Shrikant Ekbote	MIT Institute of Design, India
Siddharth Gulati	University of Manchester, UK
Wricha Mishra	MIT ADT University, India

Game Design Chairs

Malay Dhamelia	IIT Bombay, India
Sandeep Athavale	TCS, India
Aakash Johry	IIT Delhi, India

Student Research Consortium Chairs

Pranjal Borah	IIT Jodhpur, India
Saurabh Tewari	IIT Delhi, India

Posters and Demos Chairs

Sajan Pillai	DP World, India
Amaltas Khan	NID Vijayawada, India

Artworks and Installations Chairs

Jayesh S. Pillai	IIT Bombay, India
Harshit Agarwal	Adobe, India

Proceedings Team

Proceedings Chair

Pranjal Borah   IIT Jodhpur, India

Proceedings Coordinators

Sayali Tharali   IIT Bombay, India
Nimmi Thomas   IIT Bombay, India

Contents – Part I

Contents – Part II

Game Design

Student Research Consortium

Posters and Demos

Artworks and Installations

Will Changing My Phone Make My Photographs Better? Exploring the Perception of the Quality of Photographs Shot on an iPhone and an Android Phone

Palak Katiyar$^{(\boxtimes)}$ ⓘ, Ishita Sharma ⓘ, and Anirudha Joshi ⓘ

Indian Institute of Technology Bombay, Mumbai, India
palak.katiyar19@gmail.com

Abstract. As smartphone brands use strategic marketing practices to influence purchasing decisions, consumer perceptions become increasingly important. In this paper, we investigate the question: "Is there any difference in the perceived quality of photographs shot on smartphones from different brands?" In the current market, iPhones are perceived to be high-quality, high-price devices, while several Android phones are considered to be more moderate-price, moderate-quality devices. Through this study, we investigate whether photographs shot on an iPhone and on an Android phone have different Perceived Photograph Quality scores. Additionally, we explore whether the presence of a label indicating the brand of the device used affects the perception of the photograph. We present a systematic, within-subjects, counterbalanced study with 36 participants, each of whom assessed 36 photographs, 18 shot on an iPhone and 18 on an Android phone. The photographs were presented in three conditions: non-labelled, a label indicating the correct source device, and a label indicating the wrong source device. The results showed that in the non-labelled condition, there was no significant difference in the Perceived Photograph Quality scores based on the devices used (iPhone/Android) ($p = 0.793$). However, the scores increased significantly when any label (either correct or wrong) was present ($p = 0.006$). This indicates that the perceived value of a photograph increases when it is associated with a brand label.

Keywords: HCI · Perceived Value · Smartphone Camera · Mobile Photography · Brand Perception · Interaction Design

1 Introduction

In today's competitive market, branding serves as a critical tool for companies striving to differentiate themselves and capture consumer attention [54]. At the

---

P. Katiyar and I. Sharma—Contributed equally to this work.

N. Rangaswamy et al. (Eds.): IndiaHCI 2024, CCIS 2337, pp. 1–25, 2025.
https://doi.org/10.1007/978-3-031-80829-6_1

heart of effective branding lies the strategic use of brand labels, which go beyond mere visual markers to encapsulate a brand's values, personality, and positioning in the market [2,68]. Watermarked labels on smartphone photographs like "Shot on iPhone" [1] and "Shot on One Plus" [64] exemplify the strategic utilisation of brand labels in marketing. These strategies not only showcase the impressive camera capabilities of devices but also cultivate a feeling of exclusivity and community among users. By associating the brand name with premium photography experiences and social prestige, such campaigns could reinforce brand biases and shape consumer perceptions of quality.

Yet, the influence of brand labels extends far beyond their visual appeal. They serve as conduits for the formation of brand perception - the predispositions consumers hold towards certain brands based on past experiences, emotions, or societal perceptions [56]. These perceptions shape consumer behaviour, influencing purchase decisions, brand loyalty, and the overall image of a company and its products. For instance, in the smartphone industry, consumers often exhibit loyalty to specific brands like Apple or Samsung [7,57], with preferences possibly stemming from past positive experiences, perceptions of social status associated with owning certain brands, or even the influence of peer recommendations.

However, today these people are not only consumers of technology products but also active generators of content, leveraging their devices for the same [50]. This dual role necessitates smartphones with advanced specifications tailored for high-quality user-generated content as well as daily usage. Key attributes such as high-resolution cameras, robust image processing capabilities, ample storage, durability, better displays and efficient battery life are critical in consumer decision-making [27]. According to a poll [63], camera quality is often the paramount consideration, with features like multiple lenses, high megapixel counts, and advanced video capabilities being particularly sought after. Today many movies, short films, and music videos are being shot with smartphones as well, showcasing their versatility and exceeding the limits of user-generated content. This trend highlights the advanced technology of these devices, proving their efficacy in professional-grade content creation. Companies often sponsor these ventures, leveraging the association to promote their brand and demonstrate their products' superior capabilities. For example, "Jackals & Fireflies," the latest short film from Charlie Kauffman [67], was sponsored by Samsung and shot entirely on their Galaxy S22 Ultra smartphone. Through these marketing strategies, ordinary consumers' pursuit of professional-quality content drives many of them to invest in high-end devices, aiming to enhance their social media presence. In response to these market demands, smartphone manufacturers strategically position their products to highlight these attributes, ensuring they meet consumer needs for superior user-generated content creation.

Companies emphasize their devices' cutting-edge camera technologies and seamless content-sharing capabilities in their marketing campaigns and through sponsored research endeavours. However, such research is frequently sponsored by corporations, and we rarely find outcomes of research that do not show the corporation in a positive light being published. Claims regarding superior camera performance and overall quality significantly influence brand preferences, and hence there is a need for unbiased, systematic studies to provide unbiased insights into the quality of user-generated content.

We, independent of brand affiliations, aim to investigate the effect of brand perception on the quality of mobile photography. We shot 18 "identical" photograph pairs, each on an iPhone 11 and a Samsung M53 5G phone, resulting in 36 photographs. The original photograph was shot without any labels (non-labelled - NL). We created two conditions of each photograph, one which was correctly labelled (CL) with the brand of the device, and another which was wrongly labelled (WL). We systematically investigated the perceived quality of this set of photographs through a within-subjects, counterbalanced study with 36 participants (all university students).

In this study, we draw on key Human-Computer Interaction (HCI) theories to further explore the impact of design on user perception. Affective Design, which examines how design elements evoke emotional responses, is central to understanding how brand labels can influence perceived photograph quality [55]. Additionally, Social Influence Theory helps frame our investigation by considering how social cues, such as brand reputation, shape user evaluations of products [15]. By integrating these theories, we aim to provide a comprehensive analysis of how design not only affects user experience but also drives broader consumer perceptions.

We pose the following research questions:

1. Is there a difference in the perceived quality of photographs shot on an iPhone and an Android phone?
2. Does the perceived quality of a photograph get biased by the existence of a label that draws attention to a brand of the device used for capturing the image? To what extent do people get biased by the correct label? To what extent do people get biased by the wrong label?

Through this paper, we make the following contributions:

1. We propose a lab-based method to compare the perceived quality of device-created-content (photographs, in our study) associated with brands.
2. We report on the differences in the perceived quality of photographs shot on an iPhone and an Android phone (no significant difference), and how these vary by the existence of a label representing their brand, either correct or wrong (labels enhance the perceived quality of photographs, irrespective of brand and whether the label is correct or wrong).
3. We report post-hoc explorations on the effect of participant demographics (gender, field of study, and ownership of brand) on the perceived quality of photographs.
4. We discuss the implications of our study on brand perceptions and marketing.

2   Background

2.1   Smartphones, Photography and Consumers

In recent years, smartphone photography has surged in popularity, thanks to the increasing accessibility of high-quality cameras on mobile devices [60]. As a result, the definition of a good photograph has evolved to encompass not only technical proficiency but also creativity, storytelling, and the ability to capture unique moments [38]. The rise of smartphone photography has revolutionised the art form, allowing anyone with a smartphone to practice photography. According to [71], "The first mobile camera phone was sold only 20 years ago, when taking pictures with one's phone was an oddity, and sharing pictures online was unheard of. Today, the smartphone is more camera than phone." A poll conducted by [63] sought to evaluate the significance consumers attribute to camera specifications when purchasing a new smartphone. Out of 2,900 participants, 50.1% of respondents indicated that camera specifications were a key consideration and 24.2% indicated that they valued the camera above all when purchasing a smartphone. It is no wonder that smartphone brands continue focusing their efforts on building perceptions around the quality of photographs using their device.

Brands often advertise their products by commissioning pieces from renowned photographers, directors, and videographers to attach another layer of 'value' to their cameras and processing capabilities. Taking the example of Apple, they often commission feature films that they later publicise on their social media such as Instagram, X, etc. [7]. The "Shot on iPhone" and "Shot on OnePlus" campaigns both highlight their smartphones' camera capabilities through user-generated content and professional collaborations [5]. Apple's campaign, using the hashtag #ShotoniPhone, features user photos in ads, billboards, and online promotions like content for Apple's Instagram account which has gathered over 30 Million posts as of June 2023. The campaign showcases themes like night mode and short films to demonstrate iPhone cameras' versatility and quality [7] [1]. Similarly, the "Shot on OnePlus" campaign encourages users to share their best photos with the hashtag #ShotonOnePlus [64]. This campaign features ambitious projects like the feature-length film "2024," directed by Vikramaditya Motwane, which was entirely shot on the OnePlus 9 Pro, showcasing the phone's advanced camera technology and professional versatility. Oppo also revealed a campaign where they asked celebrated filmmaker S. S. Rajamouli to shoot using their device [61]. Such campaigns leverage the power of community engagement and professional artistry to highlight the photographic capabilities of their smartphones. Brands like Google Pixel, Samsung, and Huawei also have similar campaigns, namely "Night Sight [62]", "Do What You Can't [19]", and "Rewrite the Rules of Photography [65]", respectively, showcasing their camera capabilities through user-generated content. These reinforce the idea that users can also be creators and they do not require special equipment. It also pushes to 'justify' the price point of these devices.

Today, sharing images online through social media has become an integral part of life [4], enabling people to connect, communicate, and express themselves visually. Platforms like Instagram, Facebook, and Twitter have transformed the way individuals document and share their experiences with the world [69]. Such usage patterns, like social media sharing and print media, significantly impact the perceived quality of photographs, often independent of the technical capabilities of the device used [41]. On social media platforms like Instagram, the automatic compression and filters can alter image appearance, while engagement metrics like likes and shares can skew perceptions of quality [43]. Photos that align with popular influencer aesthetics may also be perceived as higher quality [28]. In print media, issues like resolution, color accuracy, and the type of paper or finish can affect how a photograph is perceived, with potential differences becoming more evident in larger formats [25,39]. Additionally, the context in which photos are displayed, such as in professional portfolios or advertising campaigns, can also elevate the perceived quality.

The evolution of smartphone photography has not only altered the socio-cultural involvement of images in our daily interactions but has also had an impact on the dynamics of image production and human-technology interaction. This transformation has been driven by advances in computational photography, which have revolutionized the way images are captured, processed, and shared [20].

Features such as image processing and post-enhancement in smartphone photography play an important role in the final photograph quality. These features play a crucial role in enhancing the quality of smartphone photographs. As proposed by [45], such advancements in smartphone cameras have been a key driver in the transition from traditional digital and video cameras to mobile devices. This transition is further facilitated by the development of new interaction techniques for smartphone cameras, which improve the picture-taking process and image quality [11]. Boissin et al. [10] found that smartphone cameras, particularly the iPhone, can produce images of comparable quality to digital cameras, making them suitable for various applications, including medical teleconsultation. The software is what makes each mobile camera unique, as different manufacturers employ their own algorithms and image processing techniques to deliver a distinct photography experience [52].

Research on default camera settings in phones has explored various aspects. Avanigadda et al. [8] proposed a method for automatically suggesting an optimum capture resolution based on the content of the preview image, aiming to save memory space and reduce power consumption. McAdam et al. [48] addressed usability issues in camera phones, such as missed icons and poorly exposed shots, by creating a camera application with novel interface elements. As brands develop software especially to ensure that the default camera setting is the best possible option for the average user, these softwares begin to play a major role in the user's experience. The average user is more likely to continue shooting in default settings than by customising them. Certain brands do not even offer 'Pro mode' in their devices. Google Pixel only recently launched Pro mode in 2024 [49].

Another important point to note is, that while many phones have advanced features, consumers do not always understand what they signify. For example, as previously mentioned, Google Pixel positions its photograph quality as one of the best in the smartphone market due to its utilization of high-quality enhancing image processing with its own ISP technology [13], while brands such as Samsung have launched devices with 200MP cameras, indicating that higher hardware specifications result in better images [51]. Such contrasting marketing may leave the average consumer confused about which is the correct evaluation metric.

A consumer may be more likely to spend money on a mobile phone based on marketing, and brand loyalty than just their own understanding of the features present [4]. Brands often make use of such gaps in knowledge to advertise and present features to users that may even appear unnecessary when broken down. For example, Apple launched a campaign in 2024 under the name of 'Don't Let Me Go' [6] that prompts users to buy the iPhone 15 for more storage space to take photographs. The purpose of this advertisement is to highlight how the iPhone 15 model options begin with a storage capacity of 128 GB (also offering options of 256 GB, 512 GB), when models from iPhone 13 onwards have the exact same storage options as iPhone 15 (128 GB, 256 GB, 512GB) [32–34]. Further, previous models had the storage option of 64 GB, making it a much cheaper option for those looking to spend less. On platforms such as Swappa [35], 75% of the consumers preferred the 64GB Model. Other brands have implemented different solutions to help users make the most of their device's storage. Google Photos has an option that lets the user delete identical pictures or quickly clear space by eliminating unnecessary files [26].

2.2   Marketing and Brand Perception

In today's consumer-driven society, brand perception subtly influences preferences, shaping market consumer choices. A popular example of this is the Pepsi Paradox [40, 66]. In 1975, PepsiCo launched the Pepsi Challenge, presenting two non-labelled glasses of cola (one with Pepsi, the other with Coke) for a taste test. Most participants indicated their preference towards Pepsi without brand knowledge. However, another study had 'semi-blind' taste tests with brand information revealed, and preferences skewed toward Coke. This begs the question, where do these brand perceptions emerge from?

Strategic advertising practices play a key role in shaping brand identities and influencing consumer purchasing decisions [3]. For example, in a competitive smartphone market, advertising campaigns strategically highlight features, aesthetics, and brand values to sway consumer preferences and foster brand loyalty [70].

One study conducted in Taiwan by [53] examined the influences of perceived brand quality and perceived brand prestige on consumer purchase likelihood of HTC and iPhone brands among Taiwanese college students. The results of this study revealed that both perceived brand quality and perceived brand prestige significantly influenced consumers' likelihood of purchasing smartphones from these brands. These findings underscore the sway that certain brands hold over consumer decisions, with perceptions of quality and prestige playing pivotal roles.

Moreover, studies by Liu et al. in China [44] and Rakib et al. in Bangladesh [59] discuss consumer behaviour in the smartphone market. Liu et al. [44] identified factors such as physical attributes and apps as influential in purchasing decisions, while Rakib et al. [59] revealed generational differences in consumer priorities, with younger consumers prioritising features and price over social factors.

A study conducted by [18] investigated the influence of brand attachment on consumers' intention to repurchase smartphones from a current brand. The findings of this study showed that brand attachment was one of the most influential driver of consumers' intention to repurchase smartphones from their current brand. Furthermore, [30] delved into studying brand loyalty differences between Males and Females. They found that male consumers were more sensitive to the influence of brand image and perceived value in developing their satisfaction and continuance intention, while female consumers relied more on perceived usefulness. [47] further studied that advertising value and brand awareness had a major impact on purchase intention. Data from 303 Portuguese respondents shows that there is also an inherent difference in the spending patterns between iPhone users and Android users [36] Although, the market cap of Android phones is greater than that of iPhones, total spending on App Store for 2023 was $108 billion as opposed to $51 billion on Play Store.

Several studies conducted in India have explored the perceptions and preferences of users regarding iPhones and Android smartphones, examining differences in operating systems [46], storage safety [21], cost perceptions, and personal preferences [58]. The study [58] states that although most users believe iPhones are generally more expensive than the average Android smartphone, a majority also believe that iPhones offer better features. Many users believe that there is greater exposure to Android marketing and advertisements in Indian media compared to Apple, which may sway the general public towards that brand. Additionally, according to Perception and Pricing Strategies, the perceived value of a product often justifies its market price, regardless of technical merits [37].

However, it is important to note that cultural differences and socioeconomic factors play a significant role in smartphone preferences, as highlighted in these studies. Android smartphones, being more cost-effective, cater to a broader segment of the population. In contrast, Apple smartphones are perceived as expensive [58]. Consequently, the pervasive marketing and affordability of Android devices further enhance their popularity among the general public in India. This interplay between brand preferences, advertising strategies, and consumer perception of quality forms the cornerstone of modern product markets, with the smartphone industry serving as a compelling case study. Furthermore, the Critical Design Perspective urges designers to critically assess the broader societal implications of their work, recognizing how design choices can shape consumer behavior and societal norms [23]. This study, therefore, not only contributes to the HCI field but also prompts a deeper reflection on the ethical responsibilities of designers.

Thus, we investigate the perception of the quality of photographs taken by different device brands, specifically iPhone and Samsung, through a systematic, within-subjects, counterbalanced study with university students (N = 36).

3 Design

3.1 Study Design

The objective of our study was to explore the existence of differences in the perceptual value of photographs. To do so, we chose to use two renowned mobile device brands, Apple and Samsung, as the platforms for capturing the photographs. For the purpose of the study we used two phone models; an iPhone 11 and a Samsung Galaxy M53 5G.

Apple, renowned for its sleek design, innovative features, seamless ecosystem, and premium image, has cultivated a loyal following, attracting affluent consumers who value performance and prestige. As mentioned previously, we used an iPhone 11, a popular iPhone model, as a representative for iPhones. Samsung is known for its wide range of products catering to different budgets and preferences, demonstrating a willingness to experiment and adapt [22]. Samsung creates the hardware for its phones and these devices mainly run on Android software that has been modified as required. For the purpose of the study, we chose a Samsung M53 5G as a representative phone. Both Apple and Samsung are major players in the market, making the devices of these brands ideal for comparative analysis.

In terms of technical capabilities of the phone models, the iPhone 11 features a dual-camera system with a 12 MP wide and ultra-wide lens. Due to its integrated Night Mode and optical image stabilization (OIS), it is able to provide high quality pictures in low light conditions [31]. The Samsung Galaxy M53 5G, on the other hand, has a 108 MP primary sensor, capturing highly detailed images in good lighting but lacking OIS, which can affect low-light performance. It also includes an 8 MP ultra-wide, 2 MP macro, and 2 MP depth sensor for added versatility [12]. While the iPhone 11 offers a more consistent camera experience, particularly in challenging conditions and for video, the Galaxy M53 5G stands out with its high-resolution photos but falls short in low-light and video capabilities.

However, it should be noted that the Apple iPhone 11 was purchased in 2020 and the Samsung M53 was purchased in 2022. Although both devices were selected partly based on convenience, and there may be some disparities in their technical specifications but they also served as suitable representatives. In 2023, the iPhone 11 was the most widely used iPhone [35], making it a great choice for the study. Additionally, we chose a Samsung device to represent Androids in the comparison, as Samsung has consistently been one of the most popular Android brands in India, being the highest shipper of mobile devices in 2023 [14]. Hence, we selected the iPhone 11 (128GB), a base model of its series (consisting of iPhone 11, iPhone 11 Pro, and iPhone 11 ProMax), and the Samsung M53, a representative mid-series mobile phone from Samsung.

We started by creating the set of photographs required for the study. To ensure a well rounded set, we took photographs with different content, angles and lighting conditions based on the categorization and work of [24] and [42]. We took 36 photographs in total (Fig. 1), 18 photographs each shot on the iPhone 11 and Samsung Galaxy M53 5G shot in identical conditions and with default values. Zoom, portrait mode, and no other modes of photography were used. The photographs were taken with the standard camera settings, on the primary photography mode.

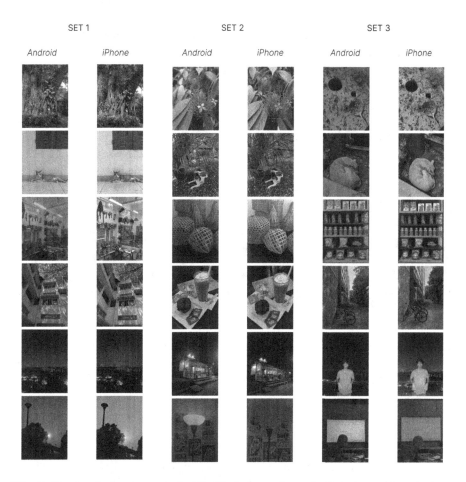

Fig. 1. Randomised sets created with 12 photographs each, 6 shot on either device.

As we wished to test the perceived value that users associate with the quality of photographs and labels, we created a counterbalanced study. The purpose of doing so was to remove the variable of primary bias. For this, we started by creating two additional sets of photographs; One which had the correct labels on it ("Shot on iPhone" for iPhone 11 and "shot with my Galaxy M53 5G" for the Android phone), and a set which was wrongly labelled ("Shot with my Galaxy M53 5G" for iPhone 11 and "Shot on iPhone" for the Android phone). We added labels of the phone models in a watermark style (see Fig. 2). For the Android phone it was straightforward as the phone had the watermark inbuilt. To get the official watermark for the phone model that we selected (Samsung M53 5G), we switched on the watermark in picture settings, took a photograph and edited the background to obtain the official watermark for the phone model. But iPhones do not inherently have a watermark that can be switched on when taking photographs, so we used the watermark "Shot on iPhone" from the popular campaign run by Apple.

This resulted in three sets of 36 photographs (i.e. 108 photographs in all); non-labelled, correctly labelled and wrongly labelled. In the rest of the paper, we use the abbreviations NL, CL and WL respectively for these. Hence, the 6 conditions of photographs would be ANL, ACL, AWL, PNL, PCL, and PWL, with 'A' for Android and 'P' for iPhone.

Fig. 2. Sample photographs with the three different label conditions: Non-labelled (NL), Correctly Labelled (CL), and Wrongly Labelled (WL). Figure 2 also depicts the "Shot on iPhone" and "Shot with my Galaxy M53 5G".

We then numbered the identical photographs from 1 to 18 for each set. After this we created three random sets (Fig. 1) each set having six "identical" pairs of photographs shot on each device, Android and iPhone (i.e. 12 photographs in total). Next, we created six unique survey forms, based on Table 1. Each form comprised one Non-labelled, one correctly labelled and one wrongly labelled set of six pairs of photographs, resulting in 36 photographs in total. The forms had a unique combination of groups to try and eliminate individual bias and ensure that each picture was counterbalanced, as can be seen in the table below. This way, every picture would be rated when correctly labelled, wrongly labelled and without a label equal number of times.

Table 1. Distribution of the 3 sets of photographs counterbalanced through 6 unique Google forms.

Form Number	Form 1	Form 2	Form 3	Form 4	Form 5	Form 6
Set Number (No Label)	Set 1 (NL)	Set 1 (NL)	Set 2 (NL)	Set 2 (NL)	Set 3 (NL)	Set 3 (NL)
Set Number (Correct Label)	Set 2 (CL)	Set 3 (CL)	Set 1 (CL)	Set 3 (CL)	Set 2 (CL)	Set 1 (CL)
Set Number (Wrong Label)	Set 3 (WL)	Set 2 (WL)	Set 3 (WL)	Set 1 (WL)	Set 1 (WL)	Set 2 (WL)

Each form had four sections. The first section asked for the participants' demographic information such as their age, gender and which department they are studying in. Section 2 had the set of 12 non-labelled photographs. The participant was asked to rate each picture on a Likert scale of 1 to 10 where 1 was 'Bad' and 10 was 'Good' (Fig. 3). We randomised the order of the 12 photographs. Section three had the sets of 12 correctly labelled (CL) and 12 wrongly labelled (WL) photographs (a total of 24), again in a randomised order and the participant was asked to rate the photographs on a Likert scale of 1 to 10 where 1 was 'Bad' and 10 was 'Good'. This was followed by a fourth section with questions regarding the participant's mobile phones such as which model and brand they have and how long they have had it for.

Fig. 3. Sample Question from the form depicting the Likert scale ratings from 1 to 10 with one being Bad and 10 being Good.

3.2   Method

We recruited 36 university students as participants for the study, each aged between 18 to 22, ensuring an equal proportion of iPhone users and Android users, with 18 participants each. There were 14 female and 22 male participants. Furthermore, based on Area of study, there was a near-equal split of engineering students and design students with 17 participants and 19 participants respectively.

As we conducted a counterbalanced study, the participants were assigned one of the six forms randomly and asked to answer the questions under our supervision. We presented the Google form to them on the same monitor (Windows Acer Predator 300, 15.6 inch LCD LED) to remove the variables of colour accuracy, brightness etc., which could have happened from using multiple devices. Each of the forms was filled by 6 participants. This resulted in each picture being given 36 ratings (twelve in the unlabelled condition, twelve in the correctly labelled condition, and twelve in the wrongly labelled condition).

Table 2. Participant distribution and demographics. It is important to note that the distribution is not equivalent across all demographics, as can be seen in Table 2, there is a higher concentration of engineering students owning iPhones while there is a higher concentration of Design students owning Android devices with only one engineering student owning an Android device.

Area of study	Android			iPhone			Total = Total 1 + Total 2
	Male	Female	Total 1	Male	Female	Total 2	
Design	10	4	14	2	3	5	19
Engineering	1	3	4	9	4	13	17
Total	11	7	18	11	7	18	36

For the purpose of analysis, the scores given by each participant for a specific condition of six photographs (i.e. ANL, ACL, AWL, PNL, PCL, PWL) were aggregated by adding up the ratings for all the photographs in that condition. This resulted in a Perceived Photograph Quality score or PPQ varying from a minimum of 6 to a maximum value of 60. Thus, each participant had 6 PPQ scores, one each for ANL, ACL, AWL, PNL, PCL, and PWL. To emphasize, we report on the perceptual value of photographs rather than the absolute value of their quality (which may depend on technical specifications).

Hence our study was a counterbalanced study where our within-subjects independent variables were Labelling (NL, CL, WL) and Device (iPhone, Android) and between-subjects independent variables were Gender (Male, Female), Phone Ownership (iPhone, Android) and Area of Study (Engineering, Design). The dependent variable was PPQ score (Likert scale ratings), control Variables as Image Content, Lighting Conditions, Image Viewing Device and the Random Variable was Image presentation order.

4   Results and Discussion

With respect to RQ1, our null hypothesis was that there is no significant difference in the PPQ scores of photographs shot on Androids vs iPhones. The observed means of the photographs shot on the Android and iPhone devices (without any labels) were 35.9 points (SD = 8.3) and 36.1 points (SD = 8.6) respectively. We conducted a paired student's t-test to investigate the differences in PPQ scores of the photographs shot on the Android device vs the iPhone device in the no-label condition (ANL vs PNL). We found that there were no significant differences ($p = 0.7925$, $N = 36$, $t = 0.139$). Thus, we cannot reject the null hypothesis - there seems to be no difference in the PPQ score for unlabelled photographs shot on Android phones and iPhones. This represents the primary endpoint of our study.

This was an interesting result, especially as the phone models themselves had a major price difference, with the iPhone 11 costing three times as much as the Samsung M53 5G. The iPhone 11 cost approximately INR 75,000 while the

Samsung M53 5G cost approximately INR 25,000 when purchased. This finding may inform consumers regarding their purchasing decisions, suggesting that higher prices do not necessarily yield better-perceived quality phone cameras and photographs.

However, it is important to note that this analysis had low statistical power (observed power = 0.464), suggesting that the sample size may have been insufficient to detect small effects. As a result, these findings should be interpreted with caution. Despite this limitation, we believe that sharing these results contributes valuable information to the public domain, particularly as independent research that may inform consumer decisions regarding smartphone photography.

To evaluate RQ2, we performed a $2 \times 3 \times 2 \times 2 \times 2$ repeated measures ANOVA with the type of Device (2, iPhone and Android, within-subjects), Label (3, no label, correct label and wrong label, within-subjects), Gender (2, between subjects), Phone ownership of a brand (2, between subjects) and Area of study (2, design and engineering, between subjects) as independent variables, and the PPQ Score as a dependent variable.

We found that there was no significant effect of the Device (F = 3.750, p = 0.063, observed power = 0.464), but there is a significant effect of the label (F = 6.326, p = 0.006, observed power = 0.862), no significant effect of Gender (F = 0.742, p = 0.396, observed power = 0.132), no significant effect of the Area of study (F = 1.458, p = 0.237, observed power = 0.215), or Phone ownership (F = 0.224, p = 0.640, observed power = 0.074). The significant interactions were label * phone ownership (F = 4.520, p = 0.020, observed power 0.722), and label * Area of study * phone ownership (F = 3.995, p = 0.030, observed power = 0.665). The interaction between Gender and Label had a borderline significant effect ((F = 3.279, p = 0.053). Refer to Table 3 and Fig. 4 for the estimated marginal means and confidence intervals. We elaborate on these results below.

We later also performed a 2×2 ANOVA comparing only non-labelled and labelled (average of CL and WL) photographs shot on iPhones and Androids with the type of Device (2, iPhone and Android, within subjects), Label (2, No label, label, within subjects), Gender (2, between subjects), Phone ownership of a brand (2, between subjects) and Area of study (2, design and engineering, between subjects) as independent variables, and the PPQ Score as a dependent variable. We found a significant effect of labels on PPQ scores (F = 12.824, p = 0.001) and that the interaction of label and gender demonstrated a significant influence (F = 6.443, p = 0.017) on participants' perceptions.

Effect of Device on Perception. As mentioned earlier, the type of device used to capture the photographs did not have a significant effect (F = 3.750, p = 0.063, observed power = 0.464) on the PPQ scores, reinforcing the finding that there is no inherent difference in the perceived quality of photographs taken on iPhones versus Android devices. Photographs shot on the Android device had a mean PPQ score of 37.014 points (95% C.I. = [33.804, 40.224]) and photographs shot on the iPhone had a mean PPQ score of 38.438 points (95% C.I. = [35.424, 41.453]) (Note that these numbers include no label, correct label and wrong label

Table 3. Estimated Marginal Means of PPQ score for NL, CL, and WL photographs shot on Android and iPhone.

	ANL	ACL	AWL	PNL	PCL	PWL
N	36	36	36	36	36	36
Mean	34.844	38.323	37.875	35.553	39.112	40.650
95% C.I. from	31.058	34.837	34.671	32.080	35.428	37.616
95% C.I. to	38.629	41.809	41.079	39.026	42.796	43.684
F = 2.477, p = 0.103						

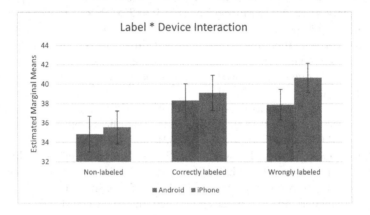

Fig. 4. Graph showing the interaction of labels and device based on the data depicted in Table 3.

conditions, and are hence different from RQ1, the unlabelled condition). This reconfirms that there was no inherent difference in the 'quality' of pictures shot on iPhone versus those shot on Android, although the presence of labels seems to have an effect, and that effect seems more pronounced for iPhone photographs.

Effects of Labels on Perception. In the first ANOVA, we found that there was a significant effect of labels (NL, CL, WL) (F = 6.326, p = 0.006). Post hoc comparisons using Bonferroni correction found that photographs with no label (NL, Mean = 35.198 points (95% C.I. = [31.770, 38.627]) had a mean difference of -3.519 points (95% C.I. = $[-6.392, -.646]$, p = 0.013) compared to correctly labelled (CL, Mean = 38.717 points (95% C.I. = [35.329, 42.106]), and -4.064 (95% C.I. = $[-6.995, -1.134]$, p = 0.004) compared to wrongly labelled (WL, Mean = 39.263, (95% C.I. = [36.300, 42.225]) photograph conditions. No significant difference was recorded between correctly labelled (CL) and wrongly labelled (WL) photographs (p = 1.000). This suggests that there was a significant difference in how participants perceived labelled versus non-labelled images.

To investigate this phenomenon further, we conducted a second 2 × 2 ANOVA between the type of device and the existence of a label on the PPQ scores. We calculated the average PPQ scores of CL and WL of Androids (ACL, AWL) and iPhones (PCL, PWL) to give us Android Labelled (AL) and iPhone Labelled (PL) and this was compared against the non-labelled photographs (ANL and PNL).

We found a significant effect of labels on PPQ scores (F = 12.824, p = 0.001). Non-labelled photographs had a mean score of 35.198 points (95% C.I. = [31.770, 38.627]), while labelled photographs had a higher mean score of 38.990 points (95% C.I. = [35.927, 42.053]).

The interaction between device and label was not significant (F = 0.628, p = 0.435) in the second ANOVA either. However, the means of non-labelled photographs were less than those of labelled photographs in both devices, corroborating the earlier finding. This suggests that labels increase the value of a photograph irrespective of its content.

However, it is important to keep in mind that the non-labelled and labelled conditions were not counterbalanced in sequence. The form given to participants presented the non-labelled (NL) images first, so they wouldn't have anticipated the labelled images in the subsequent sections. The latter sections included a mix of correctly labelled (CL) and wrongly labelled (WL) photographs. Hence, this difference could also be attributed to the order effects between the NL and labelled photographs.

Exploratory Observations. As an exploratory analysis, we also considered how participant demographics such as gender, field of study at the university, and ownership of a brand affected these variables. This analysis was opportunistic and conducted post-hoc, and the factors considered were not systematically balanced across participants. Therefore, these findings are presented as preliminary observations to be interpreted cautiously rather than conclusive evidence.

Interaction Between Label and Phone Ownership. There was no significant effect of phone ownership of participants (F = 0.224, p = 0.640) on the perceived value of photographs shot on the devices. However, the interaction effect between label and phone ownership was statistically significant (F = 4.520, p = 0.020, observed power = 0.722), suggesting that whether participants owned an iPhone or an Android device, in combination with labeling, had a significant effect on their perceptions. Figure 5 indicates that with labels, Android owners rate photographs higher and more so for wrongly labelled photographs, while iPhone owners' ratings remain largely unaffected by labels. This contrast in ratings could be because of differences in the socio-economic background of Android owners and iPhone owners, with iPhone owners generally being more affluent as iPhone owners have a 43.7% higher salary than Android owners [29,58].

Interaction Between Area of study, Phone ownership and Labels. For our study, one of the results that we had obtained centered around Area of study and perception. The interaction of label, Area of Study, and ownership of phone brand demonstrated a significant influence (p=0.030) on participants' perceptions. This result suggests that individuals from different academic backgrounds

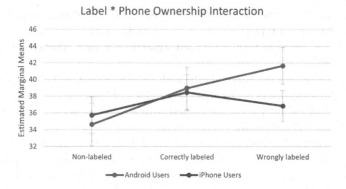

Fig. 5. Graph showing the interaction of labels and Phone Ownership on the PPQ scores.

(design vs. engineering) may have different aesthetic sensibilities, which in turn affect how they perceive labelled photographs. Interestingly, participants studying design tended to rate photographs lower (Mean = 35.945 points, 95% C.I. = [32.070, 39.820]) compared to those studying engineering (Mean = 39.507 points, 95% C.I. = [34.870, 44.144]), potentially indicating a more critical perspective among design students. However, given the uneven distribution of phone ownership across these fields (with more Android users in design and more iPhone users in engineering), this finding should be interpreted with caution (refer to Table 2 for distribution) (Fig. 6).

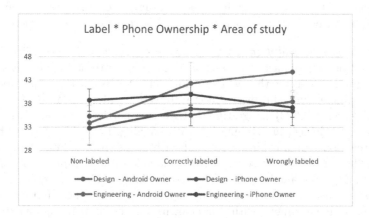

Fig. 6. Graphs showing the interaction of Label, Phone ownership, and Area of study on the PPQ scores.

Interaction Between Label and Gender. In the 2 × 2 ANOVA comparing non-labelled and labelled photographs shot on iPhones and Androids, we found that the interaction of label and gender demonstrated a significant influence (p = 0.017) on participants' perceptions. The mean PPQ score for non-labelled photographs by females was 38.812 points (95% C.I. = [34.910, 42.715]) and males was 35.376 points (95% C.I. = [30.649, 40.102]). This suggests that women tend to rate photographs higher than males but do not get affected by labels. Male participants' perception of photographs is affected by labels to a greater extent compared to females' perceptions, corroborating the findings of the study by [30] which states that male consumers are greatly influenced by the perceived value and brand image while female consumers expect higher quality and value product details more. However, these findings warrant further investigation with a larger sample size to better understand the nuances of gender differences in perception (Fig. 7).

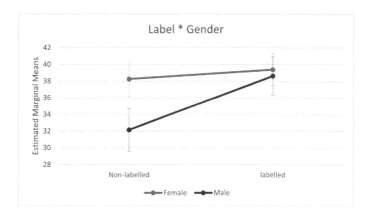

Fig. 7. Graph showing the interaction of gender and labels on the PPQ scores.

5   Conclusion

We conducted a systematic, within-subjects, counterbalanced study with 36 participants (all university students) to investigate the existence of differences in the perceptual value of photographs shot on different brands of smartphones, specifically Androids and iPhones (taking iPhone 11 and Samsung M53 as sample models in our study). We evaluated the perceptual value through the usage of label conditions on the same photograph (No label, correct label, and wrong label) to assess if the value of the photograph changed in any of the conditions. This was done using a PPQ score or Perceived Photograph Quality score, which aggregated the Likert scale ratings (1-10) for each photograph condition per user.

We found that there was no significant effect of the Device (F = 3.750, p = 0.063, observed power = 0.464) i.e. the specific device used to capture the photograph on the perceptual value of the photograph. While the observed power for this analysis was low, making it difficult to draw definitive conclusions, the importance of having this information in the public domain as part of independent research cannot be overstated. Transparency in such research helps build a more nuanced understanding of consumer perceptions. However, an interesting finding was that there was a significant effect of the label (F = 6.326, p = 0.006, observed power = 0.862) and the existence of labels (any label) increased the value of a photograph compared to one without a label.

Similar to the "Pepsi Paradox" [40,66], that states that participants prefer Pepsi in blind taste tests but Coke in semi-blind (where the labels of the brands are shown), irrespective of the perceived value of non-labelled photographs, adding a label increases the perceived quality. However, unlike the Pepsi Paradox, our study depicts that the content of the label does not have a significant effect on the perception, i.e. it does not matter if the photograph displays "Shot on iPhone" or "Shot with my Galaxy M53 5G ".

This implies that the perceived value of products, such as photographs, can be influenced by the labels or associations assigned to them. For instance, consider a simple label like "fresh" on a milk package, which, even though all competing products are fresh, still stands out and elevates consumer perception. However, a direct comparision cannot be made because a label like "Fresh" is a positive value attributed to the product.

Labels like "Shot on iPhone" or "Shot on Android" can enhance the value of photographs, irrespective of personal brand preferences. A photograph labelled "Shot by Raghu Rai" would likely carry higher perceived value among the general public due to the renowned reputation of the photographer. However, our results may suggest even a label as basic as "Shot by Palak" can potentially alter the perceived value of the same photograph. Labels carry diverse meanings and associations that vary among individuals, encompassing emotional connections, socioeconomic implications, notions of class or luxury, or personal experiences. These associations fundamentally shape how the original product can be perceived by consumers. Our finding further reinforces the reasoning behind these advertising practices. Such practices often push consumers to purchase devices from the same brands, as they look for similar experiences. This further demonstrates how even the smallest of features can have an impact on how consumers interact with devices as well as influence their purchasing decisions. This phenomenon aligns with the broader literature on consumer behaviour. As suggested by Affective Design and Social Influence Theory [55], design plays a pivotal role in shaping consumer experiences and expectations. This highlights the need for designers to engage critically with their work, possibly even directing areas for future research and exploration.

We also conducted an exploratory analysis of the effects of participant demographics (Gender, Area of study, and Phone ownership) on the perceived quality of photographs by studying their between-subjects. We found that the significant interactions were label * phone ownership ($F = 4.520$, $p = 0.020$, observed power 0.722), and label * Area of study * phone ownership ($F = 3.995$, $p = 0.030$, observed power $= 0.665$). Further, In the 2×2 ANOVA comparing only non-labelled and labelled photographs shot on iPhones and Androids, we found that the interaction of label and gender demonstrated a significant influence ($F = 6.443$, $p = 0.017$) on participants' perceptions. These findings were post-hoc observations and were not part of our original research questions. The lack of systematic investigation and the unbalanced factors across participants suggest that these results should be interpreted cautiously.

Several limitations should be acknowledged in this study. Firstly, the small sample size of 36 participants, predominantly consisting of university students, may not fully represent the broader population. This limited our ability to generalize the findings to a wider audience. Future studies should aim for a larger and more diverse participant pool to enhance the validity and generalizability of the results. Secondly, our study primarily focused on participants from a specific cultural and geographical context, which may limit the generalizability of findings to other regions and cultures. Consumer perceptions and behaviours are often influenced by cultural norms and societal factors. We would also like to understand the implications of labels and human perception in different cultures and age groups. It is interesting to note that often brands utilise different marketing strategies depending on the local cultures, similarly, it is possible that the connotations of certain labels could differ from region to region. For the purpose of this study, we aimed for a balanced distribution of all independent variables. However, our sample may not have fully represented the broader population, particularly in the exploratory analysis of demographic effects. Future studies should aim for a more diverse and representative sample to enhance the generalizability of findings.

Further, the potential underpowering of the analysis related to RQ1 in our study may undermine the reliability of our conclusions. As [16,17] emphasizes, drawing conclusions from underpowered studies can lead to inaccurate interpretations of non-significant effect sizes. This issue underscores the importance of considering the relationship between significance level, effect size, sample size, and power. Additionally, [9] highlights concerns with retrospective "observed" power, which further complicates the interpretation of our findings. While the study design and sample size were appropriate for RQ2, the conclusions drawn from RQ1 should be viewed with caution due to the limited power of the analysis.

Another limitation stems from the limited variability in the labels tested in our study. We only explored two labels ("Shot on iPhone" and "Shot with Samsung M53 5G"), which may not capture the full spectrum of label effects on perceived value. This, coupled with the exploratory nature of our demographic analysis, highlights the need for more systematic research in future work. Exploring different types of labels, including those with varied content or perceived value, and balancing participant demographics more effectively could provide deeper insights into the effects of labels on perception. A future area of study could be to test how participants react to labels with content that differs in value as mentioned above. Future work could also explore the existence of a gender bias associated with label, for example, a label stating "Shot by Ishita" versus "Shot by Anirudha". There was also limited variability in terms of the phone models selected. In future studies, it would be valuable to explore brands that are positioned differently in the market. Another important point to note is that the phone models selected in our study were released in different years (iPhone 11 was released in 2019, and Samsung M53 5G was released in 2022). To better understand the impact of technical camera capabilities on perceived quality, it would be beneficial to study phones released in the same year.

These limitations highlight the importance of future research to address these constraints by including a larger and more diverse sample size, ensuring a balanced participant pool for between-subjects testing, and exploring the impact of gender bias, cultural context, and label variability on the perceptual value of products. The preliminary findings from our exploratory analysis suggest that these are promising avenues for further study.

Acknowledgement. We sincerely thank the reviewers for their valuable feedback and constructive comments.

References

1. A Case Study on Apple's "Shot on iPhone" Brand Campaign (2024). https://thebrandhopper.com/2024/01/07/a-case-study-onapples-shot-on-iphone-brand-campaign/. Accessed 20 May 2024
2. Aaker, D.A.: Measuring brand equity across products and markets. Calif. Manag. Rev. **38**(3), 102–120 (1996). ISSN: 00081256, 21628564. https://doi.org/10.2307/41165845. http://cmr.ucpress.edu/cgi/doi/10.2307/41165845. Accessed 29 Feb 2024
3. Akkucuk, U., Esmaeili, J.: The impact of brands on consumer buying behavior: an empirical study on smartphone buyers. Int. J. Res. Bus. Soc. Sci. (2147-4478) **5**(4), 1–16 (2016). ISSN: 2147-4478. https://doi.org/10.20525/ijrbs.v5i4.551. https://www.ssbfnet.com/ojs/index.php/ijrbs/article/view/100. Accessed 25 May 2024
4. Anderson, K.E.: Getting acquainted with social networks and apps: Instagram's instant appeal. Library Hi Tech News **33**(3), 11–15 (2016). ISSN: 0741-9058. https://doi.org/10.1108/LHTN-03-2016-0011. https://doi.org/10.1108/LHTN-03-2016-0011. Accessed 25 May 2024
5. Apple. Apple on Instagram: "Commissioned by Apple. Shot on iPhone 15 Pro, "Midnight" is a thrilling ride through the neon-lit streets of Tokyo. Director Takashi Miike brings to life the drawings of legendary manga artist Osamu Tezuka, faithfully recreating frames from the original work. Music: "Midnight Klaxon Baby" by THEE MICHELLE GUN ELEPHANT Featuring: @kento_kaku @__cnp_ @yukiyoshi_ozawa #ShotoniPhone by Takashi M.". Reel (2024). https://www.instagram.com/reel/C4LjGbgRSky/. Accessed 25 May 2024
6. Apple. iPhone 15 Storage 'Don't Let Me Go' Apple (2024). https://www.youtube.com/watch?v=bks2zGnssMY. Accessed 25 May 2024
7. Apple exec explains the creation of its Shot on iPhone campaign (2021). https://9to5mac.com/2021/11/11/apple-exec-explainsthe-creation-of-its-shot-on-iphone-campaign/. Accessed 20 May 2024

8. Avanigadda, P.K., et al.: Content based selection of capture resolution in smartphone camera. In: 2015 Annual IEEE India Conference (INDICON), pp. 1–4 (2015). ISSN: 2325-9418. https://doi.org/10.1109/INDICON.2015.7443390. https://ieeexplore.ieee.org/document/7443390. Accessed 25 May 2024

9. Baguley, T.: Understanding statistical power in the context of applied research. Appl. Ergon. **35**(2), 73–80 (2004). ISSN: 0003-6870. https://doi.org/10.1016/j.apergo.2004.01.002. https://www.sciencedirect.com/science/article/pii/S0003687004000195. Accessed 04 Sept 2024

10. Boissin, C., et al.: Can we trust the use of smartphone cameras in clinical practice? Laypeople assessment of their image quality. Telemedicine e-Health **21**(11), 887–892 (2015). ISSN: 1530-5627. https://doi.org/10.1089/tmj.2014.0221. https://www.liebertpub.com/doi/10.1089/tmj.2014.0221. Accessed 25 May 2024

11. Brewster, S., et al.: Rethinking camera user interfaces. Digit. Photogr. VIII **8299**, 171–179 (2012). https://doi.org/10.1117/12.907477. https://www.spiedigitallibrary.org/conference-proceedings-of-spie/8299/82990K/Rethinking-camera-user-interfaces/10.1117/12.907477.full. Accessed 25 May 2024

12. Buy Galaxy M53 5G 6GB/128GB Blue - Price & Offer. en-IN. https://www.samsung.com/in/smartphones/galaxy-m/galaxy-m53-5g-blue-128gb-storage-6gb-ram-sm-m536bzbeinu/. Accessed 04 Sept 2024

13. Çakmak, F.: Why Google Camera is Best Camera in the Market? - Xiaomiui.Net. Fan Community. Section: Mobile (2022). https://xiaomiui.net/why-google-camera-is-best-in-the-market-15819/. Accessed 20 May 2024

14. Canalys Newsroom - India's smartphone shipments fell 3% in Q3 2023 but gaining traction amid festivities. https://www.canalys.com/newsroom/india-smartphone-shipments-Q3-2023. Accessed 25 May 2024

15. Cialdini, R., Goldstein, N.: Social influence: compliance and conformity. Annu. Rev. Psychol. **55**, 591–621 (2004). https://doi.org/10.1146/annurev.psych.55.090902.142015

16. Cohen, J.: Statistical power analysis. Curr. Dir. Psychol. Sci. **1**(3), 98–101 (1992). ISSN: 0963-7214. https://doi.org/10.1111/1467-8721.ep10768783. https://doi.org/10.1111/1467-8721.ep10768783. Accessed 04 Sept 2024

17. Cohen, J.: Things I have learned (so far). In: Methodological issues & strategies in clinical research, pp. 315–333. American Psychological Association, Washington, DC, US (1992). ISBN: 978-1-55798-154-7 978-1-55798- 167-7. https://doi.org/10.1037/10109-028

18. Cornelia, V., Pasharibu, Y.: Brand loyalty mediation in brand attachment and customer digital experience towards smartphone repurchase intentions. Benefit: Jurnal Manajemen dan Bisnis (Jurnal ini Sudah Migrasi) **5**(2), 145–157 (2020). ISSN: 2541-2604. https://doi.org/10.23917/benefit.v5i2.11278. https://journals.ums.ac.id/index.php/benefit/article/view/11278. Accessed 25 May 2024

19. COTW. Samsung #DoWhatYouCant, empowers people to overcome their barriers. Section: TV (2019). https://campaignsoftheworld.com/tv/samsung-do-what-you-cant-2019/. Accessed 25 May 2024

20. Delbracio, M., et al.: Mobile computational photography: a tour. Annu. Rev. Vis. Sci. **7**, 571–604 (2021). ISSN: 2374-4642, 2374-4650. https://doi.org/10.1146/annurev-vision-093019-115521. https://www.annualreviews.org/content/journals/10.1146/annurev-vision-093019-115521. Accessed 25 May 2024

21. Dhanush, R., Nachiappan, S.: Comparative Study of Consumer Perception between IPhone and Android Mobiles. In: 3.3 (2022)

22. Dissanayake, R., Amarasuriya, T.: Role of brand identity in developing global brands: a literature based review on case comparison between Apple Iphone vs Samsung smartphone brands. Res. J. Bus. Manag.-RJBM **2**, 430–440 (2015). https://doi.org/10.17261/Pressacademia.2015312990

23. Dunne, A., Raby, F.: Speculative Everything: Design, Fiction, and Social Dreaming. The MIT Press (2013). ISBN: 978-0-262-01984-2. https://www.jstor.org/stable/j.ctt9qf7j7. Accessed 04 Sept 2024

24. Fang, Y., et al.: Perceptual quality assessment of smartphone photography. In: 2020 IEEE/CVF Conference on Computer Vision and Pattern Recognition (CVPR), pp. 3674–3683 (2020). ISSN: 2575-7075. https://doi.org/10.1109/CVPR42600.2020.00373. https://ieeexplore.ieee.org/document/9156490. Accessed 25 May 2024

25. Firmansyah, F., et al.: How the print media industry survived in the digital era. Jurnal ASPIKOM **7**(1), 1–15 (2022). ISSN: 2548-8309. https://doi.org/10.24329/aspikom.v7i1.1013. https://jurnalaspikom.org/index.php/aspikom/article/view/1013. Accessed 04 Sept 2024

26. Free up space in Photos Storage Manager - Guidebooks with Google. https://guidebooks.google.com/storage/manage-storage-with-googlephotos/free-up-storage-space-with-google-photos?hl=en. Accessed 25 May 2024

27. Gergye, M.: Selling the Upgrade: The Top Smartphone Features Customers Want. https://www.marketsource.com/blog/selling-upgradetop-smartphone-features-customers-want/. Accessed 21 May 2024

28. Heredia-Carroza, J.: Flamenco performer's perceived value: development of a measurement index. Sci. Ann. Econ. Bus. (2019). https://doi.org/10.2478/saeb-2019-0017

29. Howarth, J.: iPhone vs Android User Stats (2024 Data) (2023). https://explodingtopics.com/blog/iphone-android-users. Accessed 24 May 2024

30. Imtiaz, S., et al.: Internet-based brand loyalty in male and female: "It is difficult to attain male customers but easier to retain, female customers are easier to attain but difficult to retain", pp. 38–49 (2018)

31. iPhone 11 - Technical Specifications - Apple Support (IN). https://support.apple.com/en-in/111865. Accessed 04 Sept 2024

32. iPhone 11 Guide, Storage. https://swappa.com/guide/appleiphone-11/storage. Accessed 25 May 2024

33. iPhone 13 - Technical Specifications. https://www.apple.com/iphone-13/specs/. Accessed 25 May 2024

34. iPhone 14 and iPhone 14 Plus - Technical Specifications. https://www.apple.com/iphone-14/specs/. Accessed 25 May 2024

35. iPhone 15 and iPhone 15 Plus - Technical Specifications. https://www.apple.com/iphone-15/specs/. Accessed 25 May 2024

36. iPhone vs. Android User & Revenue Statistics (2024). https://backlinko.com/iphone-vs-android-statistics. Accessed 15 May 2024

37. Kahneman, D., Tversky, A.: Prospect theory: an analysis of decision under risk. Econometrica **47**(2), 263–291 (1979). ISSN: 0012-9682. https://doi.org/10.2307/1914185. https://www.jstor.org/stable/1914185. Accessed 04 Sept 2024

38. Keep, D.: Artist with a camera-phone: a decade of mobile photography. In: Berry, M., Schleser, M. (eds.) Mobile Media Making in an Age of Smartphones, pp. 14–24. Palgrave Macmillan US, New York (2014). ISBN: 978-1-137-46981-6. https://doi.org/10.1057/9781137469816_2. https://doi.org/10.1057/9781137469816_2. Accessed 20 May 2024

39. Kirchner, E., et al.: Exploring the limits of color accuracy in technical photography. Heritage Sci. **9**(1), 57 (2021). ISSN: 2050-7445. https://doi.org/10.1186/s40494-021-00536-x. https://doi.org/10.1186/s40494-021-00536-x. Accessed 04 Sept 2024

40. Koenigs, M., Tranel, D.: Prefrontal cortex damage abolishes brand-cued changes in cola preference. Soc. Cogn. Affect. Neurosci. **3**(1), 1–6 (2008). ISSN: 1749-5016. https://doi.org/10.1093/scan/nsm032. https://doi.org/10.1093/scan/nsm032. Accessed 22 May 2024

41. Koh, H.-K., Burnasheva, R., Suh, Y.G.: Perceived ESG (environmental, social, governance) and consumers' responses: the mediating role of brand credibility, brand image, and perceived quality. Sustainability **14**(8), 4515 (2022). ISSN: 2071-1050. https://doi.org/10.3390/su14084515. https://www.mdpi.com/2071-1050/14/8/4515. Accessed 04 Sept 2024

42. Leder, H., et al.: Swipes and saves: a taxonomy of factors influencing aesthetic assessments and perceived beauty of mobile phone photographs. Front. Psychol. **13** (2022). ISSN: 1664-1078. https://doi.org/10.3389/fpsyg.2022.786977. https://www.frontiersin.org/journals/psychology/articles/10.3389/fpsyg.2022.786977/full. Accessed 25 May 2024

43. Li, W., Ai, P., Ding, A.: More than just numbers: how engagement metrics influence user intention to pay for online knowledge products. Sage Open **13**(1), 21582440221148620 (2023). ISSN: 2158-2440. https://doi.org/10.1177/21582440221148620. https://doi.org/10.1177/21582440221148620. Accessed 04 Sept 2024

44. Liu, N., Yu, R.: Identifying design feature factors critical to acceptance and usage behavior of smartphones. Comput. Hum. Behav. **70**, 131–142 (2017). ISSN: 0747-5632. https://doi.org/10.1016/j.chb.2016.12.073. https://www.sciencedirect.com/science/article/pii/S0747563216309013. Accessed 15 May 2024

45. Lou, H., et al.: Aesthetic evaluation and guidance for mobile photography. In: Proceedings of the 29th ACM International Conference on Multimedia. MM 2021, pp. 2780–2782. Association for Computing Machinery, New York (2021). ISBN: 978-1-4503-8651-7. https://doi.org/10.1145/3474085.3478557. https://doi.org/10.1145/3474085.3478557. Accessed 24 May 2024

46. Mahalakshmi, M.K.: A Comparative Study on Customers Satisfaction towards Android Operating System and Iphone Operating System in Mobile Phone, pp. 1752–175 (2023)

47. Martins, J., et al.: How smartphone advertising influences consumers' purchase intention. J. Bus. Res. **94**, 378–387 (2019). ISSN: 0148-2963. https://doi.org/10.1016/j.jbusres.2017.12.047. https://www.sciencedirect.com/science/article/pii/S0148296317305507. Accessed 16 May 2024

48. McAdam, C., Pinkerton, C., Brewster, S.A.: Novel interfaces for digital cameras and camera phones. In: Proceedings of the 12th International Conference on Human Computer Interaction with Mobile Devices and Services. MobileHCI 2010, pp. 143–152. Association for Computing Machinery, New York (2010). ISBN: 978-1-60558-835-3. https://doi.org/10.1145/1851600.1851625. https://doi.org/10.1145/1851600.1851625. Accessed 24 May 2024

49. McHugh Johnson, M.: How to get started with Pixel 8 Pro Camera's Pro Controls (2024). https://blog.google/products/pixel/howto-use-pixel-8-camera-pro-controls/. Accessed 25 May 2024

50. Melumad, S., Inman, J.J., Pham, M.T.: Selectively emotional: how smartphone use changes user-generated content. J. Mark. Res. **56**(2), 259–275 (2019). ISSN: 0022-2437. https://doi.org/10.1177/0022243718815429. Accessed 21 May 2024

51. Moore-Colyer, R.: Do megapixels matter in smartphone cameras? The answer may surprise you (2023). https://www.techradar.com/phones/do-megapixels-matter-in-smartphone-cameras-the-answermay-surprise-you. Accessed 25 May 2024
52. Morikawa, C., et al.: Image and video processing on mobile devices: a survey. Vis. Comput. **37**(12), 2931–2949 (2021). ISSN: 1432-2315. https://doi.org/10.1007/s00371-021-02200-8. Accessed 25 May 2024
53. Moslehpour, M., Nguyen, T.L.: The influence of perceived brand quality and perceived brand prestige on purchase likelihood of iPhone and HTC mobile phone in Taiwan. Int. J. Bus. Perform. Manag. **1** (2014). https://doi.org/10.5296/rbm.v1i1.4882
54. Nadanyiova, M., Kicova, E.: Brand as a Tool of Company's Strategic Marketing in Practice (2017)
55. Norman, D.: Emotional design: why we love (or hate) everyday things. J. Am. Cult. **27** (2004). ISBN: 978-0-465-05135-9
56. Post, K.: Brain Tattoos: Creating Unique Brands that Stick in Your Customers' Minds. Google-Books-ID: k708Bmw C2sC. AMACOM (2005). ISBN: 978-0-8144-7234-7
57. Deidre, R.: Despite Samsung's success, bias keeps company down (2015). https://www.sammobile.com/2015/04/29/despite-samsungs-success-bias-keeps-company-down/. Accessed 29 Feb 2024
58. Sanathanakrishnan, R., Ashok, S.: A critical evaluation of consumer preference between IPHONE and ANDROID mobiles. Int. J. Res. Publ. Rev. **3**(4), 2404–2407 (2022)
59. Rakib, M.R.H.K., et al.: Factors affecting young customers' smartphone purchase intention during Covid-19 pandemic. Heliyon **8**(9), e10599 (2022). ISSN: 2405-8440. https://doi.org/10.1016/j.heliyon.2022.e10599. https://www.ncbi.nlm.nih.gov/pmc/articles/PMC9476370/. Accessed 15 May 2024
60. Reynolds, F.: Camera phones: a snapshot of research and applications. IEEE Pervasive Comput. **7**(2), 16–19 (2008). ISSN: 1558-2590. https://doi.org/10.1109/MPRV.2008.28. https://ieeexplore.ieee.org/document/4487083. Accessed 25 May 2024
61. Rajamouli, S.S.: OPPO x S. S. Rajamouli — — OPPO Reno10 Series (2023). https://www.youtube.com/watch?v=mi8rn0R-jw. Accessed 25 May 2024
62. Schiffhauer, A.: See the light with Night Sight (2018). https://blog.google/products/pixel/see-light-night-sight/. Accessed 25 May 2024
63. Sharma, A.: You told us: Here's how much cameras influence your phone purchase. Independent Publication (2021). https://www.androidauthority.com/smartphone-camera-poll-results-1204074/. Accessed 20 May 2024
64. Shot on OnePlus - OnePlus (Global). https://www.oneplus.com/global/shotononeplus-rule. Accessed 20 May 2024
65. Sverdlov, E.: HUAWEI P30 — Rewrite The Rules of Photography — Gal Gadot. https://www.tomerbiran.com/huawei-p30-rewritethe-rules-of-photography-gal-gadot-1. Accessed 25 May 2024
66. Van Doorn, G., Miloyan, B.: The pepsi paradox: a review. Food Qual. Prefer. **65**, 194–197 (2018). ISSN: 0950-3293. https://doi.org/10.1016/j.foodqual.2017.11.007. https://www.sciencedirect.com/science/article/pii/S0950329317302872. Accessed 22 May 2024
67. Weisenberger, L.: The State of Smartphone Cinema — Wrapbook (2023). https://www.wrapbook.com/blog/smartphonecinema. Accessed 21 May 2024

68. Wijaya, B.S.: Dimensions of brand image: a conceptual review from the perspective of brand communication. Eur. J. Bus. Manag. **5**, 55–65 (2013). https://www.academia.edu/23496391/Dimensions_of_Brand_Image_A_Conceptual_Review_from_the_Perspective_of_Brand_Communication. Accessed 29 Feb 2024
69. Wong, L.Y.C., Burkell, J.: Motivations for sharing news on social media. In: Proceedings of the 8th International Conference on Social Media & Society. #SMSociety 2017, pp. 1–5. Association for Computing Machinery, New York (2017). ISBN: 978-1-4503-4847-8. https://doi.org/10.1145/3097286.3097343. Accessed 24 May 2024
70. Yalçýntekin, T., Saygýlý, M.: Brand loyalty at smartphones market: linking between brand passion, hedonic and utilitarian values. Mark. Manag. Innov. **1**, 274–284 (2020). ISSN: 22276718, 22184511. https://doi.org/10.21272/mmi.2020.1-23. http://mmi.fem.sumdu.edu.ua/en/journals/2020/1/274-284. Accessed 25 May 2024
71. Yang, Y.: Smartphone photography and its socio-economic life in China: an ethnographic analysis. Glob. Media China **6**(3), 259–280 (2021). ISSN: 2059 4364. https://doi.org/10.1177/20594364211005058. Accessed 25 May 2024

To Shuffle or Not to Shuffle: Evaluation of the Effect of Shuffling on Celebrity Passfaces

Ishita Sharma$^{(\boxtimes)}$ and Anirudha Joshi

Indian Institute of Technology, Bombay, Mumbai 400076, Maharashtra, India
ishitasharmadesigns@gmail.com

Abstract. Passfaces are graphical passwords that use facial images arranged in grids as password digits. A study utilized faces of celebrities as passfaces that were found to be as memorable as PINs, even among emergent users. However, the grid was not shuffled at the time of recall, raising security concerns regarding shoulder-surfing and smudge attacks. We extend their work by assessing the impact of grid shuffling on usability and memorability. We present a within-subjects, counterbalanced, longitudinal study with 100 university students that systematically compares the performance of Celebrity Passfaces presented in two conditions at recall time, one presented in the same positions (Non-shuffled) and one by shuffling the arrangement (Shuffled). Results showed no significant difference in the 10-day memorability between shuffled (98.97%) and non-shuffled (96.91%) conditions (p = 0.3033), indicating shuffled grids maintain similar usability and memorability as non-shuffled grids. While people took relatively more time to recall the shuffled passfaces in Recall 1 (31.41 s) than non-shuffled passfaces (20.78 s), and more time to recall the non-shuffled passfaces in Recall 2 and 3 (41.25, 46.10 s respectively) compared to shuffled passfaces (38.76, 45.26 s respectively), there was no significant difference between the two conditions in any of the Recalls. We present an analysis of the security and memorability of the faces used in Celebrities passfaces and compare it with the previous study.

Keywords: HCI · Usability · Security · Privacy · Graphical Passwords · Passfaces

1 Introduction

As mobile devices become repositories for an increasing amount of personal and financial data, the need for dynamic authentication systems that may cater to users becomes imperative. Knowledge-based authentication, known as "what you know" passwords, is a common method for user identification [5]. Personal Identification Numbers (PINs) are simple but have a limited security space and are not suitable for all applications. Stronger passwords, including alphanumeric combinations, offer increased security but may be simplified by users due to memory

Fig. 1. The above image depicts the Passfaces used in this study. The first page includes older male celebrities including actors and politicians, Page 2 includes older female actresses and politicians, Page 3 includes younger male actors, Page 4 includes younger female actresses, Page 5 includes male cricketers, and Page 6 has female celebrities from miscellaneous fields.

constraints [13]. Graphical passwords utilize human visual memory to enhance authentication. Passfaces, introduced by Brostoff and Sasse in 2000, are graphical passwords that use the recognition of human faces arranged in grids for user authentication. Their study showed that Passfaces could improve login accuracy compared to traditional passwords, with fewer login errors over a three-month field trial, indicating their potential for enhanced security [3]. Another study by Asif et al. [21] on 6-digit Passfaces using images of celebrities found high memorability over four days compared to unknown faces and PINs, despite Passfaces having a larger password space than PINs.

With the extended use of touch-screen-enabled smartphones, risks of over-the-shoulder attacks, where an attacker observes the user's screen or actions to obtain sensitive information, and smudge attacks, where an attacker deduces the password by analyzing the smudge patterns left on the screen, have increased. One easy mitigation for these attacks is shuffled keypads/keyboards. However, previous work has reported that users don't like shuffled keypads/keyboards both have inherent order (either numerical order, or the QWERTY sequence) that users are very familiar with [12]. However, with passfaces, there is no inherent order, and, we posit that this password mechanism is more amenable to shuffling.

This paper seeks to extend the work of Asif et al. [21] and attempt to address its two limitations. Firstly, in their study the number of recalls and the duration between Recall 1 (immediate) and Recall 2 (after 4 days) was limited, potentially impacting insights into longer-term memorability. Our study addresses this by setting 3 recalls at different intervals - Recall 1 (Immediate Recall), Recall 2 (Delayed Recall; 4 days after Recall 1), and Recall 3 (Long-term Recall; 10 days interval from Recall 2). Secondly, like many other password mechanisms, Passfaces are susceptible to smudge and shoulder-surfing attacks due to the fixed position of faces within each grid during password entry. Our study addresses this by shuffling the presentation of the Celebrity Passfaces during recalls.

In this paper, we aim to compare the performance of university students (N = 100) using shuffled and non-shuffled conditions of Celebrity Passfaces. Arguably, shuffled Celebrity Passfaces may offer protection against smudge and shoulder-surfing attacks while maintaining similar usability and memorability to the non-shuffled condition. Through a within-subjects, counterbalanced study with 100 university students, we investigated the usability, memorability, and security of Celebrity Passfaces presented in shuffled and non-shuffled conditions. To explore the reception of graphical passwords, specifically Celebrity Passfaces, within a demographic known for its technological proficiency and contrast the outcomes with those observed among emergent users, we decided to engage university students. The proximity to this population enabled a broader recruitment effort, thus facilitating increased participation in the study.

The contributions of this paper include insights into the usability and effectiveness of Celebrity Passfaces as a graphical password mechanism. Conducted with 100 participants, this study demonstrates that recall success rates for Celebrity Passfaces remain above 90% even after 10 days, indicating strong memorability and user retention. Notably, the shuffling of passfaces does not degrade performance, suggesting that enhanced security measures can be implemented without compromising user experience. The analysis of the number of attempts and success rates during password recall offers valuable data on the reliability of this authentication method. Our work also explores the relationship between the popularity of celebrities and passface memorability, offering design implications for future graphical password systems. By assessing the mental workload involved in creating and recalling passfaces using NASA TLX, we contribute to understanding the cognitive demands of these systems, emphasizing the balance between security and user burden.

2 Background

Graphical passwords are authentication systems that allow users to log in by interacting with visual elements, such as images, patterns, or drawings, rather than entering alphanumeric characters. According to a systematic literature review [18], there are four distinct categories of graphical passwords: recognition-based, recall-based, cued recall-based, and hybrid. Recognition-based methods involve selecting specific images during password creation and later identifying them during authentication. Recall-based methods require users to recreate a pattern or input based on memory without any cues. Cued recall-based methods offer visual cues to assist in recalling the password, such as PassPoints [20], where users select a sequence of points on a single image as their password and Cued-Click Points (CCP) [16], where users click on specific points across a series of images, with each click prompting the next image. Hybrid methods combine elements from the other types to create a more versatile password system.

Among these, recognition-based methods are particularly noteworthy, with Passfaces being one of the most recognized examples. Passfaces [3] are a recognition-based graphical password system where users authenticate by recognizing pre-selected human faces from a grid during multiple rounds of authentication. This method capitalizes on the human ability to remember and recognize faces more easily than text, making it a potentially more intuitive and secure alternative to traditional passwords. Studies have shown that Passfaces can reduce login errors and improve user satisfaction compared to alphanumeric passwords [3].

Despite their advantages, Passfaces and other graphical passwords are not immune to security vulnerabilities. Two significant threats to graphical password systems are shoulder-surfing and smudge attacks. Shoulder-surfing occurs when an attacker observes a user entering their password, either directly or via recording devices, potentially compromising the security of the authentication process. Smudge attacks exploit the oily residues left on a touchscreen by a user's fingers, allowing attackers to infer the password based on visible smudge patterns left on the device screen. Various methods have been proposed to counter these smudge attacks on mobile password systems, such as randomizing the layout of input mechanisms like PINs and using vibrations as a variable for input [8], modifying or extending existing password mechanisms such as the pattern lock by allowing nodes in the grid to be included multiple times [4] and using geometric image transformations, such as translation, rotation, scaling, shearing, and flipping, to increase the security of cued-recall graphical passwords [17]. Other techniques include Split pattern, Wheel lock, Random PIN lock, and Temporal lock [2], which aim to prevent or reduce the effectiveness of smudge attacks while considering usability and shoulder-surfing resistance.

A study [1] proposed a virtual keyboard where the arrangement of the keys was dynamically shuffled after each click event and the position of the keys was concealed to prevent unauthorized viewing. The analysis revealed that this improved the security of the virtual keyboard for users and made it harder for malicious software to capture authentication information, however, the time needed to input passwords was approximately two times longer than a conventional keyboard. Another study [12] shows enhanced security against smudge and shoulder-surfing attacks when using a Privacy-Enhancing Keyboard (PEK) that shuffles character positions on an alpha-numeric keyboard when a password input box is detected. Users did, however, complain that it took too long to use the mechanism which frequently resulted in the phone sleeping, and that entering their password was very challenging. Another observation from this study is that users are used to the QWERTY presentation of keys. Shuffling this every time during a new login attempt causes a significant increase in the cognitive load of users and increased frustration.

Graphical passwords can also incorporate additional security measures to prevent shoulder-surfing and smudge attacks. Studies have demonstrated the benefits of shuffling input mechanisms, showing resilience against targeted attack vectors like smudge attacks and shoulder-surfing. In a study by Joshi and Muniyal [7], a graphical password using a 3×3 grid of images was created to enhance the security of an alphanumeric password, where the images in the grid are shuffled during input to prevent eavesdropping and shoulder-surfing. The user first inputs their text password, and subsequently selects a maximum of 3 out of 9 images in the grid, in any order, to authenticate. Another study [9] proposed a circular point model whereby users' facial images, gathered at random, are distributed across designated points arranged along a circular trajectory. Users are required to input a graphical pattern by sequentially connecting these images according to a predetermined order. The shuffling pattern scheme reorganizes the input grid to counter the threat posed by shoulder-surfing attacks and modifies the main display for password input each time. Collectively, these papers provide evidence of the benefits of shuffling input mechanisms that encompass resilience against targeted attack vectors (i.e. smudge attacks and shoulder-surfing) and the potential for enhanced security when compared to conventional password systems.

As mentioned earlier, Passfaces [3] are a graphical password system where users authenticate by recognizing pre-selected human faces from a grid through multiple authentication rounds. A study [3] comparing Passfaces to traditional passwords found fewer login errors over a three-month field trial with 34 student participants. In the study by Asif et al. [21], the usability and 4-day memorability of PINs, Passfaces and Celebrity Passfaces were explored among emergent users. Celebrity Passfaces are a unique take on the password mechanism where the faces of national and local (Marathi) celebrities in India were used as Passfaces. The study by Asif et al. [21] was systematic, within-subjects, and counterbalanced, comparing PINs, Unknown Passfaces, and Celebrity Passfaces using two recall tests spaced 4 days apart. Each participant attended four sessions over 12–13 days, using the three password mechanisms. Participants received compensation for attendance and correct recalls. In the first session, participants were briefed, provided informed consent, and trained on their first password mechanism. They set and confirmed a password, then completed a 5-min distraction task before performing Recall 1. In subsequent sessions, participants did Recall 2 of the first mechanism, then set, confirmed, and recalled passwords for the remaining mechanisms. The study did not limit password attempts, allowing multiple retries until confirmation as the participants comprised of emergent users. The results confirmed that Celebrity passfaces were more memorable than Unknown Passfaces among emergent users. However, the recommended randomization of keypad layouts, as proposed by [10], was not implemented in the study by Asif et al. [21], and the passfaces were only recalled twice over 4 days, lacking insights into the long-term memorability of Celebrity Passfaces.

In this paper, we investigate the usability and memorability of Celebrity Passfaces under two conditions: shuffled and non-shuffled. Using a systematic, within-subjects, counterbalanced study design, we conducted multiple recall tests over a span of 4 days and 10 days. Recall 1 represents the mechanism's first-time usability and immediate memorability. Recall 2 represents delayed memorability (4-day) and Recall 3 represents long-term memorability (10-day).

In earlier studies, Passfaces have proved to be memorable over long periods without use. Passfaces leverage users' visual recognition skills by prompting them with mechanisms and facilitating effective consolidation as seen in multiple recall studies [6,11,14,19]. In studies conducted by Valentine, T. (1998) An Evaluation of the Passface Personal Authentication System cited in [3], participants recalled passfaces at different time intervals including 1 day, 1 week, and 1 month. Participants who had been using the mechanism every day remembered passfaces best (99.98% of participants recalled in the first attempt), while those who recalled the passfaces in a 1 week or 1 month interval, recalled it by their 3rd attempt. According to the Ebbinghaus forgetting curve [14], forgetting occurs rapidly in the first few days after learning. But over time, forgetting occurs more slowly after this initial drop in recall. As mentioned earlier, there was only a marginal difference in passface memorability between one week and thirty days in the studies conducted by Valentine (1998). The long-term memorability of Celebrity Passfaces was therefore tested using three recalls spaced four and fourteen days apart from the first recall (10 days apart from the second recall).

3 Design

3.1 Study Design and Interface

Layout randomization, or, for the context of this study, shuffling of passfaces, would improve the security of the passface by reducing the risk of smudge attacks and shoulder-surfing. As we argued in the introduction, we posit that this should not affect the usability or memorability of the password.

Without shuffling, the password space (as mentioned below) is significantly constrained due to the predictability of selections based on familiarity and grid position. Shuffling disrupts this predictability by randomizing the arrangement of Passfaces in each authentication attempt, effectively increasing the complexity of potential attack vectors. For instance, in a non-shuffled scenario, an attacker observing a user's shoulder could potentially memorize the positions of selected Passfaces, reducing the effective password space. In contrast, shuffling ensures that even if an attacker gains partial knowledge of a password, they cannot rely on consistent grid positions, thus exponentially increasing the difficulty of successful shoulder-surfing attacks. Similarly, smudge attacks, where an attacker gleans password information from the pattern of finger smudges on a screen, are mitigated by shuffling. By altering the layout of Passfaces with each use, the pattern of touch interactions becomes less predictable, thereby diminishing the effectiveness of smudge attacks.

To compare the shuffled and non-shuffled sequencing of Celebrity Passfaces, we decided to keep the design for the prototype consistent with the earlier study of passfaces with emergent users [21] on account of the design of the prototypes having undergone iterative testing by the authors. As the study was done in the cities of Mumbai and Pune, the selection of images incorporated known faces, including nationally recognizable figures as well as locally known faces such as those from the Marathi film and television industry. Each prototype allows for setting up a password, confirming the password, and recalling the password for the given participant. It also logged the time taken for each task, selected passfaces, and the results of each recall.

The objective of our study was to compare Celebrity Passfaces in two conditions of grid sequencing during recall: shuffled and non-shuffled. The design of the interface remained consistent with the one used in the study by Asif et al. [21] so that the results can be comparable. Earlier studies contributed to the design of the prototype used in both studies. Thus we maintained the parameters from Asif et al. study including the password length (6 digits), grid size (4x4), password space (16^6 or 1.7×10^7 and a guessability of $1/(1.7 \times 10^7)$) the selection of celebrity faces, and the presentation of celebrity faces per grid.

We did implement a few key differences. Firstly, given that the study was undertaken with students from the university, we decided to utilize an asterisk (*) to conceal the previously entered digits as they were being inputted (Fig. 1), ensuring only the most recent digit was visible during selection and recall. The purpose behind this to enhance security by obscuring earlier entries, aligning with common practices of masking passwords except for the most recent digit entered.

Secondly, we proceeded to carry out three recalls: immediate recall (Recall 1), delayed recall (Recall 2; interval of 4 days; as defined in [21]), and long-term recall (Recall 3; interval of 10 days). We define Recall 3 as long-term recall, because as observed in Ebbinghaus' learning curve [14], wherein the rapid loss of information occurs in the initial days post-learning, followed by a gradual decrease thereafter. By implementing a 10-day interval for Recall 3, we allow sufficient time for the forgetting curve to plateau, indicating a possible stabilization in memory retention. This extended duration enables a more comprehensive evaluation of long-term memory performance, capturing the persistence of learned information beyond the initial rapid forgetting phase.

Through this study, we attempt to explore the following research questions:

1. How do participants perform in terms of delayed (4-day) memorability, long-term (10-day) memorability, first-time usability, and time taken to set and recall shuffled and non-shuffled Celebrity Passfaces?
2. What is the effect of shuffling the presentation of images during the recall of Celebrity Passfaces on participants?

3.2 Method

We recruited a group of 100 university students from various departments, disciplines, and academic years within a university. Among these participants, 71 were male and 29 were female. The age range of the participants ranged from 17 to 27 years (The participants were chosen through convenience sampling due to the abbreviated duration of the study).

Each participant was presented with 2 types of passface grid sequencing: shuffled and non-shuffled (identical when first shown during the password creation phase), and participated in a series of five sessions, with each session being separated by a four-day interval followed by a ten-day interval per condition.

The total duration of the study per participant was 29 days. The assignment of test tasks to the participants was counterbalanced to minimize the potential influence of learning effects. All tests within the study were conducted on a hand-held device/mobile phone.

Participants were given a recall incentive per session (Rs. 50 for recalling 6 digits correctly, Rs. 40 for 5 digits, and so on) provided they attended all 5 sessions, simulating the real-life scenario where each password carries tangible consequences, emphasizing the high stakes involved. The participant would be given 4 attempts to enter their password correctly, with the accuracy of their first correct attempt or fourth attempt used to calculate their monetary compensation. If the participant failed to recall their password correctly by the fourth attempt, they would move on to the second condition within the study. Thus, each participant was compensated a maximum of Rs 300 if they recalled their passwords accurately within 4 attempts. There was no travel involved in the study as it was done remotely. Each session lasted for about 10–15 min.

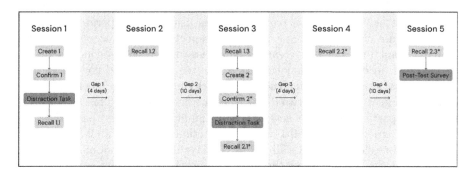

Fig. 2. The above image depicts the overview of the study methodology. The * indicates shuffling. The above methodology would follow assuming the non-shuffled condition was shown to the participant first. If the shuffled condition is shown first to the participant, Confirm 1, Recall 1.1, Recall 1.2, and Recall 1.3 would be shuffled while Confirm 2, Recall 2.1, Recall 2.2, and Recall 2.3 would be non-shuffled. Every participant participated in 5 sessions in a span of 29 days.

In the first session, the moderator briefed the participant about the study, its structure, the monetary incentives, and took their informed consent. They were told that they will need to set a password, recall it immediately, then recall it after a gap of 4 days, and then recall again after a gap of 10 days. They will then repeat the same steps after setting a second passface using the other password mechanism. They were given the option to opt out of the study at any time. The participant was given a short demo on the passfaces interface and how they could backspace or re-enter the digits they wished to choose. The participant was not informed that the study was regarding the shuffling of passfaces. The participant was then randomly assigned to either the shuffled or the non-shuffled condition as their first password mechanism. To maintain uniformity during the password creation process and consistency with Asif et al.'s work [21], we did not shuffle the grids at the time of password creation in both conditions.

The participant then created their first password. After setting their password, they were asked to confirm it by entering it again. They were then given a 5-min distraction task of a memory game that involved identifying similar faces by uncovering tiles. Once completed, they were asked to do Recall 1. The participant was given 4 attempts to recall their password. If they failed to recall it in a maximum of 4 attempts, it was recorded as a failure. In case of failure, we recorded the number of correct digits recalled (if any). This ended the first session.

The second session was held four days later. The participant was instructed to perform Recall 2 (in a maximum of 4 attempts, as earlier). If they entered the passface accurately within 4 attempts, that would conclude their second session. If the participant failed to recall, they moved to the second condition. For example, if a participant failed to recall the password set in the non-shuffled condition, they would move on and start creating the password for the shuffled condition in the current session itself.

After another 10 days, the participant was instructed to perform Recall 3 (in a maximum of 4 attempts, as earlier). Irrespective of the success or failure, the participant proceeded to create a new password for the second condition (i.e. Shuffled, in case their first condition was the non-shuffled condition, and vice versa). At this time, we instructed the participant that the second passface should not repeat more than two digits from the first passface. This was done to ensure that participants set a new password. Similar to the first password, the participant carried out a Recall 1 after a distraction task, a Recall 2 after 4 days in the fourth session, and a Recall 3 after 10 days in a fifth session.

Following the conclusion of the fifth session, the participant was informed that the study had been regarding shuffled and non-shuffled presentations of passfaces, and a post-test survey was administered to gain insight into the participant's behavior concerning password selection criteria, and perception of security for each condition, ease of use, and preferences. Furthermore, an evaluation of the participants' mental workload during passface creation and subsequent recalls of the two conditions was carried out utilizing the NASA Task Load Index [15]. The method is summarised in Fig. 2.

Thus, we conducted a within-subjects, counter-balanced systematic recall study with university students (N = 100), which had one independent variable (Celebrity Passface Grid Sequence) with two levels (Non-Shuffled or Shuffled), and a primary endpoint dependent variable of a 10-day Recall 3. We also analysed 10 other dependent variables, namely Recall 1 success (Usability), Recall 2 success (Delayed Memorability), Recall 3 success (Long-term memorability), Number of digits recalled successfully in Recall 1, Number of digits recalled successfully in Recall 2, Number of digits recalled successfully in Recall 3, Time taken to create the password, Time taken for Recall 1, Time taken for Recall 2, Time taken for Recall 3, and the number of attempts before a successful recall. Passface length, grid size, repetition of tokens, and masking of passfaces with an asterisk were treated as control variables. The grid sequence was randomized, i.e., the passfaces were shuffled during confirmation and recall but not during the creation of the password.

4   Results

4.1   Success Rates

As previously mentioned, the results from Recall 1 demonstrate the initial usability of the shuffling of Celebrity passfaces. The overall success rates in Recall 2 reflect a combination of both first-time usability and delayed memorability after 4 days, and similarly, recall 3 success rates reflect long-term memorability (10 days after Recall 2) of the passfaces. By analyzing the success rates in Recall 2 and 3 specifically for participants who were successful in previous recalls, we can isolate the impact of the 4-day and 10-day memorability. It is to be expected that individuals who failed in Recall 1 would also fail in Recall 2 and Recall 3, or those who passed Recall 1 but failed in Recall 2 would fail Recall 3. Hence, the primary endpoint of our study is the percentage of users who were successful in Recall 1 and then were also successful in Recall 2 after a gap of 4 days and Recall 3 after a gap of 10 days. We found that 94% of participants were successful in the non-shuffled condition and 88% of participants were successful in the shuffled condition in all 3 Recalls. This was our primary endpoint. Please refer to Table 1 for more detailed values.

Table 1. Success rates of the two conditions in Recall 1, Recall 2 (only those participants who were successful in Recall 1), and Recall 3 (only those participants who were successful in Recall 1 and 2). The last row also presents the results of the χ^2 test.

	Recall 1 Success		Recall 2 Success *Recall 1 Successful Participants*		Recall 3 Success *Recall 1 and 2 Successful Participants*	
	First Time Usability		4 Day Memorability		10-Day Memorability	
	Non-Shuffled	Shuffled	Non-Shuffled	Shuffled	Non-Shuffled	Shuffled
Success	99	98	96	94	95	91
Failure	1	2	3	4	1	3
Total	100	100	99	98	96	94
Proportion (%)	99.00%	98.00%	97.06%	96.08%	98.97%	96.91%
95% C.I. from	92.70%*	92.56%	91.34%	90.03%	92.49%*	90.92%
95% C.I. to	99.89%*	99.89%	99.36%	98.78%	99.89%*	99.33%
	$\chi^2 = 0.3367, p = 0.5617$		$\chi^2 = 0.158, p = 0.691$		$\chi^2 = 1.0595, p = 0.3033$	

As we can see in Recall 1 ($\chi^2 = 0.3367, p = 0.5617$), 2 ($\chi^2 = 0.158, p = 0.691$), and 3 ($\chi^2 = 1.0595, p = 0.3033$), while the non-shuffled condition is relatively more successful, the difference between the non-shuffled and shuffled conditions is not significant in any of the recalls.

In the study by Asif et al. [21], 89.39% of emergent users were successful in Recall 1 of non-shuffled Celebrity Passfaces, and 93.22% of those successful participants were successful in Recall 2, as opposed to 99% of university students successful in Recall 1 of non-shuffled Celebrity Passfaces, and 97.06% of those successful in Recall 2 in our study. However, as their study encompassed emergent users, a direct comparison cannot be made. A dependent binomial test was also conducted to assess whether there was a statistically significant difference in the success rates between the non-shuffled and shuffled conditions across these recalls which returned insignificant ($z = 0.9487$, $p = 0.3428$).

We also analysed digit-wise failures as shown in Table 2. We analysed failures in Recall 1 and 2 by coding the number of digits participants failed by as ordinal variables (If a participant failed by 1 digit, it was coded as 1, if they failed by 2 digits, then it was coded as 2, and so on) [21]. The results depicted that the non-shuffled and shuffled presentations had 1 (failed by 6 digits) and 2 (failed by 3 digits) participants respectively that failed by more than 2 digits indicating almost no difference in digit-wise failures. Even in the case of emergent users [21], only 2 users forgot more than 2 faces (non-shuffled) in the whole study.

Table 2. Digit-wise failure analysis for Recall 1, Recall 2, and Recall 3.

	Recall 1		Recall 2 Success *(Recall 1 Successful Participants)*		Recall 3 Success *(Recall 1 and 2 Successful Participants)*	
	First Time Usability		4-Day Memorability		10-Day Memorability	
	Non-Shuffled	Shuffled	Non-Shuffled	Shuffled	Non-Shuffled	Shuffled
Success	99	98	96	94	95	91
Failure	1	2	3	4	1	3
1 digit failed	1	2	0	2	0	3
2 digits failed	0	0	3	0	0	0
3 digits failed	0	0	0	2	0	0
4 digits failed	0	0	0	0	0	0
5 digits failed	0	0	0	0	0	0
6 digits failed	0	0	0	0	1	0

4.2 Time Taken

Table 3 summarizes the time taken to set up, time taken for Recall 1, Recall 2, and Recall 3 for the Celebrity Passface conditions. Setup time is reported for all 100 participants in the study while time taken for Recall 1, 2, and 3 is reported for 88 participants who were successful in all 3 recalls for both, non-shuffled and shuffled conditions. In all 3 recalls, the time includes failed attempts before a successful attempt. In qualitative observations, we noticed participants took time to carefully choose celebrities that they would remember using multiple interesting strategies. A one-way ANOVA revealed that the difference in the time taken to set up the passfaces in the two conditions was statistically insignificant ($F(1,198) = [0.439]$, $p = 0.507$) (Both conditions had the same set-up procedure).

A two-way ANOVA revealed that there was a statistically significant difference in the interaction effect of condition (Non-shuffled and Shuffled) and Recall number (1, 2, and 3) ($F (5,522) = 3.112$, $p = 0.050$) with the means plotted in Fig. 3. Pairwise comparisons using Bonferroni corrections found that the time taken for Recall 1 was significantly different from the time taken for Recall 2 ($p < 0.0005$) and Recall 3 ($p < 0.0005$). However, there was no significant difference

Table 3. Time taken (in seconds) for Setup, Recall 1, Recall 2, and Recall 3.

	Setup Time		Recall 1 Time		Recall 2 Time *Recall 1 Successful Participants*		Recall 3 Time *Recall 1 and 2 Successful Participants*	
			First Time Usability		4-Day Memorability		10-Day Memorability	
	Non-Shuffled	Shuffled	Non-Shuffled	Shuffled	Non-Shuffled	Shuffled	Non-Shuffled	Shuffled
N	100	100	88	88	88	88	88	88
Mean	89.31	84.1	20.784	31.409	41.25	38.761	46.102	45.261
95% C.I. from	76.601	72.733	17.761	25.804	33.987	32.940	37.343	39.046
95% C.I. to	102.019	95.467	23.807	37.015	48.513	44.583	54.862	51.477
	$F_{(1, 198)} = 0.439, p = 0.507$		$F_{(5, 522)} = 3.112, p = 0.050*$					

*Repeated measure 2x3 ANOVA of 88 Participants successful in all condition recalls.

Table 4. Mean Time taken (in seconds) for Non-shuffled and Shuffled conditions in all 3 Recalls.

Mean Time Taken		
	Non-Shuffled	Shuffled
N	88	88
Mean	36.045	38.477
95% C.I. from	31.569	34.383
95% C.I. to	40.522	42.572

between the time taken for Recall 2 and Recall 3 ($p = 0.131$). This result may be attributed to the fact that Recall 1 occurs immediately after the creation of the password and is therefore stored freshly in the individual's memory. In contrast, Recall 2 takes place after a period of 4 days, which necessitates a longer period for contemplation and recollection. Recall 3, occurring 10 days after recall 2, surprisingly exhibits no significant difference in performance, suggesting that the long-term memorability of Celebrity Passfaces is good, in line with studies conducted by Valentine (1998). The mean set-up time (180.06 s) and Recall 1 (47.56 s) of emergent users for the non-shuffled condition is relatively more than university students (Mean set-up time = 89.31 s, Recall 1 time = 20.784 s), however, the time taken for Recall 2 for emergent users (44.85 s) is almost similar to university students (41.25 s). In the shuffled condition, the process of inputting the password takes slightly longer as participants must search for their selected celebrities. However, it is noteworthy that no significant differences are observed in the recall times between the non-shuffled and shuffled conditions (Table 4). It is interesting to note that while Recall 1 (the immediate recall) is faster in the non-shuffled condition, it is indeed slightly slower in Recalls 2 (4-day interval) and 3 (10-day interval from Recall 2). Thus, it is safe to say that shuffling makes no difference to the time taken over a longer period of time.

4.3   Number of Attempts

In this study, we limited the attempts to only 4 because the earlier study findings reported that success was achieved up to the fourth attempt, and beyond that, participants were not able to recall their passwords [21]. We employed Friedman's test to investigate if there were any noteworthy discrepancies in the

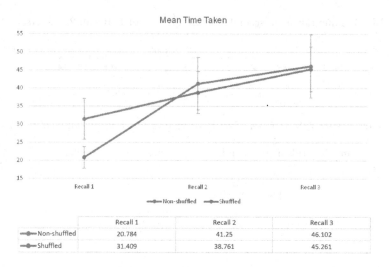

Fig. 3. The above image depicts the estimated marginal means of the time taken for Recall 1, 2, and 3 for the non-shuffled and shuffled conditions. The 95% confidence intervals are plotted in the graph as well.

number of attempts between the non-shuffled and shuffled conditions, however, no significant differences emerged ($\chi^2 = 4.099, p = 0.535$). Like with the time taken, it is interesting to note that while Recall 1 (the immediate recall) required fewer attempts in the non-shuffled condition, participants needed more attempts in the non-shuffled conditions in Recalls 2 and 3. Thus, it is also safe to say that shuffling makes no difference to the number of attempts required for a successful recall over a longer period of time.

Table 5. Number of Attempts for Recall 1, Recall 2, and Recall 3.

	Recall 1 Attempts		Recall 2 Attempts		Recall 3 Attempts	
	Non-Shuffled	Shuffled	Non-Shuffled	Shuffled	Non-Shuffled	Shuffled
N	88	88	88	88	88	88
Mean	1.068	1.114	1.227	1.057	1.193	1.102
95% C.I. from	1.014	1.020	1.078	1.007	1.069	1.1017
95% C.I. to	1.122	1.207	1.377	1.017	1.317	1.188
	$\chi^2 = 4.099, p = 0.535$					

4.4 Post-test Survey

Preferences of Passfaces: Non-shuffled or Shuffled? In the post-test survey, participants were asked to choose between non-shuffled and shuffled conditions and give their reasons. Out of 100, 62 participants preferred the non-shuffled condition because it was easier to recall, the faces could be remembered based on their positions in the grids, and it was faster to find the chosen passfaces due to muscle memory, and, 30 participants preferred the shuffled condition because it felt safer and more secure, they remembered the face more than the position, it was more fun, and people couldn't guess their password through smudge marks on their mobile. 8 participants had no preference because they weren't remembering faces based on position.

Experience, Confidence in Security, Ease of Use, and Engagement. Participants were asked to rate their experience, confidence in security, ease of use, and level of engagement during passface creation and the recall of their passface in both the non-shuffled and shuffled conditions. The ratings were on a Likert scale from 1 to 7. As seen in Fig. 4, 80 participants rated the shuffled condition 5 or greater in terms of confidence in security, compared to 60 participants for the non-shuffled condition. Thus, participants' perception of security is greater for the shuffled condition. The experience, ease of use, and level of engagement have a marginal difference among both conditions for participants that have rated it 5 or above out of 7. It is notable, however, that 33 participants rated the ease of use of the non-shuffled passface 7 while only 16 participants rated the shuffled condition a 7, which is understandable as the shuffled condition requires the participant to search for their chosen celebrities.

Mental Workload NASA Task Load Index. An evaluation of the participants' mental workload during Passface creation and subsequent recalls of the two conditions was carried out using the NASA Task Load Index (NASA TLX) [15], a standardized multi-dimensional rating procedure that provides an overall workload score based on a weighted average across six subscales: Mental Demand, Physical Demand, Temporal Demand, Own Performance, Effort, and Frustration. The NASA TLX was administered during the post-test survey, where participants were asked specific questions for each condition-creating the Passface, recalling the non-shuffled Passfaces, and recalling the shuffled Passfaces.

Participants responded to six questions tailored to each condition: How mentally demanding was the task? How physically demanding was the task? How hurried or rushed was the pace of the task? How successful were you in accomplishing what you were asked to do? How hard did you have to work to accomplish your level of performance? How insecure, discouraged, irritated, stressed, and annoyed were you? These questions were designed to capture the subjective experience of each participant concerning the demands of the task and their performance. In addition to answering these questions, participants were also

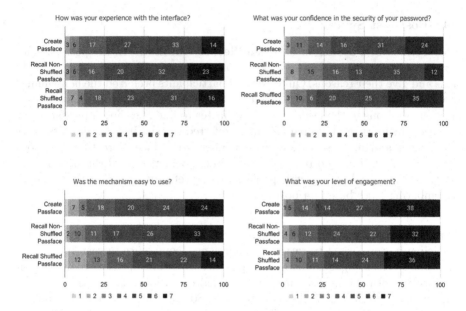

Fig. 4. Graphs depicting participant ratings of experience, confidence in security, ease of use, and engagement of creation and recall of shuffled and non-shuffled conditions. We conducted a Kolmogorov-Smirnov (K-S) test to determine if there were statistically significant differences between the ratings of non-shuffled and shuffled conditions of passfaces for the four parameters. We found that the ratings of both conditions for the parameters ease of use (D = 0.230) and confidence in security (D = 0.230) were significantly different (Critical value = 0.192) while experience (D = 0.080) and level of engagement (D = 0.060) were not significantly different.

required to determine the relative importance of each of the six subscales by making pairwise comparisons, as outlined in the NASA TLX Manual [15]. This step allowed participants to assign weightings to each subscale based on their perceived significance. The overall workload score for each condition was then calculated by averaging the weighted ratings across all subscales.

The data revealed that the overall workload for creating a Passface was 33.9, recalling non-shuffled Passfaces was 33.27, and recalling shuffled Passfaces was 50.82. These results suggest that, on average, participants perceived the workload and effort required for creating a Passface and recalling a non-shuffled Passface to be relatively low or manageable. However, recalling a shuffled Passface was perceived as moderately demanding, particularly when considering the weighted dimensions of the task, indicating that shuffling increases the cognitive load on users (Refer to Fig. 5).

4.5   Popularity of Selection

Participants made 2 passwords during their sessions, which were counterbalanced between non-shuffled and shuffled to mitigate the practice effect. Table 5

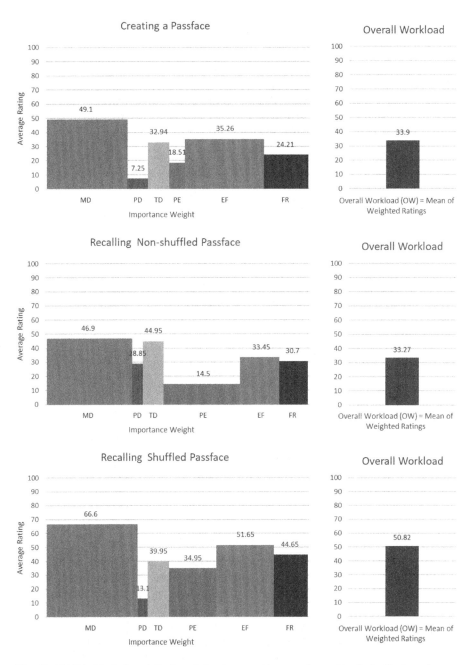

Fig. 5. NASA Task Load Index data for creation, and recall of shuffled and non-shuffled Celebrity Passfaces. The width of the bars depicts the average weight assigned by participants for a particular subscale. The 6 subscales are Mental demand (MD), Physical Demand (PD), Temporal Demand (TD), Own Performance (PE), Effort (EF), and Frustration (FR).

lists the total number of times a particular celebrity was chosen in both passwords. This revealed the popularity of 20 personalities who were chosen by 20 or more participants listed in Table 6: 1) Narendra Modi, 2) Indira Gandhi, 3) Virat Kohli, 4) Deepika Padukone, 5) Shah Rukh Khan, 6) Kalpana Chawla, 7) Amitabh Bachchan, 8) Katrina Kaif, 9) Aishwarya Rai Bachchan, 10) MS Dhoni, 11) Sachin Tendulkar, 12) APJ Abdul Kalam, 13) Priyanka Chopra Jonas, 14) Mary Kom, 15) Alia Bhatt, 16) Nita Ambani 17) Salman Khan, 18) Rekha, 19) Mamta Banerjee, and 20) Hritik Roshan.

Table 6. Popularity among the celebrities. The table shows the number of times that particular celebrity was chosen with their ranks in brackets.

Position in Page	Page 1	Page 2	Page 3	Page 4	Page 5	Page 6
Position 1	42 (7)	4	10	3	5	14
Position 2	66 (1)	8	7	31 (13)	63 (3)	1
Position 3	1	17	24 (17)	0	9	10
Position 4	0	6	6	2	14	4
Position 5	0	7	43 (5)	15	4	9
Position 6	6	6	6	2	8	0
Position 7	2	1	6	2	1	1
Position 8	12	1	11	0	6	0
Position 9	14	2	2	1	1	41 (8)
Position 10	9	23 (18)	13	40 (9)	1	4
Position 11	5	21 (19)	4	48 (4)	40 (10)	1
Position 12	4	6	16	27 (15)	3	43 (6)
Position 13	33 (12)	15	4	8	2	15
Position 14	2	5	21 (20)	3	40 (11)	30 (14)
Position 15	3	12	9	11	1	1
Position 16	1	66 (2)	18	4	2	26 (16)

The selection of local Marathi personalities was not as high as found in the study with emergent users (E.g. Sindhutai Sapkal, Sai Tamhankar, Sachin Pilgaonkar) [21], as the university corpus included students from varying locations in India, who preferred more widely known celebrities as well as celebrities from their region. This reinforces the localization of celebrity images and could enhance security further. Well-known historical personalities such as Kalpana Chawla and APJ Abdul Kalam were also chosen.

We also observed that participants' choices were influenced by the relative popularity of celebrities within a page. For instance, out of a total of 200 passwords created, Amitabh Bachchan, Narendra Modi, and APJ Abdul Kalam account for 70.5% of page 1 selections; Virat Kohli, Sachin Tendulkar, and MS Dhoni account for 71.5% of page 5 selections; and Indira Gandhi alone accounts for 33% of page 2 selections, suggesting that the popularity of a person should not be the only factor for including them in a password mechanism, rather a more balanced page should be designed. However, university students exhibit more diverse selections overall in contrast to emergent users [21].

During the creation of the second password (Referred to as Password 2), participants were advised to repeat no more than 2 faces. 40% of participants repeated no faces, 26% repeated 1 face, and 32% repeated 2 faces from their earlier password. 2 participants did not adhere to the advisory. Out of the repeated celebrities, Indira Gandhi (8), Virat Kohli (8), MS Dhoni (7), and Narendra Modi (6) were repeated the most.

Further, we analyzed the selection of celebrities and if there existed a bias for those in the first row of the grids (position bias). The results indicated that first-row celebrities made up 28.91% of total celebrity selections which is quite close to 25%, hence no position bias was observed. In the study with emergent users [21], 48% of the choices were in the first rows of the pages suggesting that there may be a primacy effect in their selections as opposed to university students.

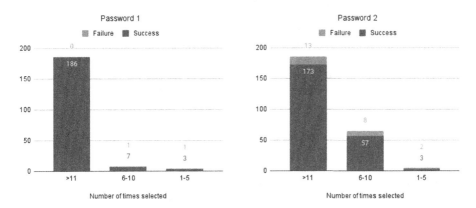

Fig. 6. The graphs compare the success and failures of the last attempts of recall where celebrity faces are categorized by popularity for both passwords. We grouped the celebrities into three groups - those who were chosen 11 or more times, those who were chosen 6–10 times, and those who were chosen 1–5 times. We also analyzed the error rates for those faces in their last recorded attempt at recall.

We also analyzed if the popularity of a celebrity also makes them more memorable at the time of recall. We grouped the celebrities into three groups - those who were chosen 11 or more times, those who were chosen 6–10 times, and those who were chosen 1–5 times (Refer to Fig. 6) in Password 1 and Password 2. We also analyzed the error rates for those faces in their last recorded attempt at recall. The error rates were found to be 0%, 12.50%, and 25% respectively in Password 1, and 6.99%, 12.31%, and 40% respectively in Password 2 for the groups mentioned above. As can be expected, the popular celebrities were also memorable. The higher error rates in Password 2 may be attributed to the confusion caused by selections made in Password 1 by participants that may have led to the exhaustion of attempts. A scatterplot depicting the popularity vs memorability of Celebrity Passfaces can be found in Fig. 7.

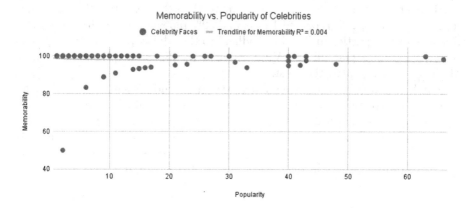

Fig. 7. The scatterplot above depicts the popularity vs memorability of Celebrity Passfaces. Each dot represents one face. The x-axis represents the number of participants who picked that face. The y-axis represents the memorability (%) of that particular face. Less popular faces are somewhat less memorable, though the effect sizes are quite small (as indicated by the R2 values).

4.6   Passface Creation Strategies

Celebrity Passfaces were a novel password mechanism that the student participants experienced or interacted with before, and the incorporation of celebrities as selectable passfaces infused an enjoyable aspect into the password creation process, customized to align with their individual preferences and interests. Given that the participant pool encompassed students aged between 17 and 27 years, the strategies employed for password creation exhibited a notable diversity beyond conventional approaches such as selecting favorite or popular choices. Numerous participants devised their passfaces by dividing the six digits into pairs, linking them through associations such as films, relationships, or public affairs. Commonly observed pairings included Amitabh Bachchan and Rekha, Ranveer Singh and Deepika Padukone, and, Shah Rukh Khan and Kajol.

Several participants indicated that exposure to trending memes or reels on platforms like Instagram influenced their selection of passfaces, such as Ranveer Singh or Mamta Banerjee. Given the considerable social media engagement within this age cohort, the frequent consumption of such content likely contributes to the heightened selection probability of certain celebrities. However, it is noteworthy that the transient nature of internet content, including memes and reels, may limit the longevity of this popularity-enhancing effect.

Some participants selected passfaces based on celebrities' physical attributes, such as age or clothing color, and interpersonal dynamics such as mutual dislike or distinctiveness within photo grids. Additionally, some participants opted for celebrities with matching initials or whose initials formed acronyms, showcasing a range of creative approaches to password creation. This highlights the potential for Celebrity Passfaces to offer a customizable, user-centric, and enjoyable authentication solution.

5 Discussion

We investigated the impact of shuffling of grids on the memorability and usability of Passfaces within the university demographic, characterized by a more technologically adept population.

Our findings indicated that the integration of shuffling did not have a significant effect on memorability and enhanced the security of Celebrity Passfaces, however, this modification introduced a trade-off in terms of the time required for password input. The observed disparity in input time between shuffled and non-shuffled Celebrity Passfaces may be attributed to the increased search time required for locating chosen passfaces within each grid. With each password comprising six digits, participants undergo a sequential process six times to complete the authentication process in Passfaces. Notably, the non-shuffled passface condition may benefit from repeated exposure, fostering a form of muscle memory wherein users develop efficient routines over time relative to the position of the chosen passface. Conversely, shuffling disrupts this memorized position process, resulting in consistent time taken to recall the shuffled passface across authentication attempts. Consequently, while non-shuffled passfaces would exhibit accelerated input times due to familiarity over time, the shuffled condition would be relatively consistent. If the password is utilised infrequently, muscle memory specific to that particular password won't develop, thus nullifying the advantage that non-shuffled passfaces have over shuffled ones, depending on the context in which the passfaces are utilized (for example, net banking).

Our study's findings align with existing research on the usability-security trade-offs in graphical password systems. While previous studies have highlighted the benefits of shuffling PINs and alphanumeric passwords in mitigating smudge and shoulder-surfing attacks, they also noted a significant decrease in usability. Our study extends this knowledge by demonstrating that shuffling Passfaces, although slightly increasing cognitive load and input time, does not compromise memorability. This finding supports the notion that graphical passwords, especially those without inherent order like Passfaces, may be better suited for shuffling than traditional passwords.

The assessment of mental workload using the NASA Task Load Index revealed a moderate level of cognitive demand associated with the recall of shuffled passfaces, with a comparatively lower workload observed during the generation and retrieval of non-shuffled passfaces. This discrepancy in workload perception likely stems from the increased cognitive effort required to search for the selected passfaces within the shuffled condition, compared to the streamlined recall process facilitated by the predictable layout of non-shuffled passfaces.

A very weak positive correlation between celebrities' popularity and memorability depicted that the more popular celebrities were, the more memorable. While leveraging moderately popular celebrities may enhance memorability without significantly escalating security risks, the inclusion of excessively renowned figures necessitates careful deliberation to mitigate the heightened vulnerability to password guessing. For example, celebrities such as Narendra Modi, Indira Gandhi, and Virat Kohli had high selection probabilities in their respective grids. In this case, while the theoretical password space of Celebrity Passfaces would be reported higher than 6-digit PINs, the practical password space may be limited to these popular selections. For any password mechanism to be deemed robust, it is imperative to ensure a balanced grid configuration wherein each token possesses an equivalent probability of selection.

As mentioned earlier, numerous participants devised their passfaces using unique strategies. By utilizing familiar celebrity pairs or associations, participants may capitalize on the mnemonic potential inherent in these connections, facilitating easier recall during authentication. However, it also raises concerns regarding the potential for predictability and susceptibility to hacking attempts if widely known associations are utilized. For instance, if a hacker discovers one digit and identifies the common pairing tendency among users, it significantly reduces the complexity of cracking the entire passface.

These observations are consistent with prior research indicating that password schemes relying on familiar or predictable patterns are more susceptible to attacks. Future work should consider strategies to diversify grid configurations to maintain security without sacrificing usability.

In our study, we observed an absence of first-row bias in celebrity selection among university participants, unlike emergent users who displayed potential primacy biases. This absence of first-row bias among university participants may be attributed to their familiarity with diverse celebrity faces, thereby reducing selections based on position within the grid. Introducing shuffling during passface creation may offer an opportunity to explore the impact of spatial arrangement on celebrity selection patterns, potentially elucidating underlying cognitive mechanisms.

6   Conclusion

We conducted a systematic, lab-based, within-subjects, counterbalanced study with university students to understand the effects of shuffling Celebrity Passfaces and compared the non-shuffled presentation of celebrity faces with the shuffled presentation during recalls. Each grid of Celebrity Passfaces had unique tokens to enhance security.

We found that while the non-shuffled condition is relatively more successful, there is no significant difference between the success rates of both conditions in Recall 1 ($\chi^2 = 0.3367, p = 0.5617$), 2 ($\chi^2 = 0.158, p = 0.691$), and 3

$(\chi^2 = 1.0595, p = 0.3033)$ indicating the efficacy of the shuffled configuration in mitigating smudge and shoulder-surfing attacks while concurrently maintaining comparable levels of memorability for participants. Recall 1 was significantly faster than Recall 2 and 3 suggesting prolonged cognitive processing to recall their Passfaces during subsequent recall attempts. Despite this discrepancy in recall time, no significant disparity was observed between the two conditions. There were no significant differences found between the number of attempts between the two shuffling conditions as well. This indicated that they had an equal probability of error during input. This finding suggests that while shuffling may introduce variability in passface presentation, its impact on error rates is negligible. Consequently, in the context of Celebrity Passfaces, this implies that implementing shuffling does not compromise usability or accessibility compared to non-shuffled configurations, thus maintaining a balanced approach to authentication.

In the post-test surveys, people who preferred the non-shuffled condition stated that it allowed them to recall their password better each time because eventually it became muscle memory by the third recall. This benefit was lost in the shuffled condition because it was equally difficult to search and input their chosen passfaces in subsequent recalls - it would never get easier. Participants who preferred the shuffled condition were more conscious of the security of their mobile. They stated that the shuffling of the passfaces made it more secure and that they weren't just remembering positions of the images but rather the faces of the chosen celebrities. Some participants stated that if the passfaces weren't shuffled, after a point it would become similar to a number pin - relying on muscle memory. Earlier studies show that shuffling of PINs and alphanumeric passwords make them less susceptible to smudge and shoulder-surfing attacks but the usability of these password mechanisms significantly decreases [1,12]. With the lack of an inherent order, passfaces are better suited for shuffling than PINs in terms of usability. Ultimately, to shuffle or not to shuffle can be a choice - one that may cater to users seeking additional security in graphical password mechanisms.

Several limitations should be acknowledged in this study. Firstly, there was limited demographic diversity in the participant pool (predominantly male students, aged 17 to 27) due to convenience sampling. In the study by Asif et al., most participants were of older age groups which led to celebrities from their time (E.g. Lata Mangeshkar, Harbhajan Singh) being chosen more often, compared to celebrities chosen in this study (E.g. Deepika Padukone, Shah Rukh Khan). Future work including a more balanced distribution of genders and incorporating participants across a broader age range would afford more comprehensive insights, particularly concerning gender-based variations.

Secondly, our research was conducted within a short time frame, focusing on immediate recall and usability. However, a longitudinal study is necessary to assess how the memorability and security of Passfaces evolve over time. Such a study could reveal patterns in long-term user behavior and the potential decline in password recall, which are critical for evaluating the long-term viability of Passfaces as an authentication mechanism.

Thirdly, it was observed that certain celebrities were chosen by a significant number of participants, potentially influencing the overall distribution of password selections and leading to possible confounding effects. Conducting a follow-up study that excludes these highly popular celebrities would yield a more stable and unbiased distribution of password choices.

Fourthly, all participants had to create 2 sets of unique passwords for both conditions. It was observed that participants made the majority of errors in the second password compared to the first (As seen in Fig. 6). This may be because participants were confusing their password 1 selections with their password 2 selections, often running out of attempts. Creating completely different sets of celebrities for both passwords may improve further studies. No direct comparison with traditional password schemes like PINs and alphanumeric passwords was made in this study. Future work could provide detailed comparisons including traditional schemes as baselines.

Additionally, the study did not delve deeply into the decision-making processes behind user image selection for Passfaces. Understanding the criteria that users apply when selecting images could provide more granular insights into both the security and memorability of graphical passwords. Future work could explore this aspect more thoroughly to develop guidelines for optimal image selection.

Future work could also involve a more rigorous analysis of security improvements by calculating the entropy of the password space before and after shuffling, offering a concrete measure of the increase in security. This could be supplemented by user studies simulating shoulder-surfing scenarios to empirically validate the enhanced security provided by shuffling.

These limitations highlight the necessity for future research to address these constraints. By expanding the participant demographics, exploring the influence of celebrity selection, and conducting more rigorous analyses regarding security enhancements, future studies can provide a deeper understanding of how shuffling impacts the security and usability of graphical passwords. Additionally, investigating user decision-making in image selection and conducting longitudinal studies will contribute to the development of more robust and user-friendly authentication systems. Addressing these areas will enhance the applicability of our findings and ensure that graphical password mechanisms like Passfaces can be effectively integrated into diverse real-world contexts.

References

1. Agarwal, M., et al.: Secure authentication using dynamic virtual keyboard layout. In: Proceedings of the International Conference & Workshop on Emerging Trends in Technology. ICWET 2011, pp. 288–291. Association for Computing Machinery, New York (2011). ISBN: 978-1-4503-0449-8. https://doi.org/10.1145/1980022.1980087. https://dl.acm.org/doi/10.1145/1980022.1980087. Accessed 08 Mar 2024
2. Amruth, M.D., Praveen, K.: Android smudge attack prevention techniques. In: Berretti, S., Thampi, S.M., Dasgupta, S. (eds.) Intelligent Systems Technologies and Applications. AISC, vol. 385, pp. 23–31. Springer, Cham (2016). https://doi.org/10.1007/978-3-319-23258-4_3

3. Brostoff, S., Sasse, M.A.: Are Passfaces more usable than passwords? A field trial investigation. In: McDonald, S., Waern, Y., Cockton, G. (eds.) People and Computers XIV - Usability or Else!, pp. 405–424. Springer, London (2000). ISBN: 978-1-4471-0515-2. https://doi.org/10.1007/978-1-4471-0515-2_27

4. Colley, A., et al.: Extending the touchscreen pattern lock mechanism with duplicated and temporal codes. Adv. Hum.-Comput. Interact. **2016**, e8762892 (2016). ISSN: 1687-5893. https://doi.org/10.1155/2016/8762892. https://www.hindawi.com/journals/ahci/2016/8762892/. Accessed 09 Mar 2024

5. Farik, M., Lal, N., Prasad, S.: A review of authentication methods. Int. J. Sci. Technol. Res. **5**, 246–249 (2016)

6. Gerbier, E., Toppino, T.C., Koenig, O.: Optimising retention through multiple study opportunities over days: the benefit of an expanding schedule of repetitions. Memory **23**(6), 943–954 (2015). https://doi.org/10.1080/09658211.2014.944916. ISSN: 0965-8211

7. Joshi, A.M., Muniyal, B.: Authentication using text and graphical password. In: 2018 International Conference on Advances in Computing, Communications and Informatics (ICACCI), pp. 381–386 (2018). https://doi.org/10.1109/ICACCI.2018.8554390. https://ieeexplore.ieee.org/document/8554390. Accessed 08 Mar 2024

8. Kabir, M.M., et al.: Enhancing smartphone lock security using vibration enabled randomly positioned numbers. In: Proceedings of the International Conference on Computing Advancements. ICCA 2020, pp. 1–7. Association for Computing Machinery, New York (2020). ISBN: 978-1-4503-7778-2. https://doi.org/10.1145/3377049.3377099. https://dl.acm.org/doi/10.1145/3377049.3377099. Accessed 09 Mar 2024

9. Kaur, R., Kaur, A.: Enhancing authentication schemes for multi-level graphical password in cloud environment. CAE **5**(8), 12–18 (2016). ISSN: 23944714. https://doi.org/10.5120/cae2016652340. http://www.caeaccess.org/archives/volume5/number8/kaur-2016-cae-652340.pdf. Accessed 09 Mar 2024

10. Kirkwood, D., et al.: PIN scrambler: assessing the impact of randomized layouts on the usability and security of PINs. In: Proceedings of the 21st International Conference on Mobile and Ubiquitous Multimedia. MUM 2022, pp. 83-88. Association for Computing Machinery, New York (2022). ISBN: 978-1-4503-9820-6. https://doi.org/10.1145/3568444.3568450. https://dl.acm.org/doi/10.1145/3568444.3568450. Accessed 13 Feb 2024

11. Küpper-Tetzel, C.E., Kapler, I.V., Wiseheart, M.: Contracting, equal, and expanding learning schedules: the optimal distribution of learning sessions depends on retention interval. Mem. Cogn. **42**(5), 729–741 (2014). https://doi.org/10.3758/s13421-014-0394-1

12. Ling, Z., et al.: A case study of usable security: usability testing of android privacy enhancing keyboard. In: Ma, L., Khreishah, A., Zhang, Y., Yan, M. (eds.) WASA 2017. LNCS, vol. 10251, pp. 716–728. Springer, Cham (2017). https://doi.org/10.1007/978-3-319-60033-8_61

13. Morris, R., Thompson, K.: Password security: a case history. Commun. ACM **22**, 594–597 (2002). https://doi.org/10.1145/359168.359172

14. Murre, J.M.J., Dros, J.: Replication and analysis of ebbinghaus' forgetting curve. PLoS ONE **10**(7), e0120644 (2015). ISSN: 1932-6203. https://doi.org/10.1371/journal.pone.0120644. https://journals.plos.org/plosone/article?id=10.1371/journal.pone.0120644. Accessed 13 Feb 2024

15. NASA Task Load Index | Digital Healthcare Research. https://digital.ahrq.gov/health-it-tools-and-resources/evaluation-resources/workflowassessment-health-it-toolkit/all-workflow-tools/nasa-task-load-index. Accessed 13 Feb 2024

16. Patra, K., et al.: Cued-click point graphical password using circular toler-
    ance to increase password space and persuasive features. Procedia Comput.
    Sci. **79**, 561–568 (2016). ISSN: 1877-0509. Proceedings of International Confer-
    ence on Communication, Computing and Virtualization (ICCCV). https://doi.
    org/10.1016/j.procs.2016.03.071. https://www.sciencedirect.com/science/article/
    pii/S1877050916002027. Accessed 13 Feb 2024
17. Schneegass, S., et al.: SmudgeSafe: geometric image transformations for smudge-
    resistant user authentication. In: Proceedings of the 2014 ACM International Joint
    Conference on Pervasive and Ubiquitous Computing. SeattleWashington: ACM,
    pp. 775–786 (2014). ISBN: 978-1-4503-2968-2. https://doi.org/10.1145/2632048.
    2636090. https://dl.acm.org/doi/10.1145/2632048.2636090. Accessed 09 Mar 2024
18. Shammee, T., et al.: A systematic literature review of graphical password schemes.
    J. Comput. Sci. Eng. **14**, 163–185 (2020). https://doi.org/10.5626/JCSE.2020.14.
    4.163
19. Smith, C.D., Scarf, D.: Spacing repetitions over long timescales: a review
    and a reconsolidation explanation. Front. Psychol. **8**, 962 (2017). ISSN: 1664-
    1078. https://doi.org/10.3389/fpsyg.2017.00962. https://www.ncbi.nlm.nih.gov/
    pmc/articles/PMC5476736/. Accessed 13 Feb 2024
20. Wiedenbeck, S., et al.: PassPoints: design and longitudinal evaluation of
    a graphical password system. Int. J. Hum.-Comput. Stud. **63**(1), 102–127
    (2005). ISSN: 1071-5819. https://doi.org/10.1016/j.ijhcs.2005.04.010. https://
    www.sciencedirect.com/science/article/pii/S1071581905000625. Accessed 13 Feb
    2024
21. Zuha, A.P., et al.: Graphical passwords for emergent users: a four-day recall com-
    parative study on PIN, passfaces and celebrities. In: Joshi, A., Sim, G.R. (eds.)
    Proceedings of the 14th Indian Conference on Human-Computer Interaction, pp.
    75–97. Springer, Singapore (2024). ISBN: 978-981-97-4335-3

Fogg Behavioural Model Based Cybersecurity Awareness Framework: An Empirical Analysis

Pintu R. Shah$^{(\boxtimes)}$

SVKM's NMIMS Mukesh Patel School of Technology Management and Engineering,
Mumbai, India
`pintu.shah@nmims.edu`

Abstract. Cyber threats have emerged as one of the significant risks facing governments, organizations and individuals. The sophistication and frequency of cyber-attacks are increasing daily despite advanced security controls. This trend indicates the need to look beyond technical security controls to prevent cyber incidents. The previous research suggests that security education, training, and awareness (SETA) programs are effective countermeasures along with other technical and administrative controls. The end user's security behaviour is critical in mitigating cyber threats. However, prior research studies indicate that most SETA programs fail to meet their objectives for various reasons. One of the reasons is the lack of systematic and theory-based design and development process of the SETA program. This paper proposes a framework for enhancing the cybersecurity behaviours of smartphone users based on the Fogg Behavioural Model (FBM). The FBM is used to design a power prompt in the proposed framework. The proposed framework was tested using a between-subjects design (n = 94) and found to be effective in creating cybersecurity awareness. The participants in the intervention group are 2.65 times more likely to adopt recommended behaviours. This framework may be useful in the design of an effective SETA program.

Keywords: Fogg Behavioural Model · Smartphone User · User Behaviour · Cybersecurity Framework · SETA Program

1 Introduction

Cybercrimes are increasing worldwide at an alarming rate. The expected annual average cost of cybercrime will be $23 trillion in 2027 [1]. Cybercrimes affect individuals, public and private organizations, and governments across the globe. They are emerging as threats to humanity. The number, severity, and sophistication of cybersecurity events are rising, suggesting that technological security controls alone cannot fully mitigate the next generation of cybersecurity threats. To enhance cybersecurity in this day and age, end users must practice excellent cyber hygiene.

The SETA program may be used to influence user behaviour. The SETA program refers to designing, developing, and implementing security awareness training efforts to improve the cybersecurity behaviour of all stakeholders, including end-users [2]. Human

N. Rangaswamy et al. (Eds.): IndiaHCI 2024, CCIS 2337, pp. 51–69, 2025.
https://doi.org/10.1007/978-3-031-80829-6_3

users cannot be blamed for cybersecurity problems if they are unaware of them [3]. The awareness about the specific issue does not lead to behavioural change [4]. The end-user should know their role in mitigating cyber threats. The SETA program aims to change cybersecurity behaviour or reinforce good security practices [2, 5, 6]. A literature review reveals consensus among security researchers on the need for effective SETA programs to protect cyberspace assets [7, 8]. International standards like ISO 27001 and PCI-DSS and regulations like GDPR and HIPAA have reiterated the need for security awareness training.

The majority of the SETA programs fail to achieve their stated goals. The ineffectiveness of SETA programs may be because of the following reasons:

- Existing SETA programs are offered as a one-size-fits-all solution [6, 9, 10]. As a result, end-users need help understanding the relevance of the SETA program, either because it is uninteresting or out of context [11].
- There is a lack of a systematic and theory-based SETA program development process [6].
- SETA programs often demand a lot of effort and skills from the participants [12]. The implementer of the SETA program expects participants to understand and digest a heap of information in a brief period [13, 14]. This may lead to security fatigue [15–17]
- The display of security threat information will not lead to behaviour change. A study by Foltz et al. [18] found that people would not adopt recommended security behaviour if they were apathetic and lacked motivation.

In this paper, the researcher proposes the framework for the design and development of the SETA program. The proposed framework addresses the issues mentioned above. The researcher designed and developed a security awareness program based on the proposed framework. The target audience for the awareness program was smartphone users. The researcher used the Fogg Behavioural Model as a part of the framework. The researcher experimented to test the effectiveness of the awareness program and, hence, the proposed framework. According to the findings, if their smartphone is stolen or lost, individuals in the intervention group are 2.65 times more likely to follow the three recommended behaviours. The organizations and the governments may use the proposed framework to design an effective security awareness program.

2 Background and Related Work

A vast body of literature discusses the role of SETA programs in cybersecurity and changing end users' behaviours. Researchers have defined the SETA program in various ways, highlighting its different perspectives. It is classified broadly into three perspectives: cognitive, behavioural, and process [19]. The NIST concurs with the process view [19]. In this study, the researcher uses a process perspective on cybersecurity awareness.

Designing an effective SETA program is complex [2, 12, 20–22]. There are four phases of a SETA program life cycle [23]. They are design, development, implementation, and evaluation. While empirical research on the SETA program's efficacy is available, they do not focus on all four phases of the SETA program life cycle [23].

They often concentrate on one or two of the life cycle phases. The proposed framework focuses on all four SETA program life cycle phases.

The analysis of existing frameworks for the SETA program indicates that the focus is mainly on shaping end-users attitudes and behavioural intentions to adopt the recommended behaviour [6, 22, 24]. The literature indicates that intention does not always translate into actual behaviour—a phenomenon known as the intention-behaviour gap, as highlighted by Sheeran and Webb [25]. This gap holds significant implications. The existing cybersecurity awareness frameworks are fragmented and lack definitive guidelines and procedures, as noted by Amankwa, Loock, and Kritzinger [24]. Consequently, there is a pressing requirement for a framework that is easy to implement, empirically tested for its efficacy, and provides clear guidelines and procedures for cybersecurity practitioners.

Cybersecurity researchers have used theories from psychology and other disciplines to understand the factors affecting end-users' cybersecurity behaviour. Previous researchers have employed behavioural theories to elucidate outcome variables, such as recommended behavioural intent or actual behaviour. The General Deterrence Theory (GDT), the Theory of Planned Behavior (TPB), and the Protection Motivation Theory (PMT) are the most widely used theories in information security awareness research [26]. These theories help predict and understand cybersecurity behaviours. However, their usage for behaviour change is limited [27, 28].

Consequently, it is necessary to explore behaviour change or persuasive design theories to shape end users' cybersecurity behaviour. A detailed literature review analysis shows that threat models are less effective in predicting behaviour than coping models. The outcomes published in the literature are inconsistent. The researcher has identified the following research gaps based on the above discussion.

1. Cybersecurity researchers agree that SETA programs should improve human cybersecurity behaviour. Current models (TPB and PMT) demonstrate only modest alignment with real-world behaviours. Despite numerous factors identified in the literature that impact cybersecurity behaviours among smartphone users, conclusive evidence regarding determinants remains elusive. Each factor contributes marginally to understanding the variability in cybersecurity behaviours.
2. Incorporating insights from behaviour change and persuasive design theories is necessary for more effective SETA program outcomes, as current SETA programs based on TPB and PMT have limited success.

This study aims to bridge the abovementioned gap by proposing a framework based on the Fogg Behavioural Model. The researcher tested the effectiveness of the proposed framework for smartphone users using a between-subjects design. The researcher selected smartphone users as the subjects because the number of smartphone users is increasing worldwide. Smartphone users are accessing more mobile services, including banking and online payment. At the same time, the number of cybersecurity threats targeting smartphone users is also growing, as indicated by multiple industry reports [29, 30]. The malware targeting smartphones is increasing. Cybercriminals use vishing and SMSishing techniques to target smartphone users. There is a need for further research on smartphone users' cybersecurity behaviours because of these new challenges and limited cybersecurity awareness of smartphone users [31–34].

3 Framework Development

Capability, opportunity, and motivation are mandatory for behaviour change [35]. The Fogg Behaviour Model (FBM) captures these crucial conditions well. According to the FBM, behaviour will take place if motivation, ability, and prompt occur simultaneously. ENISA [36] suggested using FBM to design cybersecurity behaviour interventions. All these inspired the researcher to employ the FBM for the proposed framework.

3.1 Fogg Behaviour Model

The FBM is a recent addition to the list of persuasive design models [37]. It is easy to implement and may be useful in influencing human behaviour. The FBM is a popular model in persuasive design [38–42]. Few studies have used FBM in cybersecurity [43–45]. Das et al. [44] studied the effect of various types of triggers on the security behaviour intentions of the people. A study by Shah and Agarwal [34] used the FBM to understand smartphone users' cybersecurity behaviour and practices. They found that the odds of secure behaviour and practices by respondents with high motivation and high ability were 4.64 times higher than those with low motivation and low ability.

The model states that behaviour (B) is a product of three factors given by the formula B = MAP (Motivation × Ability × Prompt), as shown in Fig. 1.

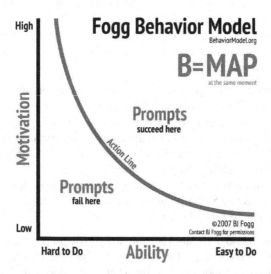

Fig. 1. The Fogg Behaviour Model (adapted from https://behaviormodel.org/)

The user will perform the target behaviour when the user has sufficient motivation and ability and is prompted for the target behaviour. The behaviour can only occur above the action line or activation threshold (green line in Fig. 1). The user will fail to perform the target behaviour below the action line despite the prompt being present because of insufficient motivation and ability. Motivation and ability have a compensatory relationship. The curved line in Fig. 1 indicates the compensatory relationship. The motivation and ability work as a teammate supporting each other to ensure the user is above the action line to perform the target behaviour when prompted.

Moreover, the model introduces three fundamental motivators, each presenting two facets. These core motivators encompass sensation, anticipation, and belonging. Within the FBM framework, the initial core motivator, sensation, manifests in two dimensions: pleasure and pain. Outcomes from this motivator typically arise swiftly, often requiring minimal cognitive processing.

The second core motivator, anticipation, centres on the anticipated consequences of behaviour, encompassing hope and fear as its two dimensions. This motivator holds significant sway in persuasive technology applications. For instance, hope may drive users to engage with matrimonial websites, while fear may prompt users to employ encryption mechanisms to safeguard their data. In many cases, anticipation can wield more significant influence than sensation; for instance, individuals may endure the discomfort of a vaccine injection to mitigate the fear of contracting COVID-19.

The third core motivator, belonging, has two dimensions: social acceptance and social rejection. Primarily utilized to regulate social conduct, this motivator incentivizes users to adhere to socially accepted norms. Social networking platforms leverage this motivator's influence to shape user behaviour.

It's noteworthy that the FBM framework does not prioritize these core motivators. Instead, designers are tasked with selecting the most suitable motivator for their specific context and objectives.

The second factor, ability, is more reliable than motivation, as motivation may change over time [46]. This factor can move users across the action line. The simplicity of target behaviour may improve the end-user's ability. Five factors, called the ability chain, affect the ability, as shown in Fig. 2.

The strength of the ability chain is contingent upon its weakest link. According to the FBM, time, money, physical effort, mental effort, and adherence to routine are all regarded as valuable resources. Should any of these resources be lacking, the user's ability to enact the desired behaviour will be compromised. It cannot be considered simple if the target behaviour necessitates more time than the user possesses. Similarly, it is deemed complex if the behaviour requires a financial investment beyond the user's means or demands excessive physical or mental effort.

Conversely, it is considered simple if the behaviour aligns with the user's routine. When the behaviour is prompted, the user's scarcest resource determines simplicity. Designers can effectively facilitate the target behaviour by addressing the barriers associated with the scarcest resource.

The third component of FBM is the prompt, which is essential for the occurrence of the target behaviour. Without the prompt, the behaviour will not occur. Various terms, such as cues, calls to action, and triggers, are used interchangeably to describe the prompt. Its role is to encourage the user to perform the behaviour at the precise moment. The model delineates three types of triggers: spark, facilitator, and signal, as depicted in Fig. 3. The spark serves to motivate the user to carry out the intended behaviour, while the facilitator simplifies the execution of the behaviour. Meanwhile, the signal serves as a reminder to the user to execute the intended behaviour.

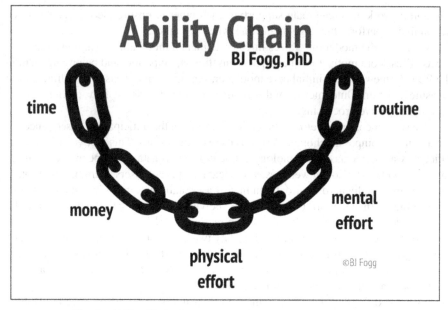

Fig. 2. Ability Chain (Source: https://behaviormodel.org/ability/)

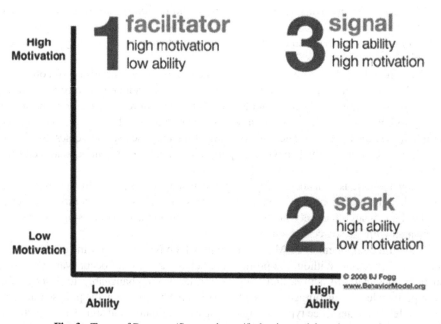

Fig. 3. Types of Prompts (Source: https://behaviormodel.org/prompts/)

3.2   Development of a Proposed Cybersecurity Awareness Framework

A recent analysis of data breaches underscores the significant risks associated with human behaviour. Consequently, security awareness training is emerging as a pivotal aspect of regulatory compliance requirements and audit standards set by regulators. Regulations such as GDPR, HIPAA, GLBA, and PCI DSS now mandate security awareness training.

Users' ability to adhere to guidelines and recommendations is limited. Human users may experience security fatigue if the cybersecurity requirements become too complex to handle [15–17, 47]. Consequently, users become insensitive when they experience security fatigue. Security fatigue occurs when users are inundated with a barrage of security messages, advice, and requests for compliance. This phenomenon leads to a decrease in secure behaviour over time. The decision to adopt recommended cybersecurity practices hinges on the end user's perceived cost-benefit analysis. If the end user believes that adhering to secure behaviour will mitigate potential losses, they are more likely to be motivated to adopt the recommended practices.

The human tendency toward inertia often deters individuals from engaging in challenging or transformative tasks. When human nature presents hurdles to adopting secure behaviours, enhancing motivation or simplifying the behaviours becomes imperative. End users require support in executing security practices to ingrain cybersecurity behaviours into habitual routines over time. Small changes will lead to lasting change [46].

Considering the above points, the researcher proposed a framework for improving smartphone users' cybersecurity behaviour, as shown in Fig. 4. Step 1 of the framework will help to reduce security fatigue as the user focuses on limited behaviours. Step 2 of the framework is used to prompt the user to adopt the recommended behaviour by using FBM. The third step provides an opportunity for the end user to implement the recommended behaviour. It also provides the opportunity for the SETA program designer to reinforce the recommended behaviour. The last step of the framework is used to measure the effectiveness of the SETA program and take any corrective actions if required.

Step 1: Define Target Behaviour: Cybersecurity poses a multifaceted challenge. Relying on a single security control is insufficient to safeguard against diverse cyber threats. Effective mitigation often necessitates the implementation of multiple security controls. For instance, to counter unauthorized access, malware, and data loss risks, smartphone users may need to employ authentication mechanisms, anti-malware solutions, and conduct regular backups and updates. However, expecting an excessive adoption of security controls from smartphone users may result in security fatigue. Hence, the initial step in the framework involves defining target behaviours for end users. These behaviours should be formulated to mitigate the risk of security fatigue. The following steps may be used to determine the target behaviour.

1. List all the cybersecurity behaviours that end-users should adopt.
2. Identify the top 3–4 behaviours that will impact the security posture most if adopted.
3. If the identified behaviour is complex, make it simple by decomposing it into multiple simple behaviours or using some tools.
4. Define security metrics to assess the success or failure of the program.

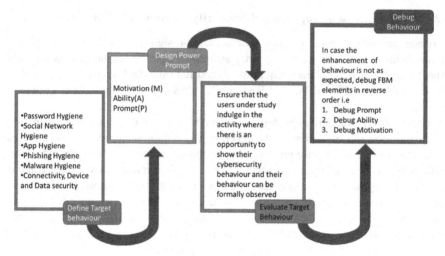

Fig. 4. Proposed Framework for Enhancing Cybersecurity Behaviour

Step 2: Design Power Prompt: The next step is to use the Fogg Behaviour Model (FBM) to design a power prompt. The power prompt includes all three components of FBM: motivation (M), ability (A), and prompt (P). It serves two purposes besides prompting the user.

1. The power prompt motivates the user to perform the desired behaviour.
2. The power prompt tries to ease the user's behaviour. There may be many ways to ease the target behaviour. For example, providing more information on how to perform the desired behaviour or providing tools to perform the behaviour may ease the behaviour.

Step 3: Evaluate Target Behaviour: Once the users are prompted for the target behaviour, the next step is to evaluate the behaviour and its success. Users should be given an opportunity to display the behaviour. Many methods are available for evaluation, including self-reporting and experimentation. The results may be compared with pre-defined security metrics to assess success or failure.

Step 4: Debug Target Behaviour: If the behaviour is not happening as expected, we need to look at each element of FBM in reverse order. Ask a few of the following questions to understand the issue/s.

Prompt:

- Are we prompting for the desired behaviour?
- Is the prompt designed effectively?
- Is the end-user bombarded with multiple prompts, leading to prompt fatigue?
- Are the prompts occurring through the effective channel?

Ability:

- Is the target behaviour still complex?
- Is there any way to make the target behaviour simple?
- Can something be integrated or embedded in the power prompt to lessen the complexity or effort, whether actual or perceived?

Motivation:

- Are there any conflicting motivational factors at the time of target behaviour?
- Is there a way to make behaviour more personal or meaningful?
- Is there a specific time when the user is naturally inclined to do the target behaviour?
- Are there any context-based factors that may be used to motivate people?
- Can we spark motivation through prompts?

4 Research Methodology

This study aims to develop a practical cybersecurity awareness framework based on the Fogg Behavioural Model.

The researcher used two methods to validate the proposed framework: the expert panel and the experimental approach. Firstly, the researcher used the expert panel approach. This method is similar to the Delphi method. The Delphi method often involves anonymous and iterative feedback from experts to reach a consensus, whereas the expert panel method requires experts to provide their opinions without anonymity or iterative feedback. The researcher approached five cybersecurity practitioners and two experienced academicians to garner their opinions on the framework's suitability for improving cybersecurity awareness and behaviour. The cybersecurity practitioners' experience ranged from 10 to 28 years. They were selected from consulting organizations, banks and multinational software product development companies. The selected professors had 25+ years of experience in industry and academia. The researcher gave a detailed presentation to each expert individually and asked for their feedback. Each presentation and discussion lasted for around 45 min to 1 h. The researcher made a few changes to the proposed framework based on the expert's feedback.

The next step was to design and develop the security awareness training program. These phases map to step 1 and step 2 of the proposed framework, i.e. to decide upon the target behaviour and design of the power prompt. The researcher selected three target behaviours related to smartphone users. These three target behaviours help to minimize the impact if the smartphone is lost or stolen. The researcher used the cybersecurity awareness game Cyber Suraksha as a power prompt [48]. The Cyber Suraksha game design is based on FBM and includes all the power prompt requirements. The game has three different cards. These cards are scenario cards, risk cards, and defence cards. The details about the design and gameplay are available in Shah & Agarwal [48]. The game uses anticipation as the core motivator. Table 1 shows the FBM components used for the validation of the framework.

After selecting target behaviours and power prompt, the researcher conducted an experiment to validate the framework's effectiveness. The researcher used a between-subject design to test the framework's efficacy. They recruited 94 participants from a leading academic institute for the experiment. Since the participants were a part of the same cohort, the researcher assumed that there was no discernible variation in the participants' knowledge levels. They were randomly allocated to the control and intervention groups to avoid self-selection bias. The gender, mobile OS, prior cybersecurity training, cybersecurity behaviours, motivation, ability, and threat awareness of the two groups were compared using Pearson's Chi-square test. The Chi-square test was conducted to

Table 1. FBM components for the target behaviours

FBM Component	Description
Behaviour (B)	1. Remote tracking of the device 2. Remote locking of the device 3. Remote wiping of data on the device
Motivation (M)	Anticipation was used as a core motivator to adopt the recommended behaviour. The risk card included a description of the severity of the threat and an individual's susceptibility to the threat
Ability (A)	The defence card included information about the recommended response's efficacy and the individual's ability to perform it. Hence, the risk card represented fear, while the defence card represented the hope aspect of FBM
Prompt (P)	The playing of the card game called Cyber Suraksha acted as a prompt for adopting the recommended behaviour

ensure the similarity of the two groups. Participants in the intervention group played the Cyber Suraksha game as a part of the experiment to evaluate the target behaviours. The demographic details of the participants are given below (Table 2).

Table 2. Demographic details of the participants

Item	Response	Frequency	
		Control Group	Intervention Group
Gender	Male	32	35
	Female	14	13
Mobile Operating System	Android	33	36
	iOS	13	12
Cybersecurity Training	Yes	10	14
	No	36	34

The researcher formulated the following hypotheses.

1. H1: Participants in the treatment group will be able to remote track their lost/stolen smartphones compared to control group participants.
2. H2: Participants in the treatment group will be able to remotely lock their lost/stolen smartphones compared to control group participants.
3. H3: Participants in the treatment group will be able to remote wipe the data from their lost/stolen smartphone compared to control group participants.
4. H4: Participants in the treatment group will display danger control behaviour.

The participants in both groups completed the survey. The researcher used two different survey questionnaires to collect the responses. The researcher used the survey, which was used by Shah and Agarwal [34], to collect responses for H1, H2, and H3. The researcher adapted the Risk Behaviour Diagnosis Scale (RBD) for the current context to collect responses for H4 [49]. The RBD serves as an evaluation instrument enabling the identification of an individual's beliefs concerning the threat and the effectiveness of the proposed response. Widely utilized within the health sector, this scale gauges audience perspectives on these crucial aspects. This scale yields three possible outcomes: 1) no response, 2) fear control, and 3) danger control. No response indicates that individuals have disregarded the risk message. Danger control occurs when individuals perceive the threat and the efficacy of recommended responses as high, motivating them to adopt said responses. Conversely, fear control responses arise when the perceived threat is high, but efficacy is low, leading individuals to reject the recommended response by denying the threat.

The objective is to elicit danger control processes and responses through risk messages. Specifically, the researcher aims to cultivate robust perceptions of cyber threats and security control efficacy among individuals, motivating them to contemplate cyber threats and embrace recommended responses. Since cybersecurity represents a risk confronting individuals, and each individual may choose whether or not to adopt recommended cybersecurity controls, the researcher has adapted the RBD scale to suit the present context. The primary variables in the scale include perceived threat, encompassing threat susceptibility and severity, and perceived efficacy, comprising response and threat efficacy. A week later, the researcher asked the players to demonstrate the target behaviours on their smartphones.

The construct validity and internal and external validity are the main threats to this study. The main construct validity threat in this study is the use of a questionnaire. The researcher mitigated the construct validity threat using a pre-validated questionnaire. Employing a pre-validated questionnaire further enhances the reliability of the instrument. The primary threat to internal validity is the researcher acting as a game master, potentially influencing participants' responses. Participants may have felt compelled to provide favourable ratings. To address this concern, the researcher implemented measures such as an anonymous survey and informing them beforehand about this anonymity. To mitigate external validity threats, real-life cyber-attack scenarios were utilized instead of abstract descriptions, enhancing the relevance and applicability of the study's findings.

5   Results and Analysis

In this section, the researcher presents the results and analysis of the experts' opinions and experiment data.

Expert Opinion Analysis: The researcher reached out to seven experts for their opinion on the effectiveness of the proposed framework. All experts agreed that creating awareness about cyber threats will help mitigate cyber risks and minimize their impact. It is mandatory to have a security awareness program for all employees in many organizations, specifically banks. Most of them said they are using a few of the awareness resources available in the market. They execute it periodically as required for compliance purposes. However, they have not evaluated their effectiveness except for phishing simulations. All experts felt that the framework would be effective in creating cybersecurity awareness. The flexibility to have a power prompt in the form of a game or short video may be effective and engaging. A much-appreciated point about the framework was allowing users to exhibit the recommended behaviour. Some of their comments are given below.

Professional 1: *I think such a framework will be quite useful in driving the creation of a structured program for cyber awareness. Understanding the challenges specific to India and incorporating those aspects in terms of localization and gamification is a great idea.*

National agencies may find great use of framework in creating impactful campaigns to drive awareness. It may also help to create specific profiles for the most vulnerable where such awareness campaigns could have the most impact.

Overall, this is a great idea and need of the hour to optimize the spend to have maximum social impact.

Professional 2: *Thank you for sharing this great piece of work the information is very insightful. Kudos for the great efforts put behind making it possible. Indeed, it is need of the hour ever since digitalization changed the world.*

With the growing use of smartphone and mobile applications, there is a need to protect consumers' data to ensure that people continue to use these technologies safely. It is essential to study issues related to data protection and cybersecurity attacks.

The proposed framework will definitely bring awareness and make people understand the importance of threats and malware.

Unlike other developing countries India lack awareness and seriousness of cyber-crimes and cyber-attack hence it is very important to understand the behaviour of the people.

Professional 3: *Motivation = As discussed, this can be driven by both Positive and Negative sentiments.*

* Positive = Good Cyber Hygiene, Gamification of Product Security Feature awareness to be rewarded via some discount codes or coupons or AMC waiver, etc.

* Negative = Advertisement showing Monetary loss, identity theft, legal lawsuit, etc. more like it was done for smoking causes Cancer campaign.

Ability = The Users Risk-cum-Ability profile can be created on basis of KYC documents like Age, Education, etc. and later supplemented by a short quiz around security awareness. Later, ongoing campaign can use a feedback or Debug loop to target or identify User categories.

Prompt = This is required and can be part of initial onboarding or a paid survey. This should not be intrusive or irritating/annoying, neither frequent or rare. Mostly pushed off-the-business hours. Should be made entertaining or fun combined with Technical questions. Look at recent GPay or Amazon quiz for example, 1 question out of 5 is awareness one.

I think this framework is simple to adopt and effective to drive required mass awareness for cyber security hygiene supplemented with enough experiment and research.

Professional 4: *I think use of a game is a good idea to engage and create cybersecurity awareness among participants. I will recommend the use of digital game to reach* *out to more number of smartphone users. I suggest that security awareness program should not be viewed as a compliance requirement. Rather it has to conducted regularly in an organization for it to be effective.*

Professional 5: *Now I know how to structure my security awareness communication with the employees. I need to engage them actively rather then just sending newsletter through an email. I will use the framework to develop awareness program at my organization.*

Based on the experts' feedback, the researcher can infer that the proposed framework will be effective in creating cybersecurity awareness.

Experiment Results and Analysis: The researcher evaluated the effectiveness of the proposed framework using four hypotheses. Three hypotheses, H1, H2, and H3, are concerned with the target behaviours, while hypothesis H4 is concerned with the participants' belief about the recommended response's threat and efficacy. The researcher used Pearson's Chi-square test of independence with a 5% significance level to test the hypotheses. The researcher found significant differences between the control and intervention groups for the target behaviours. Table 3 shows the chi-square statistics for the three-target behaviour along with the Cramer's V values.

Table 3. Chi-square statistics for target behaviours

Behaviour	Chi-square statistics	Cramer's V
Remote tracking of the device	χ^2 (1, N = 94) = 5.186, p = .023	0.235
Remote locking of the device	χ^2 (1, N = 94) = 9.691, p = .002	0.321
Remote wiping of data on the device	χ^2 (1, N = 94) = 6.098, p = .014	0.255

Table 3 displays statistically significant differences between the control and intervention groups across the three target behaviours. Cramer's V value indicates a moderate correlation between the control and intervention groups for all three behaviours [50]. The researcher conducted post-hoc analysis with Bonferroni correction to pinpoint specific cells that significantly contributed to the chi-square test of independence. Participants in the treatment group demonstrated the capability to remotely track and lock their lost or stolen smartphones and remotely wipe the data on such devices. These analyses corroborate hypotheses H1, H2, and H3.

Table 4 shows the frequency of fear control and danger control responses for the control and intervention groups. In the intervention group, more participants had a danger control response than in the control group.

The researcher used Pearson's Chi-square test of independence with a 5% significance level to test whether there is a statistically significant difference between the two groups. Results indicated a notable difference between the groups (χ^2 (1, N = 94) = 5.311, p = .021), substantiating hypothesis H4. The odds ratio, calculated by the researcher, was 2.65. This figure implies that participants in the intervention group are 2.65 times more likely to display danger control behaviour than those in the control group. Consequently, participants in the intervention group are 2.65 times more inclined to adopt the recommended behaviour.

Table 4. Responses for Fear Control and Danger Control

	Control Group	Intervention Group
Danger Control	15	27
Fear Control	31	21

One week following the intervention, the researcher requested participants in the intervention group to exhibit their proficiency in remotely tracking and locking their smartphones. Additionally, they were tasked with outlining the steps for remotely wiping their device's data. Approximately 70% of participants successfully demonstrated competence in executing the desired behaviours.

From the above analysis, the researcher can conclude that the security awareness program based on the proposed framework was effective. The participants in the intervention group were able to demonstrate the recommended security control for the targeted behaviour.

6 Discussion

Human actions are the key to ensuring cybersecurity. The literature suggests human users are the weakest link and recommends security education, training, and awareness (SETA) programs to improve the cybersecurity behaviour of human users. However, the literature review also suggests that current SETA programs are ineffective. They fail to meet their stated objectives [6, 12, 23].

The effectiveness of a SETA program depends on many factors, including the design and implementation of the program itself. Theory-based SETA programs may be effective [8]. The Theory of Planned Behaviour (TPB) and the Protection Motivation Theory (PMT) are popular theories in the behavioural cybersecurity domain. The literature indicates mixed results for intervention based on these theories. Current frameworks do not provide clear guidelines for the development of SETA programs. Traditional delivery methods like PowerPoint presentations or computer-based training fail to engage the target audience [51]. Serious Games have shown positive results in engaging the audience [52]. This research addressed these gaps by developing a theory-based framework. The proposed framework based on FBM provides clear guidelines for the design and development of the SETA program. To the researcher's knowledge, there is no framework for cybersecurity awareness based on FBM.

The researcher developed a security awareness program based on the proposed framework. Smartphones can be easily lost or stolen. A prior investigation conducted by Shah and Agarwal [34] revealed that Indian smartphone users lacked awareness regarding remote tracking, locking, and data wiping capabilities in the event of smartphone loss or theft. Consequently, the researcher opted to cultivate awareness regarding security controls applicable in such situations. Three specific target behaviours were identified for intervention. The researcher selected the Cyber Suraksha, a cybersecurity awareness card game, as a cybersecurity awareness training delivery mechanism. The game is based on FBM and serves as a power prompt [48]. The researcher observed a higher proportion of respondents exhibiting danger control behaviour in the intervention group compared to the control group. From this, it can be inferred that the security awareness program, developed according to the proposed framework, was successful. This program effectively motivated users to embrace security controls and enhanced their capability. The odds of adopting the target behaviour are 2.65 times greater in the intervention group than in the control group. This odds ratio serves as a quantitative measure of the efficacy of the security awareness program formulated based on the proposed framework.

From the above discussion, it can be concluded that theory-based interventions effectively create cybersecurity awareness. This study supports the results obtained in previous studies [51–53]. The students were the target audience for this study. The framework may be further validated with different target audiences and contexts.

The main contributions of this study are:

1. To the researcher's knowledge, this is the first study to propose a Cybersecurity Awareness Framework based on FBM. The results of this study indicate that theory-based interventions are effective in creating cybersecurity awareness and motivating users to adopt recommended cybersecurity behaviours. Hence, the researcher recommends that the SETA program designers use theory-based intervention for the program's design, specifically the models from behaviour change and persuasive design.
2. The cybersecurity awareness program developed based on the proposed framework used a game as a delivery mechanism. The game was interactive and provided opportunities for active learning. Hence, the researcher recommends that people responsible for SETA program implementation consider serious games as delivery mechanisms.
3. The FBM is mainly used in persuasive design. Very few studies have used it in the context of cybersecurity. This study successfully demonstrates the use of FBM in creating cybersecurity awareness.

7 Conclusion

A substantial percentage of cybersecurity incidents involve human errors; a human user is identified as the weakest link in the cybersecurity chain. End-users' cyber hygiene plays a critical role in mitigating cyber threats. The security researchers recommend a security education, awareness and training (SETA) program as an effective countermeasure to improve the cyber hygiene of end users. Security awareness training is becoming crucial to regulators' audit and regulatory compliance requirements. Regulations like GDPR, HIPAA, GLBA, and PCI DSS make security awareness training mandatory. However, the majority of the SETA programs are ineffective in changing the behaviour of end users. Possible explanations for the program's lack of effectiveness could include the absence of a theory-based intervention with experimental validation for designing the SETA program and the application of a one-size-fits-all approach. Existing frameworks often lack definitive guidelines and procedures for cybersecurity practitioners to effectively implement recommendations and achieve desired outcomes [24]. Thus, there is a pressing need for a user-friendly theory-based framework that offers explicit guidelines for designing and developing SETA programs.

Fogg Behaviour Model (FBM) effectively captures the requirements for behaviour change, i.e. capability, opportunity, and motivation. According to FBM, when prompted, a person with strong motivation and ability will readily adopt the target behaviour. Hence, the researcher used FBM as the theoretical model for the development of the proposed framework. The proposed framework has four steps.

1. Define Target Behaviour
2. Design Power Prompt
3. Evaluate Target Behaviour
4. Debug Behaviour

The researcher developed a security awareness program based on the proposed framework for smartphone users. The researcher considered the context of a smartphone being lost or stolen. The researcher defined three target behaviours to mitigate the impact of lost or stolen smartphone threats: remote tracking of the device, Remote Locking of the device, and Remote wiping of data on the device. The researcher used a card game called Cyber Suraksha as a power prompt.

The framework's effectiveness was tested using an experiment. The 94 participants were divided into two groups viz. Control and Intervention/Treatment Groups. The intervention group played the Cyber Suraksha game. The researcher captured the participants' responses using the Risk Behaviour Diagnosis Scale (RBD) to understand the participants' beliefs about the threat and the efficacy of the recommended response. The power prompt aims to induce danger control processes and reactions. The chi-square test was used to test the effectiveness of the power prompt and, hence, the framework. The researcher found a significant difference between the two groups in terms of the targeted behaviours. The researcher inferred from the chi-square statistic that the security awareness program based on the proposed framework effectively motivated the user to adopt the recommended security control for the targeted behaviours. The odds of danger control behaviour by the intervention group were 2.65 times more than the control group. A week later, the researcher asked the intervention group participants to demonstrate the recommended countermeasures to mitigate the risk of lost or stolen smartphones. Around 70% of the participants successfully performed the target behaviours. Hence, the researcher can conclude that a security awareness program based on the proposed framework with clear guidelines was effective.

Further research is required to better understand the effectiveness of the proposed framework and generate generalized results. This research may be conducted using different target behaviours and power prompts. The study may be repeated with different target audiences of different age groups and knowledge levels. One of the limitations of this study is that the user behaviour was evaluated only after a week. Hence, the researcher cannot comment on the sustained behaviour change of the end user. The government and private organizations may consider designing cybersecurity awareness campaigns based on the proposed framework.

References

1. Kerner, S.M.: 35 cybersecurity statistics to lose sleep over in 2024 (2024). https://www.techta rget.com/whatis/34-Cybersecurity-Statistics-to-Lose-Sleep-Over-in-2020. Accessed 19 Apr 2024

2. Hu, S., Hsu, C., Zhou, Z.: Security education, training, and awareness programs: literature review. J. Comput. Inf. Syst. **62**(4), 752–764 (2021)
3. Tu, Z., Turel, O., Yuan, Y., Archer, N.: Learning to cope with information security risks regarding mobile device loss or theft: an empirical examination. Inf. Manag., 506–517 (2015)
4. Carpenter, P.: Transformational Security Awareness: What Neuroscientists, Storytellers, and Marketers Can. Wiley, Indianapolis (2019)
5. Wilson, M., Hash, J.: NIST Special Publication 800-50: building an information technology security awareness and training program. National Institute of Standards and Technology, Gaithersburg (2003)
6. Alshaikh, M., Naseer, H., Ahmad, A., Maynard, S.B.: Toward sustainable behaviour change: an approach for cyber security education training and awareness. In: 27th European Conference on Information Systems (ECIS), Stockholm & Uppsala, Sweden (2019)
7. Khan, B., Alghathbar, K.S., Nabi, S.I., Khan, M.K.: Effectiveness of information security awareness methods based on psychological theories. Afr. J. Bus. Manag., 10862–10868 (2011)
8. Alshaikh, M., Maynard, S.B., Ahmad, A., Chang, S.: An exploratory study of current information security training and awareness practices in organizations. In: 51st Hawaii International Conference on System Sciences, Hawaii (2018)
9. Menard, P., Shropshire, J.: Training wheels: a new approach to teaching mobile device security. In: KSU Proceedings on Cybersecurity Education, Research and Practice (2016)
10. Farooq, A.: In Quest of Information Security in Higher Education Institutions. University of Turku, Turku (2019)
11. Caldwell, T.: Making security awareness training work. Comput. Fraud Secur., 8–14 (2016)
12. Bada, M., Sasse, A.M., Nurse, J.R.: Cyber security awareness campaigns: why do they fail to change behaviour?. In: International Conference on Cyber Security for Sustainable Society, Coventry, United Kingdom (2015)
13. Adams, M., Makramalla, M.: Cybersecurity skills training: an attacker-centric gamified approach. Technol. Innov. Manag. Rev., 5–14 (2015)
14. Chin, A.G., Etudo, U., Harris, M.A.: On mobile device security practices and training efficacy: an empirical study. Inf. Educ., 235–252 (2016)
15. Furnell, S., Thomson, K.-L.: Recognizing and addressing 'security fatigue'. Comput. Fraud Secur., 7–11 (2009)
16. Beautement, A., Sasse, M., Wonham, M.: The compliance budget: managing security behaviour in organizations. In: Workshop on New Security Paradigms, California, USA (2009)
17. Reeves, A., Delfabbro, P., Calic, D.: Encouraging employee engagement with cybersecurity: how to tackle cyber fatigue. Sage Open, Sage (2021)
18. Foltz, C.B., Newkirk, H.E., Schwager, P.H.: An empirical investigation of factors that influence individual behavior toward changing social networking security settings. J. Theor. Appl. Electron. Commer. Res., 1–15 (2016)
19. Dhakal, R.: Measuring the effectiveness of an information security training and awareness program (2018)
20. Zwilling, M., Klien, G., Lesjak, D., Wiechetek, Ł, Cetin, F., Basim, H.N.: Cyber security awareness, knowledge and behavior: a comparative study. J. Comput. Inf. Syst. **62**(1), 82–97 (2020)
21. Khando, K., Gao, S., Islam, S.M., Salman, A.: Enhancing employees information security awareness in private and public organizations: a systematic literature review. Comput. Secur. **106** (2021)
22. Alyami, A., Sammon, D., Neville, K., Mahony, C.: Critical success factors for Security Education, Training and Awareness (SETA) programme effectiveness: an empirical comparison of practitioner perspectives. Inf. Comput. Secur. **32**(1), 53–73 (2024)

23. Alyami, A., Sammon, D., Neville, K., Mahony, C.: The critical success factors for Security Education, Training and Awareness (SETA) program effectiveness: a lifecycle model. Inf. Technol. People **36**, 94–125 (2023)
24. Amankwa, E., Loock, M., Kritzinger, E.: A composite framework to promote information security policy compliance in organizations. In: Serrhini, M., Silva, C., Aljahdali, S. (eds.) EMENA-ISTL 2019. LAIS, vol. 7, pp. 458–468. Springer, Cham (2020). https://doi.org/10.1007/978-3-030-36778-7_51
25. Sheeran, P., Webb, T.L.: The intention–behavior gap. Soc. Pers. Psychol. Compass, 503–518 (2016)
26. Hutchinson, G., Ophoff, J.: A descriptive review and classification of organizational information security awareness research (2020)
27. Sniehotta, F.F.: Towards a theory of intentional behaviour change: plans, planning, and self-regulation. Br. J. Health Psychol. (2010)
28. Davis, R., Campbell, R., Hildon, Z., Hobbs, L., Michie, S.: Theories of behaviour and behaviour change across the social and behavioural sciences: a scoping review. Health Psychol. Rev., 323–344 (2015)
29. Symantec: Internet Security Threat Report Volume 24, Symantec (2019)
30. Check Point: Cyber Security Report, Check Point Software Technologies LTD (2024)
31. Mylonas, A., Kastania, A., Gritzalis, D.: Delegate the smartphone user? Security awareness in smartphone platforms. Comput. Secur., 47–66 (2013)
32. Vecchiato, D., Vieira, M., Martins, E.: A security configuration assessment for android devices. In: Proceedings of the 30th Annual ACM Symposium on Applied Computing, Salamanca, Spain (2015)
33. Das, A., Khan, H.U.: Security Behaviors of smartphone users. Inf. Comput. Secur., 116–134 (2016)
34. Shah, P.R., Agarwal, A.: Cybersecurity behaviour of smartphone users in India: an empirical analysis. Inf. Comput. Secur. **28**(2), 293–318 (2020)
35. Michie, S., Stralen, M.M.V., West, R.: The behaviour change wheel: a new method for characterizing and designing behaviour change interventions. Implementation Sci. (2011)
36. ENISA: Cybersecurity Culture Guidelines: Behavioural Aspects of Cybersecurity," European Union Agency For Network and Information Security (2018)
37. Fogg, B.J.: A behavior model for persuasive design. In: Persuasive 2009: Proceedings of the 4th International Conference on Persuasive Technology (2009)
38. Militello, L., Melnyk, B.M., Hekler, E.B., Small, L., Jacobson, D.: Automated behavioral text messaging and face-to-face intervention for parents of overweight or obese preschool children: results from a pilot study. JMIR Mhealth Uhealth (2016)
39. Sibanyoni, N.A., Alexander, P.M.: Insights into persuasive technology for M-learning using activity theory. In: International Conference on Cognition and Exploratory Learning in the Digital Age (CELDA), Budapest, Hungary (2020)
40. Agha, S., Tollefson, D., Paul, S., Green, D., Babigumira, J.B.: Use of the Fogg behavior model to assess the impact of a social marketing campaign on condom use in Pakistan. J. Health Commun. (2019)
41. Pintarić, A., Erjavec, J.: A framework for designing behavioural change with the use of persuasive technology. Int. J. Manag. Knowl. Learn., 75–84 (2021)
42. Edwards, L.: Seeing through the Fogg: exploring tools to enhance digital resilience to misinformation, University of Adelaide (2023)
43. Zhang-Kennedy, L., Chiasson, S., Biddle, R.: Stop clicking on "Update Later": persuading users they need up-to-date antivirus protection. In: International Conference on Persuasive Technology (2014)

44. Das, S., Dabbish, L.A., Hong, J.I.: A typology of perceived triggers for end-user security and privacy behaviors. In: USENIX Symposium on Usable Privacy and Security (SOUPS) 2019, Santa Clara, CA, USA (2019)
45. Shah, P.R., Agarwal, A.: Cybersecurity behaviour of smartphone users through the lens of Fogg behaviour model. In: 2020 3rd International Conference on Communication System, Computing and IT Applications (CSCITA), Mumbai, India (2020)
46. Fogg, B.J.: Tiny Habits. Virgin Books (2019)
47. Stanton, B., Theofanos, M.F., Prettyman, S.S., Furman, S.: Security fatigue. IT Pro, 26–32 (2016)
48. Shah, P., Agarwal, A.: Cyber suraksha: a card game for smartphone security awareness. Inf. Comput. Secur. **31**(5), 576–600 (2023)
49. Witte, K., Meyer, G., Martell, D.P.: Effective Health Risk Messages: A Step-by-Step Guide. Sage Publications, Inc. (2001)
50. Cohen, J.: Statistical Power Analysis for the Behavioural Science. Lawrence Erlbaum, USA (1988)
51. Ghazvini, A., Shukur, Z.: A framework for an effective information security awareness program in healthcare. Int. J. Adv. Comput. Sci. Appl., 193–205 (2017)
52. Alotaibi, F., Furnell, S., Stengel, I., Papadaki, M.: Enhancing cyber security awareness with mobile games. In: The 12th International Conference for Internet Technology and Secured Transactions (ICITST-2017) (2017)
53. Jansen, J., Schaik, P.V.: The design and evaluation of a theory-based intervention to promote security behaviour against phishing. Int. J. Hum.-Comput. Stud., 40–55 (2019)

Could You Hear That? Identifying Marathi Phrases Suitable for Aural Transcription Tasks

Saloni Amar Shetye[(✉)] [iD] and Anirudha Joshi [iD]

IDC School of Design, IIT Bombay, Mumbai, Maharashtra, India
{19u130005,anirudha}@iitb.ac.in

Abstract. Predetermined phrase sets are commonly used to carry out transcription tasks in evaluating text input methods. We examine the aural reliability of a set of 299 Marathi phrases that have been used in transcription studies in the past. We present a study in which 80 native Marathi speakers heard 30 randomly chosen phrases each and transcribed them, leading to 2,392 transcriptions (a repetition factor of eight per phrase). After an initial categorisation of transcription errors, we conducted a workshop with Marathi experts and arrived at an error tagging taxonomy consisting of 17 major error tags and 50 error subtags. After analysis of the transcriptions, we assigned 4,152 error subtags. Though the proportion of errors was higher than those reported in a similar study in English, surprisingly, we had a much smaller proportion of comprehension errors. We recommend 142 phrases that are aurally reliable for transcription studies but report the number and types of error subtags so that researchers can make their own assessments. The 157 phrases that we do not recommend have a value of their own, as they can inform future HCI research in Indian languages. Our contributions have potential applications in improving Marathi aural transcription tasks, spell-check and auto-correct, synthetic speech, scripting for spoken interfaces and accessibility studies.

Keywords: Transcription studies · Phrase set · Synthetic speech · Marathi · Error analysis · Error tagging taxonomy

1 Introduction

Predetermined phrase sets are often used in HCI studies where interaction techniques for communication need to be evaluated, such as transcription tasks to evaluate text input methods. For instance, to examine new virtual keyboard layouts for Marathi text input, researchers showed Marathi text to users and asked them to type the same using the keyboards while evaluating for speed

Supplementary Information The online version contains supplementary material available at https://doi.org/10.1007/978-3-031-80829-6_4.

and errors [25]. While text input studies have also explored user-composed content [17,37], mainstream text input evaluations continue to be transcription tasks [9,10,24,39,40]. This is perhaps because predetermined phrase sets enable higher internal validity in studies [29].

With the increased use of synthetic speech and speech recognition, several text input studies have also used voice technologies [16,22,33], including studies in Indian languages [4,6,7]. Phrases are sometimes presented aurally through synthetic speech (especially if the participants are visually impaired). The users enter the text using the input method, and then synthetic speech is used to play back the entered text. Such studies are especially important in making text input mechanisms accessible to blind users [4,7]. However, speech, and synthetic speech, in particular, is susceptible to being misheard by human listeners. Without checking phrases for aural reliability, it becomes challenging to determine if the resulting errors arose from the input mechanism or from difficulties in hearing the phrases. Therefore, phrase sets need to be assessed for their aural reliability before they can be used in audio-based transcription studies. When we say a phrase is "aurally reliable," we mean that there is a high likelihood that native speakers will correctly understand it when it is spoken by a synthetic speech system.

Abbott et al. [3] evaluated the aural reliability of the MacKenzie and Soukoreff [29] phrase set of 500 English phrases, contributing an aurally reliable phrase set to accessibility research in eyes-free text entry. They analysed the transcribed phrases to identify errors in aural comprehension. As expected, participants made errors. Some of these errors were acceptable and communicated the meaning, like a text entry error (e.g. "gest etiquette" instead of "guest etiquette") or extra blank space (e.g. "I like to   play tennis" instead of "I like to play tennis"). On the other hand, other errors demonstrated a lack of comprehension because phrases were presented aurally (e.g. "breathing is difficult" being transcribed as "reading is difficult"). Abbott et al. define comprehension errors in transcriptions as the usage of unassociated words. In their recommendation, they excluded phrases with comprehension errors, resulting in a subset of 92 phrases (out of 500) that were deemed aurally distinct. We draw methodological inspiration from their work in the context of Marathi (though, as we report below, we found a different error profile).

Marathi is the 13th most widely spoken language globally, with an estimated 83 million speakers as of 2011 [2]. While several voice synthesis and recognition technologies are available in Marathi, there is scope to improve the quality of both. This calls for further research in speech-based techniques for Marathi. Aurally reliable phrases are essential for evaluating newer interaction methods and systems in Marathi. A curated phrase set for Marathi transcription studies is available [12] and has been used in the past [7,11,18]. Using a method similar to Abbott et al. [3], we aim to identify aurally reliable phrases from this phrase set for voice-based transcription studies. Going beyond, we also aim to identify the type of text which is not aurally comprehensible so that corrective measures can be taken in future.

In this paper, we present a moderated study with 80 participants who heard and wrote the 299 Marathi phrases. We identified phrases that can be reliably used in transcription studies or in evaluating audio-based techniques that use synthetic speech. We analysed the transcripts, identified the occurrence and types of errors that emerged, and categorised them based on their nature. This was followed by a workshop with Marathi experts to validate our error categorisation and rationale for deeming certain errors as comprehension errors. Comparing our results with those of Abbott et al. [3], we observed significantly fewer comprehension errors in Marathi, but we identified many other error types. We present the subset of aurally reliable Marathi phrases as those where seven out of eight participants did not commit a comprehension error, and hence, these phrases can be assumed to be correctly understood by native Marathi speakers when heard using synthetic speech.

Through this paper, we make the following contributions:

- We present the errors found in the transcribed phrases, each with their corresponding error tag and subtag
- We provide an error tagging taxonomy of 17 main tags and 50 subtags based on errors that participants made while writing these phrases
- We present 142 phrases which are aurally reliable when presented through synthetic speech
- We identify phrases which are not aurally reliable and discuss potential workarounds when such text needs to be used.

2   Background

2.1   Marathi

In the landscape of technology and HCI research, English has predominantly been the language of choice for research, development and implementation. The rapid advancement in language technology in English has resulted in a substantial body of work that sometimes assumes applicability to all languages. Research in English often matures significantly before the research is done in other languages, at which stage researchers often move on towards the next horizon, assuming that the problem at hand has been "solved". However, there are differences in linguistic structures, shades of dialects, cultural contexts, user behaviours and nuances across languages, which require recognition and tailored approaches for each language. Given the colonial history and the current social, political, economic and corporate context in India, this is particularly true for Indian languages [15]. So, despite their widespread usage by millions, Indian languages receive relatively less attention in technology research compared to English.

Marathi ranks 13th globally in terms of the number of native speakers and is the third most spoken language in India after Hindi and Bengali [2]. Marathi uses the Devanagari, an abugida script and has 14 frequently used vowels, 36 consonants and two sound modifiers. The Marathi script is phonetic. The standard word order is subject-object-verb (SOV), although it can vary within certain restrictions [38]. Marathi characters have vowel signs that attach to consonants to create a combined glyph. This is shown in the script by dependent vowel signs, one for each vowel, such as *kana* (ा), *velanti* (ि, ी), *ukaar* (ु, ू), *matra* (ॆ, ॆ, ॆ, ॆ), *anusvara* (ं) and *visarga* (ः). The vowel signs also help to distinguish long (ी, ू) and short vowels (ि, ु) in the case of *velanti* and *ukaar*. Consonants can combine, forming consonant clusters known as conjuncts or *jodakshara*. When suffixes are added to words, the original word form changes, resulting in a modified word. Some Marathi consonants, like (च, ज, झ) have affricate and palatal distinctions. Additionally, some consonants are unaspirated (*alpaprana*) while others are aspirated (*mahaprana*). Like in many other languages, there are several accents of spoken Marathi and these are all different from each other and from the formal, written Marathi found in many textbooks (known as *pramaan* Marathi). One such difference is seen when the ए matra (े) at the end of words in formal Marathi is often replaced by the *shirobindu* (ं) in spoken Marathi (in words like फुले/ फुलं (flowers), माझे/ माझं (my) and हिरवे/ हिरवं (green)). Marathi has numerous dialects, including Deshi, Ahirani, Varhadi, Malvani, Nagpuri, Dangi and more. The rich nuances of Marathi and other Indian languages call for dedicated research acknowledging the depth of each language's uniqueness.

2.2 Phrase Sets

When evaluating text-entry systems, studies often require users to enter predetermined phrases one by one using the mechanism being evaluated. While users do not copy text in the real world, the spontaneous composition of text can lead to ambiguities arising from subjective composition styles and users' processing time, making it difficult for researchers to verify accuracy without a point of comparison. Therefore, to ensure internal validity, studies often involve using a standardised set of predefined reliable phrases. Popular curated phrase sets in English include the 500-word phrase set by MacKenzie and Soukoreff [29] released in 2005 and the Enron email phrase set [36] released in 2011. MacKenzie and Soukoreff [29] recommend that phrase sets should have phrases of moderate length that are easy to remember and representative of the language. Vertanen and Kristensson [36] curated and evaluated their phrase set to be memorable and have a representative character distribution, highlighting its external validity as it is derived from real emails. Recent English studies in HCI still use these two phrase sets in text-copy tasks for evaluating various novel text entry mechanisms like hand gesture recognition [9], text entry in virtual reality [39], gaze-based text entry [10], multimodal text entry in mixed reality [24] and wearable keyboard-free text entry [40]. In addition to manually curating phrase sets, researchers have also proposed various sampling techniques for generating representative phrase sets [27,28,31].

In studies involving transcription tasks in Indian languages, researchers have created their own phrase sets for users to copy, as standardised sets are not as widely established as English. Studies have used Hindi phrases from short stories [34], conversational Hindi phrases [6], conversational Marathi phrases [7], informal and formal Marathi phrases [11], paragraphs from a Marathi school textbook [25], Hindi phrases from films and textbooks and translated phrases from the MacKenzie and Soukoreff phrase set [23]. Apart from these, researchers evaluating virtual keyboards in Indian languages have used texts from popular literature [13], text from the Bengali CIIL corpus [5] and Wikipedia dumps and the EMILLE corpus [20].

Dalvi et al. [12] introduced a protocol for evaluating virtual keyboards for Indian languages using a longitudinal test to encourage further evaluations of keyboards, aiding the standardisation of text input mechanisms for Indian languages. Towards this effort, they curated phrase sets for Assamese, Bengali, Gujarati, Hindi, Kannada, Marathi, Odia, Tamil, Telugu and Urdu. The phrases are balanced between informal and formal language, sourced from various texts, including school textbooks, folk songs, poems, the national anthem and quotes by historical figures. The phrases vary in difficulty based on factors such as the presence of conjuncts, phrase length, memorability and age appropriateness. This phrase set has been used in transcription tasks such as [6,7]. Dalvi et al. report significant correlations of this curated phrase set with existing Marathi corpora, ensuring the representativeness of the language. We conducted our study using this as our source set of 299 Marathi phrases.

2.3   Aural Reliability of Synthetic Speech

Synthetic speech refers to artificial natural-sounding speech generated by text-to-speech engines. It is particularly valuable for aurally conveying dynamic content, such as voice-based virtual assistants, screen readers for individuals with vision impairments, speech generation for those who are speech-impaired or motor-speech impaired, navigation systems, public announcement systems and various other uses. However, synthetic speech can be difficult to comprehend due to poor prosody.

Researchers have previously examined the comprehension of English synthetic speech through transcription and studied the accuracy and errors in transcription. These studies include the evaluation of blind participants' ability to understand and reproduce fast synthetic speech [35], the assessment of the intelligibility of synthetic speech among participants learning English as a foreign language [8], and the comparison of various text-to-speech systems by examining intelligibility through the transcription of synthetic speech [19]. Abbott et al. [3] used a transcription task and demonstrated that synthetic speech was prone to errors when heard by human listeners, with comprehension errors as their most frequently observed error.

While the above studies show that users made errors when transcribing synthetic speech, researchers have also found that users overlooked errors within synthetic speech. Hong and Findlater [21] conducted a study demonstrating that participants faced challenges in identifying errors while listening to synthetic speech. In their study, participants performed text entry using speech input and then reviewed and edited the text through synthetic speech output (with no visuals). The study revealed that participants were unable to identify over 50% of the systems' recognition errors when listening back to the speech output of the recognised text. The errors were coded, revealing that the most common difficulty involved multiple-word errors, such as "meet" recognised as "me it" or "a while" recognised as "awhile". In a similar follow-up study with sighted and blind participants, Hong et al. [22] coded and grouped errors based on when they sounded like the original words ("prototype" recognised as "proto type") and when they didn't ("we are" recognised as "of years").

In speech-based studies in Indian languages, Bhikne et al. [7] explored accessibility in text entry. They found that integrating speech recognition into a modified Swarachakra keyboard outperformed keyboard-only input for visually impaired participants in Marathi. They used a set of 48 phrases in a text copy task where visually impaired participants read the phrases using a screen reader. Participants could speak into the phone, listen back to the text via the screen reader and edit the text if they found any recognition errors. The researchers analysed speech recognition errors in Marathi, describing error instances where the system misrecognised words by participants like मुलं (children) recognised as मुले, लख लख लख (sound word for lightning) recognised as लखलखखलख and कुऱ्हाडीचा (of the axe) recognised as कुऱ्हाडीचा. While [7, 21, 22] deal with system recognition errors, our study focuses on exploring transcription errors.

Beyond lab-based studies, researchers have identified challenges with audio comprehension in the Indian context and discussed workarounds. Rashinkar et al. [32] designed an IVR system for people living with HIV/AIDS in low-resource settings in Maharashtra and found that rewording menu prompts without changing their meaning, adding redundancy and using bilingual menu items improved understandability. Similarly, Joshi et al. [26] studied mMitra, a program delivering automated voice calls to urban poor women during pregnancy and early child care. They suggested using widely understood terms in Marathi and Hindi and locally spoken alternatives to address regional diversity and ensure information is understood.

As mentioned earlier, Abbott et al.'s [3] study served as a starting point for our study. They aimed to determine if English phrases used in text entry are sufficiently aurally distinct to people when they are heard such as in accessible eyes-free text entry. The goal was to establish a reliable set of phrases that could be used to assess both current and new text entry methods. Their rationale was that eliminating phrases with ambiguities would ensure errors are coming from the text entry technique rather than the stimuli phrases. In their method, the researchers evaluated aural comprehension of phrases based on the participant's ability to accurately reproduce them as transcribed text, and we also followed this approach.

They used phrases from the MacKenzie and Soukoreff phrase set and converted them to synthetic speech. They recruited 392 participants to listen to and transcribe 50 phrases each, resulting in 17,421 valid transcriptions. Of these, 75% were error-free. The researchers conducted automated and manual error analyses on the remaining transcriptions, identifying nine categories of errors. Comprehension errors (where participants typed an unassociated word) formed the most prevalent category of errors, comprising 44% of all errors. As is evident from this proportion, comprehension errors were a significant issue in English. They identified only 96 phrases that were free of comprehension errors. Following comprehension errors, entry errors (spelling mistakes or accidental key presses) and space errors (extra blank spaces) were the most common. Other errors, each occurring with a frequency of less than 6%, included compound break and contraction errors (adding a space between a single word or combining two words into one), addition and omission errors (adding or omitting articles and prepositions), numeric errors (using a number instead of spelling it out) and dialect errors (using alternative spellings of words). In a second follow-up study with 80 visually impaired or blind participants, only 92 of the 96 phrases were found to be aurally reliable. Overall, comprehension errors resulted in over 80% of the phrases being removed, as they were likely to be misheard and unsuitable for aural transcription tasks.

In this paper, we use the term "errors" to refer to any differences between the original Unicode phrase and its transcription, consistent with their study. This term is not meant to imply faults or failures on the part of the participants or to value-judge but rather to indicate whether the discrepancies could lead to misunderstanding the phrase when it is heard. We also adopt the definition of comprehension errors from their study.

While our approach draws inspiration from their first study, there are several key differences in our methodology that we wish to highlight. Firstly, our study was moderated with 80 native Marathi participants. Secondly, we opted for participants to write instead of type, as text input in Marathi could have introduced additional errors. Familiarising and training users on text input were not within the scope of this study, as our primary focus was on the comprehension of the phrases rather than the method used to reproduce them. Thirdly, our analysis was entirely manual and we validated our findings with Marathi language experts in an expert workshop. We additionally examined phrases that exhibited comprehension errors, identifying the kinds of phrases prone to such errors. Our findings show a different error profile from the study in English, as discussed further.

3   Method

3.1   Study

The chosen set of 299 Marathi phrases was curated by Dalvi et al. [12] and is reasonably representative of the Marathi language. We selected Google Cloud's text-to-speech service [1] as we found it to be a prominent open tool that generated acceptable quality Marathi audio clips. Each phrase was recorded in a female voice (mr-IN-Wavenet-A) and a male voice (mr-IN-Wavenet-B) available on the platform in 2023. The voice type was set to WaveNet as it provided the best prosody among the available types. Additional settings pertaining to speed and pitch were maintained as the default. Consequently, 598 audio clips in mp3 format were generated.

We conducted a pilot study with four participants to test the logistics and duration of the study for each participant. The study was conducted with one participant at a time, in the presence of a moderator, in a quiet environment. Audio clips were played aloud from a laptop speaker and the participant transcribed these. In the pilot, each participant transcribed 20 phrases. The participants could finish this task in less than 15 min, and hence, we decided to increase this number to 30 phrases per participant.

For the final study, we recruited 80 native Marathi-speaking literate participants (mean age = 39.42 years, SD = 13.38 years), comprising 50 females and 30 males. The participants held various occupations, including IT professionals, self-employed individuals, homemakers and others. To ensure fluency in Marathi, we specifically recruited individuals who could speak, understand, read and write the language. All participants had formally studied Marathi as a subject in school (35 in Marathi medium, five in semi-English medium and 40 in English medium schools). All participants had at least 12 years of schooling. The participants currently live in Pune and Mumbai in Maharashtra (a Marathi-speaking area) and are primarily from the middle-class demographic.

We randomised the 598 audio clips and assigned each participant 30 different phrases (29 in two cases). This resulted in each phrase getting repeated eight times across eight unique participants—four times in the male voice and four times in the female voice. When the participant walked in, we informed them about the goal of our study, explained that the task would be similar to a dictation task, asked for their consent to participate, and urged them to listen and write to the best of their abilities. We collected demographic information, including age, gender, where they come from (region within Maharashtra), the medium of instruction in their school and the number of years they studied Marathi in school.

The moderator played back each audio clip on a laptop so that the participant could focus on the transcription. Participants were allowed to hear the audio as many times as needed. If the participant was confused, the moderator did not help the participant but encouraged them to attempt writing whatever they heard. Unlike the approach taken by Abbott et al. [3], we opted not to have participants type the phrases but rather to write them. We made this choice because typing in Marathi is known to be challenging if participants do not have prior experience. Typing could have introduced additional, unrelated errors, which we wanted to avoid. Participants transcribed the phrases using a pencil on ruled sheets of paper, which allowed them to correct any mistakes. Figure 1 shows a sample output of the transcription task. Participants needed about 20 min each to transcribe the assigned 30 phrases.

3.2   Error Tag Identification

As mentioned, we aim to create a taxonomy of error tags and subtags that participants make while transcribing Marathi text when presented aurally, and among these tags and subtags, identify those that affect comprehension.

Error Identification and Categorisation. The first round of the data analysis process consisted of two stages: error identification and categorisation. We manually checked and documented errors by comparing each written phrase against the original Unicode phrase. As the phrases were handwritten, we opted for manual error identification. We are not aware of any image recognition

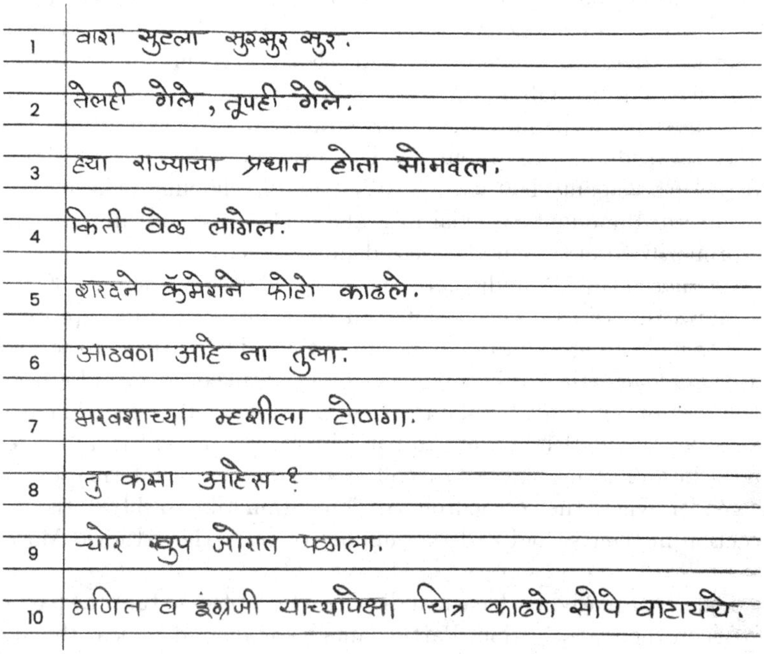

Fig. 1. Sample of Phrases Transcribed by a Participant

method capable of accurately analysing handwritten Marathi text reliably. Further, there are no reliable spell checkers and grammar checkers for Marathi. We treated any discrepancy between the transcribed text and the Unicode text as an "error", other than stylistic variations such as इ and ट्ट, ढ and द्ध, श and श्व. Identifying and noting errors from 30 phrases from a single participant required over one hour. The number of errors in the 30 transcribed phrases per participant varied from a minimum of 10 to a maximum of 120 errors.

After listing all the errors across participants, we took a bottom-up approach to categorise them by labelling each error and grouping them based on similar occurrences. We approached it qualitatively, drawing on our knowledge of the language. However (although both authors are native Marathi speakers), developing a consistent error taxonomy proved challenging. Some errors were easily grouped based on similarities and frequency, such as errors where participants had separated the suffix from the base word like मामाचा (uncle's) written as मामा चा (which is an error as Marathi is an agglutinative language), confused long and short vowel signs like कापूस (cotton) written as कापुस (commonly seen spelling mistakes), or formed a conjunct out of two consecutive consonants like उकडत (feeling hot) written as उक्डत (likely due to the quick pronunciation of these words in conversation). Nonetheless, many errors did not fit into obvious groups. To produce a systematic overview encompassing the wide range of errors encountered, we created provisional categories and noted examples of errors that seemed to fit. We iterated the categories several times and ultimately identified 11 initial error categories and 36 subcategories. The 11 main error categories are shown in Table 1. The identification and categorisation process was conducted over several months.

Table 1. Initial Error Categories

Error Category	Example of Error
Spelling Error	बक्षीस (prize) written as बक्षिस
Alpaprana Mahaprana Error	जांभुळ (java plum) written as जांबुळ
Dialect Error	सोडणार (will leave) written as सोडनार
Substitution Error	मारा (hit) written as वारा (wind)
Suffix Error	मेंदीच्या (of henna) written as मेंदी च्या
Conjunct Error	उत्कंठेने (eagerly) written as उतकंठेने
Anusvara Error	चोराच्या (thief's) written as चोरांच्या (thieves')
Word Break Error	खाताखाता (while eating) written as खाता खाता
Addition Error	पानातून हळू पाहे (slowly looking through the leaves) written as पानातून बाहेर हळू पाहे (slowly looking outside through the leaves)
Omission Error	झुक झुक झुक झुक (train sound) written as झुक झुक झुक
Hindi Error	जळ (water) written as जल

Workshop with Marathi Experts to Create a Taxonomy for Tagging Errors. After establishing the initial set of error categories, we sought to validate our taxonomy and refine the appropriateness of our error categories through a workshop with language experts. For the workshop, we recruited a panel of six experts, including two professors from IIT Bombay with expertise and experience in research involving Marathi, a senior linguist from Computation for Indian Language Technology, IIT Bombay, an independent academic consultant with prior research experience involving Marathi, an editor who formerly worked with a major Marathi newspaper and a PhD scholar from IIT Bombay who has studied Marathi literature.

Prior to the workshop, we shared our objectives and examples of each error type with the panel. We then held a three-hour session with them to evaluate our work from an expert perspective and collect feedback on the identified taxonomy. The workshop was organised in person and moderated by the authors, with notes taken by a designated note-taker.

During the workshop, we first familiarised the experts with the motivation, method and error analysis of our work, along with the error analysis from the study in English by Abbott et al. [3]. Next, we presented our preliminary error categorisation, including descriptions and examples of each type, for their review. This discussion was supplemented with the audio clips used in the study and original participant transcripts as necessary, allowing the experts to assess the nature of the errors firsthand. We invited discussion regarding the suitability of the categories, their descriptions and whether they needed to be revised through consolidation, subdivision or addition of new categories. The experts broadly agreed with our error categories and additionally pointed out several nuances and inaccuracies, which were subsequently corrected.

In the workshop, one important conclusion was to shift from using error categories to tagging errors with tags and subtags that are not mutually exclusive. For example, a participant had transcribed the word हात (hand) as हाथ. This simple error can be categorised in at least three ways. It could be called an "*Alpaprana Mahaprana* Error" as the *alpaprana* consonant त is replaced by a *mahaprana* consonant थ. But, this substitution also results in the Hindi spelling of hand, making it a "Hindi Error". Given the location of our participants, we know they are familiar with Hindi, which could have influenced their use of this spelling. Lastly, this error is not likely to affect comprehension as native Marathi speakers can understand both words, but in this case, the participant was unable to reproduce it accurately, making a "Spelling Error." Hence, in the workshop, it was decided to move away from creating rigid error categories and instead tag each error. Tagging allows multiple relevant error tags and subtags to correspond to a single error occurrence. Consequently, we opted to redefine our taxonomy to comprise of error tags and subtags. After the workshop, the first author revisited all error instances to reassign tags and subtags in a second round of analysis. The tags and subtags were reviewed by the second author and no discrepancies were detected.

The second objective of our workshop was to identify error categories affecting the aural reliability of a phrase. We asked for expert opinions on which types of errors would hinder listening comprehension and which would not. We concluded that only two out of 36 error subcategories would affect comprehension when phrases are heard. Phrases where participants' transcriptions indicated they misheard a phrase—either by writing a word that means something else or by writing words that neither exist nor seem like attempts to write the correct word—were deemed to affect comprehension. Consequently, most error types were considered acceptable as they emerged from writing and would have no impact when the phrase is heard.

Additionally, the experts highlighted that a large number of errors appeared to stem from phrases that were either from songs, poetic or idiomatic expressions. These phrases could only be reproduced correctly if the participants had heard them before. They recommended that errors arising from differences in poetic writing should be specifically tagged as such. They advised that such phrases could generally be avoided in aural transcription tasks, as they often contain words with atypical spellings or words that are rarely used in everyday or functional contexts.

4   Findings

During the transcription task, participants did not ask for the repetition of a majority of the phrases, even though they were informed that this was possible. Occasionally, a phrase was requested to be replayed two or three times, but not more than that.

Our second round of analysis after the workshop led to 17 main error tags and one "No Error" tag. Of the main error tags, 11 had 44 subtags, leading to a total of 50 unique ways to tag an error. Among these, only four (three subtags and one tag) are related to comprehension, namely the "Different Word Substitution Error" subtag, "Nonexistent Word Error" subtag, "Word Distinction Error" subtag and "Untranscribed Words Error" tag. Figure 2 visualises all the tags and subtags as a treemap. The subtags that relate to comprehension errors are highlighted through a pattern.

Table 2 in Appendix 1 provides a complete list of short description of each error tag and subtag along with an example and the number of times that tag was used. Along with this paper, we have released the error data and this taxonomy in the public domain.

Out of the total of 2,392 phrase transcriptions, 877 were transcribed accurately and had the tag "No Error". Our analysis yielded a total of 4,152 error subtags across the remaining 1,515 transcriptions (several transcriptions had multiple error tags and subtags). Among these, only 535 subtags were related to error types affecting comprehension. Figure 2 treemap visualises the relative frequencies of the 4,152 subtags (the number of subtags is proportional to the area of the rectangle representing that subtag). The tag names appear on black labels and all subtags belonging to a tag are of the same colour.

Table 3 in Appendix 2 lists the number of "No Error" tags (out of a maximum possible of 8) for each phrase in our phrase set, the number of comprehension error subtags, the number of non-comprehension error subtags, the total number of error subtags and whether we recommend the phrase or not for aural transcription tasks. Of the 299 phrases in the phrase set, eight were transcribed accurately by all the eight participants. These are in the first eight rows of Table 3. Another 101 phrases had no comprehension errors. In another 70 phrases, only one out of eight participants made a comprehension error. This gave us a candidate 179 phrases that could be potentially recommended for aural transcription

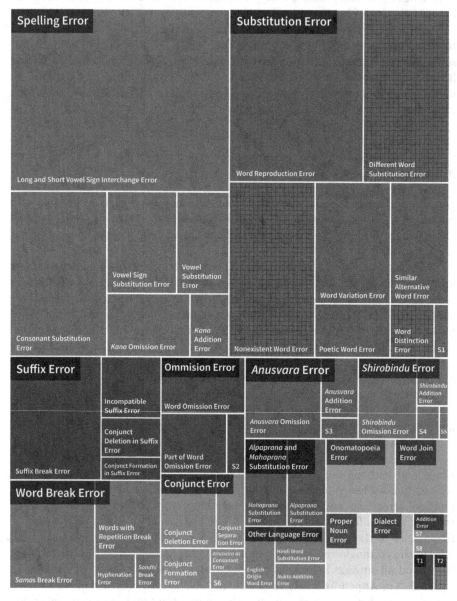

Fig. 2. Distribution of Frequencies of Error Tags and Subtags

tasks. However, among these, 16 phrases with zero comprehension errors and another 21 phrases with one comprehension error each had more than 16 non-comprehension error subtags. While these errors may not directly impact aural reliability, transcribing these phrases from audio would be more of a test of the language of a participant than the evaluation of a synthetic voice or any other technological intervention. It so happens that these phrases were either poetic, idiomatic, oddly phrased or complex, and generally "difficult". Hence we do not recommend them for aural transcription tasks. This leaves us with 142 phrases (48% of 299) that we recommend for use in aural transcription tasks involving synthetic speech because they are aurally reliable.

Of course, we encourage researchers to use their own judgement in selecting phrases based on the specific needs of their study.

4.1 Comprehension Error Subtags

Among the 535 transcriptions identified as having comprehension errors, the most frequent error subtags were "Different Word Substitution Error" and "Nonexistent Word Error" which were used 244 times each. The "Different Word Substitution Error" subtag was designated for errors where a participant substituted a word with an unrelated word, changing the meaning of the phrase. For example, in the phrase मित्राचे काम करण्यात कसला आला आहे कमीपणा, the participant wrote मित्राचे पाय धरण्यात कसला आला आहे कमीपणा, changing the meaning of the words from "doing a friend's work..." to "holding a friend's feet...". Other examples of such word substitutions include टक्का (percent/bribe) written as चटका (burn), गाऊ (will sing) written as खाऊ (will eat), and सदर (these) written as खबर (news). These errors seem to be clear cases of mishearing a phrase. In cases where words are substituted with words that do not exist and also do not seem like an attempt to reproduce the original word, we use the "Nonexistent Word Error" subtag, indicating an inability to comprehend the word, such as बैलगाडी (bullock cart) written as डौतदार, पिच्छा (chase) written as पुखावे and लडिवाळा (dear baby) written as हीनवाडा. These errors seem to arise from participants guessing the word and attempting to write down whatever they heard regardless of whether it made sense. We also observed instances where participants were unable to distinctively identify two or more words and instead combined parts of those words to form different words. For example, मित्र आला (friend came) written as मित्राला (to a friend) and राजाझाच ती तिचे (it was the king's order) written as राजाया स्थीती चे. Such errors have been subtagged as "Word Distinction Error" and this subtag has been used 38 times. These errors indicate that participants could not hear consecutive words as distinct and attempted to write similar-sounding words, resulting in either different words or nonexistent words. These three error subtags fall within the "Substitution Error" tag and have been identified as those substitution errors which affect the aural reliability of a phrase. Additionally, we observed nine instances where participants left certain parts of a phrase unwritten. These errors belong to a separate tag called "Untranscribed Words Error" and are not simply word omission errors; rather, participants began writing but gave up the effort, as we observed in person that they asked to move to the next phrase. As mentioned earlier, we observed a total of 535 subtags involving the above four types of errors and phrases involving these tags and subtags have been deemed as aurally unreliable as participants have had difficulty identifying words in these phrases.

4.2   Other Frequent Error Subtags

Overall, the most frequently observed error tag was the "Spelling Error" tag with a frequency of 1,248. Arguably, nearly every other tag and subtag could be labelled as a spelling error. However, we have specifically defined spelling errors to only include mistakes at the character level. Additionally, to maintain a two-level structure for tags and subtags, we have separated out other types of errors.

More than half of the subtags within the "Spelling Error" tag (657) belonged to the "Long and Short Vowel Sign Interchange Error" subtag. As most Indian language speakers would agree, this is perhaps the most common kind of error people make. Participants mistook short vowel signs for long vowel signs and vice versa, as seen in the transcriptions like कापूस (cotton) written as कापुस and बांधुन (tied up) written as बांधून involving the *ukaar*; and भीती (fear) written as भिती and शिकत (learning/studying) written as शीकत involving the *velanti*. These errors are largely knowledge-based, as one needs to know when to use each vowel sign. These errors likely occurred because participants knew the word but were either unaware of the correct spelling or had forgotten it. Differentiating between these solely by sound can be challenging due to the very slight difference and synthetic speech systems are currently not capable of pronouncing that slight difference accurately.

Another 265 subtags within this tag belonged to the "Consonant Substitution Error" subtag where participants replaced a consonant with another. Examples involving this error often led to other kinds of errors like पलटण (platoon) written as पलटन is also tagged as a "Dialect Error" and अडचण (difficulty) written as अढचण also had the subtag of "*Alpaprana* Substitution Error".

The second most frequent tag was the "Substitution Error Tag" used 1,245 times. The three subtags within this tag that affect comprehension have already been discussed ("Different Word Substitution Error", "Nonexistent Word Error" and "Word Distinction Error"). The "Word Reproduction Error" subtag was the most used subtag (375 times) involving substitution but not affecting comprehension. It was used when a word was substituted with one that appeared to have incorrect spelling. However, the transcribed word suggested that the participant likely heard the word correctly but faced challenges in accurately reproducing its spelling. Examples include पक्षी (bird) written as पक्शी, म्हणजे (meaning) written as मंजे, जाऊन (to go) written as जावून and शहाणी (wise) written as शाणी. Although the transcribed word appears different from the original word, based on our judgement, these errors have emerged from the writing rather than the audio and, therefore, we opted not to label them as a "Nonexistent Word Error". It was possible to discern that the words were attempts at the original word and not unintelligible.

Another subtag involving substitution but not affecting comprehension is where the substitution is acceptable because the participant has used an acceptable alternative of the original word, such as अन् (and) written as आणि and ह्या (these) written as या. This subtag is called "Similar Alternative Word Error" and was used 117 times.

"Suffix Errors" accounted for the third most frequent error tags with a frequency of 305. The most common subtag was the "Suffix Break Error," where participants wrote the suffix separately from the base word, such as writing दीपाने (Deepa did) as दीपा ने and त्याच्याकडे (to him) as त्याचा कडे. This subtag was used for these errors 186 times; however, this error is inconsequential to aural comprehension.

Please refer to Table 2 in Appendix 1 for a complete listing of all the error tags and subtags.

5   Discussion and Future Work

Towards the goal of identifying an aurally reliable phrase set in Marathi, we conducted a study in which we presented 299 phrases in the form of synthetic speech to 80 participants (30 phrases each). We collected a total of 2,392 transcriptions and manually analysed them, identifying 4,152 errors. A detailed error analysis, followed by validation through an expert workshop, allowed us to define 17 main error tags and 50 subtags, that represent the nature of the errors observed in the transcriptions. While 13% of the errors were comprehension errors, we tagged 87% of the errors as non-comprehension related. The error tags and subtags provided the basis for identifying 142 aurally reliable phrases, which are presented in Table 3 in Appendix 2.

Our findings show that compared to the study by Abbott et al. [3], there seem to be more ways in which a transcriber can make an error in Marathi compared to English. On average, we found 52 error subtags per participant and 1.73 error subtags per transcribed phrase. In contrast, Abbott et al. had found 0.25 errors per transcribed phrase. On the other hand, only about 13% of our errors were comprehension errors compared to 44% in their case. Thus, they had to eliminate 82% of their 500 phrases from the MacKenzie and Soukoreff phrase set, recommending only 92 (18%) as aurally reliable. We could recommend 142 of 299 phrases as aurally reliable (48%).

This difference in the proportion of comprehension and non-comprehension errors could be attributed to the differences in the nature and textures of the languages. However, we need to be careful in interpreting this assertion. There were methodological differences between the two studies. Ours was a moderated study in which the device (laptop) was controlled. Abbott et al.'s [3] study was crowd-sourced using Amazon Mechanical Turk. The use of the device was up to the participant and the study was not moderated. So participants in our study likely approached the task with more focus and intent than in Abbott et al.'s study. If we had crowd-sourced our study, we may have possibly had an even larger number of errors.

We recommend a set of 142 aurally reliable Marathi phrases for use in aural transcription tasks. These aurally reliable phrases can also be used in studies evaluating synthetic speech, and to optimise parameters like synthesis engine or algorithm, gender, dialect and speed. Additionally, these phrases are valuable for conducting accessibility studies for eyes-free text entry. We further present error rates in all 299 phrases of the phrase set, allowing researchers to use their own judgement in selecting phrases for their study.

Aural communication in real-life situations may require conveying all types of information. Hence, the 157 phrases that we do not recommend for aural transcription tasks are also valuable. These phrases could be examined to identify language styles that could be avoided and to find strategies for rephrasing them to improve communication (like [32] and [26]). Such phrases are also valuable for scriptwriters of voice-based interfaces that use predetermined scripts. By analysing phrases with comprehension errors, scriptwriters can improve their scripts for clear and effective communication in systems where information has to be communicated aurally. A large majority of phrases that had comprehension errors were also poetic, idiomatic, oddly phrased or complex, used atypical word order, had words from old Marathi and were generally difficult. Possible strategies to improve the aural reliability of content could be opting for simple, common and familiar words rather than complex and rare words, maintaining typical word order in sentences, providing additional contextual clues, using prose instead of stylistic or poetic forms, slowing the pace of synthetic speech for some difficult words, or repeating of key information. Further studies are required to validate these strategies.

Unlike Abbott et al. [3], we moved from categorising errors to tagging errors. Our error tagging approach can be extended to studies involving error analysis in other languages where forming discrete error categories is not the best approach.

We would like to note that despite Google Cloud's text-to-speech yielding the best results among current tools (in 2023), there were noticeable issues with the pronunciation, prosody and enunciation of the phrases in the generated audio clips. The phrases involving many comprehension errors can be useful for evaluating and improving the prosody of synthetic speech technology in Marathi.

The transcription errors identified in this study showcase the wide range of mistakes people make while writing (and possibly could make while typing) Marathi. These can be useful in developing Marathi spell checkers and auto-correct tools for text input correction. Errors similar to those found in this study are likely to occur in other Marathi transcription studies. The error tags and subtags can serve as a reference for researchers, with the possibility of expanding our list of tags and subtags if additional errors are discovered.

For the purpose of our study, we defined "aurally reliable" phrases to be those that either contain no errors or contain errors that do not hinder comprehension. There are several ways to define "comprehension" errors in transcription, but in this study, we mean the use of unassociated words (like Abbott et al. [3]), nonexistent words and untranscribed words. These errors have the potential to alter meaning, introduce ambiguities, render sentences grammatically incorrect and possibly cause confusion. Thus in our study, comprehension refers to a participant hearing a phrase well enough to reproduce it through transcription.

As we evaluated aural comprehension of phrases through writing, many non-comprehension errors stemmed from participants' unfamiliarity with the word itself or its spelling, leading to difficulties for them in reconstructing the word. This could be due to forgetting spellings or not being in the habit of writing in Marathi. The complexity of Devanagari could also be a cause. The script has many characters "near" each other, such as long and short vowels or unaspirated and aspirated consonants (*alpaprana and mahaprana*). Our interpretation of participants' handwriting could have also introduced errors.

In our study, the transcriptions were performed by native speakers, not language experts, so many errors were expected and should not be overly scrutinised. While transcription allowed for a detailed examination of errors, our intent was not to judge our participants' language skills. Interpretation of audio and transcription are significantly influenced by an individual's cultural background, exposure to the language, current language usage and social context. Further, Marathi is a diverse language with several accents and dialects, often captured by the expression "चांदा ते बांदा" (from Chandrapur to Banda). The study's sample size of 80 participants, mainly from Pune and Mumbai, may not be representative of the entire Marathi-speaking population and may not have included people speaking other dialects spoken in different regions.

Our use of the term "error" in this study refers solely to discrepancies between transcriptions and the original Unicode text (phrases used for synthetic speech generation). In the context of Marathi, there are historical and social dimensions to determining what constitutes a spelling "mistake". Deshpande [14] has explored the history of debates over standardised spelling conventions (*shuddhalekhan* or *pramaanalekhan*) in Marathi, including issues surrounding long and short vowel signs. She argues that standard Marathi largely derives from the speech of the *Puneri Brahmin* and was historically chosen as a benchmark. Written Marathi, or textbook language, adheres to those strict spelling rules. In contrast, the spoken language is much more fluid, with significant regional diversity. Hence, in aural transcription studies like ours, participants' writing mistakes should not be overly scrutinised in any case.

Future studies could employ methods beyond transcription to assess the comprehension of audio. Researchers can measure subjective comprehension through judgement of understandability on a scale. This approach has been used in previous research by Moos and Trouvain [30] in measuring comprehension of natural and synthetic speech. Incorporating a Likert scale and comprehension questions in addition to transcription tasks, as done by Bione and Cardoso [8], could provide more information about participants' comprehension levels. Beyond self-reports, studies could also ask participants to verbally reproduce or explain what they heard.

6 Conclusion

Reliable predetermined phrase sets in empirical studies help to ensure that observations result from user interactions rather than ambiguities in the phrase sets presented. To identify an aurally reliable phrase set in Marathi, we examined 299 Marathi phrases, inspired by a study in English by Abbott et al. [3]. Participants transcribed these phrases after hearing them in synthetic speech, resulting in 2,392 transcriptions. Through detailed manual error analysis of the transcriptions, we developed a taxonomy of 17 error tags and 50 subtags, identifying a total of 4,152 subtags. Our taxonomy of error tags and subtags is an original contribution representing the kinds of errors people make while writing Marathi. Although we identified more error subtags per transcription than Abbott et al., we found a smaller proportion of errors impacting comprehension.

Another outcome of our work is the set of 142 aurally reliable Marathi phrases that we recommend can be readily used for aural transcription tasks. We recommend phrases without errors that affect comprehension and those with few overall errors as aurally reliable. Further, our study can inform several other areas of research. The 157 phrases that we do not recommend due to a high occurrence of errors could be used for identifying strategies to improve aural scripts in Marathi and to improve the quality of synthetic speech in Marathi. The taxonomy of tags and subtags that we identified can inform research in Marathi error correction mechanisms, such as spell checkers and auto-correct. The tags and subtags can be used by researchers in other related Indian languages as starting points for developing their taxonomies. We expect the errors in Indian languages to resemble our tags and subtags more than the error categories identified by Abbott et al. [3]. Our approach to tagging errors (instead of strictly categorising them) can inform other languages where errors may be difficult to categorise. Lastly, our work shows that the errors made by users while transcribing Marathi text need to be analysed differently from those made by users while transcribing English text, highlighting the need for independent research in every language.

Acknowledgements. We thank the reviewers for their thorough analysis and helpful commentary on the paper. We thank the experts Prof Malhar Kulkarni, Prof Girish Dalvi, Mrs Irawati Kulkarni, Mr Salil Badodekar, Mr Niraj Pandit and Ms Sayali Tharali for their contribution to our Marathi expert workshop. We also extend our thanks to Yash Kothari and Avani Bhagdikar for their assistance in conducting the study. Finally, we thank all the participants for their willingness to participate in our study.

Disclosure of Interests. The authors have no competing interests to declare that are relevant to the content of this article.

Appendix 1

Table 2. Marathi Error Tag and Subtag Taxonomy with Examples

Error Tag	Error Subtag	Description	Example	Freq.
No Error	No Error	Accurate transcription of a phrase compared to the Unicode text used to generate the synthetic audio	-	877
Spelling Error	Long and Short Vowel Sign Interchange Error	A long vowel sign (*ukaar* or *velanti* on a consonant) is replaced by a short vowel sign (and vice versa)	महिना written as म्हिना	657
Spelling Error	*Kana* Addition Error	A *kana* vowel sign is added to a consonant	टपए written as टपाए	40
Spelling Error	*Kana* Omission Error	A *kana* vowel sign is deleted from a consonant	अर्थग written as अर्थग	84
Spelling Error	Vowel Sign Substitution Error	A *kana, velanti, ukaar* or *matra* on a consonant is replaced by another	झाडे written as झाडी	115
Spelling Error	Vowel Substitution Error	A vowel is replaced by another	इमानी written as एमानी	87
Spelling Error	Consonant Substitution Error	A consonant is replaced by another, typically one that is "near"-sounding	वैडले written as वैडले	265
Alpaprana and *Mahaprana* Substitution Error	*Alpaprana* Substitution Error	An *alpaprana* consonant is replaced by a "near"-sounding *mahaprana* consonant	गुड्यांला written as गुड्यांला	55
Alpaprana and *Mahaprana* Substitution Error	*Mahaprana* Substitution Error	An *mahaprana* consonant is replaced by a "near"-sounding *alpaprana* consonant	तंबाखू written as तंबाकू	61
Dialect Error	Dialect Error	A word is spelt incorrectly according to standard Marathi but reflects its pronunciation in a regional dialect	आपण written as आपन	54
Substitution Error	Synonymous Word Error	A word is replaced by its synonym, which has a different sound and spelling	औषध written as वडू	13
Substitution Error	Similar Alternative Word Error	A word is replaced by an acceptable alternative to it, which is similar in sound and spelling	कुणी written as कोणी	117

(continued)

Table 2. (*continued*)

Error Tag	Error Subtag	Description	Example	Freq.
Substitution Error	Poetic Word Error	Any spelling mistake involving a word that is spelt atypically due to its poetic form	दाऊ written as राधु	65
Substitution Error	Word Reproduction Error	A word is transcribed incorrectly but likely heard correctly (with the transcribed form of the word being "near" the original word)	कौतुक written as कवतुक	375
Substitution Error	Word Variation Error	A word is spelt with the same base word but with slight variation in spelling (changing tense, gender or plurality)	द्यावित written as द्यावे	149
Substitution Error	Word Distinction Error	Two or more consecutive words are replaced by different or non-existent words	राजाज्याच ती written as राजा अज्ञासती	38
Substitution Error	Different Word Substitution Error	A word is replaced by another word with a different meaning	बरा written as भरला	244
Substitution Error	Nonexistent Word Error	A word is spelt incorrectly resulting in an unintelligible, nonexistent word (not "near" the original word)	रसिसारखे written as प्रतिसकिया	244
Untranscribed Words Error	Untranscribed Words Error	Portions of a phrase are left untranscribed	द्योवे अंगा वारे कारया थरथरे written as द्योवे अंगा	9
Suffix Error	Suffix Break Error	The suffix is separated from the base word and written as a separate word	शेतावर written as शेता वर	186
Suffix Error	Conjunct Formation in Suffix Error	A consonant from the suffix of a word is replaced by a conjunct, keeping the base word same	मीठा written as मीठ्या	22
Suffix Error	Conjunct Deletion in Suffix Error	A conjunct in the suffix of a word is replaced by a consonant, keeping the base word same	जिव्या written as जिया	38
Suffix Error	Incompatible Suffix Error	A suffix of a word is changed, making resulting new word grammatically inconsistent with the rest of the phrase	राच्या संग्रह्याकन... written as राच्या संग्रह्याकन...	59
Conjunct Error	Conjunct Separation Error	A conjunct replaced by its separate component consonants	कल्पना written as कलपना	35

(*continued*)

Table 2. (*continued*)

Error Tag	Error Subtag	Description	Example	Freq.
Conjunct Error	*Anusvara* as Consonant Error	An *anusvara* is replaced by the corresponding consonant	बंदूक written as बन्दूक	13
Conjunct Error	Conjunct Formation Error	Two consecutive consonants are replaced by their conjunct form	शिकरण written as शिक्रण	33
Conjunct Error	Conjunct Deletion Error	A conjunct in a word is replaced by a consonant (involved in the conjunct)	न्हला written as न्हला	67
Conjunct Error	Jumbled Letters of Conjunct Error	The order of consonants involved in and around a conjunct is altered	ब्रह्मज्ञान written as ब्रम्हज्ञान	10
Anusvara Error	*Anusvara* Addition Error	An *anusvara* is added to a word	चोरीच्या written as चोरींच्या	36
Anusvara Error	*Anusvara* Omission Error	An *anusvara* is deleted from a word	घरच्यांत written as घरच्यात	100
Anusvara Error	*Anusvara* Placement Error	An *anusvara* is misplaced on a neighboring consonant	लंगडी written as लगंडी	12
Shirobindu Error	*Shirobindu* Omission Error	A *shirobindu* is omitted from the last consonant of a word	म्हणां written as म्हणत	77
Shirobindu Error	*Shirobindu* Addition Error	A *shirobindu* is added over the last consonant of a word	पोट written as पोटं	25
Shirobindu Error	*Shirobindu* Substitution Error	A *shirobindu* on the last consonant of a word is replaced by an ए *matra*	खोटं written as खोटे	12
Shirobindu Error	ए-*Matra* Substitution Error	An ए *matra* on the last consonant of a word is replaced by a *shirobindu*	राहावे written as राहावं	5
Word Break Error	Words with Repetition Break Error	An exact reduplicated word is replaced by its two separate duplicating words	किरकिरिला written as किरा फिरा	78
Word Break Error	*Samas* Break Error	A *samasik* word is replaced by its separate component words	सुईदोरा written as सुई दोरा	155
Word Break Error	*Sandhi* Break Error	A *sandhi* word is replaced by its separate component words	पूर्वायुष्य written as पूर्व आयुष्य	14

(*continued*)

Table 2. (*continued*)

Error Tag	Error Subtag	Description	Example	Freq.
Word Break Error	Hyphenation Error	A single word is replaced by its hyphenated form	रिमझिम written as रिम-झिम	23
Word Join Error	Word Join Error	Two separate words are replaced by one word combining them	सगळे जग written as सगळेजग	65
Word Position Interchange Error	Word Position Interchange Error	The position of two words is swapped	कशी नाहीबाने थट्टा आज मांडली written as कशी नाहीबाने आज थट्टा मांडली	12
Addition Error	Word Addition Error	A word that is not part of the phrase is added	पानातून हळू पाहे ढोकावून खार written as पानातून हळू बाहेर पाहे ढोकावून खार	14
Addition Error	Suffix Addition Error	A suffix is added to a word	मना written as मनात	9
Omission Error	Word Omission Error	A word from the phrase is omitted	देव देते आणि कर्म नेते written as देव देते कर्म नेते	77
Omission Error	Part of Word Omission Error	Letter(s) of a word are omitted, keeping the base word same	आावडत written as आवड	64
Omission Error	Repeating Word Omission Error	A word is omitted in a repeated sequence of the word	लुख लुख written as लुख	18
Onomatopoeia Error	Onomatopoeia Error	Any spelling mistake in a Marathi onomatopoeic word	झरझर written as झुजर	82
Proper Noun Error	Proper Noun Error	Any spelling mistake involving a proper noun	विनू written as विनु	56
Other Language Error	Hindi Word Substitution Error	A Marathi word is replaced by its Hindi counterpart in spelling	हात written as हाथ	30
Other Language Error	*Nukta* Addition Error	A *nukta* is added to a consonant	पहले written as पढ़ले	21
Other Language Error	English-Origin Word Error	Any spelling mistake within a word that originally is an English word	कॅमेऱ्याने written as कॅमेरानी	32

Appendix 2

Table 3. List of 299 Phrases with Error Subtag Counts and Recommendations

ID[1]	Phrase	No errors	Comp. errors[2]	Non-Comp. errors[3]	Total errors	Rec.[4]
94	घरी सगळे कसे आहेत	8	0	0	0	Yes
1	चहा गरम आहे	8	0	0	0	Yes
37	झाली सकाळ सरली रात	8	0	0	0	Yes
31	तो सकाळी लवकर उठला	8	0	0	0	Yes
21	भारत माझा देश आहे	8	0	0	0	Yes
48	माती नाही तर शेती नाही	8	0	0	0	Yes
6	रमेश जेवण कर	8	0	0	0	Yes
47	वारा जोरात वाहतो आहे	8	0	0	0	Yes
136	आज गोकुळात रंग खेळतो हरी	7	0	1	1	Yes
7	विजय पाट उचल	7	0	1	1	Yes
87	विमान आकाशात उडत आहे	7	0	1	1	Yes
22	ससा ससा दिसतो कसा	7	0	1	1	Yes
99	सागरा प्राण तळमळला	7	0	1	1	Yes
135	विंध्य हिमाचल यमुना गंगा	6	0	1	1	Yes
33	कावळा करतो काव काव	7	0	2	2	Yes
41	थेंबे थेंबे तळे साचे	7	0	2	2	Yes
92	आठवण आहे ना तुला	6	0	2	2	Yes
118	काखेत कळसा गावाला वळसा	6	0	2	2	Yes
148	बाळाचे पाय पाळण्यात दिसतात	6	0	2	2	Yes
90	मग मी काय करू	6	0	2	2	Yes
95	मला हाक का मारलीस	6	0	2	2	Yes
13	हे खूप महाग आहे	6	0	2	2	Yes
104	चोराच्या मनात चांदणे	7	0	3	3	Yes
27	जय हे जय हे जय हे	7	0	3	3	Yes
228	तो मात्र रुमालातून भाकरी आणतो	7	0	3	3	Yes
12	बळी तो कान पिळी	7	0	3	3	Yes
113	चोराच्या उलट्या बोंबा	6	0	3	3	Yes
67	जिकडे तिकडे झाडेच झाडे	6	0	3	3	Yes
190	फिटे अंधाराचे जाळे झाले मोकळे आकाश	6	0	3	3	Yes
73	वडाचे झाड खूप मोठे होते	6	0	3	3	Yes
68	तुझी माझी जोडी जमली रे	5	0	3	3	Yes
2	तू कसा आहेस	5	0	3	3	Yes
150	दोघांची बरीच बाचाबाची झाली	5	0	3	3	Yes
75	आकांक्षा शहरात शिकत होती	5	0	4	4	Yes
129	ते माझं कौतुक करू लागले	5	0	4	4	Yes
207	मी कोणाशीही जास्त बोलत नसे	5	0	4	4	Yes
103	अरे तू इकडे कसा काय	4	0	4	4	Yes
25	खेळणी आमची मातीची	7	0	5	5	Yes
3	तू कशी आहेस	4	0	5	5	Yes
131	दिव्याखाली अंधार	4	0	5	5	Yes

(*continued*)

Table 3. (*continued*)

ID	Phrase	No errors	Comp. errors	Non-Comp. errors	Total errors	Rec.
121	हा पक्षी इमानी निघाला	4	0	5	5	Yes
69	हवेत उडतो लाल लाल फुगा	3	0	5	5	Yes
56	दात आहेत तर चणे नाहीत	6	0	6	6	Yes
28	पी हळद आणि हो गोरी	6	0	6	6	Yes
84	फारच मोठी अडचण आहे	6	0	6	6	Yes
133	थेंब थेंब तळ्यात नाचती रे	5	0	6	6	Yes
219	पवनचक्की म्हणजे काय हो गुरुजी	5	0	6	6	Yes
202	दैव देते आणि कर्म नेते	4	0	6	6	Yes
49	मुलं बागेत खेळत होती	4	0	6	6	Yes
117	वासरात लंगडी गाय शहाणी	4	0	6	6	Yes
170	साखरेचे खाणार त्याला देव देणार	4	0	6	6	Yes
16	कालदेखील पाऊस पडला	2	0	6	6	Yes
205	असा बालगंधर्व आता न होणे	7	0	7	7	Yes
93	आता काय बोलणार मी	6	0	7	7	Yes
45	इकडे झाडे तिकडे झाडे	5	0	7	7	Yes
20	राव चढले पंत पडले	5	0	7	7	Yes
78	माकडाने रंगवले आपले तोंड	4	0	7	7	Yes
156	सारे भारतीय माझे बांधव आहेत	4	0	7	7	Yes
17	अजयने चेंडू आणला	3	0	7	7	Yes
11	जय जय जय जय है	3	0	7	7	Yes
53	मोठाली नखे ठेवूच नका	3	0	7	7	Yes
248	शाळेमधल्या पोरांना हा वाटे दुसरा यम	5	0	8	8	Yes
155	दोघांनीही आपापले पैसे मोजले	4	0	8	8	Yes
108	आमची माती आमची माणसं	3	0	8	8	Yes
259	कधीही स्वार्थाला त्याने थारा दिला नाही	3	0	8	8	Yes
34	चिमणी करते चिव चिव	3	0	8	8	Yes
119	दुष्काळात तेरावा महिना	4	0	9	9	Yes
32	विमान बनवले दीपाने	2	0	9	9	Yes
294	कुठल्या बाजूने चालावे हेसुद्धा त्याला कळत नाही	1	0	9	9	Yes
116	माझा फोन खूप जुना आहे	1	0	9	9	Yes
225	पाखरे घरट्यात जाऊन बसली आहेत	0	0	9	9	Yes
43	जिकडे तिकडे लख लख लख	4	0	10	10	Yes
4	सीता दूध पी	4	0	10	10	Yes
290	त्याने आपले पूर्वायुष्य परोपकारात घालवले होते	3	0	10	10	Yes
143	किती चिमुकली आहेत ही फुलं	2	0	11	11	Yes
114	नदीनाल्यांना आला पूर	1	0	11	11	Yes
76	पावसाची रिमझिम थांबली रे	3	0	12	12	Yes
198	पोरांची पलटण चेंडूला शोधायला बाहेर पडली	3	0	12	12	Yes
151	मी तुला कधीच विसरणार नाही	3	0	12	12	Yes
214	त्याची खाकी पँट तर नीट बघा	3	0	13	13	Yes
236	पुढे मला काही कल्पना सुचू लागल्या	3	0	13	13	Yes
154	अति शहाणा त्याचा बैल रिकामा	2	0	13	13	Yes
271	चार आण्याची कोंबडी अन बारा आण्याचा मसाला	2	0	13	13	Yes
30	वीज चमकली चक चक चक	2	0	13	13	Yes

(*continued*)

Table 3. (*continued*)

ID	Phrase	No errors	Comp. errors	Non-Comp. errors	Total errors	Rec.
256	बाईंनी प्रथम नदीबद्दल माहिती सांगितली	1	0	13	13	Yes
80	काळाकाळा कापूस पिंजला रे	0	0	13	13	Yes
239	स्वतः मेल्याशिवाय स्वर्ग दिसत नाही	3	0	14	14	Yes
54	तेलही गेले तूपही गेले	2	0	14	14	Yes
242	स्वराज्य हा माझा जन्मसिद्ध हक्क आहे	2	0	14	14	Yes
40	चला घासू या आपले दात	1	0	14	14	Yes
184	पळस गेलं कोकणात तीन पानं चुकेनात	2	0	15	15	Yes
171	छडी लागे छमछम विद्या येई घमघम	4	0	16	16	Yes
5	दीपक पाणी आण	2	0	16	16	Yes
81	आज पाऊस पडला नाही	7	1	1	2	Yes
65	चिमण आता मोठा झाला आहे	7	1	1	2	Yes
26	घर झाडून केर काढा	6	1	2	3	Yes
55	तळे राखी तो पाणी चाखी	6	1	2	3	Yes
8	दूर तयांची घरे	6	1	2	3	Yes
9	किती वेळ लागेल	5	1	2	3	Yes
79	पंजाब सिंध गुजरात मराठा	7	1	3	4	Yes
58	जोवरी पैसा तोवरी बैसा	6	1	3	4	Yes
18	तव शुभ नामे जागे	6	1	3	4	Yes
60	सारखी सारखी फिरते गोल	6	1	3	4	Yes
100	पण लक्षात कोण घेतो	6	1	4	5	Yes
223	शेतात राबणाऱ्या बैलांचा हा सण	5	1	4	5	Yes
160	आज शाळेत बक्षीस समारंभ होता	4	1	4	5	Yes
168	मागे उभा मंगेश पुढे उभा मंगेश	4	1	4	5	Yes
158	अडला नारायण गाढवाचे पाय धरी	6	1	5	6	Yes
188	कावळा बसायला आणि फांदी तुटायला गाठ	5	1	5	6	Yes
85	मला थोडे पाणी देता का	5	1	5	6	Yes
98	तू रागावला का आहेस	4	1	5	6	Yes
83	चोर खूप जोरात पळाला	3	1	5	6	Yes
211	चेंडू मनोमन अगदी धन्य झाला	6	1	6	7	Yes
88	सगळी मुलं हसायला लागली	4	1	6	7	Yes
226	सोनेरी तेजामध्ये जग खुलले आहे	3	1	6	7	Yes
97	द्राविड उत्कल बंग	2	1	6	7	Yes
101	तो अजयच्या घरी आला	5	1	7	8	Yes
105	पालथ्या घागरीवर पाणी	5	1	7	8	Yes
62	जन गण मंगलदायक जय हे	3	1	7	8	Yes
227	पोरेही काही कमी वस्ताद नव्हती	2	1	7	8	Yes
63	नाचता येईना अंगण वाकडे	2	1	8	9	Yes
66	घरी कशी मग सांगा जातिल	1	1	8	9	Yes
102	आंधळा मागतो एक डोळा	5	1	9	10	Yes
134	गांधीजींना मुले खूप आवडत	5	1	9	10	Yes
106	मीना गोष्ट वाचत होती	4	1	9	10	Yes
109	आपला हात जगन्नाथ	3	1	10	11	Yes
71	औषध घेतले दुखणे थांबले	3	1	10	11	Yes
255	दुपारी चारच्या सुमारास पाऊस सुरू झाला	3	1	10	11	Yes
128	दिनूचे वडील डॉक्टर होते	2	1	10	11	Yes

(*continued*)

Table 3. (*continued*)

ID	Phrase	No errors	Comp. errors	Non-Comp. errors	Total errors	Rec.
193	कुठूनही गेले तरी पोरांची नजर पडणारच	4	1	11	12	Yes
166	आभाळात छानछान सातरंगी कमान	2	1	12	13	Yes
145	सरड्याची धाव कुंपणापर्यंत	2	1	12	13	Yes
217	जिवलगा राहिले रे दूर घर माझे	1	1	12	13	Yes
110	सेवक आम्ही ह्या देशाचे	2	1	13	14	Yes
195	मामाची बायको सुगरण रोजरोज पोळी शिकरण	0	1	13	14	Yes
89	आपण कुठून आलात	3	1	14	15	Yes
185	मेंदीच्या पानावर मन अजून झुलते ग	2	1	14	15	Yes
181	हवा निघून जाऊन आपण चुरगाळून जाऊ	3	1	15	16	Yes
224	कुलस्त्री जसे हास्य ओठात शोभे	1	1	15	16	Yes
247	टपटप पडती अंगावरती प्राजक्ताची फुले	4	1	16	17	Yes
240	मोठ्या मोठ्या मिश्या डोळे एवढे लाल	1	1	16	17	Yes
186	हिरव्याहिरव्या रंगाची झाडी घनदाट	0	1	16	17	Yes
70	ताटात घेतली भाजीभाकरी	0	0	17	17	No
283	राजाने त्याला कारागृहात बंदिवान करून ठेवले	3	0	19	19	No
300	शरदने कॅमेऱ्याने फोटो काढले	3	0	19	19	No
152	अगं अगं म्हशी मला कुठे नेशी	1	0	19	19	No
276	तीच मला हिऱ्यांच्या हारासारखी वाटते आहे	1	0	20	20	No
149	कानामागून आली अन तिखट झाली	1	0	21	21	No
178	कामापुरता मामा आणि ताकापुरती आजी	1	0	24	24	No
221	कुणाच्या खांद्यावर कुणाचे ओझे	4	0	26	26	No
282	पोलिसांना खूपच तंदुरुस्त राहावे लागत असेल	0	0	29	29	No
296	सर्वांनी एकमुखाने त्याच्या गरिबीचे दाखले द्यावेत	2	0	31	31	No
189	तुझंमाझं जमेना तुझ्यावाचून करमेना	0	0	31	31	No
125	जिथे राबती हात तेथे हरी	1	0	33	33	No
52	कोंबडा आरवतो कुकुच कू	0	0	33	33	No
272	झाडावरदेखील खूपशा पक्ष्यांची घरटी होती	0	0	38	38	No
77	झुक झुक झुक झुक आगीनगाडी	0	0	38	38	No
253	आभाळगत माया तुजी आम्हांवरी ऱ्हाऊ दे	0	0	62	62	No
268	पळती झाडे पाहू या मामाच्या गावाला जाऊ या	1	1	18	19	No
267	निळ्याजांभळ्या जळात केशर सायंकाळी मिळे	0	1	18	19	No
82	आपण बॅट बॉल खेळू	2	1	19	20	No
265	आले राजाजीच्या मना तेथे कोणाचे चालेना	2	1	20	21	No
72	जनगणमन अधिनायक जय है	2	1	20	21	No
251	मामाचा गाव मोठा सोन्याचांदीच्या पेठा	2	1	20	21	No
220	उषःकाल होताहोता काळरात्र झाली	0	1	20	21	No
38	आभाळ वाजलं थडाड धूम	1	1	21	22	No
299	मी बऱ्याच पोलिसांच्या पट्ट्याजवळ बंदूक पाहिली आहे	1	1	21	22	No
29	झरझर झरझर आला वारा	1	1	22	23	No
273	दोघांच्या डोळ्यांतून आनंदाश्रू ओघळू लागले	0	1	22	23	No
230	पचापचा शिव्या देई खाताखाता पान	2	1	23	24	No
144	चल रे भोपळ्या टुणुकटुणुक	0	1	24	25	No
199	गाढवापुढे वाचली गीता कालचा गोंधळ बरा होता	1	1	25	26	No
169	कुणी दिली मोराला ही रंगीत पिसं	0	1	25	26	No
182	मी तुमची उत्कंठेने वाट पाहत आहे	0	1	25	26	No

(*continued*)

Table 3. (*continued*)

ID	Phrase	No errors	Comp. errors	Non-Comp. errors	Total errors	Rec.
258	पक्ष्यांनी त्याच्याकडे दुर्लक्ष केले	1	1	27	28	No
284	अनेक माणसांपेक्षा पशुपक्षी अधिक इमानी असतात	1	1	28	29	No
250	दरीखोऱ्यांतून वाहे एक प्रकाश प्रकाश	0	1	29	30	No
285	गणित व इंग्रजी ह्यांच्यापेक्षा चित्र काढणे सोपे वाटायचे	0	1	33	34	No
42	वारा सुटला सू सू सुम	0	1	33	34	No
238	आपल्या सद्याने त्याला कोरडे केले	6	2	1	3	No
24	बरेच ढग दिसत आहेत	5	2	2	4	No
157	नाच रे मोरा आंब्याच्या वनात	7	2	3	5	No
39	आज खूप उकडत आहे	5	2	3	5	No
187	चेंडू पळून जायची संधी बघू लागला	5	2	3	5	No
280	मित्राचे काम करण्यात कसला आला आहे कमीपणा	4	2	3	5	No
61	चिऊताई चिऊताई दार उघड	5	2	4	6	No
167	तो गावोगावी जाऊन माल विकायचा	6	2	5	7	No
64	दात कोरून पोट भरत नाही	2	2	5	7	No
233	मधल्या सुट्टीत आम्ही डबा उघडतो	4	2	6	8	No
122	भाते पिकुनी पिवळी झाली	3	2	6	8	No
86	मुलं पळतच गावात गेली	3	2	6	8	No
35	मामाची बैलगाडी आली	4	2	7	9	No
218	दुसऱ्या दिवशी दिनू सकाळी उठला	3	2	7	9	No
14	केरकचरा गेला दूर	2	2	7	9	No
96	भारतभाग्यविधाता	1	2	7	9	No
147	हातच्या काकणाला आरसा कशाला	4	2	8	10	No
120	झाकली मूठ सव्वा लाखाची	3	2	8	10	No
127	ता म्हणता ताकभात समजावा	3	2	8	10	No
138	धुरांच्या रेघा हवेत काढी	3	2	8	10	No
36	बागेभोवती भिंत आहे	3	2	8	10	No
153	खाईन तर तुपाशी नाहीतर उपाशी	2	2	8	10	No
126	भरवशाच्या म्हशीला टोणगा	2	2	9	11	No
269	मद्र देशात वेदत्त राजा राज्य करत होता	3	2	10	12	No
146	उन्हाळ्यात फार ऊन पडतं ना	1	2	10	12	No
50	फिरताफिरता जातो तोल	0	2	10	12	No
237	सुखकर्ता दुखहर्ता वार्ता विघ्नाची	3	2	11	13	No
139	ठेविले अनंते तैसेची रहावे	1	2	11	13	No
172	सांग सांग भोलानाथ पाऊस पडेल काय	1	2	12	14	No
196	लोका सांगे ब्रह्मज्ञान आपण कोरडे पाषाण	1	2	13	15	No
176	एवढासा ससा त्याचे एवढे मोठे कान	3	2	16	18	No
246	डेबू मामाच्या शेतावर कष्ट करू लागला	1	2	18	20	No
130	गाढव हळुहळू चालू लागले	0	2	18	20	No
44	हात लावता पंख फाटतिल	0	2	18	20	No
263	प्रत्येकाने चेंडू हातात घेऊन कुरवाळला	2	2	19	21	No
278	चेकाळून सगळे जण चेंडूला लाथेने ठोकरत होते	2	2	21	23	No
249	माझे माहेर पंढरी आहे भीवरेच्या तीरी	1	2	23	25	No
163	मना सज्जना भक्तिपंथेचि जावे	0	2	23	25	No
275	बिचाऱ्या चेंडूची हाडे खिळखिळी होऊ लागली	3	2	24	26	No
266	ह्या अश्रूंचे मात्र हिरे व्हायला नकोत	0	2	25	27	No

(*continued*)

Table 3. (*continued*)

ID	Phrase	No errors	Comp. errors	Non-Comp. errors	Total errors	Rec.
177	पावसाच्या रेघांत खेळ खेळू दोघांत	1	2	27	29	No
264	आधी त्या फळ्यावरचं माझं नाव पुसून टाका	1	2	28	30	No
74	दोरा बांधुन पायहि तुटतिल	0	2	31	33	No
292	पांढऱ्या कपड्यांतील पोलिस हे वाहतूकनियंत्रक असतात	0	2	38	40	No
59	ढगांशी वारा झुंजला रे	7	3	0	3	No
23	हपापाचा माल गपापा	5	3	1	4	No
19	तव शुभ आशिष मागे	5	3	2	5	No
123	सगळे विश्व हेच आपले घर	5	3	2	5	No
210	घे ब्रश की हाण फरकांड्या	4	3	6	9	No
183	बेफाम झालेला बैल उधळत निघून गेला	4	3	7	10	No
161	आता तुझी पाळी वीज देते टाळी	3	3	7	10	No
270	दिवस गेला रेटारेटी चांदण्यात कापूस वेची	3	3	7	10	No
204	रम्य ही स्वर्गाहून लंका	3	3	7	10	No
57	फुलांवर उडती फुलपाखरे	1	3	7	10	No
132	पावसात न्हाऊ काहीतरी गाऊ	2	3	8	11	No
124	शितावरून भाताची परीक्षा	1	3	9	12	No
192	घनश्याम सुंदरा श्रीधरा अरुणोदय झाला	4	3	10	13	No
137	पावसात न्हाली धरणी हसली	1	3	11	14	No
213	कशी नशिबाने थट्टा आज मांडली	0	3	11	14	No
180	गुरे झाडांखाली निवारा शोधत आहेत	3	3	12	15	No
286	शिक्षकांनी प्रयत्नपूर्वक मुलगा अचूक निवडावा	3	3	12	15	No
209	सर्वांनी एकच नाव उच्चारले	4	3	14	17	No
51	कोकीळ बोले कुहू कुहू	3	3	14	17	No
287	तुम्ही पिशवी आणून देणाऱ्यास काही बक्षीस ठेवा	1	3	14	17	No
231	नकटीच्या लग्नाला सतराशे विघ्ने	2	3	15	18	No
164	जागोजागी जळ तुडुंब भरले आहे	0	3	16	19	No
234	वाघांचे भांडण आणि गवताचा विस्फोट	3	3	17	20	No
46	टपटप पानांत वाजती रे	0	3	17	20	No
141	नाठाळाच्या माथी हाणू काठी	0	3	19	22	No
257	शस्त्रधारी सैनिकांचा कडेकोट बंदोबस्त	2	3	22	25	No
288	चंद्राला किंवा सूर्याला झाडाआडून येताना दाखवायचो	0	3	22	25	No
279	जिच्या हाती पाळण्याची दोरी ती जगा उद्धारी	1	3	31	34	No
261	ऐरणीच्या देवा तुला ठिणगीठिणगी वाहु दे	0	3	39	42	No
15	झरझर धार झरली रे	3	4	4	8	No
216	उतावळा नवरा गुडघ्याला बाशिंग	2	4	6	10	No
232	नखाने काम होते तर कुऱ्हाड कशाला	4	4	7	11	No
175	एका छान अनुभवाला तो मुकला होता	3	4	11	15	No
200	शेळी जाते जिवानिशी खाणारा म्हणतो वातड कशी	2	4	14	18	No
91	उच्छल जलधितरंग	1	4	15	19	No
293	कारभारी राबतात दुसऱ्याच्या शेतात त्यांच्यासाठी	1	4	15	19	No
289	सटवाईला नव्हता नवरा अन् म्हसोबाला नव्हती बायको	0	4	16	20	No
229	मग ती काही पिच्छा सोडणार नाहीत	1	4	17	21	No
179	घननिळा लडिवाळा झुलवू नको हिंदोळा	1	4	19	23	No
235	लवलव करी पातं डोळं नाही थाऱ्याला	1	4	19	23	No
245	ह्या राजाचा प्रधान होता सोमदत्त	0	4	20	24	No

(*continued*)

Table 3. (*continued*)

ID	Phrase	No errors	Comp. errors	Non-Comp. errors	Total errors	Rec.
197	शूर आम्ही सरदार आम्हाला काय कुणाची भीती	1	4	21	25	No
262	सुईदोरा घ्यायचा आणि चटकन टाका मारायचा	1	4	27	31	No
277	तंबाखूच्या पिचकाऱ्यांनी भिंती झाल्या घाण	0	4	33	37	No
201	कोण म्हणतं टक्का दिला	1	5	7	12	No
208	कुऱ्हाडीचा दांडा गोतास काळ	1	5	10	15	No
112	बैल गेला नि झोपा केला	1	5	10	15	No
10	गाहे तव जयगाथा	0	5	11	16	No
162	खायला कोंडा नि निजेला धोंडा	0	5	12	17	No
165	पानातून हळू पाहे डोकावून खार	2	5	14	19	No
191	आवडतो मज अफाट सागर अथांग पाणी निळे	1	5	20	25	No
298	त्याने आजूबाजूची बरीच राज्ये स्वपराक्रमाने जिंकली	2	5	26	31	No
297	त्याच्या सांगण्यावरून आलो घेऊन तुमच्याजवळ सोडायला	1	5	26	31	No
295	हद्दीत गुन्हे घडू नयेत म्हणून पोलिस सावध राहतात	1	5	32	37	No
291	महिन्यातून एकदा बंदुकींच्या फैरी झाडल्या जातात	0	5	32	37	No
206	पावसाच्या धारा डोईवर मारा	3	6	2	8	No
140	भले तरी देऊ कासेची लंगोटी	3	6	6	12	No
107	तिकडून दुसरी बस पकडा	1	6	6	12	No
194	राजाझाच ती तिचे तंतोतंत पालन झाले	0	6	13	19	No
260	दंतोजींचा पत्ता नाही खप्पड दोन्ही गाल	3	6	17	23	No
244	उठि लवकरी वनमाळी उदयाचळीं मित्र आला	0	6	17	23	No
174	येईन भेटायास वनी तुजला वारंवार	1	6	28	34	No
281	जांभुळपिकल्या झाडाखाली ढोल कुनाचा वाजं जी	0	6	61	67	No
203	सरणार कथी रण प्रभू तरी	3	7	2	9	No
252	कराग्रे वसते लक्ष्मी करमध्ये सरस्वती	2	7	12	19	No
243	उठा उठा हो सकळिक वाचे स्मरावे गजमुख	0	7	14	21	No
173	वल्हव रे नाखवा हो वल्हव रे रामा	1	7	18	25	No
222	परहित आधी नंतर स्वहित साधावे	1	8	8	16	No
254	मंत्रीमहोदय सोमदत्त यांसी सदर प्रणाम	0	8	25	33	No
274	हिच्या कीर्तिच्या सागरलहरी नादविती डंका	0	8	26	34	No
159	झोंबे अंगा वारे काया थरथरे	1	9	3	12	No
241	खऱ्याचं खोटं अनु लबाडाचं तोंड मोठं	0	9	30	39	No
215	सुधेसारखा साद स्वर्गीय गाणे	0	11	23	34	No
212	रतीसारखे जया रुपलावण्य लाभे	0	13	8	21	No
115	झाडांची भिजली इरली रे	0	14	17	31	No
142	वेडात मराठे वीर दौडले सात	0	19	24	43	No

[1] Phrase ID as assigned in Dalvi et al.'s [12] original phrase set
[2] Number of comprehension errors
[3] Number of non-comprehension errors
[4] Recommendation for use of the phrase in aural transcription tasks

References

1. Google cloud text-to-speech. https://cloud.google.com/text-to-speech#demo. Accessed 1 Jan 2023
2. Marathi language, wikipedia, the free encyclopedia. https://en.wikipedia.org/w/index.php?title=Marathi_language&oldid=1224770056. Accessed 1 June 2023
3. Abbott, J., Kaye, J., Clawson, J.: Identifying an aurally distinct phrase set for text entry techniques. In: Proceedings of the 2022 CHI Conference on Human Factors in Computing Systems, CHI 2022. Association for Computing Machinery, New York, NY, USA (2022). https://doi.org/10.1145/3491102.3501897
4. Anu Bharath, P., Jadhav, C., Ahire, S., Joshi, M., Ahirwar, R., Joshi, A.: Performance of accessible gesture-based Indic keyboard. In: Bernhaupt, R., Dalvi, G., Joshi, A., Balkrishan, D.K., O'Neill, J., Winckler, M. (eds.) INTERACT 2017. LNCS, vol. 10513, pp. 205–220. Springer, Cham (2017). https://doi.org/10.1007/978-3-319-67744-6_14
5. Bhattacharya, S., Laha, S.: Bengali text input interface design for mobile devices. Univ. Access Inf. Soc. **12**(4), 441–451 (2013). https://doi.org/10.1007/s10209-012-0280-1
6. Bhikne, B., Joshi, A., Joshi, M., Ahire, S., Maravi, N.: How much faster can you type by speaking in Hindi? Comparing keyboard-only and keyboard+speech text entry. In: Proceedings of the 9th Indian Conference on Human-Computer Interaction, IndiaHCI 2018, pp. 20–28. Association for Computing Machinery, New York, NY, USA (2018). https://doi.org/10.1145/3297121.3297123
7. Bhikne, B., Joshi, A., Joshi, M., Jadhav, C., Sakhardande, P.: Faster and less error-prone: supplementing an accessible keyboard with speech input. In: Lamas, D., Loizides, F., Nacke, L., Petrie, H., Winckler, M., Zaphiris, P. (eds.) INTERACT 2019. LNCS, vol. 11746, pp. 288–304. Springer, Cham (2019). https://doi.org/10.1007/978-3-030-29381-9_18
8. Bione, T., Cardoso, W.: Synthetic voices in the Foreign language context. Lang. Learn. Technol. **24**(1), 169–186 (2020). https://doi.org/10125/44715
9. Chu, Q., Chen, C.P., Hu, H., Wu, X., Han, B.: iHand: hand recognition-based text input method for wearable devices. Computers **13**(3), 80 (2024). https://doi.org/10.3390/computers13030080, https://www.mdpi.com/2073-431X/13/3/80
10. Cui, W., et al.: GlanceWriter: writing text by glancing over letters with gaze. In: Proceedings of the 2023 CHI Conference on Human Factors in Computing Systems, CHI 2023. Association for Computing Machinery, New York, NY, USA (2023). https://doi.org/10.1145/3544548.3581269
11. Dalvi, G., et al.: Does prediction really help in Marathi text input? Empirical analysis of a longitudinal study. In: Proceedings of the 18th International Conference on Human-Computer Interaction with Mobile Devices and Services, MobileHCI 2016, pp. 35–46. Association for Computing Machinery, New York, NY, USA (2016). https://doi.org/10.1145/2935334.2935366
12. Dalvi, G., et al.: A protocol to evaluate virtual keyboards for Indian languages. In: Proceedings of the 7th Indian Conference on Human-Computer Interaction, IndiaHCI 2015, pp. 27–38. Association for Computing Machinery, New York, NY, USA (2015). https://doi.org/10.1145/2835966.2835970
13. Debasis Samanta, S.S., Ghosh, S.: An approach to design virtual keyboards for text composition in Indian languages. Int. J. Hum.-Comput. Interact. **29**(8), 516–540 (2013). https://doi.org/10.1080/10447318.2012.728483

14. Deshpande, P.: Shuddhalekhan: orthography, community and the Marathi public sphere. Econ. Polit. Weekly **51**(6), 72–82 (2016). http://www.jstor.org/stable/44004357
15. Devy, G.: Between Diversity and Aphasia: The Future of Languages in India, pp. 411–424. AuthorsUpFront (2017)
16. Foley, M., Casiez, G., Vogel, D.: Comparing smartphone speech recognition and touchscreen typing for composition and transcription. In: Proceedings of the 2020 CHI Conference on Human Factors in Computing Systems, CHI 2020, pp. 1–11. Association for Computing Machinery, New York, NY, USA (2020). https://doi.org/10.1145/3313831.3376861
17. Gaines, D., Kristensson, P.O., Vertanen, K.: Enhancing the composition task in text entry studies: eliciting difficult text and improving error rate calculation. In: Proceedings of the 2021 CHI Conference on Human Factors in Computing Systems, CHI 2021. Association for Computing Machinery, New York, NY, USA (2021). https://doi.org/10.1145/3411764.3445199
18. Ghosh, S., et al.: Shift+tap or tap+longpress? The upper bound of typing speed on InScript. In: Proceedings of the 2017 CHI Conference on Human Factors in Computing Systems, CHI 2017, pp. 2059–2063. Association for Computing Machinery, New York, NY, USA (2017). https://doi.org/10.1145/3025453.3025944
19. Grimshaw, J., Bione, T., Cardoso, W.: Who's got talent? Comparing TTS systems for comprehensibility, naturalness, and intelligibility. In: Future-Proof CALL: Language Learning as Exploration and Encounters–Short Papers from EUROCALL, pp. 83–88 (2018). https://doi.org/10.14705/rpnet.2018.26.817
20. Hinkle, L., Brouillette, A., Jayakar, S., Gathings, L., Lezcano, M., Kalita, J.: Design and evaluation of soft keyboards for Brahmic scripts. ACM Trans. Asian Lang. Inf. Process. **12**(2), 1–37 (2013). https://doi.org/10.1145/2461316.2461318
21. Hong, J., Findlater, L.: Identifying speech input errors through audio-only interaction. In: Proceedings of the 2018 CHI Conference on Human Factors in Computing Systems, CHI 2018, pp. 1–12. Association for Computing Machinery, New York, NY, USA (2018). https://doi.org/10.1145/3173574.3174141
22. Hong, J., Vaing, C., Kacorri, H., Findlater, L.: Reviewing speech input with audio: differences between blind and sighted users. ACM Trans. Access. Comput. **13**(1), 1–28 (2020). https://doi.org/10.1145/3382039
23. Jain, M., Tekchandani, K., Truong, K.N.: Evaluating the effect of phrase set in Hindi text entry. In: Kotzé, P., Marsden, G., Lindgaard, G., Wesson, J., Winckler, M. (eds.) INTERACT 2013. LNCS, vol. 8120, pp. 195–202. Springer, Heidelberg (2013). https://doi.org/10.1007/978-3-642-40498-6_14
24. Janaka, N., et al.: GlassMessaging: towards ubiquitous messaging using OHMDs. Proc. ACM Interact. Mob. Wearable Ubiquit. Technol. **7**(3), 1–32 (2023). https://doi.org/10.1145/3610931
25. Joshi, A., Dalvi, G., Joshi, M., Rashinkar, P., Sarangdhar, A.: Design and evaluation of Devanagari virtual keyboards for touch screen mobile phones. In: Proceedings of the 13th International Conference on Human Computer Interaction with Mobile Devices and Services, MobileHCI 2011. Association for Computing Machinery, New York, NY, USA (2011). https://doi.org/10.1145/2037373.2037422, https://doi.org/10.1145/2037373.2037422
26. Joshi, A., Roy, D., Ganju, A., Joshi, M., Sharma, S.: ICT acceptance for information seeking amongst pre- and postnatal women in urban slums. In: Lamas, D., Loizides, F., Nacke, L., Petrie, H., Winckler, M., Zaphiris, P. (eds.) INTERACT 2019. LNCS, vol. 11748, pp. 152–160. Springer, Cham (2019). https://doi.org/10.1007/978-3-030-29387-1_9

27. Leiva, L.A., Sanchis-Trilles, G.: Representatively memorable: sampling the right phrase set to get the text entry experiment right. In: Proceedings of the SIGCHI Conference on Human Factors in Computing Systems, CHI 2014, pp. 1709–1712. Association for Computing Machinery, New York, NY, USA (2014). https://doi.org/10.1145/2556288.2557024

28. Ljubic, S., Salkanovic, A.: Generating representative phrase sets for text entry experiments by GA-based text corpora sampling. Mathematics 11(11), 2550 (2023). https://doi.org/10.3390/math11112550, https://www.mdpi.com/2227-7390/11/11/2550

29. MacKenzie, I.S., Soukoreff, R.W.: Phrase sets for evaluating text entry techniques. In: CHI 2003 Extended Abstracts on Human Factors in Computing Systems, CHI EA 2003, pp. 754–755. Association for Computing Machinery, New York, NY, USA (2003). https://doi.org/10.1145/765891.765971

30. Moos, A., Trouvain, J.: Comprehension of ultra-fast speech–blind vs."normally hearing" persons. In: Proceedings of the 16th International Congress of Phonetic Sciences, vol. 1, pp. 677–680. Saarland University Saarbrücken Germany (2007)

31. Paek, T., Hsu, B.J.P.: Sampling representative phrase sets for text entry experiments: a procedure and public resource. In: Proceedings of the SIGCHI Conference on Human Factors in Computing Systems, CHI 2011, pp. 2477–2480. Association for Computing Machinery, New York, NY, USA (2011). https://doi.org/10.1145/1978942.1979304

32. Rashinkar, P.G., et al.: Healthcare IVRS for non-tech-savvy users. In: Holzinger, A., Simonic, K.-M. (eds.) USAB 2011. LNCS, vol. 7058, pp. 263–282. Springer, Heidelberg (2011). https://doi.org/10.1007/978-3-642-25364-5_20

33. Ruan, S., Wobbrock, J.O., Liou, K., Ng, A., Landay, J.A.: Comparing speech and keyboard text entry for short messages in two languages on touchscreen phones. Proc. ACM Interact. Mob. Wearable Ubiquit. Technol. 1(4), 1–23 (2018). https://doi.org/10.1145/3161187

34. Sarcar, S., Panwar, P.: Eyeboard++: an enhanced eye gaze-based text entry system in Hindi. In: Proceedings of the 11th Asia Pacific Conference on Computer Human Interaction, APCHI 2013, pp. 354–363. Association for Computing Machinery, New York, NY, USA (2013). https://doi.org/10.1145/2525194.2525304

35. Stent, A., Syrdal, A., Mishra, T.: On the intelligibility of fast synthesized speech for individuals with early-onset blindness. In: The Proceedings of the 13th International ACM SIGACCESS Conference on Computers and Accessibility, ASSETS 2011, pp. 211–218. Association for Computing Machinery, New York, NY, USA (2011). https://doi.org/10.1145/2049536.2049574

36. Vertanen, K., Kristensson, P.O.: A versatile dataset for text entry evaluations based on genuine mobile emails. In: Proceedings of the 13th International Conference on Human Computer Interaction with Mobile Devices and Services, MobileHCI 2011, pp. 295–298. Association for Computing Machinery, New York, NY, USA (2011). https://doi.org/10.1145/2037373.2037418

37. Vertanen, K., Kristensson, P.O.: Complementing text entry evaluations with a composition task. ACM Trans. Comput.-Hum. Interact. 21(2), 1–33 (2014). https://doi.org/10.1145/2555691

38. Wali, K.: Marathi. In: Brown, K. (ed.) Encyclopedia of Language & Linguistics (Second Edition), pp. 488–490. Elsevier, Oxford (2006). https://doi.org/10.1016/B0-08-044854-2/02228-8, https://www.sciencedirect.com/science/article/pii/B0080448542022288

39. Wu, J., Wang, Z., Wang, L., Duan, Y., Li, J.: FanPad: a fan layout touchpad keyboard for text entry in VR. In: 2024 IEEE Conference Virtual Reality and 3D User Interfaces (VR), pp. 222–232 (2024). https://doi.org/10.1109/VR58804.2024. 00045

40. Zhang, M.R., Zhai, S., Wobbrock, J.O.: TypeAnywhere: a QWERTY-based text entry solution for ubiquitous computing. In: Proceedings of the 2022 CHI Conference on Human Factors in Computing Systems, CHI 2022. Association for Computing Machinery, New York, NY, USA (2022). https://doi.org/10.1145/3491102. 3517686

IDCText: An Application for Conducting Text Input Research Studies in Indian Languages

Vedant Deshmukh[1]([✉])[ID] and Anirudha Joshi[2][ID]

[1] Sardar Patel Institute of Technology (SPIT), Mumbai, India
vedantdeshmukh3108@gmail.com
[2] Indian Institute of Technology (IIT), Bombay, Mumbai, India
anirudha@iitb.ac.in

Abstract. Some might argue that text-input-related HCI research in English is verging towards saturation. On the other hand, a lot more work remains to be done in Indian languages (and in fact, in several other languages around the world). Through this paper, we release in the public domain IDCText, a web based tool that makes it easier for researchers to conduct text entry studies for Indian (and other) languages. This application is compatible with all contemporary web browsers and supports studies using any keyboard that can enter text in a web browser text field. The tool has many features that have been used in text input studies (including some special features that Indian language HCI researchers might need), and automatically calculates several metrics that text input studies report. To test our tool, and also to demonstrate its capabilities, we conducted an empirical within-subjects counterbalanced systematic longitudinal study (N = 10) to compare the performance of two experimental Marathi keyboards, namely Swarachakra and Swaravarna. We present the metrics that emerged from IDCText. We also reflect on the current capabilities of the tool and the future possibilities for improvement. The tool is hosted on a website and is accompanied by a video tutorial that shows how a HCI researcher can set up and conduct a new text input study. Through this paper, we also release IDCText code in the public domain in the open source, so that other researchers can continue to build on it.

Keywords: IDCText · Web application · Text entry metrics · Indian languages · Swarachakra keyboard · Swaravarna keyboard · Open source · Public domain · Tool

1 Introduction

HCI research in text input studies is extensive. With the advent of mobile phones in 1990s, the focus of text input studies shifted to mobile devices. Given the constraints of size of the device, the focus in this research has been primarily

N. Rangaswamy et al. (Eds.): IndiaHCI 2024, CCIS 2337, pp. 104–124, 2025.
https://doi.org/10.1007/978-3-031-80829-6_5

on speed of entry and errors. Given that text input is a frequent task, and given that the participant performance on text entry systems improves a lot by practice, HCI researchers are usually not interested in the first-time usability of these mechanisms, but rather on the effect of longitudinal practice on speed and errors.

For example, Silverberg et al. present a model for predicting expert text entry rates of 41 words per minute (WPM) for one-handed thumb input to 46 WPM for two-handed thumb input on a 12-key mobile phone keypad using different input methods [24]. It incorporates a movement component based on Fitts' law [17] and a linguistic component based on digraph probabilities, providing predictions for both one-handed thumb and two-handed index finger input methods. Text input studies on mobile devices changed dramatically when mobile phones with touch screens started becoming available. Early work involved use of styluses. For example, Zhai et al. [35] propose a method for touchscreen-based speed writing "shape writing" (participants could learn shorthand symbols of 15 words in a session) that enhances stylus keyboarding with shorthand gesturing (later called swyping [23] [36]). The technique of shape writing improved the speeds of English text input on smartphones to 25 WPM for novice users, and 46.5 WPM for practiced user [20]. With the advent of devices such as smart watches and virtual reality headsets, HCI research in text input moved to these devices. Vertanen et al. proposed a sentence-based text entry approach achieving a 41 CPM on a smartwatch-sized keyboard 40 mm wide for novice users [29]. More recently, Speicher et al. shows text entry in VR by selecting characters on virtual keyboard [26].

While much has been done, research in text input studies in English seem to be saturating, particularly on smartphones and other common devices. However, a lot still needs to be done in text input in Indian languages, particularly with respect to speed and errors. For example, after conducting a between-subject longitudinal study with novice users lasting several weeks and providing about 300 min of typing practice, Dalvi et al. [13] reported peak speeds between 35 to 45 CPM on four Marathi keyboards, namely Swarachakra Marathi [3], CDAC InScript Devanagari [11], Swiftkey Marathi [4] and Sparsh Marathi [2]. Bhikne et al. proposed a method which shows that novice users could achieve mean speeds of up to 118 CPM with speech, compared to 47 CPM without speech [9]. For visually impaired users, the gains are even more impressive, reaching 182 CPM [10]. However, despite these advantages, speech has not yet become the dominant text input mechanism even for Indian langentuges.

Though five Indian languages are among the top 20 most spoken languages in the world by number of speakers [33], the text input in these languages remains low. One evidence of this is the number of articles in Wikipedia, viz. 161,554 for Hindi, 153,377 for Bengali, 96,534 for Marathi, 78,934 for Telugu and 165,666 for Tamil, compared to an average of 1,626,797 articles for each of the other fifteen languages [31]. On the whole, a lot more research needs to be done in the area of text input in Indian languages.

However, doing text input research with high scientific rigour is challenging. For novice HCI researchers, getting started in the realm of text input studies presents substantial obstacles. A HCI researcher new to text input needs to first understand the intricacies of the script. Once a new text input mechanism is conceptualised, it needs to be developed with sufficient fidelity. Low-fidelity or wireframe prototypes are insufficient; a high-fidelity prototype must be created. The researcher must also be familiar with the standard metrics for evaluating speed and errors [25]. Past researchers have had to custom-build apps for conducting studies, further adding to the difficulties. The custom applications like one in [14] are developed for recording text input metrics for that specific protocol. In most of the case the application is not up-to-date and thus is not compatible with recent technologies. These custom made applications are developed keeping in mind a particular evaluation technique, thus cannot be used in other studies.

This paper releases IDCText, a tool that makes it easier for HCI researchers to conduct text input studies with high scientific rigour. The tool helps the researcher specify the design of the study and to automatically calculate several metrics that are commonly reported in text input studies. There are several unique peculiarities about how some Indian languages have been implemented in Unicode [27] (the current standard of text input storage). We describe some of these peculiarities below. Our tool has features that makes it easier to evaluate text input mechanisms by working around such peculiarities. Also, (unlike studies in English, where most participants are familiar with typing on QWERTY keyboards), several participants in an Indian language text input study could be absolute novices to typing (or at least to typing in the chosen Indian language). Our tool enables researchers to account for this aspect of our society.

Thus, through this paper, we make the following contributions:

- We release a tool IDCText that makes it easier for HCI researcher to conduct text input studies and report common metrics.
- We report on a study in Marathi to test IDCText and to demonstrate its capabilities.
- Through this paper we will release a hosted version of IDCText in the public domain [5]. HCI researchers who are interested in conducting a text input study will be able to use it and download the data that they need.
- Through this paper, we also release the source code of IDCText in open source [19]. HCI researchers who want to add to the tool (e.g. more metrics, more study designs etc.) will be able to customise the tool for their needs beyond the features that we have already provided.

2   Background

2.1   Tools for Text Input Studies

Although not very common, it is not unusual for HCI researchers to release tools for each other via research papers. For example, Eiselmayer et al. released Touchstone 2, a tool that helps HCI researchers to design quantitative experiments [15]. In the field of text input, MacKenzie et al. [21] released a corpus of 500 phrases for evaluating text entry methods (in English), including utility programs to analyze their statistical properties and addressing the benefits and methodological considerations of using a predefined phrase set. Dalvi et al. developed a comprehensive protocol for evaluating input mechanisms on touch-screen devices across 14 major Indian languages, incorporating extensive training and usability tests, and provided an Android app for data collection and analysis [14].

Arif et al. introduced WebTEM, a web application for recording text entry metrics compatible with any device and keyboard [8]. This application has been a significant contributor to recording various text entry metrics, and it recently added a feature for uploading custom phrases. However, the application is currently limited to the English language. Our tool IDCText comes closest to WebTEM, but adds several features specific to Indian language text input studies.

2.2   Issues Related to the Design of Text Input Studies

In this section, we summarise the key issues that a HCI researcher needs to consider while conducting a text input study. Approaches to text input studies can be broadly classified into transcription studies and composition studies. Composition studies are considered to have higher external validity, while transcription studies have a higher internal validity. Composition studies may be conducted either in the lab [28] or in the wild [16]. These studies are relatively rare. The more typical ones are transcription studies, which we now describe in detail.

The most common form of a transcription study involves participants evaluating one or more text input mechanisms such as a keyboard (possibly designed by the HCI researcher conducting the study). If only a single mechanism is being evaluated, it is called a one-shot study. However, it is not uncommon to compare two or more novel text input mechanisms, or to compare a novel mechanism with an existing benchmark. The study could either be between-subjects, in which the cohort of participants is randomised into two or more groups, where each group evaluates one mechanism, or it could be within-subjects, in which the whole cohort of participants evaluates two or more mechanisms one at a time, in a counterbalanced order. A within-subjects-counterbalanced study accounts for individual variations across participants (such as dexterity, eye sight, language knowledge etc.). Within-subjects study is preferable, unless there are asymmetric learning effects, in which case a between-subjects study is used. As we see below, IDCText supports both kinds of studies.

In a typical transcription study, the participant is shown one phrase at a time and is asked to transcribe it using the assigned mechanism. Participants usually transcribe several such phrases in a "session". Since the speed of text input increases with practice, it is not uncommon to have multiple sessions, which may be conducted on the same day, or may be spread across multiple days. The phrases come from a predetermined corpus, and attempt is made to ensure that the corpus is representative of the language. As can be expected, some phrases could be longer or otherwise harder to type than other phrases. Since we are mainly interested in evaluating the text input mechanisms, it is important to eliminate the effect of phrase difficulty and the sequence of phrases. Hence it is common to randomise the sequence of phrases within a session and phrases across sessions. Since the participant's performance improves with practice, several studies are longitudinal. In any case, the researcher is usually interested in reporting the average text input speed at the granularity of sessions (rather than phrases).

The speed of text input for a particular transcribed phrase is measured in characters per minute (CPM) or words per minute (WPM). These are first calculated for each phrase and then averaged across a session. The task time for transcribing a phrase is taken to be the duration between the input of first character and last modification to the transcribed phrase either by input of the last character or its last edit. The speed in CPM is calculated by dividing n − 1 (where n was the number of characters typed) by the phrase task time M (in minutes), as shown in formula 1 [22]. If the CPM speed is divided by the average number of characters in a word in that language (5 in case of English), we get the WPM, as shown in formula 2.

$$CPM = \frac{n-1}{M} \tag{1}$$

$$WPM = \frac{n-1}{M} \times \frac{1}{5} \tag{2}$$

A participant in a text input study follows a speed-accuracy tradeoff that is common to several HCI studies. Some participants may be careful and accurate, but slow, while other participants may be fast but reckless and error-prone. Speed of text entry is considered to be the main variable of interest in a transcription study, but it is considered to be valid only if the error rates are within reasonable limits (e.g. 5% on average). So before reporting speed, the HCI researcher is also interested in reporting errors made by participants.

Soukoreff et al. define several standard metrics for calculating errors in a transcription study [25]. The first is the Minimum String Distance (MSD) Error Rate, as shown in Eq. 3. Here, C stands for "correct" characters that are common between the presented phrase and transcribed phrase and INF stands for "incorrect but not fixed" characters in the transcribed phrase including extra characters (insertions), incorrect characters (substitutions), and omitted characters (deletions).

$$\text{MSD Error rate} = \frac{INF}{C + INF} \times 100\% \tag{3}$$

Please note that, MSD error rate is based only on the finally transcribed phrase and does not include incorrect characters that were typed by the participant but were later deleted. Hence, Soukoreff et al. define another metric called Uncorrected Error Rate (UER), which can be calculated using Eq. 4. Here, additionally, IF stands for "incorrect but fixed" characters which were incorrect characters typed and subsequently deleted by the participant before submitting the phrase.

$$\text{Uncorrected Error Rate} = \frac{INF}{C + INF + IF} \times 100\% \tag{4}$$

Soukoreff et al. additionally describe a third metric called Corrected Error Rate (CER), which describes the effort the participant took while correcting the phrase, which can be calculated using Eq. 5.

$$\text{Corrected Error rate} = \frac{IF}{C + INF + IF} \times 100\% \tag{5}$$

As per Soukoreff et al., UER + CER represents the total error rate (TER). Please note that IF does not include keystrokes such as backspace, delete, cursor movement and modifier keys such as shift, alt and control. These keystrokes are captured in another parameter called F (standing for "fixes keystroke"), using which Soukoreff et al. define two more related metrics, namely keystrokes per character (KSPC, Eq. 6) and correction efficiency (Eq. 7).

$$KSPC = \frac{C + INF + F + IF}{C + INF} \tag{6}$$

$$\text{Correction Efficiency} = \frac{IF}{F} \tag{7}$$

There seems to be some confusion about whether C, INF and IF represents characters or keystrokes. Soukoreff et al. seem to use these words interchangeably. Since they mainly describe text input studies in English (and more specifically English studies without capitalisation and punctuation marks), this distinction does not matter much. However, this could be important in case of text input in Indian languages, which is often more complex. In some cases, a single key press may lead to multiple Unicode characters. Several Indians may assume क्ष or ज्ञ to be consonants, but in fact they are implemented as conjuncts (of consonants क + ् + ष and ज + ् + ञ respectively). Both conjuncts can often be typed by pressing one or two keys on most keyboards (e.g. on Inscript [11] 2 keystrokes, Google Indic [1] 1 keystroke, Sparsh [2] 2 keystroke, and Swarachakra [3] 1 keystroke), though they are stored as 3 Unicode characters each. Conversely, several Unicode characters in Indian languages need multiple key presses. For example, the consonants ख, घ, छ, झ, ठ, ढ, ध, फ, भ require two keystrokes on the Inscript keyboard (shift plus one other key), though they are represented with a single Unicode character. Unlike in English (and several languages that use the Latin script), these are not merely "capital" forms of their lower case equivalents, but entirely different consonants with a different pronunciation. The participant needs to press two keys (shift plus one other key) to type standalone vowels अ, आ, इ, ई, उ, ऊ, ए, ऐ, ओ, औ on the Inscript keyboard, each of which results in one Unicode character. These characters are neither rare, and nor are they "replaceable" by their unshifted equivalents.

This issue of many-to-one and one-to-many mapping between keystrokes and characters is not unique to Indian languages. In Pinyin, which is a romanised system for entering Mandarin text, multiple keystrokes are used to input a single

Chinese character [34]. Typing a single Chinese character usually involves typing multiple keystrokes corresponding to the phonetic components of the character, which are then converted into the desired character by an input method editor (IME). Similar is the case of entering Japanese Kanji [32].

Further, keystroke to character mapping is not a standard and is dependent on the design of the keyboard and its interaction technique. Often, competing keyboards differentiate themselves on such designs. Additionally, when the keyboard includes word completion and next word prediction technologies, multiple characters are often entered in one keystroke, and there is no easy way to compute error rates for such systems at "keystroke" level. Hence we argue that it is best to use Unicode characters for calculating C, INF and IF (rather than keystrokes) because these are standard and are independent of the design of the keyboard.

Another noteworthy issue with Indian language text input studies is the (limited) prior exposure of participants to typing. In almost all contemporary text input studies in English, participants are familiar with typing on the QWERTY layout. The same may not be the case with Indian language studies, and participants may need to be trained. During such training, it may be desirable to expose them to "simpler" phrases first, and gradually "ramp up" the difficulty, as was done by [14] and [7].

To aid this activity, Dalvi et al. described Difficulty Index (DI) for evaluating a phrase, which is an ordinal scale varying from 3 to 9 [14]. It is a sum of three components: Typing Difficulty (TD, scale 1 to 3), Phrase Length (PL, scale 1 to 3), and Memorability and Age appropriateness (MA, scale 1 to 3). For Indian languages, conjuncts are hard to type. Dalvi et al. suggest that if a phrase has no conjuncts, use TD = 1, if a phrase has one or two conjuncts, use TD = 2, and if a phrase has three or more conjuncts, use TD = 3. Longer phrases are known to be more difficult to type. Based on the number of Unicode characters, they can classify PL as follows: use PL = 1 if the phrase has up to 25 Unicode characters, use PL = 2 if the phrase has 26–40 Unicode characters, and use PL = 3 if the phrase has 41–55 Unicode characters. Similarly, use MA = 1 if the participant needs to read the phrase only once to memorise it before typing, use MA = 2 if the participant needs to read it carefully once or twice, and use MA = 3 if the participant needs to read the phrase several times, including while typing. This parameter is subjective and depends on the language and the judgement of the researcher. The sum of TD, PL, and MA gives the DI, ranging from 3 to 9. DI could be used to ramp up a text input study from simple to more difficult.

A further issue arises because of the way Unicode or the keyboards have been historically implemented in some scripts / languages. For example, in Devanagari, there are multiple ways to type a consonant with a nukta such as ग़. It could be typed either as a single consonant ग़ (Unicode character 095A) or as a combination of the consonant ग (Unicode character 0917) followed by the nukta character ़ (Unicode character 093C). In most implementations of operating systems, both combinations render in exactly the same way. To make matters worse, most keyboards support only one of the two methods.

A similar issue arises due to the way some keyboards are designed. For example the Devanagari standalone vowel ॲ (Unicode character 0972) is not available in the current version of the Google Indic Marathi keyboard [1]. If one were to type the Devanagari standalone vowel अ (Unicode character 0905) followed by the vowel modifier ॅ (Unicode character 0945), we can (on several devices) see a glyph that looks like the desired ॲ. If left unchecked, these Unicode level and Keyboard level differences could show up as uncorrected errors (because the Unicode characters in the shown phrase and the transcribed phrase vary). Any tool that supports text input studies needs to support the handling of such exceptions in a way that the participant is not unfairly penalised for the errors he did not make.

Thus, text input studies in Indian (and other languages) need somewhat different types of supports from a tool to conduct the study than the traditional English tools.

3 IDCText

IDCText is an open-source, freely available web application developed using HTML5, CSS3, PHP and Javascript. IDCText allows HCI researchers to design studies in Indian languages, offering the flexibility to use custom phrases and configure various study parameters to meet their specific needs. Application is hosted and is freely accessible from the url [5] and the source code is available here [19] .

In this section, we first describe how a HCI researcher can set up a new study, how they can add participants in the study, and how they can retrieve the metrics that the study provides.

Setting up a New Text Input Study. IDCText is hosted on a website [5] and is accompanied by a video tutorial [6] that shows how a HCI researcher can set up and conduct a new text input study. To set up a study, they will have to specify some study parameters. Figure 1 shows the screenshot of the application page that sets up the study. To begin with, the HCI researcher inputs a unique Study ID (e.g. "My_Study_01"). The researcher then specifies the number of sessions (an integer) they would want the participant to participate in, and the number of phrases the participant would need to transcribe in each session (another integer). The researcher also inputs a "repetition factor" (also an integer). The researcher must upload a "Phrases File" in a CSV format. The researcher may, optionally, upload a "Ramping File" and a "Unicode Exceptions File", both in CSV formats. The researcher may download templates of each of these to ensure that it is in the correct format so that the application can read it. (See explanations and samples of all three files below)

The researcher also specifies whether they require the phrases to be presented in a randomised order (the usual way). If the researcher chooses not to, the application will display the phrases in the sequence in which they appear in the

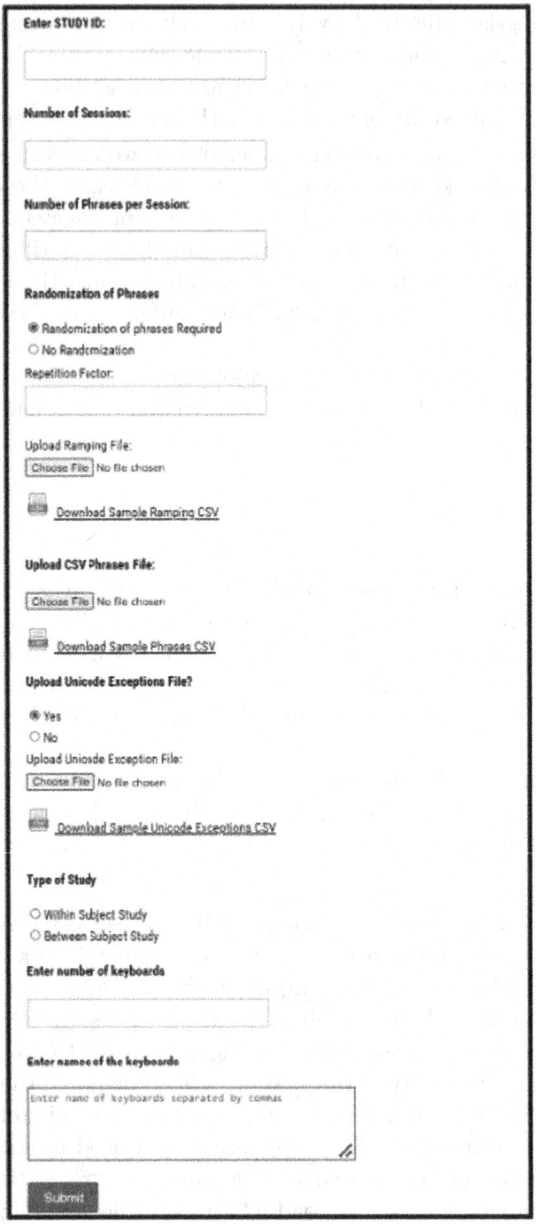

Fig. 1. Page for setting up a new text input study.

Phrases File. Next, researcher specifies the design of the study (either between-subjects or within-subjects). As mentioned above, a text input study could be a between-subjects study, in which the cohort of participants is divided into N approximately equal groups (where N is the number of text input mechanisms being evaluated in the study). Alternatively, it could be a within-subjects study, where the whole cohort of participants uses each input mechanism one at a time in a counterbalanced sequence. Lastly, the HCI researcher specifies the number of text input mechanisms to be evaluated in the study, and the names of these mechanism (for reference of the participants and the researcher herself).

Three aspects of the study need clarification. Firstly, the repetition factor is the maximum number of times a phrase is allowed to be repeated across sessions in a study. So, if the repetition factor is 1, the application will ensure that each phrase is presented to each participant no more than once. The researcher will need to ensure that they have uploaded a sufficient number of phrases to satisfy the chosen numbers of sessions, phrases per session and the repetition factor. For example, if the researcher specified a study with 20 sessions, and 10 phrases per session with a repetition factor of 1, they need to upload a CSV file with at least 200 phrases. On the other hand, if the repetition factor were 2, they would need to upload a CSV file with at least 100 phrases. If the researcher uploads more phrases than the minimum number required, the application randomly chooses a set of phrases for each participant within the repetition factor constraints.

```
\\sample Phrases File
\\format is phrase, difficulty index, language tag
phrase one goes here,2,mr
phrase two goes here,4,mr
phrase three goes here,6,mr
```

Secondly, as mentioned above, ramping refers to a gradual increase in difficulty of the phrases to be typed. In the Phrases file, the researcher has the option to indicate an integer specifying the Difficulty Index (DI) of the phrase (How to calculate DI for each phrase is up to the researcher). In the Ramping File, the researcher may, for example, specify that the first three sessions should contain phrases with a maximum DI of 2, while the next three sessions should contain phrases with a maximum DI of 4, followed by a random set of phrases in the remaining sessions. Of course, the researcher must ensure that their corpus contains the required number of phrases of each DI in the corpus. Please note that if the researcher does not choose to randomise the sequence of phrases, the application ignores the Ramping File and shows phrases exactly in the sequence in the Phrases File.

```
\\sample Ramping File
\\format is from session,to session,maximum Difficulty Index allowed
1,3,2
4,6,4
```

Thirdly, as discussed above, Indian (and perhaps other) languages have exceptions because of the way the scripts have been implemented in Unicode or in keyboards. The Exceptions File is a list of exceptions, where each line contains a comma separated pairs of Unicode combinations that can be considered as "equivalent" for error calculation. Optionally, the researcher may further specify that an exception is applicable only when the participant is entering text with a particular keyboard. Thus, using this feature a researcher may specify (for example) that अ (Unicode character 0905) + ॅ (Unicode character 0945) to be a alternative Unicode to type ऒ (Unicode character 0972), when the participant is using a particular keyboard. The application calculates all error parameters in two ways. The error rates calculated after considering exceptions are displayed in the participant feedback and are also stored in the database. The error rates calculated without considering exceptions are stored in the database, but are not displayed in the participant feedback.

```
\\sample Exceptions File
\\format is Unicode text, alternative Unicode text
\\Unicode level exceptions
Alternative Unicode for exception 1, Unicode for exception 1
Alternative Unicode for exception 2, Unicode for exception 2
Alternative Unicode for exception 3, Unicode for exception 3

\\Keyboard level exceptions
Alternative Unicode for exception 4,Unicode for exception 4,
KeyboardName
Alternative Unicode for exception 5,Unicode for exception 5,
KeyboardName
```

Once the researcher submits the form, a study is created, and the researcher gets a unique URL for the study. The HCI researcher needs to save this URL and use it to launch the study dashboard every time. Using this URL, the HCI researcher can add participants to the study, review performance of each participant, and retrieve the unique URL for each participant (see below).

On the same study URL upon clicking Results , the HCI researcher can review three types of tables. The first table shows an overall summary of the average speed and errors for each participant (one row per participant). The second table shows session-wise summary that shows the average speed and errors for each participant for each session (one row for each session). A third, detailed table shows the speed and errors for each phrase of each session typed by each participant. These tables can be downloaded by the HCI researcher in CSV format for further analysis.

Adding a Participant to the Study. After creating a study the researcher can then add participants to the study (Fig. 2). The researcher adds a participant by entering a participant ID (which can be name of the participant, or a code to represent the participant). If the study follows a within-subjects design, the researchers will specify the order of keyboards (the specific counterbalancing strategy for each participant is left to the researcher). If the study follows a between-subjects design, the researcher specifies the assigned keyboard (the specific randomisation strategy is left to the researcher). After a participant has been added, the application generates a URL which will be unique for each participant. The researcher may either send the URL to the participant (in a remote study), or load the URL on a specific device before handing over the device to the participant (in a lab-based study). The URL remains the same for a particular participant for all his sessions throughout the study.

Participant Experience During Sessions. When the participant's unique URL is launched, for the first time, the application displays the first assigned phrase of the first session for that participant (Fig. 3). When the URL is launched after a phrase has been transcribed, the application displays the first untyped phrase of the first incomplete session. As the participant transcribes the first character of a phrase, the application displays the current speed (in CPM) and the current MSD Error rate and updates these metrics after each keystroke. For this purpose, strings are divided into individual characters using JavaScript's built-in capabilities to provide dynamic browser-side functionality. When the participant taps the submit button for the phrase, all metrics including the speed in CPM, and error rates including the MSD error rate, the corrected error rate, the uncorrected error rate, the total error rate, and the parameters C, INF, IF and F (all calculated twice, once by considering the specified exceptions, and a second time by not considering the exceptions) are transferred to the server's MySQL database for secure archiving.

At the end of each sessions, metrics are calculated by retrieving data from the database and performing computations on the client side. Overall summaries for all participants are generated in the same manner and can be downloaded in CSV format for further analysis. We used Chart.js, a JavaScript library, to create interactive, responsive, and customisable graph using its "HTML Canvas" element [12]. After the participant completes all the phrases in a session, a table displaying speed and MSD error rates for all previous sessions is shown. Additionally, a line graph showing the average speed in CPM (characters per minute) for each session is also displayed (Fig. 3).

4   A Study Comparing Swarachakra and Swaravarna

To evaluate IDCText, and also to demonstrate its capabilities, we conducted an empirical within-subjects counterbalanced systematic longitudinal study (N = 10) to compare the performance of two experimental keyboards, namely Swarachakra and Swaravarna (Fig. 4). Our study was conducted in Marathi, which uses the Devanagari - an Abugida script [30]. We chose an accelerated learning approach similar to [18].

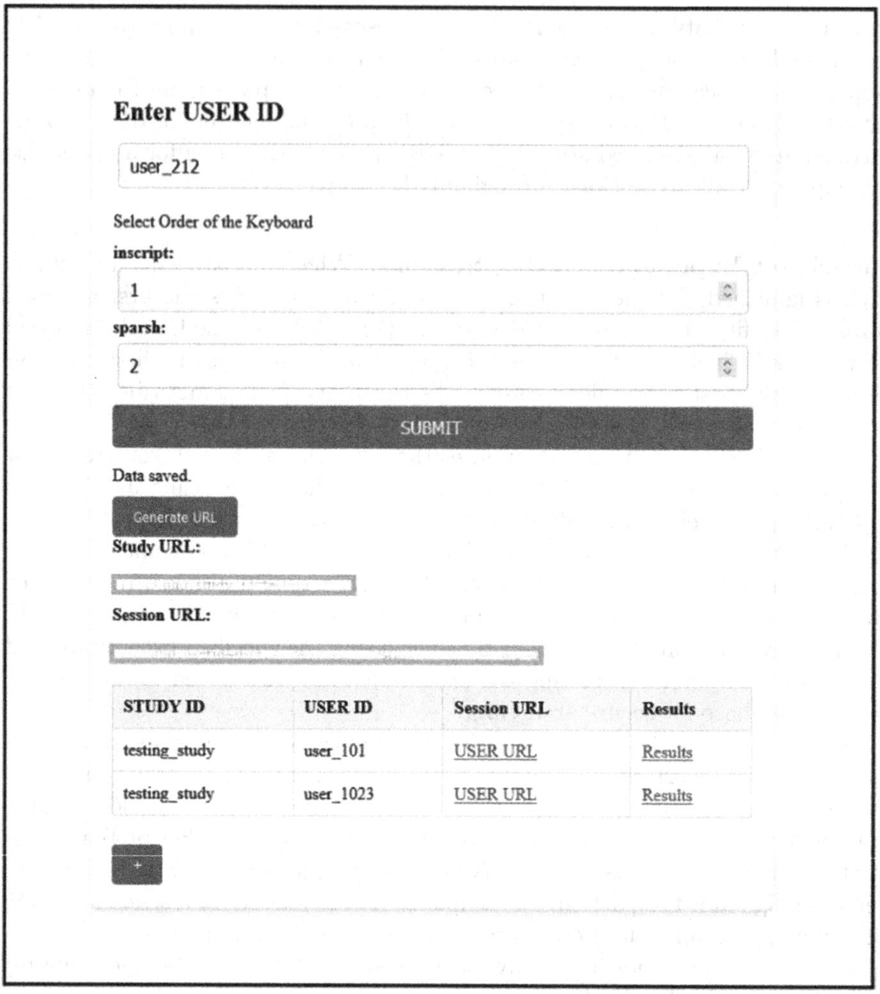

Fig. 2. A screen showing how a researcher can add a participant to the study. The researcher needs to provide a participant id and specify the sequence of keyboards in a within-subjects study. Once the participant is created, the researcher can generate URLs for that user id. The participant id appears in a table below along with a URL for the participant to start their session and a URL for the researcher to view the results for that participant.

Swarachakra Marathi [3] is an experimental keyboard available on Google Play Store for Android phones. The unique aspect of this keyboard is its interaction technique for entering vowel modifiers (matras). Swarachakra shows 34 frequently used Devanagari consonants on a single level (i.e. without using a shift key). Once a participant touches a consonant, the keyboard inputs it in the text box, and at the same time displays a "chakra"(a wheel) around the conso-

(a)   (b)

Fig. 3. a) Participant typing a phrase. Note the current speed and MSD error rate shown while the participant is typing the phrase. b) At the end of the session, the participant is shown a table with summary of their session performances so far, including average, minimum and maximum error rates, and average, minimum and maximum speed in CPM for each session that the participant has finished so far. The speed is also visualised as a line graph.

nant, which acts as a pie menu that previews 9 frequently used Devanagari vowel modifiers on the selected consonant as well as the Devanagari Virama sign (also called the Halant). If the participant lifts his finger, only the consonant remains typed. If the participant drags his finger towards an item in the pie menu, the corresponding vowel modifier or the Virama sign is added. Swarachakra also displays the standalone vowel अ, and in its chakra, displays the 10 most frequently used standalone vowels in Devanagari.

Swaravarna Marathi is another experimental keyboard developed by Rupesh Nath that he kindly made available to the authors. It has a layout of consonants that is identical to Swarachakra. The main difference is in the interaction technique. Swaravarna does not display a chakra around the consonant, but instead provides all the vowel modifiers and standalone vowels in the left margin and in a top row respectively (Fig. 4).

The theoretical position that we take is that the chakra will be a faster method to input text than individual keys for vowel modifiers. This is because

118   V. Deshmukh and A. Joshi

(all other things being constant), the chakra needs less hand movement and
almost no zoning time. Since there are significant numbers of vowel modifiers
in Marathi text, this should lead to a significant effect. Any additional learning
time that may be needed to master a new interaction technique will be small
after a bit of practice. Thus, the objective of our study was to evaluate the effect
of the presence of the unique interaction technique of the chakra through an
empirical study.

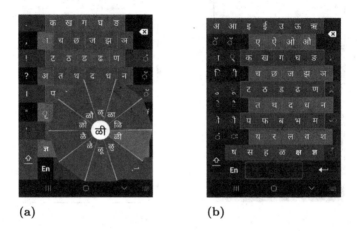

(a)   (b)

Fig. 4. Swarachakra Marathi (left) and Swaravarna Marathi (right)

We selected our corpus of phrases based on previous work. To select our
phrases, we referred to the raw data from the authors of [13]. Theirs was a
between-subjects longitudinal study with 300 phrases typed on four keyboards,
namely InScript [11], SwiftKey [4], Swarachakra [3], and Sparsh [2]. We calculated the standard deviation for the typing speed for each phrase across the four
keyboards. We also derived average typing speed for each phrase and sorted the
phrases based on this metric. We then divided the 300 phrases into 5 groups of
60 phrases each starting with the lowest CPM to the highest. From each group
of 60 phrases, we selected a phrase with the lowest standard deviation across
keyboards in that group. This ensured that we had phrases with five text input
speeds (thus representing five levels of difficulty of typing), and with minimum
typing speed variation across keyboards. Table 1 lists the phrases and their typing speeds across the four keyboards.

With these phrases as our corpus, we set up a study using IDCText with
50 sessions, 5 phrases per session and a repetition factor of 50. We decided to
consider the average speed in the last 5 sessions (session 46 to 50) as the primary
outcome of the study. While we did not use ramping in this study, participants
were first provided training on both keyboards. For participants who were new
to typing Marathi text, a separate training study was created in IDCText with
10 phrases (different from the above phrases). Participants were allowed to start

Table 1. Marathi Phrases selected for study

Phrase Length (chars)	Phrase	Inscript CPM	Sparsh CPM	Swara-chakra CPM	Swift-key CPM	Average CPM
27	मना सज्जना भक्तिपंथेचि जावे	25.64	21.68	22.22	22.74	23.07
20	विमान आकाशात उडत आहे	31.3	33.71	31.19	31.06	31.82
22	सगळी मुलं हसायला लागली	33.83	36.49	35.38	33.27	34.73
26	मी कोणाशीही जास्त बोलत नसे	39.23	37.21	36.52	34.69	36.91
21	बैल गेला नि झोपा केला	42.91	44.23	42.58	40.35	42.53

the main study only if they could consistently achieve a session average speed of 45 CPM (which was the highest average speed reported in the last 5 sessions of [13]). The training data was not analysed beyond this requirement.

The study involved 10 volunteers aged between 21 and 55, 5 male and 5 female. All participants were native Marathi speakers recruited through our social network, including acquaintances and colleagues. None of the participants were lab members. They took part in their free time and did not receive any compensation. On recruitment, a participant was briefed on the experimental protocol and carried out the first session under the supervision of a moderator. Participants were instructed to keep the smartphone on a table or hold it in the palm of the non-dominant hand and type with only index finger of the dominant hand. In case of any technical issue like phrase not getting rendered or loss of the internet connection, participants were instructed to refresh the browser and restart the phrase being typed. The participants were instructed to complete a maximum of 10 sessions per day, divided into two slots of 5 sessions each, with a break of at least 20 min after the first 5 sessions to mitigate fatigue and retain interest.

5   Results

We could conduct this longitudinal study with 10 participants. Five participants used Swarachakra first, followed by Swaravarna. The other 5 participants followed the opposite sequence. Initially, each session lasted 3 to 4 min. As the study progressed, muscle memory developed, reducing the time per session. Each participant took approximately 150 min to complete 50 sessions with one keyboard. The total time required per participant for completing this study was approximately 300 min. At the end of the study, we had data from 5 phrases × 50 repetitions × 2 input methods × 10 participants = 5000 phrases in total. To minimize bias in analyzing speed, we considered only phrases with an error rate below 20%. Out of 5000 phrases, only 5 had an error rate exceeding 20% (0.1%). These phrases were excluded from the speed analysis.

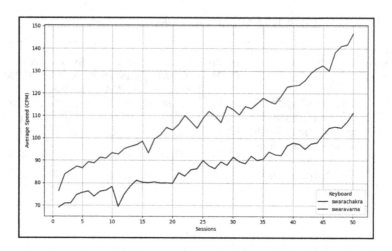

Fig. 5. Session wise mean speeds (CPM) of the keyboards for all sessions 1–50.

Table 2. Speed Statistics (CPM) for Swarachakra and Swaravarna Keyboards (Sessions 1 to 45) & (Sessions 46–50) with 95 % C.I

	Swarachakra		Swaravarna	
	Sessions (1–50)	Sessions (46–50)	Sessions (1–50)	Sessions (46–50)
Mean	109.1	139.5	86.9	106.5
Lower bound	97.2	123.2	80.4	99.6
Upper bound	121	155.9	93.4	113.5

Speed. Figure 5 illustrates the session-wise average typing speed in characters per minute (CPM) for the two keyboards. As we can see, the speed continues to rise during sessions 45–50 and has not yet plateaued. This indicates that future studies need a higher repetition factor. Table 2 shows means and upper and lower bounds of 95 % confidence intervals for speeds of these keyboards achieved in the sessions 1–50 and peak sessions 46–50. We performed a paired t test to compare speeds for Swarachakra and Swaravarna. For sessions 46–50, we found a significant difference in speeds ($t = 5.420$, $n = 9$, $p = 0.0004$). Similarly, we found a significant difference in speeds for sessions 1–50 ($t = 4.682$, $n = 9$, $p = 0.0011$). The presence of a chakra gives a significant advantage of about 33 CPM. Though it may not be completely appropriate to compare text input speeds across languages, we restate here for reference the typical speeds achieved in English text input studies on touch screens that mentioned above – between 25 WPM/150 CPM to 46 WPM/230 CPM.

Error Rates. The purpose of performing error rate analysis was to observe any variations in the pattern of errors while using Swarachakra and Swaravarna keyboards. Since our study with Marathi participants had phrases repeated exten-

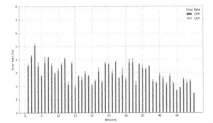
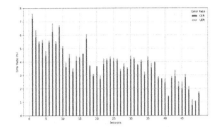

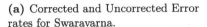

(a) Corrected and Uncorrected Error rates for Swaravarna.

(b) Corrected and Uncorrected Error rates for Swarachakra.

Fig. 6. Comparison of error rates.

sively, the errors observed were quite low. Figure 6 (a),(b) shows Corrected and Uncorrected Error rates for Swaravarna and Swarachakra keyboards respectively. Corrected error rates (CER) largely outnumbered the uncorrected error rates (UER), as expected. We were interested in observing the variation in error rates with respect to the amount of practice. For Swaravarna for initial sessions corrected error rate was 3.535% (UER 0.167%) which significantly decreased to 1.454% (UER 0.157 %) as sessions progressed as shown in Fig. 6. Similarly for Swarachakra initial sessions had corrected error rate of 7.225 % (UER 0.360 %) which significantly decreased to 1.637% (UER 0.138 %) by the end of 50 sessions as shown in Fig. 6.

We conducted paired t-test for different ranges of sessions across keyboards, but did not find any significant differences. When we compared CER for Swarachakra and Swaravarna keyboards for peak sessions 46–50 with a paired t-test, we did not find a significant difference (t = –0.892, df = 9, p = 0.3958). Similarly, when we compared CER for all sessions 1–50 with a paired t-test, we did not find a significant difference (t = 0.924, df = 9, p = 0.3797).

6   Conclusion

We presented IDCText, a customizable tool for conducting text input studies for Indian languages. IDCText is compatible with all modern devices and keyboards. It allows the researcher to add custom phrases, set number of sessions, adjust repetition factor, add ramping to their study and take care of exceptions introduced by issues with Unicode implementations. By open-sourcing the code, IDCText paves the way for future work in text input by HCI researchers.

IDCText is suitable for conducting a variety of text input studies. It has features such as user management which enables longitudinal (multi-session) studies, and option to choose between a within-subjects or a between-subjects study, features that are not available in current tools (e.g. [8]). Further, IDCText has special features for text input studies in Indian languages such as accounting for Unicode exceptions and variations and option for a ramped study design (which makes it easier for first-time text inputters). These complexities highlight the need for a more nuanced approach to character and keystroke counting. Since text input in all languages is now based on Unicode, IDCText can also support non-Indian languages as well (though the interface may need to be localised if participants can't read English). Through this paper, we release IDCText source code in open source [19], so that additional features can be added by other researchers, if needed.

We evaluated IDCText and demonstrated its use through an empirical study in which we compared the performance of participants on two experimental Marathi keyboards Swaracharka and Swaravarna. The two keyboards are mainly different from each other by the presence of a chakra (a pie menu of vowel modifiers). As expected, the presence of a chakra in Swarachakra gives it a significant advantage of about 33 CPM in peak average session speeds in our study. Even after conducting an accelerated longitudinal study with a repetition factor of 50, there seems to be no evidence of saturation in speeds. Future research with more sessions is needed to establish the actual saturation point (something we hope IDCText will make easier to replicate).

In this empirical study, we assessed the overall effect of the two keyboards. An alternative study design (e.g. with a corpus of pairs of phrases that differ only in one vowel modifier) could be used to discover the specific effects on speed and accuracy of the two interaction techniques. IDCText will help conducting such a study very easily and could be attempted in future.

Through this paper, we release a hosted version of IDCText [5] (and accompanying tutorial videos [6]) to make it easier for HCI researchers to conduct Indian language text input studies. A lot more work needs to be done for Indian languages and there is a lot of room for improving upon the metrics provided by IDCText.

Acknowledgements. We would like to express our gratitude to all the participants for their time and valuable inputs during the study. We also extend our thanks to Rupesh Nath for providing the Swaravarna keyboard, which greatly contributed to the successful completion of this research.

Disclosure of Interests. The authors have no competing interests to declare that are relevant to the content of this article.

References

1. Google indic keyboard. https://play.google.com/store/apps/details?id=com.google.android.inputmethod.latin
2. Sparsh marathi keyboard. https://play.google.com/store/apps/details?id=com.sparsh.inputmethod.marathi
3. Swarachakra marathi keyboard. https://play.google.com/store/apps/details?id=iit.android.swarachakraMarathi
4. Swiftkey keyboard. https://play.google.com/store/apps/details?id=com.touchtype.swiftkey
5. IDCText hosted and available on website with URL link (2024). http://idid.in/IDCtext/

6. Setup and conduct a new text input study using IDCText: Tutorial video (2024). https://www.youtube.com/watch?v=zjOIJ0RGGFE

7. Anu Bharath, P., Jadhav, C., Ahire, S., Joshi, M., Ahirwar, R., Joshi, A.: Performance of accessible gesture-based indic keyboard. In: Bernhaupt, R., Dalvi, G., Joshi, A., Balkrishan, D.K., O'Neill, J., Winckler, M. (eds.) INTERACT 2017. LNCS, vol. 10513, pp. 205–220. Springer, Cham (2017). https://doi.org/10.1007/978-3-319-67744-6_14

8. Arif, A.S., Mazalek, A.: Webtem: a web application to record text entry metrics. In: Proceedings of the 2016 ACM International Conference on Interactive Surfaces and Spaces, pp. 415–420 (2016)

9. Bhikne, B., Joshi, A., Joshi, M., Ahire, S., Maravi, N.: How much faster can you type by speaking in hindi? comparing keyboard-only and keyboard+ speech text entry. In: Proceedings of the 9th Indian Conference on Human-Computer Interaction, pp. 20–28 (2018)

10. Bhikne, B., Joshi, A., Joshi, M., Jadhav, C., Sakhardande, P.: Faster and less error-prone: supplementing an accessible keyboard with speech input. In: Lamas, D., Loizides, F., Nacke, L., Petrie, H., Winckler, M., Zaphiris, P. (eds.) INTERACT 2019. LNCS, vol. 11746, pp. 288–304. Springer, Cham (2019). https://doi.org/10.1007/978-3-030-29381-9_18

11. CDAC: Inscript: Unified virtual keyboard for indian languages. http://www.cdac.in/index.aspx?id=dl_android_uvkil

12. Chart.js: Open-source javascript library for data visualization (2024). https://www.chartjs.org/docs/latest/

13. Dalvi, G., Aet al.: Does prediction really help in marathi text input? empirical analysis of a longitudinal study. In: Proceedings of the 18th International Conference on Human-Computer Interaction with Mobile Devices and Services, pp. 35–46 (2016)

14. Dalvi, G., et al.: A protocol to evaluate virtual keyboards for Indian languages. In: Proceedings of the 7th Indian Conference on Human-Computer Interaction, pp. 27–38 (2015)

15. Eiselmayer, A., Wacharamanotham, C., Beaudouin-Lafon, M., Mackay, W.E.: Touchstone2: an interactive environment for exploring trade-offs in hci experiment design. In: Proceedings of the 2019 CHI Conference on Human Factors in Computing Systems, pp. 1–11 (2019)

16. Evans, A., Wobbrock, J.: Taming wild behavior: the input observer for obtaining text entry and mouse pointing measures from everyday computer use. In: Proceedings of the SIGCHI Conference on Human Factors in Computing Systems, pp. 1947–1956 (2012)

17. Fitts, P.M.: The information capacity of the human motor system in controlling the amplitude of movement. J. Exp. Psychol. **47**(6), 381 (1954)

18. Ghosh, S., et al.: Shift+ tap or tap+ longpress? the upper bound of typing speed on inscript. In: Proceedings of the 2017 CHI Conference on Human Factors in Computing Systems, pp. 2059–2063 (2017)

19. IDCText: Link for open source on github (2024). https://github.com/IDCText/IDCText-app

20. Kristensson, P.O.: Discrete and continuous shape writing for text entry and control. Ph.D. thesis, Institutionen för datavetenskap (2007)

21. MacKenzie, I.S., Soukoreff, R.W.: Phrase sets for evaluating text entry techniques. In: CHI'03 Extended Abstracts on Human Factors in Computing Systems, pp. 754–755 (2003)

22. MacKenzie, I.S., Tanaka-Ishii, K.: Text Entry Systems: Mobility, Accessibility. Universality. Elsevier, Amsterdam (2010)

23. Markussen, A., Jakobsen, M.R., Hornbæk, K.: Vulture: a mid-air word-gesture keyboard. In: Proceedings of the SIGCHI Conference on Human Factors in Computing Systems, pp. 1073–1082 (2014)

24. Silfverberg, M., MacKenzie, I.S., Korhonen, P.: Predicting text entry speed on mobile phones. In: Proceedings of the SIGCHI Conference on Human Factors in Computing Systems, pp. 9–16 (2000)

25. Soukoreff, R.W., MacKenzie, I.S.: Metrics for text entry research: an evaluation of msd and kspc, and a new unified error metric. In: Proceedings of the SIGCHI Conference on Human Factors in Computing Systems, pp. 113–120 (2003)

26. Speicher, M., Feit, A.M., Ziegler, P., Krüger, A.: Selection-based text entry in virtual reality. In: Proceedings of the 2018 CHI Conference on Human Factors in Computing Systems, pp. 1–13 (2018)

27. Unicode Consortium: Unicode for Indian languages (2003). https://www.unicode.org/L2/L2003/03102-indic-ov.pdf. Accessed 05 June 2024

28. Vertanen, K., Kristensson, P.O.: Complementing text entry evaluations with a composition task. ACM Trans. Comput.-Human Interact. (TOCHI) 21(2), 1–33 (2014)

29. Vertanen, K., Memmi, H., Emge, J., Reyal, S., Kristensson, P.O.: Velocitap: investigating fast mobile text entry using sentence-based decoding of touchscreen keyboard input. In: Proceedings of the 33rd Annual ACM Conference on Human Factors in Computing Systems, pp. 659–668 (2015)

30. Wikipedia: Abugida. https://en.wikipedia.org/wiki/Abugida. Accessed 7 June 2024

31. Wikipedia: Article counts. https://en.wikipedia.org/wiki/Wikipedia:Multilingual_statistics#Number_of_article_milestones. Accessed 7 June 2024

32. Wikipedia: Kanji. https://en.wikipedia.org/wiki/Kanji. Accessed 7 May 2024

33. Wikipedia: List of languages by total number of speakers. https://en.wikipedia.org/wiki/List_of_languages_by_total_number_of_speakers. Accessed 7 May 2024

34. Wikipedia: Pinyin wikipedia. https://en.wikipedia.org/wiki/Pinyin. Accessed 7 May 2024

35. Zhai, S., Kristensson, P.O.: Shorthand writing on stylus keyboard. In: Proceedings of the SIGCHI Conference on Human Factors in Computing Systems, pp. 97–104 (2003)

36. Zhu, S., Zheng, J., Zhai, S., Bi, X.: i'sfree: eyes-free gesture typing via a touch-enabled remote control. In: Proceedings of the 2019 CHI Conference on Human Factors in Computing Systems, pp. 1–12 (2019)

Comparative Evaluation of Speech Interfaces of Conversational Agents in Hindi

Shivangi[✉], Anirudha Joshi, and Anurag Kumar Singh

IDC School of Design, IIT Bombay, Mumbai, Maharashtra, India
ux.shivangi@gmail.com, anirudha@iitb.ac.in

Abstract. Personal Digital Assistants have gained a great momentum and many innovations are happening in this field in recent years. They are now being widely used in the form of home-based smart speakers such as Amazon's Alexa, Google's Home and Apple's Homepod Mini etc. As voice assistants are becoming popular in India, people are discovering different ways in which they can use them. For more and more people to be able to use them, it not only relies on people to learn and adapt to how they work but also the speakers to adapt to the multilingual Indian audience. More than half of the population of India is predominantly Hindi speaking, therefore it is necessary for the voice assistants to not only function in the language but also be able to understand what the user is expecting, feel natural while responding and adapt to the language. This paper presents the results of an evaluation of the two smart personal voice assistants that support Hindi i.e. Amazon's Alexa and Google's Assistant in the dimensions of response rate, success rate and how helpful or correct and natural the responses feel to the users. The paper also tries to explore what participants considered as a good answer when given by a machine assistant and the rationale behind modifying their command to the assistant when they could not get the desired response. Eight people participated in the experiment and the results show that Amazon's Alexa had a better success and response rate than Google's Assistant and the participants also rated Amazon Alexa's responses slightly good in terms of it's way of responding and more helpful in terms of precision of response. But, Amazon's Alexa had a significantly high interruption rate as the participants lost patience due to lengthy responses when compared to Google Assistant whose responses were short and crisp. The overall impact of this research is to serve a basis for finding gaps in the existing popular voice assistant devices and hence can be used as a guide towards a better experience of usage. Further studies could also help serve as a basis for understanding what native hindi speaking audience expects as a response and how differently they can frame the question even when the task given at hand is the same based on how they rated responses to be successful, failed or invalid.

Keywords: voice interfaces · HCI for Indian languages · smart speakers

© The Author(s), under exclusive license to Springer Nature Switzerland AG 2025
N. Rangaswamy et al. (Eds.): IndiaHCI 2024, CCIS 2337, pp. 125–145, 2025.
https://doi.org/10.1007/978-3-031-80829-6_6

1   Introduction

As the internet can reach all over the world and a large number of people in multiple languages, these smart speakers have the potential to overcome not only literacy barriers but also dependence on sight, touching, typing or temporary situational disabilities like while cooking one would not be able to constantly read or interact with the screen. As these technologies are now spread out widely and are being rapidly adopted by various groups in India, therefore it makes sense to access these technologies for Indian languages. These devices can not only help low-literate and older people who are not well equipped with the technology to not only have access to the information available on the internet but would also help in simplifying their day-to-day tasks like setting up an alarm and making calls and many more.

Having access to the internet helps people know better and expand mental horizons. In a mainstream bollywood movie Jayeshbhai Jordar, the male protagonist is motivated to oppose his patriarchal family and skedaddle with his wife to save their unborn daughter from foeticide. Beyond education, it is his 9-year-old daughter who introduces him to the world of Google and YouTube, expanding his mental horizons beyond their regressive environment. A voice assistant named 'Sarla' plays a crucial role in supporting the family during difficult times. Sarla is depicted as a device that seamlessly understands and responds to every prompt given by the actors, setting an ideal standard for real-world VUIs.

Our motivation is to understand how predominantly Hindi speaking people in India interact with these devices to assess how effective they are in Indian languages and consider ways of improving current user interaction from insights gathered. Another motivation for this study is to evaluate both the assistants with many users, not just the personal experience of a single person.

This paper makes a comparison of two intelligent personal assistants available on home-based smart speakers (i.e. Google's Assistant on Google Home Mini and Amazon's Alexa on Echo Dot) that have been developed to aid people in performing tasks by giving commands in Hindi. We kept speech-to-text services like Apple Dictation, Google Speech-to-Text, Liv.ai and other built-in smartphones and search bars like in Amazon mobile application and Google search engine out of scope due to their lack of being somewhat conversational and dependence on having to visually access the output. Although there are many other mainstream assistants like Apple's Siri, Microsoft's Cortana and Samsung's Bixby, none of them support Indian languages. There are other smart speakers available in the market like MI Smart Speaker, Ptron Music bot cube, Zebronics Zeb-Music Bomb X Mini, Sonos One and Yamaha YAS-209 which make use of the same assistants, like Amazon Alexa or Google Assistant but these assistants were developed by Amazon and Google respectively so the performance seemed to be better on the devices produced by the respective companies. These assistants were selected for this study due to their popularity in Indian market and for their similar characteristics [1]. These were chosen due to their similar characteristics (functions, physical appearance) and the similar budget friendly price point as our sample was a low-income group.

Both Google Home Mini and Amazon Echo Dot are very similar devices as they not only lie in the same price range of Rupees 2,600–3,300 but were also released around the same time, Google home mini in October, 2017 and Amazon Echo Dot in March, 2016. Moreover, both the smart-speakers used were of the same charcoal black color and had similar dough like shape and size of about 9 cm diameter as seen in Fig. 1 and Fig. 2.

Fig. 1. Voice-Assistant supporting smart speakers used for the study. Left: Google's Home Mini supporting Google Assistant. Right: Amazon's Echo Dot supporting Amazon Alexa

2   Related Work

Even after voice-assistants being mainstream, evaluating them is a challenge due to the variety of tasks they support on different devices and their specialties in different areas. For example, 1. The assistants on an average smartphone supports a wide range of tasks such as making a call, setting a reminder, playing music and several others. Due to the numerous variety of tasks that can be performed using a voice-assistant, studies that attempt to measure the effectiveness or compare them tend to focus on a narrow field of usage scenario in which authors perform measurements by themselves (for example, assistance during their day-to-day email writing). 2. Amazon's Alexa being an Amazon product that owns Amazon E-commerce specializes in product recommendation and ease in selecting and buying products directly whereas Google's Assistant being a product from Google that owns Google web browser and maps, specializes in searching data from the internet and accurately describing the time and directions to navigate. Therefore, the study was narrowed down to home-based smart speakers supporting hindi that are popular in the Indian market for convenience.

128   Shivangi et al.

Device Name	Color	Height	Diameter	Weight	Lights
Amazon Echo Dot	Black	43 mm	99 mm	300 g	Ultraviolet Ring Light
Google Home Mini	Charcoal Black	42 mm	97.8 mm	173 g	Blue, Red, Yellow, Green

Fig. 2. Comparing physical aspects of the devices. The physical attributes needed to be similar in order to avoid any cognitive biases

Personal Assistants can be evaluated in different ways based on the response they give. While sometimes the creators of the assistants offer an evaluation mechanism, like in the case of Alexa, Amazon offers an evaluation guide where one task is to create notifications [4]. However this allows for the evaluation of Alexa to execute the task, it does not consider the user experience of the device. Therefore, apart from measuring the capacity the device has to perform a specific task it would also be valuable to measure the user experience with these digital assistants. There have been several studies where user experience is extensively evaluated. Aung Pyae et al. investigated the usability, user experiences, and usefulness of the Google Home smart speaker. The findings showed that Google Home is usable and user-friendly for the user [6], but the study did not include other assistants like Alexa or Cortana.

While most of the literature works related to voice assistants are focussed on the evaluation of a single assistant and the tasks that it can perform from searches and configuration notification, among other tasks the papers "Alexa, Siri, Cortana, and More: An Introduction to Voice Assistants" [3] by Matthew B Hoy are examples which not only make an evaluation of the tasks that the assistants offer but also include a comparative analysis of the available digital assistants.

Another approach is that of the authors Ana Berdasco et al. [2]. They proposed a study in which they evaluated the answers of the assistants based on the goodness and correctness of the response of the devices. This maintains the focus of evaluating the tasks that the assistants perform but also considers the quality of the user-assistant interaction. However, in this paper the participants who rated the devices did not directly interact with the devices but were only shown a video of both the devices answering the same question one after the other. Our work is partially based on this paper, which served as a reference for the evaluation of intelligent personal assistants but in Hindi language.

On the other hand, there are also studies that not only focus on comparing machine-powered digital voice-assistants amongst themselves but to human powered voice assistants. Jennifer Pearson et al. carried out a study that was set up for the challenging context of public spaces in slums and makes use of conversational speech question and answer systems to help improve machine-powered smart speakers; and, highlight the potential benefits of multi-sited public speech installations within slum environments. [5]

Another study done in the Indian context for regional language by S. B. Rajeshwari et al. recognizes that a multilingual society such as India has grown quite comfortable using a combination of two or more languages while communicating, commonly referenced as code-switching and evaluated the models on standardized classification metrics. [7]

3 Methodology

3.1 Recruitment and Lab Testing Pilot

The next stage was to perform an unscripted pilot, so we recruited 4 emergent users (2M;2F) for a short pilot study to help test and improve the study before deployment. All participants were mess workers for different hostels working for the same university and had primary school level of literacy in their local language (Hindi or Marathi). We selected this group as they were predominantly hindi speaking and first time voice assistant users. The goal was to understand how they naturally interacted with the personal assistants when given a few of the scripted scenarios (Fig. 5), with minimal guidance. A scenario in this context is defined as a hypothetical situation that is given to the participant in which they would want the assistant's help. These scenarios were carefully selected to make sure it includes a wide range of activities and type of answers that voice-assistants perform or answer. In an informal workshop-like setting, we asked participants to pose questions to both the smart speakers, and observed their interactions and any challenges. Later, we gave them a few scenarios based on which they had to ask some more questions. The users were initially not given any question format that they should ask the VUIs, however when they were getting stuck for more than 3 times, they were suggested to use these specific prompts to allow users get a better idea of what the response by VUIs (Voice User Interfaces) would be in an ideal or happy case scenario. These prompts were different for both devices as per our trials before starting the research study. After finishing the set prompts required for our study, we asked the participants if they would like to ask any questions of their own, very few of them ended up asking barely one question at max. We understood that this audience might require more frequent and prolonged exposure to adapt to using VUIs more confidently. Each participant was then asked to evaluate both the devices in terms of helpfulness and goodness of the responses and shared why they considered responses as a failure or a success and the rationale behind modifying their articulated questions iteratively. This can be seen in as shown in Fig. 3

These interactions of people with the smart devices enabled gathering of natural commands put forth by people in an attempt to get the desired activity done by the smart devices. An example of the guidance provided to the members of the pilot is: "Imagine that you are going to sleep now but you have to go to the market for shopping at 6pm and you want the device to wake you up before that". Each participant asked questions the the smart devices in slightly different

Metric	Method
Helpfulness	How helpful were the answers? Rate on the scale of 1-5 where 1 is bad and 5 is excellent.
Goodness	How good were the answers? Rate on the scale of 1-5 where 1 is bad and 5 is excellent.

Fig. 3. Method used for evaluation performance of the smart speakers in pilot study

ways, such as one of them asked, (I am going to sleep now. I have to go to the market in the evening. Remind me.) while the other asked (Set up an alarm for 6 pm). So, we got to know that it was necessary to mention the time the reminder has to be set up for when asking Google Assistant which was missing in the first articulation of command else the command will fail whereas Amazon Alexa would ask follow up questions to confirm the time, information like this could be used to give hints to the participants in the final study whenever they would feel stuck.

This pilot also identified a range of improvements, such as the need to give a demo with a few simple questions prior to starting the interview(Fig. 4), a few of the scripted scenarios were added, removed or clubbed and the suggestion to have some commands handy that we had already tested and were working for each of the scripted scenarios (Fig. 5) for both the smart speakers.

We recognized that the methods used for evaluating the devices in terms of goodness and helpfulness was confusing for people and so we should mention clearly what we meant by these terms and what all should they consider while rating the devices. Also, it was difficult to say if the participant considered a particular response as successful, therefore we decided to ask the user to vote for each response as satisfactory or not.

Usually, participants would reiterate the command and ask if they were dissatisfied but while some participants could keep going some would lose patience and start to feel frustrated if they had any time constraints during the experiment. So, we decided to restrict the number of attempts per scripted scenario to 3 for each of the two smart speakers.

For the final study, we recruited 8 more participants (4M;4F) as given in Fig. 4. To balance the study, half the participants were asked to ask for help from Amazon Alexa first and the rest from Google Assistant.

3.2   Evaluation Design

Demo. After the assistants were identified and the pilot study was done, the next step was to design the study. As the participants were emergent users, initially we had to give a demo of how both the devices work, how they can sometimes fail or give irrelevant responses to some commands while responding perfectly when the same command was articulated differently. During this phase

Code	Gender	First Device	Age
1MG	Male	Google Assistant	25
2MG	Male	Google Assistant	21
3MA	Male	Amazon Alexa	20
4FA	Female	Google Assistant	40
5FA	Female	Amazon Alexa	37
6FG	Female	Google Assistant	35
7MA	Male	Amazon Alexa	21
8FA	Female	Amazon Alexa	43

Fig. 4. List of people that participated in the final study

the interviewer posed these questions to both the smart speakers while simultaneously explaining about how they work. This was done using the sequence of commands in (Fig. 5).

Own Questions. The participants were then asked to ask a few questions of their own from both the devices, in order to get used to it.

Scripted Scenarios. The scenarios were carefully selected after exploring what all types of commands voice-assistants support and what are the popular types of commands that people use in their day-to-day life. The selected scenarios and some questions that could be suggested or be given hints for if the user failed to form then to get the desired response are in below (Figs. 6, 7, 8, 9)

Participants were given 3 tries per assistant for each scenario to get desired output, sometimes if they fail to frame the command correctly the examiner will suggest a few modifications or questions that were pre-tested to be working, so that the user can analyze the voice-assistants in a better way.

Scenario context	Digital Voice Assistant	Command - Hindi	Command - Translation in English	Expected Response
To find Date and weather of the place	Alexa	आज कौन सी तारीख है?	What is the date today?	Correct
	Google	आज कौन सी तारीख है?	What is the date today?	Correct
	Alexa	आज मौसम कैसा रहेगा?	How will the weather be today?	Correct
	Google	आज मौसम कैसा रहेगा?	How will the weather be today?	Correct
To find What 'banana' is called in hindi	Alexa	हिंदी में "बनाना" को क्या कहते हैं?	What is "banana" called in hindi?	Doesn't know
	Alexa	"बनाना" हिंदी में?	"Banana" in Hindi?	Plays Song
	Alexa	"बनाना" को हिंदी में क्या कहेंगे?	How to say "banana" in Hindi?	Correct
	Google	हिंदी में "बनाना" को क्या कहते हैं?	What is "banana" called in Hindi?	Incorrect Definition
	Google	हिंदी में "बनाना" फल को क्या कहते हैं?	What is "banana" fruit called in Hindi?	Correct

Fig. 5. List of questions asked to Digital Voice Assistant for giving a demo to the participants

3.3 Data Analysis Method

The analysis method used was based both, the experience and emotions of the participants while getting a response for the articulated query and the statistical approach for measuring the success rate and response rate. (Fig. 10)

4 Results

After carrying out the study, with all the participants, the recordings of each study were transcribed for further analysis. The transcription was done in a way to capture the tone of voice, emotions, satisfaction level with each response and patience. Along with the device name, question framed by the participants and the response provided by the assistant, it also mentions if the participant's response of the assistant to be a successful one or a failed one with description of why they considered it to be so. The data also mentioned their rationale behind reiterating the articulated question posed by the participants (Fig. 11).

Sr. No.	Scenario Category	Scenario Name	Script - Hindi	Script - Translation	Suggested commands - Hindi	Suggested commands - Translation
1	Task based	Reminder; Story/Joke/Shayari	एमाज़ॉन अलेक्सा या गूगल असिस्टेंट से बोलिये: - की वो आपको शाम 6 बजे मार्केट जाने के लिए याद दिला दे। - की वो आपको एक छोटी सी कहानी, शायरी, गाना या चुटकुला सुना दे।	Tell Amazon Alexa or Google Assistant: - That she should remind you to go to the market at 6 pm. - That she should tell you a short story, poetry, song or joke.	Q: Alexa/Google शाम 6 बजे बाजार जाने के लिए रिमाइंडर सेट करो। Q: Alexa/Google मुझे एक छोटी सी कहानी बताओ।	Q: Alexa/Google Set a reminder to go to the market at 6 pm. Q: Alexa/Google Tell me a little story.
2	Recommendation based	Buying a phone	सोचिये अगर आप फ़ोन पानी में गिर जाये और काम कर बंद कर दे। अब आपको एक नया फ़ोन खरीदना है लेकिन आप नहीं जानते कि कौनसा फ़ोन आपकी जरूर के लिए पर्याप्त रहेगा। तो ये जानन के लिए एमाज़ॉन अलेक्सा या गूगल	Imagine if your phone falls in water and stops working. Now you have to buy a new phone but you don't know which phone will be good enough for	Q: Alexa/Google मुझे कौन सा फ़ोन खरीदना चाहिए?	Q: Alexa/Google Which phone should I buy

Fig. 6. 1 of 4 Scripted scenarios for the participants and some questions that could be suggested or be given hints for if the user failed to form then to get the desired response

4.1 Quantitative Analysis

A total of 387 questions were posed during the experiment, out of which only 175 responses were successful and 212 had failed out of which 103 were invalid (Fig. 12). Invalid here is defined as responses where the smart speaker could not understand the command, did not know the answer, beep sound, gibberish or did not respond at all.

Sr. No.	Scenario Category	Scenario Name	Script - Hindi	Script - Translation	Suggested commands - Hindi	Suggested commands - Translation
			असिस्टेंट से सवाल पूछिए।	your needs. So to find out, ask a question to Amazon Alexa or Google Assistant.		
3	Suggestion based	Places to visit in Mumbai	मान लीजिए, आप हाल ही में मुंबई शिफ्ट हुए हैं और आपको नहीं पता कि यहां घूमने के लिए कौन सी अच्छी जगह हैं। सुझाव मांगें।	Suppose, you have recently shifted to Mumbai and you do not know which are the best places to visit here. Ask for suggestions	Q: Alexa/Google मुंबई में घूमने लिए सबसे अच्छी जगह कौन सी हैं?	Q: Alexa/Google Which are the best places to visit in Mumbai
4	Fact based	Leaders of US & Canada	जैसे की आप जानते हैं की श्री नरेंद्र मोदी जी इंडिया के प्रधानमंत्री हैं। उसी तरह से अमेरिका और कनाडा में उनकी जगह पे कौन है? ये आप एमाज़ॉन अलेक्सा या गूगल असिस्टेंट की मदद से जानने कि कोशिश करिये।	As you know that Shri Narendra Modi ji is the Prime Minister of India. In the same way, who is in his place in America and Canada? Try to find out with the help of Amazon Alexa or Google Assistant.	Q: Alexa/Google अमेरिका के प्रधान मंत्री कौन हैं? Q: Alexa/Google कनाडा के प्रधान मंत्री कौन हैं?	Q: Alexa/Google Who is the Prime Minister of America? Q: Alexa/Google Who is the Prime Minister of Canada?
5	Descriptive	Explanation for	एमाज़ॉन अलेक्सा गूगल असिस्टेंट के	Try using Amazon	Q: Alexa/Google	Q: Alexa/Google

Fig. 7. 2 of 4 Scripted scenarios for the participants and some questions that could be suggested or be given hints for if the user failed to form then to get the desired response

Sr. No.	Scenario Category	Scenario Name	Script - Hindi	Script - Translation	Suggested commands - Hindi	Suggested commands - Translation
		nightmares	माध्यम से जानने कोशिश करिये की हमें सपने क्यों आते हैं।	Alexa or Google Assistant to find out why we dream.	हम क्यों सपने देखते हैं?	Why do we dream?
6	Procedural	Cooking	मान लीजिए कि आप आज एक नया व्यंजन बनाने की कोशिश करना चाहते हैं, तो एमाज़ॉन अलेक्सा या गूगल असिस्टेंट से सामग्री और नुस्खा के लिए पूछें।	Let's say you want to try a new recipe today, ask Amazon Alexa or Google Assistant for ingredients and a recipe.	Q: Alexa/Google भिंडी की सब्जी बनाने की प्रक्रिया क्या है?	Q: Alexa/Google What is the process of making Bhindi curry?
7	Navigation	Going place	अगर आप नहीं जानते की आई आई टी बॉम्बे के कैंपस में पोस्ट ऑफिस कहाँ पर है तो आप एमाज़ॉन अलेक्सा असिस्टेंट से वहाँ जाने का रास्ता कैसे पूछेंगे?	If you don't know where the post office is located on the campus of IIT Bombay, how do you ask Amazon Alexa or Assistant how to get there?	Q: Alexa/Google मैं हॉस्टल 11 IIT कैंपस पोस्ट ऑफिस कैसे जा सकता हूँ?	Q: Alexa/Google How do I go from Hostel 11 to IIT Campus Post Office?
8	Philosophical	Egg or Hen; Death	आपको क्या लगता है पहले क्या आया - मुर्गी या अंडा? क्या आप यही सवाल स्मार्ट स्पीकर्स से पूछ सकते हैं? आपको क्या लगता है मरने के बाद लोग कहाँ	Which do you think came first - the chicken or the egg? Can you ask the same question to Smart Speakers?	Q: Alexa/Google पहले मुर्गी आई या अंडा? Q: Alexa/Google लोग मरने बाद कहा जाते हैं?	Q: Alexa/Google came first, the chicken or the egg? Q: Alexa/Google Where do people go after dying?

Fig. 8. 3 of 4 Scripted scenarios for the participants and some questions that could be suggested or be given hints for if the user failed to form then to get the desired response

Sr. No.	Scenario Category	Scenario Name	Script - Hindi	Script - Translation	Suggested commands - Hindi	Suggested commands - Translation
			जाते हैं?क्या आप वही सवाल स्मार्ट स्पीकर से पूछ सकते हैं?	Where do you think people go after dying?Can you ask the same question to Smart Speakers?		
9	Personification	Human assistant	सोचिये की अलेक्सा और गूगल असिस्टेंट हमारी तरह एक इंसान है और उससे उसकी पसंद या नापसंद के बारे में कोई सवाल पूछिए।	Imagine that Alexa and Google Assistant are human beings just like us and ask her a question about her likes or dislikes.	Q: Alexa/Google तुम्हे कौनसी मूवी पसंद है? Q: Alexa/Google आपका पसंदीदा रंग क्या है? Q: Alexa/Google मुझसे शादी करोगी?	Q: Alexa/Google Which movie do you like? Q: Alexa/Google What's your favorite color? Q: Alexa/Google will you marry me?

Fig. 9. 4 of 4 Scripted scenarios for the participants and some questions that could be suggested or be given hints for if the user failed to form then to get the desired response

Amazon Alexa was asked a total of 180 queries out of which 93 were successful and 87 failed in which 25 were invalid responses. Whereas, Google Assistant was asked a total of 207 queries, out of which 82 were successful and 125 failed in which 78 were invalid (Fig. 13).

We calculated and compared [Sum of successful queries/(Total queries - Sum of invalid queries)] and [Sum of failed queries/(Total queries - Sum of invalid queries] for each of the assistants. It was observed that Alexa performed better in terms of both Response rate and success rate, due to its less dependence on sentence structure and grammar in general, it was able to correctly respond to what the participant wished for. Whereas, with Google Assistant participants struggled a lot with getting their queries through.

Metric	Definition	Method
Success Rate	Measures the number of times the user was satisfied with the response given by the smart speaker.	It is a measured as a percentage of (Total Successful Responses/Total number of Queries) for both the smart speakers
Response Rate	Measures how many times a device responded with a logical relevant answer to the command. This setdoes not include invalid responseslike when the response was thatthey could not understand thecommand, did not know the answer,beep sound, gibberish or did notrespond at all.	It is measured as a percentage of ((Total Queries - Invalid Responses)/Total Queries) for both the smart speakers.
Helpfulness	Measures that to what extent the user's query was resolved. It considers the satisfaction of the user and the precision of the answer. It may be based on the users preconceptions about the issue and if they agree with the response or not.	People were asked "How helpful did you find the responses in terms of precision and quality of the responses?". They had to rate both the devices on the likert scale (1) very poor, (2) poor, (3) average, (4) good, and (5) excellent. An average of all the ratings were then calculated.
Goodness	Measures the quality of the response based on the way the device responds. Considering the words used, tone of voice, emotions expressed etc.	People were asked "How good were the answers? in terms of tone of voice, emotions and engagement of the responses?". They had to rate both the devices on the likert scale (1) very poor, (2) poor, (3) average, (4) good, and (5) excellent. An average of all the ratings were then calculated.
Length of Response	Average number of words used by the devices to respond in order to solve a query put forth by the participants.	It is calculated as, (Total number of words used by a smart speaker while responding to a query/Total number of queries that were put forth)
Interruption Rate	The number of times a participant interrupts the smart speaker in the middle of its response either to stop or ask another query. This could happen due to two reasons, one is that the response is too long and the participant does not have the patience to listen to the full response and secondly, the participant has identified that the response is incorrect or repetitive and then chooses to interrupt. In this case, the later one is not considered.	It is calculated as, (Total number of times response was interrupted due to losing patience / Total number of questions)

Fig. 10. Descriptions and methods for the metrics evaluated for the study

4.2 Qualitative Analysis

As illustrated in Fig. 4 on an average, the participants found Amazon Alexa's responses to be more helpful and good (Fig. 14). Only participant 7MA found Google Assistant's responses to be more helpful than Amazon Alexa, the reason they gave for doing so was due to the short and crisp responses given by Google Assistant. Whereas, in terms of helpfulness 2 out of 8 i.e. 3MA and 6FG found Alexa's expressive nature of responding irritating due to the tone of voice.

Metric	Amazon Alexa	Google Assistant
Response Rate	89.17%	65.81%
Success Rate	51.66%	39.61%
Helpfulness	3.37/5	2.75/5
Goodness	3.25/5	2.62/5
Length of Response	39.45 words	25.97 words
Interruption Rate	7.22%	1.40%

Fig. 11. Results obtained for each metric for both the smart speakers

5   Discussion

5.1   Follow up Questions

The user gets confused when answering to follow up questions asked by alexa like, , the user's response was always selecting an option, to which alexa repeated the question as it was expecting a "Yes" or "No" As an answer. An example of statements that seem to be pretty long and unnecessary include,

5.2   Hints:

A total of only 14 hints were given to users for framing the question, out of which 8 were for Google assistant and 6 for Alexa. It was observed that even after giving the hints, only 5 (Amazon Alexa: 3, Google Assistant: 2) number of modified queries were able to get a successful response whereas 9 (Amazon Alexa: 3, Google Assistant: 6) still failed in their immediately after query, but only 1 was successful in the consecutive queries. Most number of hints were given for the "get recommendations for buying a new phone" question for which 4 hints were given in total across different participants.

5.3   Length of Response

Average number of words used by Alexa for one response was 39.45 which is significantly higher than 25.97 which is the count for Google Assistant. Users liked longer responses than required only when the response includes terms that confirm that the command was heard correctly Eg. When Asked to set up a alarm to Google assistant it responded just by saying, "Okay done" Whereas,

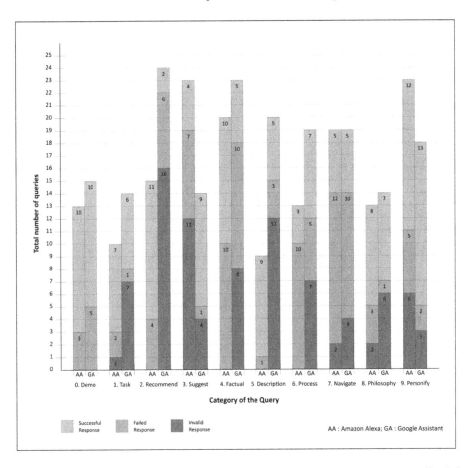

Fig. 12. Figure illustrates the overall and category breakdown of responses to all valid interactions on each system. Shown as a percentage, the blue areas indicate relevant responses, green are irrelevant responses and yellow are invalid responses. (Color figure online)

when asked Alexa, it responded by saying. "Okay, done. The alarm is set for 6 tomorrow evening." Otherwise, the participants liked crisp reponses by Google assistant more and lost patience many times while Amazon Alexa was answering and tried to stop the device themselves by saying "Alexa, Stop!" Eg. Participant: Alexa: Google Assistant: Even if Google used some statements like, "I don't know if I know the answer, but I found this on the Internet..." and when asked a joke, the response always started with, "This makes me laugh, let's see what you think about it..." on the other hand Alexa's response started immediately with the joke, shayari or story but count of words per response was significantly huge in Alexa as it had more process based follow up questions, when cooking related questions were asked to set up a timer Eg. Like when asked cooking related questions such as recipe or ingredients, Alexa tries to offer a quick way

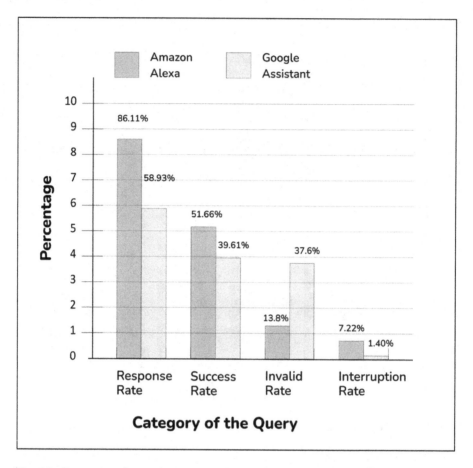

Fig. 13. Comparing the average score of Amazon Alexa and Google Assistant in terms of Success Rate, Response Rate, Invalid Rate and Interruption Rate

to cut through layers of information hierarchy. Due to its invisible information architecture, a well-designed voice interface is designed to be more flexible and adaptable to specific users and use cases, as well as new product features.

5.4   Repetition of Words

In Hindi some words get repeated when asking a question about a variety of options like, When asked Alexa it was not able to process such questions. Eg. but it answer successfully to, which was not the case with Google Home.

5.5   Feedback

Alexa seemed to ask for feedback for a response whenever it was asked, to which the response was perfectly correct but never seemed to ask for feedback for any

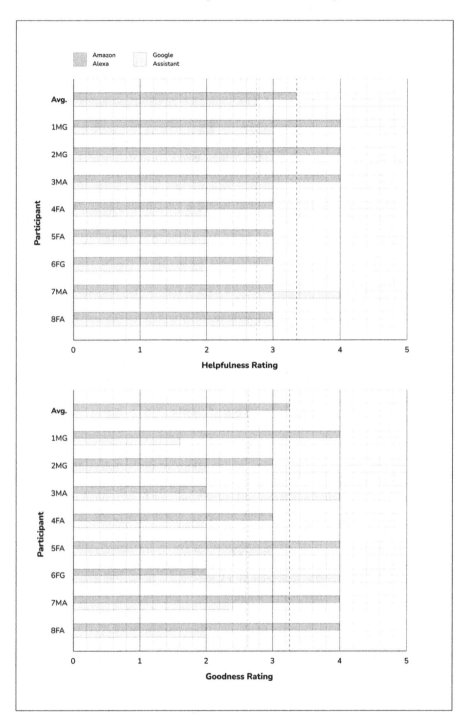

Fig. 14. Comparing the scores given by each of the participants in terms of helpfulness and goodness

other questions even if some of them were similar in nature. But for the later participants it stopped asking for this particular feedback as well. While Alexa asked for feedback when prompted with a specific question, Google assistant never seemed to ask for any in the duration of the entire study.

5.6   Sentence Formation

Even if the words used in the question are same, the placement of words matters makes difference in the response. Eg. when asked, response was whereas for, response was, about Britain's Prime minister Rishi Sunak. The responses were likely to be more successful when the question formation was similar to the structure of what it would have been in English. Usually in hindi, the sentence formation is like, (Noun + Question word + verb) as in whereas in English it is like (Question word + noun + verb) as in "What are you doing?"

5.7   Participant's Breakpoint

The total number of breakpoints for Amazon Alexa were 24 which is significantly higher than Google Assistant that was only 8. In which for Alexa, 13 were due to long responses and 11 due to participants recognizing that the response was either invalid or incorrect. Whereas, for Google assistant, 3 were due to long response and 5 due to invalid or incorrect response. The breakpoints for Alexa mostly occurred when asking for a recipe from alexa.

5.8   Rational for Reframing Questions

The Intention was also to explore the relationship between the "response given by the machine" to the "reiteration of question formed by the human" and understand the rationale behind the human reiterating the question which would explain the requirements for a good and correct answer from a machine and also explore what humans think about how the voice assistants work.

5.9   Rating Assistants Qualitatively

Instead of just getting the participant to rate each device at the end of the session, if they could share their feelings and reasoning for accepting or not accepting an answer and the rationale behind reframing the question. Eg. first they asked to which the response was so they removed the word from the question itself and shortened the question to: to which they got a desired answer .

5.10   Response Expectation

Since in our study the questions were formed by participants themselves and they had the choice to reframe the question or ask again or not, the study has a potential to find out what according to humans is considered as a good answer when given by a machine. Eg. In the question where participants had to ask the location of the place, they were able to get the time it will take to travel by when asked about how to reach there the answers included names of roads and distance from landmarks nearby in km which is not ubiquitous. Person asks and response was but the participant felt satisfied with the response.

5.11 Technological Advancement

Advancements in deep learning and generative AI are set to greatly enhance voice assistants like Alexa and Google Assistant. These technologies can significantly improve natural language understanding, enabling the assistants to generate more accurate and context-aware responses. They can also handle complex queries more effectively, thereby addressing many of the current limitations in voice assistant interactions. This progress will lead to more intuitive and satisfying user experiences, making voice assistants more reliable and versatile in various applications.

6 Conclusion

In this research paper, we explored the human perception of conversational agents' responses to questions in Hindi, a low-resource language. We conducted a user study with 8 participants who interacted with two devices, Google Home and Amazon Echo, and asked them to rate the quality, relevance, and satisfaction of the answers. We found that the participants preferred Amazon Echo over Google Home, as it provided more accurate, informative, and natural responses. We also found that the participants had different expectations and preferences for the answers depending on the type and context of the questions. For example, they valued factual information for location and general knowledge questions, but they also appreciated personalization and humor for personal and opinion questions. We also analyzed the feedback and suggestions from the participants, and identified some areas for improvement and future research, such as providing more local and contextual information, supporting more complex and follow-up questions, and enhancing the voice and tone of the conversational agents.

7 Future Work

The target group selected for the study were people working in a university in Mumbai, Maharashtra employed in the food preparation activities in different hostels of the same university. The population could have been more diverse.

If all the people selected for the study could be given the device for regular use for about a week and from those the most common type of questions were taken out for the study. The sample size of the study could have been larger and more actionable insights could have been generated. But due to constraint of time and lack of previous work we limited our study to these numbers and methods.

Adding more scenarios like when playing a game (song quiz is a common game across both the devices) would help the study.

'Language appropriateness' could be measured with more number of participants. As part of the results of the pilot, it was identified that depending on how the questions were posed, the device may or may not be able to understand. Therefore, it became important to note what are the most common ways of giving the command in a specific scenario and if the smart device was able to give favorable responses to those questions. We listed this metric as 'language appropriateness' to guarantee that the performance of all the assistants was mature under fair and equal circumstances, in which they are evaluated based on if they would be able to understand the most common ways of a question being asked.

It would have been interesting to recruit bilingual participants and give them the same scenarios to work with in both english in hindi and see if framing similar sentences in hindi as formed in english give a better response. Eg. In english the activity expected to be done by the assistant is put forth first using words like tell me, explain, search, play, help, suggest whereas in hindi these words as usually placed at the end of the sentence like

If we did not limit the number of questions that were allowed for a person to be asked in one scenario to 3 and had let them ask any number of questions until they felt satisfied with the response, would help in a better study of satisfaction and patience levels. The only issue with this was that participants had limited time to spare for the study so there was a chance of them losing patience easily. It could be balanced or countered by bringing incentive, by paying some money per hour they might be willing to spare a little more time. Patience is an important factor and might vary from scenario to scenario, Eg. When asking a factual or philosophical question, it would be easy to keep going but for cooking and navigation, when the person is in process of doing what is being told, it is quick to lose patience. Patience can also be measured by how often or after how much time people feel the response is getting stretched and ask the device to stop. Further scope could be to carry a prolonged study with people and help them develop a habit of using these devices in their day-to-day life while recording the conversations with VUIs while complying to the ethical and privacy implications of it.

References

1. Basuroy, T.: Amazon alexa and google assistant were among the most popular digital assistants used by Indians (2024). https://www.statista.com/statistics/1351068/india-voice-enabled-assistantusage/
2. Berdasco, A., López, G., Diaz, I., Quesada, L., Guerrero, L.A.: User experience comparison of intelligent personal assistants: alexa, google assistant, siri and cortana. Proceedings **31**(1) (2019). https://doi.org/10.3390/proceedings2019031051. https://www.mdpi.com/2504-3900/31/1/51
3. Hoy, M.: Alexa, siri, cortana, and more: an introduction to voice assistants. Med. Ref. Serv. Q. **37**, 81–88 (2018). https://doi.org/10.1080/02763869.2018.1404391

4. Inc., A.: Alexa skills kit available online (2024). https://developer.amazon.com/public/

5. Pearson, J., et al.: Streetwise: smart speakers vs human help in public slum settings. In: Proceedings of the 2019 CHI Conference on Human Factors in Computing Systems, CHI '19, pp. 1–13. Association for Computing Machinery, New York (2019). https://doi.org/10.1145/3290605.3300326

6. Pyae, A., Joelsson, T.: Investigating the usability and user experiences of voice user interface: a case of google home smart speaker, pp. 127–131 (2018). https://doi.org/10.1145/3236112.3236130

7. Rajeshwari, S.B., Kallimani, J.S.: Regional language code-switching for natural language understanding and intelligent digital assistants. In: Mekhilef, S., Favorskaya, M., Pandey, R.K., Shaw, R.N. (eds.) Innovations in Electrical and Electronic Engineering. LNEE, vol. 756, pp. 927–948. Springer, Singapore (2021). https://doi.org/10.1007/978-981-16-0749-3_71

Exploring the Impact of Foot-Based Haptic Feedback on User Experience in Virtual Reality Navigation

Nayan Borah[1], Pradnya Mungi[2], R. Sneha[2], Pragya Sachdeva[2], and Pranjal Protim Borah[2(✉)] (iD)

[1] Tezpur University, Tezpur, Assam, India
[2] Indian Institute of Technology (IIT) Jodhpur, Jodhpur, Rajasthan, India
pranjalborah777@gmail.com

Abstract. Haptic feedback in Virtual Reality (VR) navigation transforms the digital experience into an immersive tangible experience. Haptic feedback, particularly on the legs and feet, augments VR experiences by imitating real-world actions, such as stepping on or encountering objects. It is beneficial for training, simulations, therapeutic interventions, and gaming. Providing haptic feedback on feet can not only enhance user immersion and presence but also enable more natural and emotionally involved user experiences. Although the use of haptics is prevalent in VR devices like handheld controllers, its influence on user experience and workload during VR navigation, especially accompanied by vibrotactile feedback on feet, needs further investigation. In this two-phase study, we investigated vibrotactile feedback on feet during VR navigation using a mixed-method approach. This work's results indicate that foot-based haptic feedback enhances participants' perception, spatial awareness, collision information, and path guidance without solely depending on visual feedback while reducing mental and temporal demands and effort.

Keywords: Human-Computer Interaction (HCI) · Virtual Reality (VR) · Multisensory User Experience · Haptic Feedback on Feet

1 Introduction and Background

VR offers users an immersive three-dimensional (3D) environment where interaction is facilitated by stimulating various senses, such as, visual, auditory and tactile, thereby crafting a life-like experience. The richness of this perception is often governed by the fidelity of sensors and actuators employed. Vibrotactile feedback in VR devices refers to the use of vibrations or tactile sensations to provide users with a sense of touch during virtual reality experiences. These sensations are typically generated by vibration motors or actuators embedded in VR controllers or other wearable devices. Including tactile and haptic feedback in

VR applications offers the user a emotionally involved [19] and immersive experience by approximating real-world sensations [6,29]. For instance, augmenting a typical controller functionality with haptic feedback for grasping virtual objects, touching virtual surfaces, and triggering [5] and haptic feedback during simulation training [17]. Similarly, full body experiences, such as heat in the desert or cold in the snow mountain or partial body experiences, such as heating the iron or quenching the hot iron [11]. In comparison, the majority of the VR setups facilitate devices like hand-held controllers [2] and haptic gloves [18], primarily focusing on providing feedback on the hands and upper body, often overlooking the lower body, especially the leg and foot. This omission is noteworthy, considering the potential the foot holds for haptic feedback to offer emotionally involved experiences [30], provided its natural sensitivity to stimuli and the feasibility of embedding miniature devices on footwear. For instance, Strohmeier et al. developed shoes that could simulate walking on different materials, potentially enhancing user experience [28]. In addition, audio feedback is often provided to users along with visual feedback to enhance presence and immersion, especially in VR tasks involving lower limbs, such as walking [15]. For individuals with auditory impairments, limited or no access to audio feedback can affect their overall experience. In this context, providing vibrotactile feedback along with visual feedback has the potential to offer more inclusive VR experiences.

Existing literature underscores a marked preference for vibrotactile feedback on foot over fingertips, asserting its viability for haptic interactions [10]. Unlike hands, which are frequently preoccupied with various tasks, potentially disrupting feedback reception, legs are predominantly free, making them ideal feedback recipients [29]. This potential has been realised with studies delving into the nuances of vibrotactile feedback on foot explorations that promise to revolutionise athletic training and rehabilitation [24]. Innovations such as the bARefoot [28] and RealWalk [27] prototype shoes provide tactile sensations mirroring real-world physical properties like elasticity and friction. Furthermore, innovative methods, such as the one proposed by Chi Wang et al., employ two-dimensional skin stretching techniques to impart haptic sensations on the legs [32]. This increase in vibrotactile feedback innovations is a testament to the number of ways such feedback can enrich VR experiences, especially in domains like motor learning [13]. The continuous presence of this feedback is crucial in ensuring a genuine "realness" in virtual worlds [14], a concept actualized by creations like the Pace-sync shoes by Watanabe and Ando [33], designed to optimize walking rhythms through strategic vibrational cues. Introducing haptic feedback not only amplifies spatial awareness but also enhances overall emotional involvement [19], emotional competences [4], engagement and precision and reduces mental load [22]. Beyond rehabilitation, envisioning a gaming scenario where haptic feedback imitates in-game obstacles could elevate user experiences [8,25]. However, there is a limited investigation of user experience during VR navigation accompanied by haptic feedback on the feet.

In this research work, we took the opportunity to investigate haptic feedback during navigation in a Virtual Environment (VE) and carried out two user studies. We conducted a preliminary study that aims to determine whether participants can differentiate among the three distinct one-point feedback and distinguish between one-point and compound feedback for each foot. Here one-point feedback refers to providing vibrotactile feedback at a single point or location of the foot at a time (using one actuator). In contrast, compound feedback refers to providing vibrotactile feedback at multiple points or locations of the foot at a time (using multiple actuators). We found that, unlike compound feedback, all the participants were able to identify all the three one-point vibrotactile feedback and their respective locations on each foot. Considering these three one-point vibrotactile feedback, we conducted the main study to compare participants' experiences and workload in situations where vibrotactile feedback is provided on feet using the Wizard of Oz approach to instances where no vibrotactile feedback is provided during encounters with obstacles in the VE. In the context of a virtual environment (VE), "encounter" refers to the act of coming into contact with a virtual object within the digital space. We explored three scenarios of encountering an obstacle, including coming across an obstacle either in front, on the sides during forward movement or behind during backward movement. We found that navigation in VE supported by vibrotactile feedback on feet to indicate these encounters with virtual objects improves the participants' perception, spatial awareness, collision information, and path guidance without solely depending on visual feedback and reduces the participants' mental and temporal demands and efforts. The core contribution of this research is the demonstration of how a minimalistic design using three one-point vibrotactile feedback on the foot enhances spatial awareness during navigation in virtual environments. The findings show that this feedback improves obstacle detection and reduces cognitive load compared to scenarios without feedback, offering practical implications for haptic design and human-computer interaction. The findings provide valuable insights for designers and researchers in Haptics and Human-Computer Interaction, highlighting the effectiveness of targeted vibrotactile cues for immersive experiences.

2   Preliminary Study

According to existing literature [3, 9, 20, 26, 31, 33], five primary zones on the feet are commonly utilised for delivering vibrotactile feedback, as depicted in Fig. 1a. Of these, we chose three commonly investigated zones in the existing literature [3, 9] for further investigation, highlighted with green dots in Fig. 1b. We excluded the two zones (highlighted with red in Fig. 1b), primarily the inner side of the feet, considering these areas rarely come into contact with other objects during real-world walking on plane surfaces. Moreover, by focusing on these three selected zones, we aimed to design a more minimalist vibrotactile feedback system. With these zones in consideration, we conducted this preliminary study.

2.1 Methodology

In this work, we investigated two feedback types. Firstly, the 'one-point feedback', wherein vibrotactile feedback is provided to a single location (toes, near the base of little toe, or heel as depicted in Fig. 1d). Conversely, for the 'compound feedback', the vibrotactile feedback was provided simultaneously across all these three locations. This preliminary study aims to determine whether participants can differentiate between the three distinct one-point feedback and distinguish between one-point and compound feedback for each foot. Furthermore, we aim to understand the participants' ability to associate these tactile cues (one-point and compound feedback) with real-life situations, such as encountering obstacles while manoeuvring their feet.

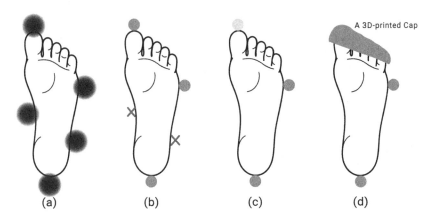

Fig. 1. (a) Five commonly utilized zones on the feet for delivering vibrotactile feedback, (b) three zones selected for further investigation in this research work, (c) weak stimuli on toes using only one vibrotactile actuator and (d) a 3D-printed cap, with a vibration motor mounted on it to envelop the majority of the toes.

Task: The participants were asked to sit comfortably and put on socks equipped with vibrotactile actuators. Their main task involved identifying and reporting the location and type of vibrotactile stimuli they experienced. Additionally, they were asked to share their thoughts regarding the potential of these stimuli to imitate sensations similar to encounters with obstacles within a virtual environment (VE).

Participants: To gather participants for this study, we reached out to university students and invited them for their voluntary participation. A total of 20 students, comprising 10 males and 10 females, aged between 18 to 25 years, participated. Each of these participants had prior experience using VR applications with head-mounted display devices. We selected participants with prior VR experience for this preliminary study to ensure they could primarily focus on perceiving and distinguishing the vibrotactile feedback without needing to be in an immersive setup, while still being able to relate this feedback to collisions scenarios during VR navigation. None of the participants have any known disabilities. No remuneration was provided to the participants.

Apparatus: For this research work, we developed a prototype to provide vibro-tactile feedback on feet. This prototype incorporates three linear resonant actuators (LRA), each measuring 10mm in diameter and 3mm in thickness, for each foot. In this prototype, we utilised a Polylactic Acid (PLA) 3D-printed cap (Fig. 1d), with a vibration motor mounted on it to provide feedback on toes instead of placing a single motor on just one toe (Fig. 1c). The 3D-printed cap ensures a uniform vibration across the majority of the toes. For the location near the base of the little toe, we employed the second LRA. The heel area featured the third LRA of the same specification. This configuration was consistent for both feet. As depicted in Fig. 2a, all the LRAs were attached at the three chosen locations on each sock for better grasp and user perception of vibrations. As illustrated in Fig. 2a, participants wore this feedback system on their feet throughout the experiment.

As showcased in Fig. 2b, these vibrotactile motors were connected to an Arduino Uno microcontroller board via independent output pins. A PWM (Pulse Width Modulation) value of 255 was applied to each LRA vibration motor, resulting in a continuous vibration for a duration of 125 ms. The moderator, using a 4 × 4 matrix membrane keypad linked to the Arduino Uno, could activate these motors by pressing respective buttons.

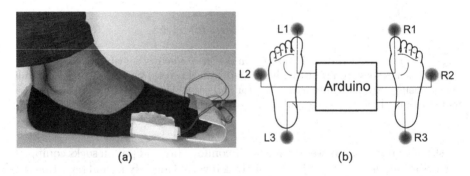

(a)   (b)

Fig. 2. (a) A participant wearing the vibrotactile feedback system on the right foot and (b) a basic block diagram of the feedback system with six LRAs connected to a single micro-controller board.

Procedure: The study was conducted in a controlled environment, adhering to the ethical standards for research involving human subjects. At first, the moderator explained the objectives of the preliminary study to the participants. Subsequently, they were verbally acquainted with the potential scenarios of utilizing haptic feedback on feet, such as, walking or stepping on an object and encountering obstacles while navigating in a VE, which could be in front and to the sides during forward movements or behind during backward movements.

Throughout the experiment, participants were instructed to sit comfortably on a chair (without wearing any VR headset), wear socks equipped with vibrotactile actuators and rest their feet flat on the floor. The moderator initiated the experiment by activating one LRA vibration motor at a time and then all three together on either foot. The participant was then asked to distinguish the feedback as either one-point or compound and then report the precise location of the stimuli they perceived. This process was repeated thrice for each type of feedback on each foot. After completing the identification task, the participant was asked to share his or her opinions regarding the potential of the stimuli to imitate sensations similar to encounters with obstacles by VR avatars during navigation within a VE. The same process was repeated for each participant, with the sequence of feedback randomized. Each session spanned approximately 15 min per participant.

2.2   Results of the Preliminary Study

We analysed the frequency of participants who accurately identified the location and type of vibrotactile stimuli. We also reviewed their responses regarding association with potential scenarios in a VE. We found that all the participants (100%) were able to identify all the one-point vibrotactile feedback and their respective locations on each foot. Conversely, for the compound feedback, 45% (9 out of 20) and 40% (8 out of 20) of the participants were able to accurately distinguish and identify it on the left and right foot, respectively. Analysing the results, we comprehend that since vibrations travel through a medium, giving compound feedback disoriented participants as they struggled to perceive the feedback provided to their feet.

Similarly, based on the participants' verbal responses, we found that the majority of the participants associated the one-point feedback positively with potential obstacle encounters in a VE, whether these obstacles appeared in front (for feedback on toes), to the sides (for feedback near the base of little toe) during forward movement, or behind (for feedback on the heel) during backward movement. Referring to the backward movement, one participant mentioned, "This feedback would be valuable in a shooting game to move backwards without visually monitoring the obstacles behind me". Another participant mentioned, "With these feedback on our feet, we can realise the objects around us and relate to the world". Similar comparisons with real-world scenarios and potential improvements in VR experiences with haptic feedback on lower limbs were also reported in the literature [10]. However, due to the difficulty in distinguishing the compound feedback, the majority of the participants failed to associate it with specific scenarios, such as walking or stepping on an object. One probable reason could be the identical vibration intensity utilised for both one-point and compound feedback. Another probable reason could be the selected feedback locations which are on the edges of the feet instead of the base of the feet. Further investigation on compound feedback on the base of the feet could give promising results. Considering the findings of this preliminary study, we decided to focus solely on one-point feedback for subsequent investigations in this research work.

3   Study on Haptic Feedback During Navigation

This main study aims to compare participants' experiences and workload in situations where vibrotactile feedback is provided on the feet using the Wizard of Oz approach against situations where no vibrotactile feedback is provided during encounters with obstacles in the VE. This study explored three scenarios of encountering obstacles, including coming across obstacles either in front and on the sides during forward movement or behind during backward movement.

3.1   Methodology

Task. The participants were instructed to navigate a predefined path in the Virtual Environment (VE), simulating a plant nursery, while avoiding collisions with surrounding virtual objects such as virtual plants along the way. Each participant navigated this path twice: once with vibrotactile feedback on their feet and once without.

Participants. To gather participants for this study, we reached out to university students and invited them for their voluntary participation. A total of 10 students, comprising 5 males and 5 females, aged between 18 to 23 years (Mean $= 19.7$ and SD $= 1.57$), participated in this study. The participants had no prior experience of using VR applications with head-mounted display devices. We selected participants with no prior VR experience to minimize the bias that could arise from the prior knowledge of experienced participants, particularly regarding joystick-based navigation in VR environments without collision. However, investigating such foot-based haptic feedback with experienced users could also provide promising insights, given their expertise with VR navigation. In this study, none of the participants have any known disabilities. No remuneration was provided to the participants.

Apparatus. For this study, we developed a VE simulating a plant nursery using Unity and Unity Assets Store. The participant, acting as a customer in the virtual plant nursery, was instructed to navigate cautiously to avoid damaging the virtual plants in the surroundings. As depicted in Fig. 3a, the path in the simulated plant nursery consisted of two diagonal trajectories (from the Starting Point to Point A and from Point B to Point C) and two linear trajectories (from Point A to Point B and from Point C to the End Point). Participants were instructed to locomote forward during the diagonal trajectories and the first linear trajectory. For the second linear trajectory, participants were instructed to locomote backward until they reached the End Point. We integrated both diagonal and linear trajectories along with both forward and backward locomotion to cover a comprehensive range of ways of navigation and also to heighten the potential encounters with the surrounding virtual objects. The path's floor colour incorporates multiple shades of the surrounding objects, and the diagonal trajectories' uneven borders make it challenging to estimate the path without cautious navigation. We utilized repeated low-poly objects of varying sizes as virtual plants in the environment to minimize distractions for the user.

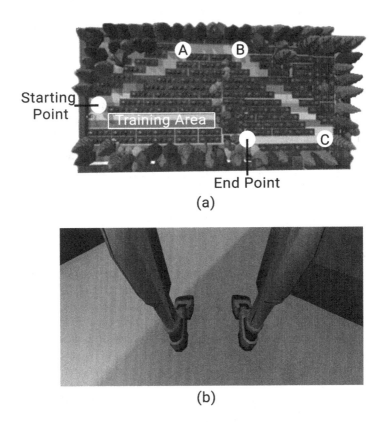

(a)

(b)

Fig. 3. (a) A virtual environment simulating a plant nursery. Here, the straight path marked as Training Area is used during the training of the participants. The other path from the Starting Point to the End Point via A, B, and C points is used during the study. (b) A third-person view of the user's feet in the Virtual Environment using a secondary camera.

The experiment setup includes an Oculus Quest-2 with controllers and a laptop computer. Unity was employed for virtual simulation, running directly on the Oculus Quest-2 headset via a USB Type-C cable. Participants navigated the Virtual Environment (VE) using the hand-held controllers, with locomotion controlled by the left joystick and rotation controlled by the right joystick. We selected this controller-based continuous locomotion technique due to its better spatial awareness [23], and its suitability for limited physical spaces. Additionally, we provided a training area for participants to familiarize themselves with navigation in VR. During this study, we utilized the prototype developed for the preliminary study to provide the vibrotactile feedback on feet. The Wizard of Oz technique [7,34] was used to activate the vibrotactile feedback on a foot when the participant's avatar foot touches or steps on the border of the path in the VE. The moderator observed the participant's avatar through a secondary camera and triggered the respective vibration motor attached to the feet. The secondary camera was placed behind the legs and tilted towards the feet so that the moderator could closely focus on the feet and observe the upcoming collisions, as shown in Fig. 3b. The Avatar's legs and feet are intentionally kept thin to avoid any potential occlusion.

We explored three distinct scenarios involving potential encounters with obstacles. For instance, during backward locomotion, the LRA vibration motor on the heel was activated when the participant approached an obstacle after touching or stepping on the border of the path. Similarly, the LRA vibration motor at the toes was triggered when the participant approached an obstacle in front. Additionally, the LRA vibration motor placed near the base of the little toe of the left foot responded on approaching an obstacle on the left side, while the counterpart on the right foot responded on approaching an obstacle on the right side.

Procedure. The study was conducted in a controlled environment, adhering to the ethical standards for research involving human subjects. At first, the moderator explained the objectives of this study to the participants. Participants were then asked to wear the VR headset and familiarise themselves with using the controllers to navigate within the training area in the VE (Fig. 3a). During this training phase, participants experienced both conditions: navigation with vibrotactile feedback and without vibrotactile feedback. The study commenced once participants reported confidence and were ready to use the controllers' joysticks to navigate in the VE.

The participant was tasked with navigating the path depicted in Fig. 3a without vibrotactile feedback. After completing the plant nursery navigation task, the participant was asked to complete a questionnaire. In the next step, the participant was equipped with the vibrotactile feedback system to provide feedback on feet. The participant was asked to confirm if the participant could perceive the vibrations on feet. Then the participant undertook the same navigation task again, this time with vibrotactile feedback on feet. Upon completion, the participant filled out the same questionnaire based on the experience during navigation that was accompanied by vibrotactile feedback on feet. This sequence of not providing and providing vibrotactile feedback on feet is counterbalanced among the participants.

Since this work focuses on investigating user experience and workload in navigating in a VE accompanied by vibrotactile feedback, we asked a total of eighteen questions to collect participants' responses. A 7-point Likert scale was employed in nine questions to evaluate the participants' experience in terms of perception [24], realism [29], naturalness [16], spatial awareness [29], reliance on visual feedback [24], collision information, path guidance [28], immersiveness [21], and fun. Furthermore, the NASA Task Load Index (NASA TLX) [12] was incorporated to measure participants' perceived workload during the navigation task in the VE. NASA TLX [12] calculates an overall workload score based on a multi-dimensional rating technique, encompassing mental demand, physical demand, temporal demand, performance, effort, and frustration level. We also asked the participants to respond to dichotomous questions regarding the convenience, usefulness, and contribution of vibrotactile feedback towards their decision-making during navigation.

3.2   Results and Discussion

We collected and analysed the participants' ratings on a 7-point Likert Scale for the nine user experience attributes and on a 10-point Likert Scale for the NASA TLX questionnaire. Given that the collected data followed a normal distribution, we employed a parametric test (T-test with a confidence level of 95%) to interpret the collected data.

Based on the T-Test results, statistically significant differences were identified for perception (p = 0.011), spatial awareness (p = 0.002), visual feedback (p = 0.026), collision information (p = 0.006), and path guidance (p = 0.041) among the nine user experience attributes evaluated (Fig. 4a). However, no statistically significant differences were identified for realism (p = 0.111), naturalness (p = 0.051), immersiveness (p = 0.129), and fun (p = 0.05). The results demonstrate that navigation in a Virtual Environment (VE) supported by vibrotactile feedback on feet to indicate encounters with virtual objects enhanced the ability of the participants to recognise and interpret sensory information to avoid collision without solely depending on visual feedback. Similar findings regarding enhanced sensory information were also reported in the literature [24]. While we did not find statistically significant differences in realism, naturalness, immersiveness, and fun, the participants' verbal feedback indicated a positive influence. In this context, one participant mentioned, "This feedback helped me to feel the environment and made things clear to me". Another participant mentioned, "When I feel something on my feet, it appears more real than the usual VR experience". Moreover, according to the results, the vibrotactile feedback on feet also enhances the capability of the participants to be aware of the surroundings in the VE, which aligns with existing literature [29]. In this context, one participant mentioned, "While moving backwards, I was able to get a clear understanding of where the obstacles were and what was behind me". Similar to the findings reported in existing literature [28], providing the vibrotactile feedback on feet also reduces the participants' potential deviation from the intended path. In this context, one participant mentioned, "Getting this feedback helped me to change and orient myself to the right path". However, in this work, we did not investigate user point of view analysis; further investigation in this direction could yield promising findings.

Based on the T-Test results, we also found statistically significant differences for the NASA TLX's mental demand (p = 0.009), temporal demand (p = 0.019), and effort (p = 0.011). However, no statistically significant differences were identified for physical demand (p = 0.083), performance (p = 0.39), and frustration

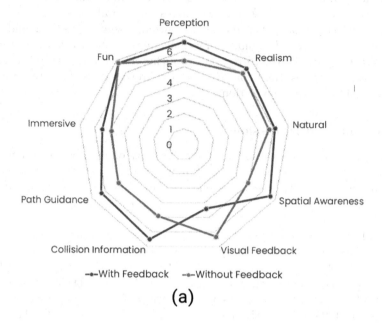

(a)

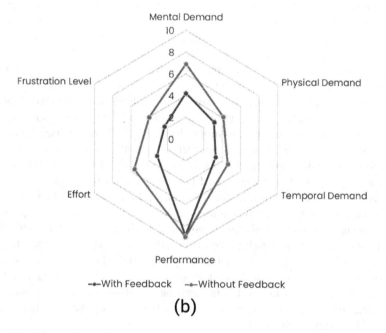

(b)

Fig. 4. (a) Comparison of 9 attributes selected to evaluate user experience and (b) comparison of 6 attributes of NASA TLX.

level (p = 0.061). This indicates that introducing vibrotactile feedback on feet during VR navigation reduces the participants' mental and temporal demands and effort (Fig. 4b). This is consistent with the observation that decreasing reliance on visual cues lessens mental demand and effort. In this context, one participant mentioned, "This feedback on feet makes the navigation task easy, interesting, and fun". Similar findings regarding workload were also reported for haptic feedback on hand [22]. Moreover, the reduced necessity to frequently glance downwards due to the presence of haptic feedback also diminishes the temporal demand. In this context, one participant mentioned, "This feedback makes the task easy as I need to look less on the ground during navigation".

We also calculated the participants' responses to the dichotomous questions regarding convenience, usefulness, and contribution towards decision-making. All participants (100%) stated that the provision of vibrotactile feedback on feet was convenient, useful, and contributed to decision-making during navigation. Similar findings on the usefulness of haptic feedback were also reported in the literature [1]. It was also observed that such feedback simplified the entire navigation process, in particular, making it simpler and less frustrating during backward locomotion. This haptic feedback on the feet indirectly contributed to collision avoidance, closely mimicking one of the essential uses of real-world tactile perception through the feet. According to the participants' verbal responses, this vibrotactile feedback on feet gives them the confidence to navigate easily and enables them to feel an emotionally and physically involved, interesting, immersive and realistic experience of true walking.

4 Conclusion and Future Work

In this work, we carried out two studies to investigate the use of vibrotactile feedback on feet during navigation in a Virtual Environment (VE). The preliminary study aimed to determine whether participants could differentiate between three distinct one-point feedback and distinguish between one-point and compound feedback. We found that all participants were able to differentiate all one-point vibrotactile feedback and identify their specific locations. However, distinguishing compound feedback was found to be more challenging, with only 45% and 40% success on the left and right foot, respectively. According to the participants' verbal responses, the majority of the participants associated the one-point stimuli positively with potential obstacle encounters in the VE.

Building on the results of the preliminary study, our main study on haptic feedback during navigation aimed to compare user experiences and workload in situations where vibrotactile feedback is provided on feet using the Wizard of Oz approach to instances where no vibrotactile feedback is provided during encounters with obstacles in the VE. We explored three scenarios of encountering obstacles, including coming across obstacles either in front and on the sides during forward movement or behind during backward movement. We found that navigation in VE accompanied by vibrotactile feedback on feet to indicate encounters with virtual objects enhances the participants' perception, spatial awareness, collision information, and path guidance without solely depending on visual feedback and reduces the participants' mental and temporal demands and effort. We also found that such feedback simplifies the navigation process, especially making it less frustrating during backward locomotion.

While the findings of this study offer valuable insights for designers and researchers working in the domain of haptics, one major limitation of this work is the application of the Wizard of Oz approach. This method, though effective, may introduce inconsistencies due to human intervention. In our subsequent research, we aim to address this limitation by implementing an automated system, ensuring more consistent and scalable outcomes. We also aim to investigate the challenges associated with compound feedback by exploring a more extensive range of feedback locations and vibration intensities to provide compound feedback.

References

1. Achibet, M., Girard, A., Talvas, A., Marchal, M., Lécuyer, A.: Elastic-arm: human-scale passive haptic feedback for augmenting interaction and perception in virtual environments. In: 2015 IEEE Virtual Reality (VR), pp. 63–68. IEEE (2015)
2. Adilkhanov, A., Rubagotti, M., Kappassov, Z.: Haptic devices: wearability-based taxonomy and literature review. IEEE Access **10**, 91923–91947 (2022)
3. Anlauff, J., Kim, T., Cooperstock, J.R.: Feel-a-bump: haptic feedback for foot-based angular menu selection. In: 2018 IEEE Haptics Symposium (HAPTICS), pp. 175–179. IEEE (2018)
4. Changeon, G., Graeff, D., Anastassova, M., Lozada, J.: Tactile emotions: a vibro-tactile tactile gamepad for transmitting emotional messages to children with autism. In: Isokoski, P., Springare, J. (eds.) EuroHaptics 2012. LNCS, vol. 7282, pp. 79–90. Springer, Heidelberg (2012). https://doi.org/10.1007/978-3-642-31401-8_8
5. Choi, I., Ofek, E., Benko, H., Sinclair, M., Holz, C.: Claw: a multifunctional hand-held haptic controller for grasping, touching, and triggering in virtual reality. In: Proceedings of the 2018 CHI Conference on Human Factors in Computing Systems, pp. 1–13 (2018)
6. Cui, D., Mousas, C.: Evaluating wearable tactile feedback patterns during a virtual reality fighting game. In: 2021 IEEE International Symposium on Mixed and Augmented Reality Adjunct (ISMAR-Adjunct), pp. 328–333. IEEE (2021)
7. Dahlbäck, N., Jönsson, A., Ahrenberg, L.: Wizard of oz studies: why and how. In: Proceedings of the 1st International Conference on Intelligent User Interfaces, pp. 193–200 (1993)
8. Danieau, F., Lécuyer, A., Guillotel, P., Fleureau, J., Mollet, N., Christie, M.: Enhancing audiovisual experience with haptic feedback: a survey on hav. IEEE Trans. Haptics **6**(2), 193–205 (2012)
9. Gibson, A., Webb, A., Stirling, L.: User abilities in detecting vibrotactile signals on the feet under varying attention loads. In: Schmorrow, D.D.D., Fidopiastis, C.M.M. (eds.) AC 2016. LNCS (LNAI), vol. 9743, pp. 322–331. Springer, Cham (2016). https://doi.org/10.1007/978-3-319-39955-3_30
10. Gurari, N., Smith, K., Madhav, M., Okamura, A.M.: Environment discrimination with vibration feedback to the foot, arm, and fingertip. In: 2009 IEEE International Conference on Rehabilitation Robotics, pp. 343–348. IEEE (2009)

11. Han, P.H., et al.: Haptic around: multiple tactile sensations for immersive environment and interaction in virtual reality. In: Proceedings of the 24th ACM Symposium on Virtual Reality Software and Technology, pp. 1–10 (2018)
12. Hart, S.G., Staveland, L.E.: Development of nasa-tlx (task load index): Results of empirical and theoretical research. In: Advances in Psychology, vol. 52, pp. 139–183. Elsevier (1988)
13. Islam, M.S., Lim, S.: Vibrotactile feedback in virtual motor learning: a systematic review. Appl. Ergon. **101**, 103694 (2022)
14. Lind, S., Thomsen, L., Egeberg, M., Nilsson, N., Nordahl, R., Serafin, S.: Effects of vibrotactile stimulation during virtual sandboarding. In: 2016 IEEE Virtual Reality (VR), pp. 219–220. IEEE (2016)
15. Nilsson, N.C., Serafin, S., Steinicke, F., Nordahl, R.: Natural walking in virtual reality: a review. Comput. Entertain. (CIE) **16**(2), 1–22 (2018)
16. Nordahl, R., Nilsson, N.C., Turchet, L., Serafin, S.: Vertical illusory self-motion through haptic stimulation of the feet. In: 2012 IEEE VR Workshop on Perceptual Illusions in Virtual Environments, pp. 21–26. IEEE (2012)
17. Panait, L., Akkary, E., Bell, R.L., Roberts, K.E., Dudrick, S.J., Duffy, A.J.: The role of haptic feedback in laparoscopic simulation training. J. Surg. Res. **156**(2), 312–316 (2009)
18. Perret, J., Vander Poorten, E.: Touching virtual reality: a review of haptic gloves. In: ACTUATOR 2018; 16th International Conference on New Actuators, pp. 1–5. VDE (2018)
19. Pietra, A.: Promoting eco-driving behavior through multisensory stimulation: a preliminary study on the use of visual and haptic feedback in a virtual reality driving simulator. Virt. Real. **25**(4), 945–959 (2021). https://doi.org/10.1007/s10055-021-00499-1
20. Plauché, A., Villarreal, D., Gregg, R.D.: A haptic feedback system for phase-based sensory restoration in above-knee prosthetic leg users. IEEE Trans. Haptics **9**(3), 421–426 (2016)
21. Rahimi, K., Banigan, C., Ragan, E.D.: Scene transitions and teleportation in virtual reality and the implications for spatial awareness and sickness. IEEE Trans. Visual Comput. Graph. **26**(6), 2273–2287 (2018)
22. Ramírez-Fernández, C., Morán, A.L., García-Canseco, E.: Haptic feedback in motor hand virtual therapy increases precision and generates less mental workload. In: 2015 9th International Conference on Pervasive Computing Technologies for Healthcare (PervasiveHealth), pp. 280–286. IEEE (2015)
23. Rantala, J., Kangas, J., Koskinen, O., Nukarinen, T., Raisamo, R.: Comparison of controller-based locomotion techniques for visual observation in virtual reality. Multimodal Technol. Interact. **5**(7), 31 (2021)
24. Recinos, E., Demircan, E.: Understanding human perception of vibrotactile feedback on the foot in a virtual reality framework for applications in sports performance. In: 2021 18th International Conference on Ubiquitous Robots (UR), pp. 205–210. IEEE (2021)
25. Singhal, T., Schneider, O.: Juicy haptic design: vibrotactile embellishments can improve player experience in games. In: Proceedings of the 2021 CHI Conference on Human Factors in Computing Systems, pp. 1–11 (2021)
26. Son, H., Gil, H., Byeon, S., Kim, S.Y., Kim, J.R.: Realwalk: feeling ground surfaces while walking in virtual reality. In: Extended Abstracts of the 2018 CHI Conference on Human Factors in Computing Systems, pp. 1–4 (2018)

27. Son, H., Hwang, I., Yang, T.H., Choi, S., Kim, S.Y., Kim, J.R.: Realwalk: haptic shoes using actuated mr fluid for walking in vr. In: 2019 IEEE World Haptics Conference (WHC), pp. 241–246. IEEE (2019)

28. Strohmeier, P., Güngör, S., Herres, L., Gudea, D., Fruchard, B., Steimle, J.: barefoot: generating virtual materials using motion coupled vibration in shoes. In: Proceedings of the 33rd Annual ACM Symposium on User Interface Software and Technology, pp. 579–593 (2020)

29. Turchet, L., Burelli, P., Serafin, S.: Haptic feedback for enhancing realism of walking simulations. IEEE Trans. Haptics 6(1), 35–45 (2012)

30. Turchet, L., Zanotto, D., Minto, S., Roda, A., Agrawal, S.K.: Emotion rendering in plantar vibro-tactile simulations of imagined walking styles. IEEE Trans. Affect. Comput. 8(3), 340–354 (2016)

31. Vyas, P., Al Taha, F., Blum, J.R., Weill-Duflos, A., Cooperstock, J.R.: Ten little fingers, ten little toes: can toes match fingers for haptic discrimination? IEEE Trans. Haptics 13(1), 130–136 (2020)

32. Wang, C., et al.: Gaiters: exploring skin stretch feedback on legs for enhancing virtual reality experiences. In: Proceedings of the 2020 CHI Conference on Human Factors in Computing Systems, pp. 1–14 (2020)

33. Watanabe, J., Ando, H.: Pace-sync shoes: intuitive walking-pace guidance based on cyclic vibro-tactile stimulation for the foot. Virt. Real. 14, 213–219 (2010)

34. Weiss, A., Bernhaupt, R., Schwaiger, D., Altmaninger, M., Buchner, R., Tscheligi, M.: User experience evaluation with a wizard of oz approach: technical and methodological considerations. In: 2009 9th IEEE-RAS International Conference on Humanoid Robots, pp. 303–308. IEEE (2009)

Investigating Contextual Factors in Technology-Based Solutions Designed to Support Health and Fitness Routines for Older Adults: A Systematic Review

Pallavi Rao[1]([⊠]) [iD], Anirudha Joshi[1] [iD], and Nicole D'Souza[2] [iD]

[1] IDC School of Design, IIT Bombay, Mumbai, India
{pallavi.rao,anirudha}@iitb.ac.in
[2] NMIMS University, Mumbai, India

Abstract. Technology-based solutions can potentially support older adults in managing their health and fitness routines. However, their adoption among this demographic is low. In this systematic review, we explore the research landscape in this domain by investigating 78 publications published over the past decade from two prominent databases. Our primary objective is to understand how these studies integrate essential contextual factors, particularly cultural and socio-economic influences, in their design and development phases. Our analysis identifies various contextual factors, with social factors emerging as a prominent influence. Additionally, our analysis reveals disparities in research across countries with varying levels of economic development. Based on these findings, our recommendations include promoting research initiatives in economically disadvantaged areas, considering older adults' diverse cultural and socio-economic backgrounds and incorporating relevant contextual factors in the design of technology solutions, long-term assessments to gauge the sustained impact of these solutions on older adults.

Keywords: Technology Solutions · Health and Fitness Routines · Older Adults · Contextual Factors · Systematic Review

1 Introduction

Population aging is a global phenomenon. As life expectancies rise, the world is witnessing a shift towards an increase in the older adult demographic. While increasing longevity is a matter to celebrate, studies have found multiple morbidities and disabilities linked to the advancement of age [87]. To live an active and healthy life, older adults need to manage their Health and Fitness (H&F) routines, including physical activities, diet, and health check-ups. Despite the benefits, older adults do not adhere to these routines [67,76,89]. Recognizing this, the role of technology in supporting H&F routines in older adults has gained prominence as a promising avenue for intervention.

© The Author(s), under exclusive license to Springer Nature Switzerland AG 2025
N. Rangaswamy et al. (Eds.): IndiaHCI 2024, CCIS 2337, pp. 161–192, 2025.
https://doi.org/10.1007/978-3-031-80829-6_8

Technology-based solutions can potentially support older adults in engaging in H&F routines. From wearable devices monitoring H&F activities to mobile applications guiding exercise regimens, technology-based solutions promote healthy living among older adults. These solutions can provide real-time feedback and deliver personalized guidance, helping older adults take charge of their H&F goals. Research has shown that while technology-based solutions can assist older adults in adhering to H&F routines, their adoption among this demographic remains low [63, 64, 79, 91, 102]. This can be attributed to the fact that these technologies are often not designed based on older adults' needs, preferences, and prior experiences [43, 49]; also, their involvement in the design process is limited [96].

Additionally, the design of technology-based solutions cannot exist in isolation. Neither can we expect a single solution to work globally. Integrating contextual factors in technology-based solutions is essential to ensure that these solutions align with the needs and preferences of older adults. Contextual factors are "factors which reflect a particular context, characteristics unique to a particular group, community, society and individuals" [11]. They refer to diverse external influences, encompassing cultural norms, socio-economic conditions, individual backgrounds, environmental settings, and other situational elements that impact a specific situation [52]. Investigating social, cultural, and other contextual factors in the design and evaluation is important in mainstream Human-Computer Interaction (HCI) research [52]. Contextual factors help ensure the solutions are relevant and appropriate to the target population. By considering contextual factors, designers can develop solutions better suited to the unique requirements and challenges presented by the specific context. Users are more likely to embrace technologies that fit into their daily lives and address their unique needs and challenges. Older adults are mostly rooted in society and have the least willingness to change. Thus, the importance of contextual factors in the design of technology solutions is much greater for this population.

In light of the intersection between technology-based solutions, healthy aging, and contextual factors in design, we conducted a systematic literature review to examine existing research on technology-based solutions designed to support H&F routines for older adults globally. We review the literature from prominent computing publications. This review does not aim to provide an exhaustive overview of the entire literature across multiple subfields. Instead, we focus on the HCI literature and investigate the existing research on technology-based solutions supporting older adults' H&F routines worldwide. Specifically, we address the following two research questions:

1. What research has been conducted on technology-based solutions designed to support health and fitness routines for older adults on a global scale?
2. To what extent do these research studies incorporate contextual factors, including cultural and socio-economic influences, in designing and developing technology-based solutions for supporting health and fitness routines for older adults?

Through this review, we aim to add to the ongoing discourse about technology's role in fostering healthy aging. We also aim to inspire the development of innovative solutions that cater to the diverse needs of older adults worldwide.

2   Background

2.1   Contextual Factors

Contextual factors are context-specific and have been extensively studied in HCI research. For instance, in a study on reducing technology abuse by adolescents, Hung et al. [53] highlighted contextual factors such as *cultural* and *social influences* affecting technology abuse. Similarly, Jung et al. [61], in their research on designing a personal informatics system for stress management, associate stress with contextual factors such as *location, social setting,* and *time.* Additionally, Padhi et al. [74] found that using the *local language,* a crucial contextual factor, in video interventions, immensely helped enhance parents' involvement in their children's education.

In summary, while the broad concept of contextual factors remains consistent–encompassing various external influences, their relevance can differ significantly depending on the domain in question. In the healthcare domain, previous research suggests that users' socio-cultural background may significantly influence how they think about health and thus should be considered in how health technologies are designed [75]. Harrington and Piper [47] assert that analyzing health technologies through inter-sectional socio-cultural dimensions helps reveal new approaches to technology among various user populations and subgroups within those populations.

2.2   Past Reviews on Technology for Older Adults' Health and Fitness

Several studies have reviewed technologies targeting older adults' health or fitness, each with distinct objectives. For instance, [9] addressed critical challenges in enhancing Human-Computer Interaction within technology-enhanced healthcare systems for older adults, while [96] focused on wearable physical activity tracking systems tailored for this demographic. Additionally, [40] explored the incorporation of the active aging model in research and technology design, [43] provided a comprehensive review with an emphasis on identity dimensions such as ethnicity, age, and socio-economic status, and [73] focused on the uses, challenges, and future directions of digital healthcare technologies for older adults.

Our systematic review is motivated by the work of [43] though we differ in focus and methodology. Our review highlights the significance of contextual factors, including cultural and socio-economic influences, in the design and evaluation of these solutions. In contrast, [43] centers on historically marginalized groups in technology design, emphasizing identity dimensions like ethnicity, age, socio-economic status, and geographic residence.

It is important to distinguish between contextual factors and identity dimensions. Contextual factors encompass diverse external influences that impact situations, extending beyond individual attributes. On the other hand, identity dimensions refer to demographic and socio-economic characteristics shaping an individual's sense of identity. While identity dimensions offer insights into users' backgrounds and their influence on interactions with technology, contextual factors span broader influences, including cultural and environmental contexts. In essence, contextual factors encompass external influences, while identity dimensions are specific demographic and socio-economic attributes shaping an individual's identity and experiences.

3   Method

We explored many full-text databases. As our work aims to provide an overview of designing technology-based solutions, we did not include databases from other fields such as medicine (e.g., PubMed database). Given our emphasis on technology design and development, we prioritized databases that predominantly house research pertinent to HCI and Engineering. Among the databases that predominantly have literature on HCI and Engineering, we chose ACM digital library and IEEE Xplore databases. The search functionalities of these two databases are well-suited for systematic reviews. They allow for precise and efficient retrieval of relevant articles, which is crucial for maintaining the quality and manageability of the review process. Steps to perform this systematic review were taken from [19, 43, 77].

Our primary objective was to explore the body of research dedicated to technology-based solutions tailored to support H&F routines for older adults across the globe. A key focus was determining the extent to which these studies considered contextual factors within their design processes. We specifically concentrated on research studies that focused on technologies intended for use by older adults, as opposed to those aimed at medical professionals in clinical settings or caregivers. Moreover, our review was explicitly focused on H&F routines, not on any ailment-specific solutions.

3.1   Search Strategy

To ensure a comprehensive review, we included a broad range of keywords related to health, fitness, older adults, and technology. The selection was informed by prior literature and brainstorming among the authors, aiming to capture all relevant studies in our targeted research area. This diverse range of terms ensured we encompassed various possibilities and did not overlook significant studies indexed under different terminologies.

The search terms were a combination of the following three areas: 1 - domain ("*health*", "*fitness*", "*physical activity*", "*physical activities*", "*wellness*", "*well-being*"), 2 - population terms ("*older adults*", "*senior citizens*", "*elderly*", "*aging*", "*ageing*"), and 3 - intervention terms ("*design*", "*device*", "*system*", "*technology*", "*wearable*", "*app*", "*mhealth*", "*m-health*", "*mobile health*", "*ehealth*", "*e-health*", "*digital*", "*IoT*", "*chatbot*") to catch all possible papers that may be relevant.

The technology landscape has evolved rapidly over the past decade, with significant advancements in areas such as IoT, wearable devices, and AI, which have profound implications for health and fitness technologies. Hence, our review included research articles published in the last 10 years (between January 2013 and June 2023). By concentrating on the last ten years, we aimed to capture the latest trends, innovations, and design methodologies that are pertinent to contemporary technology-based solutions for older adults.

Table 1 shows the search string applied in ACM and IEEE databases and their results.

3.2 Paper Selection

Our database search returned 199 results from ACM and 336 results from IEEE. Out of the total 535 results returned from the initial search, we excluded 72 results that were abstracts, short papers, posters, tutorials, extended abstracts, demonstrations, panels, work in progress, magazines, books, and early access from both databases, leaving behind only peer-reviewed research articles (conference papers and journal papers). We only selected peer-reviewed research articles as they undergo a rigorous evaluation by experts in the field and also provide comprehensive research results. This process resulted in the selection of 135 papers from ACM and 328 from IEEE, totaling 463 papers.

Title and Abstract Screening. The first two authors decided on the inclusion and exclusion criteria.

We included papers that met the following criteria:

1. Publication Date: Papers published between January 2013 and June 2023. We chose this period to capture the trends in technology over the past decade.
2. Language: Only papers published in English were included.
3. Focus on H&F Technologies: We included papers that specifically discussed, designed, or developed technologies aimed at supporting the H&F routines of older adults.
4. Direct Use by Older Adults: We focused on technologies intended for direct use by older adults themselves.

We excluded papers that met the following criteria:

1. Not relevant to H&F Routines: Papers that did not directly focus on H&F routines were excluded. For instance, studies on leisure activities, privacy concerns, or non-health-related technology use among older adults were not included.
2. Healthcare Settings: We excluded papers focused on healthcare settings, such as hospital-based technologies or patient-centered equipment primarily used by healthcare professionals or caregivers, rather than the older adults themselves.

Table 1. Search string applied at ACM and IEEE databases

Database	Search String	Results
ACM Digital Library	[[Abstract:"health"] OR [Abstract: "fitness"] OR [Abstract: "physical activity"] OR [Abstract: "physical activities"] OR [Abstract: "wellness"] OR [Abstract: "well-being"] OR [Abstract: "wellbeing"]] AND [[Title: "older adults"] OR [Title: "senior citizens"] OR [Title: "elderly"] OR [Title: "aging"] OR [Title: "ageing"]] AND [[Abstract: "design"] OR [Abstract: "device"] OR [Abstract: "system"] OR [Abstract: "technology"] OR [Abstract: "wearable"] OR [Abstract: "app"] OR [Abstract: "mhealth"] OR [Abstract: "m-health"] OR [Abstract: "mobile health"] OR [Abstract: "ehealth"] OR [Abstract: "e-health"] OR [Abstract: "digital"] OR [Abstract: "IoT"]] AND [E-Publication Date: (01/01/2013 TO 06/30/2023)]	Research Article = 135, Abstract = 21, Short Paper = 18, Poster = 14, Tutorial = 5, Extended Abstract = 3/, Demonstration = 1, Panel = 1, Work in Progress = 1
IEEE Xplore	("Abstract":"health" OR "Abstract":"fitness" OR "Abstract":"physical activity" OR "Abstract":"physical activities" OR "Abstract":"wellness" OR "Abstract":"well-being" OR "Abstract":"wellbeing") AND ("Document Title":"older adults" OR "Document Title":"senior citizens" OR "Document Title":"elderly" OR "Document Title":"aging" OR "Document Title":"ageing") AND ("Document Title":"design" OR "Document Title":"device" OR "Document Title":"system" OR "Document Title":"technology" OR "Document Title":"wearable" OR "Document Title":"app" OR "Document Title":"mhealth" OR "Document Title":"m-health" OR "Document Title":"mobile health" OR "Document Title":"ehealth" OR "Document Title":"e-health" OR "Document Title":"digital" OR "Document Title":"IoT")	Conference papers = 306, Journal papers = 22, Magazines = 4, Books = 3, Early access = 1

3. Medical and Disease Management: Papers that focused on medication management, medical care, disease-specific technologies (e.g., diabetes management systems), fall detection/prevention devices, or blood pressure monitoring tools were not included, as our focus was on preventive health and fitness rather than medical treatment or disease management.
4. Mental Health and Cognitive Activities: We excluded studies focusing on mental health interventions, cognitive training, or technologies designed to enhance cognitive functioning.
5. Non-Personal Use Technologies: Papers on smart home designs, ambient assisted living technologies, or similar systems not meant for direct interaction by older adults were excluded. For example, studies on home automation systems controlled by caregivers were not considered relevant.

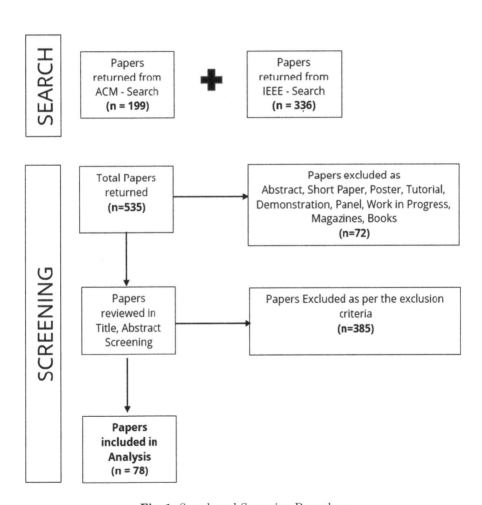

Fig. 1. Search and Screening Procedure

Two coders (the first and the third author) reviewed the titles and abstracts of all 463 papers following the predetermined inclusion and exclusion criteria. Each coder independently evaluated the papers and assigned them one of two codes: "Select" or "Not Select," aligning with the established criteria. When a coder encountered any uncertainty regarding a paper, it was marked as "Discuss." A final decision regarding including such papers in the corpus was reached through mutual discussions. Inter-rater reliability (IRR) was assessed using Cohen's Kappa to ensure the consistency and reliability of the screening process, yielding a high value of 0.95. This screening process identified 78 relevant papers for further analysis, excluding 385 papers based on the exclusion criteria. The complete list of 78 papers selected for the study is given in Appendix A.

Figure 1 shows the search and screening procedure.

3.3   Data Extraction

To address the research questions, the first two authors discussed and established a comprehensive set of codes for extracting essential data from the selected 78 papers. These codes were derived deductively based on the research questions, as explained in [19, 43, 77]. The purpose of using a deductive coding approach was to ensure that our analysis remained focused and aligned with our specific research questions, allowing us to systematically identify and categorize relevant information. While alternative approaches, such as fully open coding, could provide a broader exploratory perspective, our goal was to directly address predefined research questions that required a more structured analysis.

To address the research questions, we would want to extract information on the country of research, type of research, involvement of older adult participants in the study, technologies used/discussed/designed, and contextual factors considered. Accordingly, we identified five primary codes: *Research Country, Type of Research, Involvement of Older Adults, Description of Technologies,* and *Contextual Factors.*

The coding process involved discussing and refining these codes collaboratively with all authors to ensure a common understanding. Notably, *Research Country* primarily denotes the geographic location where the selected papers conducted their study, while *Involvement of Older Adults* serves as a binary indicator (Yes/No) denoting whether older adult participants were involved in the study.

Moving beyond, we further divided *Type of Research* into five distinct subcodes:

1. Exploratory: This includes early-stage research that focuses on understanding older adults, experience reports, and generating design ideas.
2. Design & Evaluation: This includes research centered around designing and evaluating prototypes or products.
3. Evaluative: Papers under this sub-code aim to evaluate previously designed prototypes or developed products.
4. System Development: This includes research primarily focused on the development of technologies.

5. Review: Papers in this sub-code are literature reviews or discourse analyses.

The purpose behind creating these sub-codes was to capture the varied and mutually exclusive methodological approaches employed across the selected papers. Each sub-code represents a unique approach, enriching our understanding of the research landscape in this domain.

Similarly, we divided *Description of Technologies* into diverse sub-codes, reflecting the range of existing technologies discussed in the literature. These sub-codes include *Web & Mobile Apps*, *Assistants*, *AI/ML-based Apps*, *IoT & Wearables*, and *Games*. Each sub-code represents a genre of technology, ensuring a comprehensive overview of the technological landscape associated with H&F routines for older adults. However, these genres may not always be mutually exclusive. For example, *Assistants* can comprise any of the technologies that assist older adults, such as robots, text, or voice assistants/bots. At the same time, these *Assistants* may have been developed using other technologies, such as Artificial Intelligence. The papers were assigned these sub-codes based on the main technology focus of each paper. Furthermore, we introduced an additional sub-code labeled as *No Technologies* for papers that did not specifically discuss any particular technology. Additionally, we included an *Other* sub-code for open coding to accommodate any emerging or unconventional technologies not explicitly captured by the predefined sub-codes. This is to acknowledge the dynamic nature of technological advancements, allowing for flexibility in coding when encountering innovations beyond the initially identified sub-codes.

Lastly, we divided *Contextual Factors* into many sub-codes, informed by insights gained from our prior research involving older adult participants and medical experts [38]. Accordingly, we selected cultural and socio-economic factors such as, *Language*, *Local Tradition & Practices*, *Local Food*, *Social*, *Literacy* and *Access & Affordability*. These sub-codes encompass various contextual factors deemed crucial in the design and development of technology-based solutions for supporting H&F among older adults as observed through our empirical studies. In addition to these sub-codes, we included an *Other* sub-code for open coding to ensure flexibility in accounting for additional, unforeseen contextual factors that may emerge during the analysis.

The complete coding tree, detailing the hierarchical structure of these codes and sub-codes, is provided in Fig. 2. The coding tree ensures a comprehensive and systematic extraction of key information from the corpus.

The first author reviewed all 78 selected papers individually and recorded the details in a shared spreadsheet, summarizing their contents in accordance with the predefined codes. Several papers did not fit into the predefined codes, particularly under *Description of Technologies* and *Contextual Factors*. Hence, the first author conducted an open coding process to capture these emergent concepts.

To ensure the accuracy and consistency of this data, the third author conducted a thorough cross-verification of the data extracted from these 78 papers. This verification encompassed both the predefined codes and the newly identified codes resulting from the open coding process.

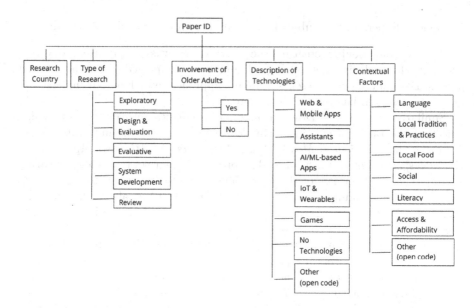

Fig. 2. Coding Tree

4   Results

This section addresses our research questions by discussing the results in four sub-sections.

4.1   Country of Research

Our systematic review offers a comprehensive global perspective on technology-based solutions for older adults, encompassing research from diverse countries. A total of 28 countries were represented in the 78 papers analyzed. Notably, the majority of these studies (n = 15) were conducted in the United States, followed by China (n = 7). Table 2 shows the detailed breakdown of these countries along with their respective per-capita GDP (PPP)[1] ranges and corresponding papers.

Figure 3 further illustrates the global distribution of countries by per-capita GDP range and provides insights into our paper distribution within these categories. Interestingly, while there are 73 countries with a per-capita GDP within the range of 5–20K, our review exhibited a modest representation of only nine papers (from four countries). In contrast, the 20–40K and 40–60K GDP ranges, comprising 27 and 28 countries, showed more substantial representation with 16 papers (from six countries) and 15 papers (from eight countries), respectively. Notably, the 60K+ per-capita GDP range, encompassing 28 countries, had the highest number of papers, totaling 38 (from 10 countries). Our review did not identify any papers from countries with a per-capita GDP below 5K, comprising

---

[1] Gross Domestic Product adjusted for Purchasing Power Parity [2].

42 countries, pointing to a potential research gap in regions with lower economic development.

4.2   Types of Research

As shown in Table 3, most papers belong to the *Exploratory* sub-code (n = 35), followed by *System Development* (n = 23). Within the *Exploratory* sub-code, we observed the involvement of older adults in 28 papers. These studies have adopted diverse methodologies, including interviews, surveys, focus groups,

Table 2. Country of Research

GDP (PPP) range	Country	# of Papers	Papers
5-20K	India	5	[13, 25, 73, 79, 80]
	Philippines	1	[32]
	Sri Lanka	1	[90]
	Brazil	2	[84, 111]
20-40K	Thailand	3	[81, 82, 99]
	China	7	[15, 16, 37, 66, 105–107]
	Mexico	1	[8]
	Chile& Ecuador	1	[18]
	Malaysia	3	[17, 72, 109]
	Greece	1	[31]
40-60K	Portugal	3	[24, 30, 65]
	Spain	2	[7, 57]
	Japan	3	[62, 78, 83]
	New Zealand	1	[39]
	Italy	1	[14]
	UK	3	[69, 71, 97]
	South Korea	1	[56]
	France	1	[50]
60K+	Canada	4	[23, 88, 108, 110]
	Australia	3	[22, 55, 93]
	Belgium	4	[27, 40, 95, 96]
	Sweden	1	[9]
	Germany	3	[6, 35, 54]
	Austria	1	[94]
	Taiwan	4	[42, 68, 98, 104]
	USA	15	[10, 20, 26, 28, 33, 34, 36, 43–48, 70, 103]
	Singapore	2	[58, 100]
	Ireland	1	[29]

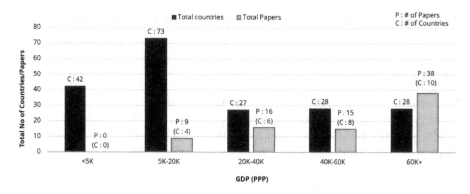

Fig. 3. Distribution of Countries, Research papers by GDP (PPP). The total number of countries taken from [2].

and participatory design/co-design approaches to understand older adults. The remaining seven papers [30,47,88,106–108,110] within this sub-code did not involve older adults in their studies. Instead, these papers delved into various aspects of technology design for older adults. For instance, they explored the merits of participatory design methodologies, ethical challenges associated with technology design for older adults, and behavioral theories relevant to this demographic.

In the *Design & Evaluation* as well as the *Evaluative* types of research, which inherently involve methods incorporating evaluation, active involvement of older adults is commonly observed. However, some evaluations within these codes were conducted using specific checklists, such as usability guidelines, which did not necessarily involve direct participation of older adults.

In the *System Development* type of research, encompassing 23 papers, only eight incorporated older adult participants. Their studies involved older adults either during the initial evaluation of the developed technology [36,50,58,69, 84] or to assess the accuracy of the developed system [95]. Additionally, two studies [13,33] developed their technologies based on input from older adult participants. However, the remaining 15 papers exclusively focused on technology development without involving older adult participants in either the initial design or subsequent evaluation stages.

The *Review* type predominantly comprises literature reviews without direct studies involving older adults. Five of the six papers in this sub-code were systematic reviews, each with distinct objectives. For example, [9] reviewed critical challenges in enhancing Human-Computer Interaction within technology-enhanced healthcare systems for older adults, identifying trust, personal integrity, technology acceptance, e-health literacy, and accessibility as the key challenges. [96] focused on reviewing wearable physical activity tracking systems tailored for this demographic, highlights that most wearable activity trackers are aimed at disease and frailty management than promoting rehabilitation and self-monitoring. [40] looked into incorporating the active aging model in research and technology design, highlighting its strengths and shortcomings to guide future HCI work. [43] provided a comprehensive review in this field, explicitly emphasizing identity dimensions like ethnicity, age, and socio-economic status, highlighting gaps in inclusivity, and suggesting that more diverse participation could improve technology adoption and address health inequities among marginalized populations. [73] explored the digital healthcare technologies for older adults, focusing on their uses, challenges, and future directions. Further, [97] conducted a discourse analysis of aging in HCI, shedding light on potential future research directions.

Table 3. Type of Research

Type of Research	# of Papers	Papers
Exploratory	35	$[10, 14$–$16, 18, 23, 25$–$27, 30, 32, 35, 37, 44$–$48, 65, 66, 70, 71, 79$–$82, 88, 93, 95, 103, 104, 106$–$108, 110]$
Design & Evaluation	4	$[7, 29, 39, 57]$
Evaluative	10	$[6, 8, 20, 22, 28, 34, 54, 55, 72, 78]$
System Development	23	$[13, 17, 24, 33, 36, 42, 50, 55, 56, 58, 62, 68, 69, 83, 84,$ $90, 94, 98$–$100, 105, 109, 111]$
Review	6	$[9, 40, 43, 73, 96, 97]$

4.3   Description of Technologies

Out of the 78 papers reviewed, a significant number ($n = 33$) did not focus on any specific technology. These papers predominantly fell into *Exploratory* or *Review* type of research which are oriented towards broader aspects of the field rather than delving into the intricacies of particular technologies.

Among the papers that did discuss specific technologies, *IoT & Wearables* ($n = 14$) and *Web & Mobile Apps* ($n = 11$) emerged as the most frequently discussed. Eight papers have discussed *Games* - specifically, exercise-based games such as Xbox Kinect [1] and Nintendo Wii [3]. We grouped robots, voice assistants, and chatbots as *Assistants*, and found six papers discussing these technologies. Furthermore, we identified four papers that have implemented applications using AI/ML algorithms. Additionally, two papers delved into the data collected by technologies, contributing to the emergence of *Data* as a new code through open coding. Table 4 shows the technologies and the corresponding papers. *Web & Mobile Apps* have been a focal point of discussion in this research domain since 2013. Majority of the papers in this sub-code were predominantly associated with the design of health management systems. The *Games* sub-code, which primarily featured studies on designing exercises through gaming interfaces, has also been a notable area of exploration since 2013. Research efforts related to *IoT & Wearables* gained prominence starting in 2018, focusing largely on monitoring

Table 4. Description of Technologies

Technology Used	# of Papers	Papers
Web & Mobile Apps	11	$[20, 29, 42, 50, 56, 58, 68, 84, 100, 107, 109]$
Assistants (Chatbots, Robots, Voice assistants)	6	$[10, 39, 45, 46, 69, 83]$
AI/ML-based Apps	4	$[62, 90, 98, 99]$
IoT & Wearables	14	$[7, 13, 17, 24, 36, 54, 57, 80-82, 95, 96, 105, 111]$
Games	8	$[6, 8, 22, 31, 33, 55, 65, 78]$
No Technologies	33	$[9, 14-16, 18, 23, 25-27, 30, 32, 34, 35, 37, 40, 43, 44, 47, 48, 66, 70-73, 79, 88, 93, 97, 103, 104, 106, 108, 110]$
Data	2	$[28, 94]$

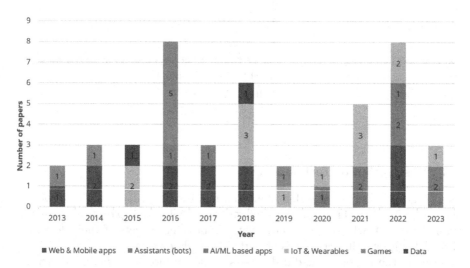

Fig. 4. Technology Trends over the Years

physical activities. Notably, there is an uptrend in studies concerning *AI/ML-based Apps*, centered around personalization of H&F activities, which became more prominent since 2020. Additionally, a recent surge in research related to *Assistants*, encompassing chatbots, robots, and voice assistants, emerged as a noteworthy trend, especially from 2022. Within this sub-code, the primary focus was on assisting older adults in exercises or health information seeking. Despite being identified through open coding, the sub-code *Data* yielded only two papers. Figure 4 shows the technology trends over the years.

4.4   Contextual Factors Considered

Out of 78 papers, 33 (approximately 42%) did not discuss contextual factors. Among these 33 papers that did not discuss contextual factors, IEEE accounts for 21 papers, surpassing ACM's 12 papers. The majority of these papers were primarily focused on either the development of a system or its subsequent evaluation. Additionally, some papers [15,25,30,35,70,71,81,104,108], coded as *Exploratory* type of research, aimed to understand older adults and explore the design of technology-based solutions in this space, but they did not discuss incorporating contextual factors in the design.

Among the 45 papers, that have discussed contextual factors, a significant portion (n = 25) emphasized incorporating social factors in designing technology-based solutions for older adults. Specifically, papers falling under the *Exploratory* type of research [14,23,26,27,48,79,82,95,103,106,110], spanning various countries, emphasized the significance of social factors such as "social interactions within a group", "social sharing of information", "social engagement", and "community involvement" in the lives of older adults. These studies advocated for the inclusion of these factors in the design and development of technology-based solutions. Another cluster of papers, falling under *System Development* type of research [13,33,42,50,84,100], developed technology-based solutions incorporating social factors like community platforms, exercise sharing platforms, applications facilitating interactions with family members, and peer activity tracking. Notably, these studies did not deploy their solutions to assess their impact on older adults. Additionally, some papers [20,22,54] fell under the *Evaluative* type of research, evaluated existing technologies, and discussed the impact of social factors such as "social interactions" and "gamification elements among a social group" in enhancing older adults' engagement with physical activities. Finally, two papers from the *Review* type [96,97] explored the profound impact of social interactions on the general well-being of older adults. Collectively, these papers highlight that social interactions serve as a means of companionship and a motivating factor for promoting healthy aging.

Some papers (n = 9) have addressed the issues related to *Access & Affordability*. Interestingly, seven of these nine papers were conducted in economically developed countries, with only two originating from the Philippines [32] and China [107]. This finding raises significant questions about the research landscape in this domain, particularly in developing countries. While access and affordability are often more pressing concerns for older adults in economically disadvantaged regions, our results suggest that research efforts in some developing countries may be directed toward older adults who already have access to and can afford technologies. Conversely, studies in the developed countries focused on low-income older adults (e.g., [44,47] and marginalized groups (e.g., [88]).

Further, five papers delved into the topic of *Literacy*, which extends beyond traditional literacy and includes health literacy among older adults. These studies have emphasized health literacy as essential in designing technologies [39,88,107] and technology adoption among older adults [9,93]. These studies highlighted the importance of tailoring technologies to accommodate varying levels of literacy among this demographic. All these papers on *Literacy* are from economically developed countries, except one from China [107]. Another five papers emphasized the significance of considering older adults' *Language* diversity while designing technologies. These studies highlighted the need to address language barriers that older adults may encounter while using technologies.

Further, three papers stressed on an understanding of *Local Tradition & Practices* when designing technology-based solutions. These papers discussed game localization [62,78] and advocated for understanding local context [37] in technology design for better adoption and effectiveness.

Notably, we identified six papers that discussed *broad cultural aspects*, comprehensively addressing culture and its significant influence on technology design without getting into specific elements. Additionally, three papers examined the influence of *race and ethnicity*. These papers emphasized the importance of recognizing and addressing potential disparities that may arise due to racial and ethnic differences, thereby promoting more inclusive technology design. Both *broad cultural aspects* and *race and ethnicity* are new codes that emerged through open coding.

Table 5 shows the contextual factors and the corresponding papers. Figure 5 further illustrates the distribution of papers for each contextual factor among economically developed and developing countries.

Table 5. Contextual Factors

Contextual Factors	# of Papers	Papers
Language	5	[39, 72, 79, 80, 88]
Local Tradition & Practices	3	[37, 62, 78]
Social	25	[10, 13, 14, 20, 22, 23, 26, 27, 29, 33, 42, 48, 50, 54, 79, 82, 84, 88, 95– 97, 100, 103, 106, 110]
Literacy	5	[9, 39, 88, 93, 107]
Access & Affordability	9	[32, 40, 43, 44, 47, 65, 88, 107, 110]
Broad cultural aspects	6	[14, 16, 18, 46, 66, 84]
Race, Ethnicity	3	[10, 43, 45]

Some papers have addressed multiple contextual factors. For instance, in [79], authors highlighted *Language* as a barrier to technology use and *Social* activities as a significant motivator for physical activity among older adults. [43]'s systematic review discussed *Access & Affordability*, *Race*, and *Ethnicity* (referred as identity dimensions). In a study on developing an assistive robot [39], discussions included the health and technical *Literacy* of older adults and the importance of *Language* in design. Further, while discussing ethical challenges in aging and technology, [88] discusses the importance of considering *Literacy*, *Affordability*, *Language*, and *Social* activities in designing age-related technologies. [110],

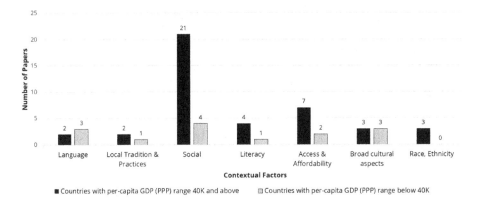

Fig. 5. Contextual Factors considered between Developed and Developing Countries

focused on requirements for technology-supported healthy aging, discussed contextual factors like *Social* relations and *Affordability*. Lastly, the importance of considering *Literacy* and *Affordability* was emphasized in a discussion about mismatches of product design with older adults' needs [107].

While most of the papers explicitly discussed contextual factors, we found two exceptions. [72], which focused on designing mobile exergames for older adults, integrated *Language* into the design guidelines, although this was not explicitly discussed by the authors. Similarly, [62] centered on developing stick exercises for older adults in Japan without explicitly mentioning these exercises are based on a *Local Practice* in Japan.

Finally, despite coding *Local Food* under contextual factors (as shown in Fig. 2), our review did not find any papers discussing its role in the design of technology-based solutions.

5 Discussion

Our review presents a focused effort to assess the global landscape of technology solutions designed to support H&F routines of older adults. Despite the increasing global population of older adults, our analysis found only 78 relevant papers published over the past decade from the two databases selected. This number is relatively modest compared to the extensive research in fields like Human-Computer Interaction for Development (HCI4D) or Information Communication Technology for Development (ICT4D). Although studies concerning the H&F of older adults do intersect with HCI4D and ICT4D in several contexts, it is important to recognize that older adults do not uniformly face the same barriers as marginalized populations. While some older adults may face similar challenges, such as access, affordability, and literacy, others face unique issues like mobility limitations and difficulties with technology adoption. Consequently, research focused on older adults warrants specific attention due to the distinct needs of this demographic. Preventive healthcare for older adults is becoming an increasingly important area of research, highlighting the need to improve technological support for older adults in maintaining their H&F regimens.

Our analysis identifies significant implications for research and practice in designing technology-based solutions to support the H&F of older adults and avenues for future research. These are discussed in detail below.

5.1   Promoting Research in Economically Disadvantaged Areas: Lot of Opportunities

Several HCI labs in developing countries, including India, have conducted extensive research on various health topics such as women's health, mental health, and disease-specific healthcare, addressing challenges like access, affordability, and literacy (e.g., [12,59,60,86,92]). However, similar research focused on the H&F of older adults remains limited, leaving a significant gap in preventive healthcare research that specifically addresses these challenges for older adults in economically disadvantaged regions.

While the percentage of the aging population in developing countries is smaller than in developed ones, the absolute numbers are more significant than in developed nations. There is concern that these countries may experience demographic aging before achieving significant economic growth. Preventive healthcare measures are often overlooked in many developing countries due to the absence of immediate health implications and the urgent need to treat existing illnesses within the population [101].

The scarcity of research from regions with lower economic development raises questions about the inclusivity of research efforts in this field, emphasizing the need for increased contributions from these countries. Research on technology for older adults has primarily been conducted in economically developed regions, where the context may differ significantly from less developed areas. To address this gap, funding agencies should support research initiatives in preventive healthcare for older adults, facilitating the development of impactful projects that effectively bridge this critical research gap.

Moreover, *Access & Affordability* and *Literacy* are pressing concerns for older adults in economically disadvantaged regions. However, our analysis revealed that of the 14 papers discussing these contextual factors, only two originated from developing countries (China and the Philippines). This disparity suggests a difference in research focus between economically developed and developing countries. While the former may concentrate on optimizing existing solutions for their aging populations, the latter struggles with broader challenges. Even the two papers from developing countries focus on older adults from middle-class segments who already have access to and can afford technologies. Our findings align with the assertion made in two studies from India [79,80], indicating that research in developing countries often targets older adults who already have access to and can afford technologies. Therefore, more research is needed to explore access, affordability, and literacy issues in relation to the H&F of older adults in economically disadvantaged regions.

5.2 Incorporating Contextual Factors in Technology Design: Mixed Findings

Contextual factors are frequently discussed in HCI research. The need to consider relevant contextual factors is greater in designing H&F solutions than other solutions, as various factors significantly influence individual outcomes.

Our analysis showed that several papers report contextual factors pertinent to H&F among older adults. However, a significant portion of the papers, mainly focusing on implementing technology solutions, failed to incorporate contextual factors into their tech solutions. Notably, this trend was more prominent in papers from the IEEE database, which predominantly focuses on technology development, compared to those in the ACM database. It is also possible that papers predominantly focused on technology development have incorporated some contextual factors (e.g., location, an essential feature in fitness apps) but did not mention them in their paper.

We are not arguing that past research that has not considered contextual factors in technology design for older adults is wrong or of poor quality. Instead, we emphasize the crucial role of identifying and incorporating relevant contextual factors in designing technology-based solutions catering to H&F of older adults. There is a huge opportunity in this area, as much remains to be explored. One advantage of including contextual factors in the design and development of technology-based solutions is it can significantly influence the adoption of such solutions among older adults, as discussed in several papers (e.g., [9, 14, 27, 37, 43, 66, 79, 80, 82, 93]).

The importance of contextual factors is notably higher for older adults, who tend to have established habits, such as food preferences. Surprisingly, our review found no papers discussing *Local Food* in technology design, despite the widespread availability of food and nutrition-related content online. *Local Food* plays a crucial role in the daily lives of individuals, reflecting their cultural heritage, dietary preferences, and nutritional intake. It is closely tied to older adults' cultural identity and well-being. The lack of research on this topic highlights a significant gap in our understanding of the relationship between older adults, technology-based solutions, and dietary practices.

HCI researchers should address this gap by exploring how technology can be designed to support diverse food practices among older adults. Artificial Intelligence (AI) can play a pivotal role by enabling the creation of databases of local recipes, offering personalized meal planning that incorporates traditional foods, and providing tailored nutritional information based on local diets. AI-driven health monitoring technologies like wearables or mobile health apps can combine real-time health data with local food recommendations to offer personalized dietary advice. By integrating *Local Food* considerations into technology design, we can promote healthier eating habits and enhance the overall well-being of older adults across different regions.

Older adults are also habituated to their *Local Tradition & Practices*. However, our review found only three papers discussing this aspect. Local traditions and practices represent rich cultural heritage and can significantly impact overall

H&F. For instance, in various Indian cultural traditions, including those observed by older adults, traditional dance practices (such as *Garbha* [5], *Bhangra* [4] and many more) are commonly performed during festivals across different Indian subcultures, promoting physical activity. These dance practices are primarily performed together in a community, enhancing social interactions. Many similar local traditions are practiced by older adults in communities worldwide. Our review has shown that such social interactions are a motivating factor for promoting healthy aging. Thus, integrating these traditional practices into regular community engagement may enhance overall fitness among older adults. Additionally, many cultures have traditional exercises that contribute to fitness and well-being. Technology-based community interventions can be developed to organize regular events promoting these practices, thus enhancing physical activity and social interaction among older adults. Exploring the incorporation of *Local Tradition & Practices* into technology design can thus help preserve cultural heritage while fostering healthier lifestyles among older adults worldwide.

However, there are challenges associated with integrating these practices into tech solutions. These traditions may need rigorous validation. We do not advocate for immediate deployment but aim to highlight future opportunities for such integration. Our focus is on identifying areas for exploration, emphasizing the need for careful study and validation before broader implementation. Given the enduring nature of these traditions, passed down through generations, they present valuable insights for potential integration into technology-based H&F solutions. They are deeply ingrained in cultural practices and have demonstrated value in promoting engagement and social interaction. This could offer motivational benefits and improved adherence to fitness routines. For instance, Japan's stick exercise tracking system [62], which aligns with Japanese cultural practices, is a promising example observed in our review.

5.3 Involving Older Adults in the Design Process: Methodological Considerations

Our review identified two categories of papers: those that did not involve older adult participants and those that did. The papers that did not involve older adult participants primarily focused on system development, revealing a disconnect between technology development and user-centric design. These studies often emphasize emerging technologies like IoT, wearables, AI/ML-based applications, and chatbots, which promise personalized support-an essential feature for older adults. However, they often prioritize algorithmic advancements over direct user engagement, neglecting to assess whether design decisions align with older adults' specific needs, preferences, and contexts.

Holtzblatt and Beyer [51] stress the importance of understanding users within their context, arguing that "because life and technology are so closely knit, users must be understood in their own context." They caution that traditional data-gathering techniques with fixed questions and predefined tasks can "take the user out of context," failing to capture the real-life situations in which they interact with technology.

Capturing users' authentic experiences, needs, and behaviors within their natural environment is crucial for designing solutions that support their daily lives. To bridge the gap between technological innovation and the unique needs of older adults, involving them actively throughout the design process using various methodologies is essential.

Researchers capture users' experiences, behaviors, and interactions through qualitative research methods such as Grounded Theory [41], Thematic Analysis [21], Contextual Design [51], and Participatory Design [85]. These approaches often involve interviews, contextual inquiry, observations, or focus groups to collect data. Grounded Theory and Thematic Analysis focus on analyzing data to identify patterns or develop theories. At the same time, Contextual Design and Participatory Design emphasize understanding user context and involving users directly in the design process. Notably, designers play a more active role in contextual design than participatory design.

Our review also identified numerous papers that involved older adult participants, either in preliminary research to understand their needs or in evaluating the solutions post-development. Methods such as semi-structured interviews [23,45,71,79,80,103], contextual inquiry [65], and focus group studies [14,16,78] have been effectively used to include older adults in the design process. However, these studies are conducted in various parts of the world, making transferring findings across different cultural contexts challenging. Embracing these approaches in localized contexts can address culture-specific challenges, such as H&F routines. For instance, when designing technology solutions that reflect older adults' dietary habits and preferences, engaging local community members is crucial. Involving community members in the design process ensures that healthcare interventions address specific needs, preferences, and cultural considerations, leading to more effective solutions for larger groups.

Some papers have employed participatory and co-design approaches involving communities in the design process [10,18,26,39,44,48,70,95]. These approaches emphasize community-based experiences and position older adults as co-creators rather than mere consumers of technology. By promoting collaboration between designers and end-users, participatory methods facilitate ongoing feedback and iterative improvements to technology solutions, potentially leading to designs more attuned to users' contextual needs. For example, in designing H&F apps for older adults, Harrington et al. [48] demonstrate how co-design amplifies the benefits of user-centered design by providing older adults-often an overlooked demographic in technology development-with a platform to contribute their voice and input.

In conclusion, to effectively design technology solutions that resonate with older adults, it is essential to bridge the gap between technological innovation and the specific needs of this demographic. Involving older adults throughout the design process, using diverse methods, ensures that their voices are heard and their unique contexts are understood. By doing so, researchers and designers can develop more inclusive, contextually relevant, and user-centered technologies that truly enhance older adults' well-being and quality of life.

5.4   Addressing the Absence of Longitudinal Studies: Critical Gaps and Future Directions

Longitudinal interventional studies are relatively rare in HCI research related to healthcare. While our review identified numerous papers involving older adults, most of these studies primarily focus on the design or evaluation of technology rather than on long-term impacts. Surprisingly, we found only two papers [29,43] that conducted longitudinal field studies with older adult participants. In [29], the authors reported findings from a 5-month home deployment of a technology designed to help older adults manage their health and receive feedback on their well-being. Although the study did not assess the application's direct health benefits, the authors suggested that long-term adherence to self-management tools is achieved through personalization. Similarly, in [43], researchers carried out longitudinal interventions that included personalized training sessions to help overcome barriers to using wearable activity trackers. Post-intervention observations indicated that these trackers positively influenced some participants' physical activities.

In healthcare, it is crucial not only to design technology solutions that consider the context of older adults but also to assess how these solutions affect their adherence to H&F routines and overall well-being over time. Long-term studies are essential for understanding the sustained impact of these technologies. However, several challenges arise when conducting such studies.

Firstly, maintaining participant engagement over extended periods can be challenging, especially with older adults who may experience fluctuating health. Participant dropout rates can impact the reliability of findings. Secondly, continuous data collection and monitoring over months or even years require substantial resources, including time, funding, and specialized equipment, which may not always be readily available. Despite these challenges, research efforts should prioritize understanding the long-term effects of these solutions on the H&F routines of older adults. Longitudinal studies provide valuable insights for the ongoing refinement of technology-based interventions. By focusing on long-term assessments, researchers can contribute to a deeper understanding of the challenges and opportunities in enhancing the well-being of older adults, ultimately leading to the development of more effective and sustainable technology solutions for this population.

6   Limitations

We recognize and acknowledge certain limitations in our systematic review. Firstly, our paper selection process was confined to two prominent databases, ACM and IEEE. While these databases are reputable sources for research in HCI and related fields, and our review included a substantial number of papers (78) from these sources, it is important to acknowledge the potential limitation that valuable research articles may be present in other databases beyond our selection. However, our focus on these two databases helped us to understand the importance, trends, and potential future avenues of integrating contextual factors in designing technology solutions for the H&F of older adults.

Secondly, research on aging in HCI has a long history. However, as we aimed to focus on the recent trends and developments in this domain, our review is limited to research conducted within the last 10 years. While this approach helps to understand current trends, it might not cover all research in this diverse field.

7   Conclusion

The aging population worldwide exhibits diverse cultural practices, economic situations, and social contexts, necessitating tailored approaches. Our review highlights the critical importance of integrating relevant contextual factors when designing technology-based solutions to support H&F for older adults. Doing so not only empowers older adults to manage their H&F routines effectively but also foster greater acceptance and utilization of these solutions, thereby addressing pertinent challenges.

By discussing implications for both research and practice and providing future research directions, we shed light on critical areas that demand attention from the HCI community. Researchers and practitioners can collaborate and develop solutions that cater to the multifaceted needs of older adults worldwide, ultimately enhancing their overall quality of life.

References

1. Kinect (2023). https://en.wikipedia.org/wiki/Kinect. Accessed 1 Sept 2023
2. List of countries by gdp (ppp) per capita (2023). https://en.wikipedia.org/wiki/List_of_countries_by_GDP_(PPP)_per_capita. Accessed 1 Sept 2023
3. Wii (2023). https://en.wikipedia.org/wiki/Wii. Accessed 1 Sept 2023
4. Bhangra (dance) (2024). https://en.wikipedia.org/wiki/Bhangra_(dance). Accessed 1 Feb 2024
5. Garba (dance) (2024). https://en.wikipedia.org/wiki/Garba_(dance). Accessed 1 Feb 2024
6. Barenbrock, A., Herrlich, M., Malaka, R.: Design lessons from mainstream motion-based games for exergames for older adults. In: 2014 IEEE Games Media Entertainment, pp. 1–8 (2014). https://doi.org/10.1109/GEM.2014.7048096
7. Sarria-Ereño, A., Méndez-Zorrilla, A., García-Zapirain, B., Gialelis, J.: Wearable sensor-based system to promote physical activity among elderly people. In: 2015 IEEE International Symposium on Signal Processing and Information Technology (ISSPIT), pp. 100–104 (2015). https://doi.org/10.1109/ISSPIT.2015.7394248
8. Velazquez, A., Martinez-Garcia, A.I., Favela, J., Hernandez, A., Ochoa, S.F.: Design of exergames with the collaborative participation of older adults. In: Proceedings of the 2013 IEEE 17th International Conference on Computer Supported Cooperative Work in Design (CSCWD), pp. 521–526 (2013). https://doi.org/10.1109/CSCWD.2013.6581016

9. Ahmad, A., Mozelius, P.: Critical factors for human computer interaction of EHealth for older adults. In: Proceedings of the 5th International Conference on E-Society, e-Learning and e-Technologies, ICSLT 2019, pp. 58–62. Association for Computing Machinery, New York (2019). https://doi.org/10.1145/3312714.3312730

10. Antony, V.N., Cho, S.M., Huang, C.M.: Co-designing with older adults, for older adults: robots to promote physical activity. In: Proceedings of the 2023 ACM/IEEE International Conference on Human-Robot Interaction, HRI 2023, pp. 506–515. Association for Computing Machinery, New York (2023). https://doi.org/10.1145/3568162.3576995

11. Barzilai-Nahon, K., Gomez, R., Ambikar, R.: Conceptualizing a contextual measurement for digital divide/s: using an integrated narrative. In: Handbook of Research on Overcoming Digital Divides: Constructing an Equitable and Competitive Information Society, pp. 630–644. IGI Global (2010)

12. Bhatnagar, G., Singh, P., Kumar, N., Tuli, A.: Unpacking tensions in designing annotation system for public toilets to support menstrual mobilities. In: Proceedings of the 2022 International Conference on Information and Communication Technologies and Development, pp. 1–6 (2022)

13. Bhayana, R., Agrawal, K., Aggarwal, M., Devgon, R., Kar, R.: Sahayak: an application for social and physical well-being for the elderly. In: Proceedings of the 11th Indian Conference on Human-Computer Interaction, IndiaHCI 2020, pp. 124–129. Association for Computing Machinery, New York (2021). https://doi.org/10.1145/3429290.3429300

14. Buccoliero, L., Bellio, E.: The adoption of "Silver" e-health technologies: first hints on technology acceptance factors for elderly in Italy. In: Proceedings of the 8th International Conference on Theory and Practice of Electronic Governance, ICEGOV 2014, pp. 304–307. Association for Computing Machinery, New York (2014). https://doi.org/10.1145/2691195.2691303

15. Li, C., Xu, S.: Interaction design for smart healthcare system considering older adults' healthy and wellbeing lifestyles. In: 2020 IEEE 2nd Eurasia Conference on Biomedical Engineering, Healthcare and Sustainability (ECBIOS), pp. 151–153 (2020). https://doi.org/10.1109/ECBIOS50299.2020.9203625

16. Li, C., Xu, S.: How older adults' user experiences of smart healthcare system are affected by their cultural differences. In: 2021 IEEE 3rd Eurasia Conference on Biomedical Engineering, Healthcare and Sustainability (ECBIOS), pp. 100–104 (2021). https://doi.org/10.1109/ECBIOS51820.2021.9510513

17. Hew, C.W., Ramasamy, M.: Development of a IoT based low cost wearable smart health monitoring system for elderly. In: 2022 IEEE 8th International Conference on Smart Instrumentation, Measurement and Applications (ICSIMA), pp. 42–47 (2022). https://doi.org/10.1109/ICSIMA55652.2022.9929133

18. Cajamarca, G., Herskovic, V., Lucero, A., Aldunate, A.: A co-design approach to explore health data representation for older adults in Chile and Ecuador. In: Proceedings of the 2022 ACM Designing Interactive Systems Conference, DIS 2022, pp. 1802–1817. Association for Computing Machinery, New York (2022). https://doi.org/10.1145/3532106.3533558

19. Carrera-Rivera, A., Ochoa-Agurto, W., Larrinaga, F., Lasa, G.: How-to conduct a systematic literature review: a quick guide for computer science research. MethodsX p. 101895 (2022)

20. Chaudhry, B.M., Dasgupta, D., Chawla, N.: Formative evaluation of a tablet application to support goal-oriented care in community-dwelling older adults. Proc. ACM Hum.-Comput. Interact. **6**(MHCI) (2022). https://doi.org/10.1145/3546743
21. Clarke, V., Braun, V.: Thematic analysis. J. Posit. Psychol. **12**(3), 297–298 (2017)
22. Cyarto, E.V., Batchelor, F., Baker, S., Dow, B.: Active ageing with avatars: a virtual exercise class for older adults. In: Proceedings of the 28th Australian Conference on Computer-Human Interaction, OzCHI 2016, pp. 302–309. Association for Computing Machinery, New York (2016). https://doi.org/10.1145/3010915.3010944
23. Kappen, D.L., Nacke, L.E., Gerling, K.M., Tsotsos, L.E.: Design strategies for gamified physical activity applications for older adults. In: 2016 49th Hawaii International Conference on System Sciences (HICSS), pp. 1309–1318 (2016). https://doi.org/10.1109/HICSS.2016.166
24. Lourenço, D., Postolache, O.: IoT health status monitoring system for elderly people. In: 2021 International Conference on e-Health and Bioengineering (EHB), pp. 1–4 (2021). https://doi.org/10.1109/EHB52898.2021.9657727
25. Padaliya, D., Arya, B.: Usage of mHealth apps for meditation: a study on older adults. In: 2022 2nd International Conference on Innovative Sustainable Computational Technologies (CISCT), pp. 1–4 (2022). https://doi.org/10.1109/CISCT55310.2022.10046544
26. Davidson, J.L., Jensen, C.: What health topics older adults want to track: a participatory design study. In: Proceedings of the 15th International ACM SIGACCESS Conference on Computers and Accessibility, ASSETS 2013. Association for Computing Machinery, New York (2013). https://doi.org/10.1145/2513383.2513451
27. D'Haeseleer, I., Gerling, K., Schreurs, D., Vanrumste, B., Vanden Abeele, V.: Ageing is not a disease: pitfalls for the acceptance of self-management health systems supporting healthy ageing. In: Proceedings of the 21st International ACM SIGACCESS Conference on Computers and Accessibility, ASSETS 2019, pp. 286–298. Association for Computing Machinery, New York (2019). https://doi.org/10.1145/3308561.3353794
28. Doyle, J., Caprani, N., Bond, R.: Older adults' attitudes to self-management of health and wellness through smart home data. In: Proceedings of the 9th International Conference on Pervasive Computing Technologies for Healthcare, PervasiveHealth 2015, pp. 129–136. ICST (Institute for Computer Sciences, Social-Informatics and Telecommunications Engineering), Brussels (2015)
29. Doyle, J., Walsh, L., Sassu, A., McDonagh, T.: Designing a wellness self-management tool for older adults: results from a field trial of your wellness. In: Proceedings of the 8th International Conference on Pervasive Computing Technologies for Healthcare, PervasiveHealth '14, pp. 134–141. ICST (Institute for Computer Sciences, Social-Informatics and Telecommunications Engineering), Brussels (2014). https://doi.org/10.4108/icst.pervasivehealth.2014.254950
30. Spanakis, E.G., Santana, S., Ben-David, B., Marias, K., Tziraki, C.: Persuasive technology for healthy aging and wellbeing. In: 2014 4th International Conference on Wireless Mobile Communication and Healthcare - Transforming Healthcare Through Innovations in Mobile and Wireless Technologies (MOBIHEALTH), pp. 23–23 (2014). https://doi.org/10.1109/MOBIHEALTH.2014.7015899

31. Konstantinidis, E.I., Billis, A.S., Mouzakidis, C.A., Zilidou, V.I., Antoniou, P.E., Bamidis, P.D.: Design, implementation, and wide pilot deployment of fitforall: an easy to use exergaming platform improving physical fitness and life quality of senior citizens. IEEE J. Biomed. Health Inform. **20**(1), 189–200 (2016). https://doi.org/10.1109/JBHI.2014.2378814

32. Albina, E.M., Hernandez, A.A.: Assessment of the elderly on perceived needs, benefits and barriers: inputs for the design of intelligent assistive technology. In: 2018 16th International Conference on ICT and Knowledge Engineering (ICT&KE), pp. 1–10 (2018). https://doi.org/10.1109/ICTKE.2018.8612447

33. Ofli, F., Kurillo, G., Obdržálek, Š, Bajcsy, R., Jimison, H.B., Pavel, M.: Design and evaluation of an interactive exercise coaching system for older adults: lessons learned. IEEE J. Biomed. Health Inform. **20**(1), 201–212 (2016). https://doi.org/10.1109/JBHI.2015.2391671

34. Franklin, A., Myneni, S.: Engagement and design barriers of MHealth applications for older adults. In: Proceedings of the Technology, Mind, and Society. TechMindSociety 2018. Association for Computing Machinery, New York (2018). https://doi.org/10.1145/3183654.3183695

35. Fronemann, N., Pollmann, K., Weisener, A., Peissner, M.: Happily ever after: positive aging through positive design. In: Proceedings of the 9th Nordic Conference on Human-Computer Interaction. NordiCHI 2016. Association for Computing Machinery, New York (2016). https://doi.org/10.1145/2971485.2996740

36. Boateng, G., Batsis, J.A., Proctor, P., Halter, R., Kotz, D.: GeriActive: wearable app for monitoring and encouraging physical activity among older adults. In: 2018 IEEE 15th International Conference on Wearable and Implantable Body Sensor Networks (BSN), pp. 46–49 (2018). https://doi.org/10.1109/BSN.2018.8329655

37. Peng, G., Sepulveda Garcia, L.M., Nunes, M., Zhang, N.: Identifying user requirements of wearable healthcare technologies for Chinese ageing population. In: 2016 IEEE International Smart Cities Conference (ISC2), pp. 1–6 (2016). https://doi.org/10.1109/ISC2.2016.7580787

38. Gadahad, P.R., Joshi, A.: "so, should i walk today or not?" understanding concerns and queries on health and fitness among Indian older adults. In: Indian Conference on Human-Computer Interaction, pp. 23–49. Springer, Heidelberg (2023). https://doi.org/10.1007/978-981-97-4335-3_2

39. Gasteiger, N., et al.: Participatory design, development, and testing of assistive health robots with older adults: an international four-year project. J. Hum.-Robot Interact. **11**(4) (2022). https://doi.org/10.1145/3533726

40. Gerling, K., Ray, M., Abeele, V.V., Evans, A.B.: Critical reflections on technology to support physical activity among older adults: an exploration of leading HCI venues. ACM Trans. Access. Comput. **13**(1) (2020). https://doi.org/10.1145/3374660

41. Glaser, B., Strauss, A.: Discovery of Grounded Theory: Strategies for Qualitative Research. Routledge, Abingdon (2017)

42. Wu, H.-K., Yu, N.-C., Tsai, C.-H.: The development of a sport management and feedback system for the healthcare of the elderly. In: 2017 IEEE International Conference on Consumer Electronics - Taiwan (ICCE-TW), pp. 401–402 (2017). https://doi.org/10.1109/ICCE-China.2017.7991165

43. Harrington, C., Martin-Hammond, A., Bray, K.E.: Examining identity as a variable of health technology research for older adults: a systematic review. In: Proceedings of the 2022 CHI Conference on Human Factors in Computing Systems. CHI 2022. Association for Computing Machinery, New York (2022), https://doi.org/10.1145/3491102.3517621

44. Harrington, C.N., Borgos-Rodriguez, K., Piper, A.M.: Engaging low-income African American older adults in health discussions through community-based design workshops. In: Proceedings of the 2019 CHI Conference on Human Factors in Computing Systems, CHI 2019, pp. 1–15. Association for Computing Machinery, New York (2019). https://doi.org/10.1145/3290605.3300823

45. Harrington, C.N., Egede, L.: Trust, comfort and relatability: understanding black older adults' perceptions of chatbot design for health information seeking. In: Proceedings of the 2023 CHI Conference on Human Factors in Computing Systems. CHI 2023. Association for Computing Machinery, New York (2023). https://doi. org/10.1145/3544548.3580719

46. Harrington, C.N., Garg, R., Woodward, A., Williams, D.: "It's Kind of Like Code-Switching": black older adults' experiences with a voice assistant for health information seeking. In: Proceedings of the 2022 CHI Conference on Human Factors in Computing Systems. CHI 2022. Association for Computing Machinery, New York (2022). https://doi.org/10.1145/3491102.3501995

47. Harrington, C.N., Piper, A.M.: Informing design through sociocultural values: co-creation with low-income African-American older adults. In: Proceedings of the 12th EAI International Conference on Pervasive Computing Technologies for Healthcare, PervasiveHealth 2018, pp. 294–298. Association for Computing Machinery, New York (2018). https://doi.org/10.1145/3240925.3240966

48. Harrington, C.N., Wilcox, L., Connelly, K., Rogers, W., Sanford, J.: Designing health and fitness apps with older adults: examining the value of experience-based co-design. In: Proceedings of the 12th EAI International Conference on Pervasive Computing Technologies for Healthcare, PervasiveHealth 2018, pp. 15–24. Association for Computing Machinery, New York (2018). https://doi.org/10.1145/3240925.3240929

49. Helbostad, J.L., et al.: Mobile health applications to promote active and healthy ageing. Sensors **17**(3), 622 (2017)

50. Hina, M.D., Ramdane-Cherif, A., Dourlens, S.: Serious gaming: autonomy and better health for the elderly. In: Proceedings of the 17th International Conference on Computer Systems and Technologies 2016, CompSysTech 2016, pp. 245–252. Association for Computing Machinery, New York (2016). https://doi.org/10.1145/2983468.2983519

51. Holtzblatt, K., Beyer, H.: Introduction. In: Holtzblatt, K., Beyer, H. (eds.) Contextual Design: Evolved, pp. 1–3. Springer, Cham (2015). https://doi.org/10.1007/978-3-031-02207-4_1

52. Huh, J., Ackerman, M.S., Erickson, T., Harrison, S., Sengers, P.: Beyond usability: taking social, situational, cultural, and other contextual factors into account. In: CHI '07 Extended Abstracts on Human Factors in Computing Systems, pp. 2113–2116. ACM, San Jose (2007). https://doi.org/10.1145/1240866.1240961

53. Hung, M.W., et al.: To use or abuse: opportunities and difficulties in the use of multi-channel support to reduce technology abuse by adolescents. Proc. ACM Hum.-Comput. Interact. **6**(CSCW1), 1–27 (2022)

54. Buchem, I., Merceron, A., Kreutel, J., Haesner, M., Steinert, A.: Gamification designs in Wearable Enhanced Learning for healthy ageing. In: 2015 International Conference on Interactive Mobile Communication Technologies and Learning (IMCL), pp. 9–15 (2015). https://doi.org/10.1109/IMCTL.2015.7359545

55. Garcia, J.A., Sundara, N., Tabor, G., Gay, V.C., Leong, T.W.: Solitaire fitness: design of an asynchronous exergame for the elderly to enhance cognitive and physical ability. In: 2019 IEEE 7th International Conference on Serious Games and Applications for Health (SeGAH), pp. 1–6 (2019). https://doi.org/10.1109/SeGAH.2019.8882471

56. Jung, J., Lee, J., Lee, J., Kim, Y.T.: Personalized health support system for elderly people based on an application for the web and smartphone. In: The 18th IEEE International Symposium on Consumer Electronics (ISCE 2014), pp. 1–2 (2014). https://doi.org/10.1109/ISCE.2014.6884297

57. Carús, J.L., Peláez, V., García, S., Á. Fernández, M., Díaz, G., Álvarez, E.: A non-invasive and autonomous physical activity measurement system for the elderly. In: 2013 IEEE 10th International Conference on Ubiquitous Intelligence and Computing and 2013 IEEE 10th International Conference on Autonomic and Trusted Computing, pp. 619–624 (2013). https://doi.org/10.1109/UIC-ATC.2013.101

58. Li, J., Erdt, M., Lee, J.C.B., Vijayakumar, H., Robert, C., Theng, Y.-L.: Designing a digital fitness game system for older adults in community settings. In: 2018 International Conference on Cyberworlds (CW), pp. 296–299 (2018). https://doi.org/10.1109/CW.2018.00061

59. Joshi, A., et al.: Supporting treatment of people living with hiv/aids in resource limited settings with ivrs. In: Proceedings of the SIGCHI Conference on Human Factors in Computing Systems, pp. 1595–1604 (2014)

60. Joshi, A., et al.: Design opportunities for supporting treatment of people living with HIV/AIDS in India. In: Campos, P., Graham, N., Jorge, J., Nunes, N., Palanque, P., Winckler, M. (eds.) INTERACT 2011. LNCS, vol. 6947, pp. 315–332. Springer, Heidelberg (2011). https://doi.org/10.1007/978-3-642-23771-3_24

61. Jung, G., Park, S., Lee, U.: Deepstress: supporting stressful context sensemaking in personal informatics systems using a quasi-experimental approach. In: Proceedings of the CHI Conference on Human Factors in Computing Systems, pp. 1–18 (2024)

62. Oi, K., Nakamura, Y., Matsuda, Y., Fujimoto, M., Yasumoto, K.: Short stick exercise tracking system for elderly rehabilitation using IMU sensor. In: 2022 2nd International Workshop on Cyber-Physical-Human System Design and Implementation (CPHS), pp. 13–18 (2022). https://doi.org/10.1109/CPHS56133.2022.9804564

63. Kalimullah, K., Sushmitha, D.: Influence of design elements in mobile applications on user experience of elderly people. Procedia Comput. Sci. 113, 352–359 (2017)

64. Kekade, S., et al.: The usefulness and actual use of wearable devices among the elderly population. Comput. Methods Programs Biomed. 153, 137–159 (2018)

65. Costa, L.V., Veloso, A.I.: "Game-based psychotherapy" for active ageing: a game design proposal in non-game context. In: 2016 1st International Conference on Technology and Innovation in Sports, Health and Wellbeing (TISHW), pp. 1–8 (2016). https://doi.org/10.1109/TISHW.2016.7847788

66. Lan, Z., Liu, H., Yang, C., Liu, X., Sorwar, G.: Investigating influencing factors of chinese elderly users' intention to adopt MHealth based on the UTAUT2 model. In: Proceedings of the Fourth International Conference on Biological Information and Biomedical Engineering. BIBE2020. Association for Computing Machinery, New York (2020). https://doi.org/10.1145/3403782.3403798

67. Laranjo, L., et al.: Do smartphone applications and activity trackers increase physical activity in adults? systematic review, meta-analysis and metaregression. Br. J. Sports Med. 55(8), 422–432 (2021)

68. Lee, M.P., Hu, H.Y., Jafar, N.: Life chasing: a location-based game prototype for elderly health promotion. In: Proceedings of the International Conference on Healthcare Service Management 2018, ICHSM 2018, pp. 265–271. Association for Computing Machinery, New York (2018). https://doi.org/10.1145/3242789. 3242834

69. Lotfi, A., Langensiepen, C., Wada, Y.S.: Active and healthy ageing: development of a robotic platform as an exercise trainer. In: Proceedings of the 10th International Conference on PErvasive Technologies Related to Assistive Environments, PETRA 2017, pp. 275–279. Association for Computing Machinery, New York (2017). https://doi.org/10.1145/3056540.3076195

70. Martin-Hammond, A., Vemireddy, S., Rao, K.: Engaging older adults in the participatory design of intelligent health search tools. In: Proceedings of the 12th EAI International Conference on Pervasive Computing Technologies for Healthcare, PervasiveHealth 2018, pp. 280–284. Association for Computing Machinery, New York (2018). https://doi.org/10.1145/3240925.3240972

71. McNeill, A., Briggs, P., Pywell, J., Coventry, L.: Functional privacy concerns of older adults about pervasive health-monitoring systems. In: Proceedings of the 10th International Conference on PErvasive Technologies Related to Assistive Environments, PETRA 2017, pp. 96–102. Association for Computing Machinery, New York (2017). https://doi.org/10.1145/3056540.3056559

72. Pindeh, N., Kamaruddin, A., Norowi, N.M., Rahmat, R.W.O.: Exploring design guidelines of mobile exergame for older adults. In: 2022 8th International HCI and UX Conference in Indonesia (CHIuXiD), vol. 1, pp. 71–76 (2022). https:// doi.org/10.1109/CHIuXiD57244.2022.10009875

73. Nautiyal, S., Shrivastava, A., Deka, C., Chauhan, P.: Role of digital healthcare in the well-being of elderly people: a systematic review. In: Proceedings of the 13th Indian Conference on Human-Computer Interaction, IndiaHCI 2022, pp. 30–41. Association for Computing Machinery, New York (2023). https://doi.org/10. 1145/3570211.3570214

74. Padhi, D.R., Jhunja, R., Joshi, A.: Enabling adults with less education to support their child's education through hyperlocal educational videos. In: Proceedings of the 32nd Australian Conference on Human-Computer Interaction, pp. 210–219 (2020)

75. Perchonok, J., Montague, E.: The need to examine culture in health technology. In: Proceedings of the Human Factors and Ergonomics Society Annual Meeting, vol. 56, pp. 1847–1851. SAGE Publications Sage CA, Los Angeles (2012)

76. Podder, V., et al.: Physical activity patterns in India stratified by zones, age, region, BMI and implications for COVID-19: a nationwide study. Ann. Neurosci. **27**(3–4), 193 (2020)

77. Purssell, E., McCrae, N.: How to perform a systematic literature review: a guide for healthcare researchers, practitioners and students. Springer, Heidelberg (2020)

78. Pyae, A., Liukkonen, T.N., Saarenpää, T., Luimula, M., Granholm, P., Smed, J.: When Japanese elderly people play a finnish physical exercise game: a usability study. J. Usabil. Stud. **11**(4), 131–152 (2016)

79. Rao, P., Joshi, A.: Design opportunities for supporting elderly in India in managing their health and fitness post-COVID-19. In: Proceedings of the 11th Indian Conference on Human-Computer Interaction, IndiaHCI 2020, pp. 34–41. Association for Computing Machinery, New York (2021). https://doi.org/10.1145/ 3429290.3429294

80. Rao Gadahad, P., Joshi, A.: Wearable activity trackers in managing routine health and fitness of Indian older adults: exploring barriers to usage. In: Nordic Human-Computer Interaction Conference. NordiCHI 2022. Association for Computing Machinery, New York (2022). https://doi.org/10.1145/3546155.3546645

81. S. Phetnuam, C. Pintavirooj, S. Tungjitkusolmun: design and development of equipment wrist and forearm physical therapeutic in elderly persons. In: 2018 11th Biomedical Engineering International Conference (BMEiCON), pp. 1–5 (2018). https://doi.org/10.1109/BMEiCON.2018.8609991

82. Srizongkhram, S., Shirahada, K., Chiadamrong, N.: Critical factors for adoption of wearable technology for the elderly: case study of Thailand. In: 2018 Portland International Conference on Management of Engineering and Technology (PICMET), pp. 1–9 (2018). https://doi.org/10.23919/PICMET.2018.8481990

83. Sun, S., Obo, T., Loo, C.K., Kubota, N.: Health promotion using smart device interlocked robot partners for elderly people. In: 2016 Joint 8th International Conference on Soft Computing and Intelligent Systems (SCIS) and 17th International Symposium on Advanced Intelligent Systems (ISIS), pp. 317–322 (2016). https://doi.org/10.1109/SCIS-ISIS.2016.0073

84. dos Santos, M.M.T., Antonelli, H.L., Rodrigues, S.S., de O. Silva, C.L., Fortes, R.P.M., Castro, P.C.: Personalizing health-related ICT interface and application: older adults and elderly caregivers preferences. In: Proceedings of the 7th International Conference on Software Development and Technologies for Enhancing Accessibility and Fighting Info-Exclusion, DSAI 2016, pp. 331–338. Association for Computing Machinery, New York (2016). https://doi.org/10.1145/3019943.3019991

85. Schuler, D., Namioka, A.: Participatory Design: Principles and Practices. CRC Press, Boca Raton (1993)

86. Sinha Deb, K., et al.: Is india ready for mental health apps (mhapps)? a quantitative-qualitative exploration of caregivers' perspective on smartphone-based solutions for managing severe mental illnesses in low resource settings. PLoS ONE **13**(9), e0203353 (2018)

87. Sivaraju, S., Moneer, A., Gangadharan, K.R., Syamala, T., Supriya, V., Nidhi, G.: Caring for our elders: early responses India ageing report - 2017 (2017). https://india.unfpa.org/sites/default/files/pub-pdf/India%20Ageing%20Report%20-%202017%20%28Final%20Version%29.pdf. Accessed 21 Feb 2022

88. Sixsmith, A.: Ethical challenges in aging and technology. In: Proceedings of the 15th International Conference on PErvasive Technologies Related to Assistive Environments, PETRA 2022, pp. 552–555. Association for Computing Machinery, New York (2022). https://doi.org/10.1145/3529190.3534756

89. Sullivan, A.N., Lachman, M.E.: Behavior change with fitness technology in sedentary adults: a review of the evidence for increasing physical activity. Front. Public Health **4**, 289 (2017)

90. Sitparoopan, T., Chellapillai, V., Arulmoli, J., Chandrasiri, S., Kugathasan, A.: Home bridge - smart elderly care system. In: 2021 2nd International Informatics and Software Engineering Conference (IISEC), pp. 1–5 (2021). https://doi.org/10.1109/IISEC54230.2021.9672411

91. Talukder, M.S., Sorwar, G., Bao, Y., Ahmed, J.U., Palash, M.A.S.: Predicting antecedents of wearable healthcare technology acceptance by elderly: a combined sem-neural network approach. Technol. Forecast. Soc. Chang. **150**, 119793 (2020)

92. Tuli, A., Dalvi, S., Kumar, N., Singh, P.: "it'sa girl thing" examining challenges and opportunities around menstrual health education in India. ACM Trans. Comput.-Hum. Interact. (TOCHI) **26**(5), 1–24 (2019)

93. Khan, U.R., Zia, T., Perera, K.: An exploratory study of the role of eHealth in healthy ageing. In: 2016 IEEE 18th International Conference on e-Health Networking, Applications and Services (Healthcom), pp. 1–5 (2016). https://doi.org/10.1109/HealthCom.2016.7749422

94. Urbauer, P., Frohner, M., David, V., Sauermann, S.: Wearable activity trackers supporting elderly living independently: a standards based approach for data integration to health information systems. In: Proceedings of the 8th International Conference on Software Development and Technologies for Enhancing Accessibility and Fighting Info-Exclusion, DSAI 2018, pp. 302–309. Association for Computing Machinery, New York (2018). https://doi.org/10.1145/3218585.3218679

95. Vargemidis, D., Gerling, K., Abeele, V.V., Geurts, L., Spiel, K.: Irrelevant gadgets or a source of worry: exploring wearable activity trackers with older adults. ACM Trans. Access. Comput. **14**(3) (2021). https://doi.org/10.1145/3473463

96. Vargemidis, D., Gerling, K., Spiel, K., Abeele, V.V., Geurts, L.: Wearable physical activity tracking systems for older adults-a systematic review. ACM Trans. Comput. Healthcare **1**(4) (2020). https://doi.org/10.1145/3402523

97. Vines, J., Pritchard, G., Wright, P., Olivier, P., Brittain, K.: An age-old problem: examining the discourses of ageing in hci and strategies for future research. ACM Trans. Comput.-Hum. Interact. **22**(1) (2015). https://doi.org/10.1145/2696867

98. Chang, W.-J., et al: iFitness: a deep learning-based physical fitness motion detection system for elderly people. In: 2021 IEEE 10th Global Conference on Consumer Electronics (GCCE), pp. 458–459 (2021). https://doi.org/10.1109/GCCE53005.2021.9621944

99. Sansrimahachai, W.: Personalized walking exercise support system for elderly based on machine learning. In: 2020 17th International Joint Conference on Computer Science and Software Engineering (JCSSE), pp. 6–11 (2020). https://doi.org/10.1109/JCSSE49651.2020.9268327

100. Wang, D., Tan, A.H.: EHealthPortal: a social support hub for the active living of the elderly. In: Proceedings of the 2nd International Conference on Crowd Science and Engineering, ICCSE 2017, pp. 19–25. Association for Computing Machinery, New York (2017). https://doi.org/10.1145/3126973.3126989

101. Wang, F., Wang, J.-D., Huang, Y.-X.: Health expenditures spent for prevention, economic performance, and social welfare. Heal. Econ. Rev. **6**(1), 1–10 (2016). https://doi.org/10.1186/s13561-016-0119-1

102. Wang, S., et al.: Technology to support aging in place: Older adults' perspectives. In: Healthcare, vol. 7, p. 60. Multidisciplinary Digital Publishing Institute (2019)

103. Wang, X., Knearem, T., Carroll, J.M.: Never stop creating: a preliminary inquiry in older adults' everyday innovations. In: Proceedings of the 13th EAI International Conference on Pervasive Computing Technologies for Healthcare, PervasiveHealth 2019, pp. 111–118. Association for Computing Machinery, New York (2019). https://doi.org/10.1145/3329189.3329192

104. Wu, I.Y., Yu, Y., Cheng, S.J., Tu, W.J., Sung, T.J.: Acceptance and sustainability of health promotion solutions for the elderly in Taiwan: evidence from SHI-LIN elderly university in Taipei. In: Proceedings of the 12th ACM International Conference on PErvasive Technologies Related to Assistive Environments, PETRA 2019, pp. 21–27. Association for Computing Machinery, New York (2019). https://doi.org/10.1145/3316782.3321529

105. Yi, X., Yan, Z., Zhou, X., Liu, Y., Huang, F., Liu, Z.: Design of intelligent wearable devices for the elderly based on ARM. In: 2023 3rd Asia-Pacific Conference on Communications Technology and Computer Science (ACCTCS), pp. 263–266 (2023). https://doi.org/10.1109/ACCTCS58815.2023.00047

106. Zeng, X., Liao, Y., Wu, Q.: Study on the design strategy of outdoor fitness equipment for elderly users. In: 2020 International Conference on Artificial Intelligence and Electromechanical Automation (AIEA), pp. 469–473 (2020). https://doi.org/10.1109/AIEA51086.2020.00106

107. Lin, Y.-X., Zhang, B.-Y.: Research on health education plate design for elderly based on QFD and TRIZ. In: 2022 15th International Symposium on Computational Intelligence and Design (ISCID), pp. 114–117 (2022). https://doi.org/10.1109/ISCID56505.2022.00033

108. Yang, M.: Supporting physical activity in later life: perspectives from older adults. SIGACCESS Access. Comput. (135) (2023). https://doi.org/10.1145/3584732.3584736

109. Dahari, Z., et al.: Development of smart elderly care mobile application for health management system. In: 2022 IEEE International Conference on Artificial Intelligence in Engineering and Technology (IICAIET), pp. 1–6 (2022). DOIurl-https://doi.org/10.1109/IICAIET55139.2022.9936853

110. Wei, Z., Liu, Y., Liu, L., Yu, E., Mylopoulos, J., Chang, C.K.: Understanding requirements for technology-supported healthy aging. In: 2020 IEEE First International Workshop on Requirements Engineering for Well-Being, Aging, and Health (REWBAH), pp. 47–56 (2020). https://doi.org/10.1109/REWBAH51211.2020.00017

111. Zimmermann, L.C., Rodrigues, K.R.d.H., Pimentel, M.D.G.C.: EPARS: elderly physical activity reminder system using smartphone and wearable sensors. In: Adjunct Proceedings of the 2019 ACM International Joint Conference on Pervasive and Ubiquitous Computing and Proceedings of the 2019 ACM International Symposium on Wearable Computers, UbiComp/ISWC 2019 Adjunct, pp. 1139–1145. Association for Computing Machinery, New York (2019). https://doi.org/10.1145/3341162.3350845

Is ChatGPT Ready for Indian-Language Speakers? Findings From a Preliminary Mixed Methods Study

C. R. Chaitra[(✉)] [iD], Prajna Upadhyay [iD], and Dipanjan Chakraborty [iD]

BITS Pilani Hyderabad Campus, Secunderabad, India
{p20210024,prajna.u,dipanjan}@hyderabad.bits-pilani.ac.in

Abstract. Recent developments in Artificial Intelligence (AI) technology, especially Generative AI (GenAI), are helping individuals in content generation and collaborative work, thus enhancing the quality of the work. In this paper, we investigate if ChatGPT, one of the most popular GenAI tools, is ready to cater to the capabilities, expectations and needs of the non-English speaking, emergent users of digital technologies. To understand this space among non-English speakers, we conducted a user study with 15 non-English speakers in the state of Telangana, India. To assess the experience of emergent users using ChatGPT, we set them tasks of querying ChatGPT, and contrasted it with the same tasks on Google, a traditional search engine. We asked them to rate the platforms for ease of use and the understanding of the users' language. We draw insights from the study through user ratings of the interactions and logging user observations during the interactions. We derive a few design recommendations for designers and researchers working on voice-based conversational GenAI tools.

Keywords: ChatGPT · Google · Indian Language

1 Introduction

Recent advancements in conversational AI, particularly Generative AI and GPT models, have transformed how users interact with technology and complete everyday tasks, such as writing emails, completing assignments, and more [25]. While extensive literature highlights the benefits of these tools for literate users across various domains [11,23,25,42], the effectiveness of ChatGPT as an information-seeking tool for non-English speakers and low-literate users remains under-explored. This study aims to evaluate whether ChatGPT can serve as an effective alternative information-seeking tool for non-English users, focusing specifically on its ease of use and language comprehension capabilities[1].

---

[1] The 'Information Seeking Process' is defined as a series of cognitive and behavioural steps that include problem identification, need articulation, query formulation, and results evaluation in order to find and extract useful information from various sources, such as the Web. An Information Seeking tool is a tool or group of tools which facilitate information-seeking [13].

N. Rangaswamy et al. (Eds.): IndiaHCI 2024, CCIS 2337, pp. 193–214, 2025.
https://doi.org/10.1007/978-3-031-80829-6_9

With the rise of Generative AI, large language models (LLMs) like ChatGPT are increasingly influencing content generation and collaborative work [32,39,46]. GenAI tools, like ChatGPT, offer voice support, offering significant advantages to non-English language speakers and oral literates [34]. This demography of emergent users, often lacking reading and writing skills, can benefit greatly from this technology, reshaping the landscape of learning methodologies. While numerous scholars, students, and proficient individuals are embracing diverse AI tools to enhance efficiency, one question arises: can these productivity-boosting AI tools be accessible to individuals with low literacy levels or those who primarily communicate in non-English languages? Historically, it has been documented that when significant progress is made in digital technologies, market dynamics result in user groups with lower resources and capabilities being left behind, thus widening the digital divide [17,22]. While technological progress offers a great number of advantages, one persistent challenge remains: bridging the gap between technological advancements and user capabilities.

In this paper, we aim to assess how ready ChatGPT is for non-English speaking emergent users, which can provide leads into whether emergent users are a group of interest for the designers of the ChatGPT interfaces. For this, we wish to understand if ChatGPT can cater to the information-seeking behaviour and expectations of emergent users in comparison to searching on a popular search engine: Google. We compare the interactions with Google as Google is one of the de-facto information-seeking platforms for these users, and the users are more familiar with Google than any other information-seeking platforms [31]. To understand this, we attempt to answer the following research question:

RQ: Is the quality of experience and interactions with ChatGPT and Google influenced by:

(a) Non-English Language
(b) Gender
(c) Age
(d) Educational Background

To answer the question, we conducted a mixed methods study with 15 users. The study comprised a structured interview with emergent users and a user observation study with tasks set for the users on ChatGPT and Google Search. We draw the findings from the interviews, user ratings of the interaction and observation logs. We wish to clarify that we are evaluating the suitability of the ChatGPT application with Non-English speakers and not evaluating its performance against Natural Language Processing benchmarks like MEGA [1] and MEGAVERSE [2]. The study is described in detail in Sect. 3.

2 Related Work

2.1 Information Seeking Behaviour of Emergent Users

Information seeking involves searching, finding and retrieving information. Various theories have been proposed to understand the information-seeking behaviours of individuals. Zipf's Theory of Least Effort suggests that the users tend to use information systems which require less effort to understand and use [70]. Brenda Dervin's Sense-Making theory postulates that information-seeking is a personal and contextual process influenced by an individual's situation, emotions, and past experiences [19]. Chatman [10] postulates that people belonging to marginalized communities rely on trusted, close-knit sources and are less likely to seek out or accept information that challenges their existing beliefs. This theory has been validated by other researchers as well [21]. Robinson's [60] research on information-seeking behaviour in the workplace suggests that people rely on other people and also information systems, spending an equal amount of time with both the sources (people and information systems). These theories highlight that both the literacy level and the socio-cultural context of users play crucial roles in shaping information-seeking behaviour and the effectiveness of information systems. Literate users can easily navigate information systems and efficiently find the information they are looking for, whereas semi-literate and emergent users face certain challenges in searching and retrieving information.

People with low literacy levels often choose to get information based on how easy it is to access and understand the information systems [67]. Most emergent users prefer information, whether health- or money-related, to be available in a voice format, as it is easier for them to understand [50]. The literature highlights various methods for delivering essential information to users, including IVRS [7, 8,38,40,54,63] (Interactive Voice Response System), Android applications [7,9, 16,50,62], and, more recently, Conversational Agents (CA) [36,56,57,68]. IVRS has been highly successful in disseminating information because it is entirely text-free, easy to use, and also there is a human agent involved, which makes it trustable [48].

While IVRS has been successful in disseminating information without requiring text, the rise of smartphones has led to the development of various Android applications to deliver information to users. WhatsApp, in particular, has become a favourite among users for passive communication and information distribution [4]. During the COVID crisis, critical information was conveyed through WhatsApp, and users tended to trust it more because it was sent to them by people they knew [20]. Researchers have provided various guidelines for designing application interfaces, such as keeping the interface text-free and avoiding deep menu hierarchies [50,51,64]. However, using applications to disseminate information may not be as successful as IVRS, as emergent users struggle to navigate them and require literacy to obtain information [16,21].

Despite the availability of user-friendly applications, emergent users often struggle with identifying the correct information from among a deluge of information returned by different information systems. Kodagoda et al. [43], in their survey with 10 UK participants, found that emergent users tend to stop their search as soon as they find relevant or interesting information, assuming it to be correct. This behaviour is often driven by confirmation bias, where users are more likely to accept information that aligns with their pre-existing beliefs or expectations [47]. If they do not find any relevant or interesting information, they tend to abandon the search altogether.

To address the issue of information overload and the difficulty in identifying correct information, Conversational Agents (CAs) have emerged as a promising solution [24,65]. With Conversational Agents, this problem can be solved, as the answers to questions can be precise and accurate. An added advantage of CAs is that they support voice input, which is a natural mode of communication for all able-bodied humans [14]. Interacting with CAs can mimic a human-like conversation, which is particularly appealing to emergent users [21]. With advancements in technology, these CAs are now backed by Generative AI (GenAI) models. One such CA is ChatGPT. However, the literature shows that while ChatGPT performs well with high-resource languages, it struggles with low-resource languages [55,58]. However, these studies approach the issue from an NLP perspective rather than from the users' point of view. In our work, we evaluate ChatGPT from a User Experience (UX) standpoint for ease of use and language understanding, compared to Google, a well-known information-seeking tool.

2.2   Conversational Agent (CA)

With the advancement of technology, conversational systems have become integral to how users interact with machines, enabling natural language communication and providing information or completing tasks. These systems, known by various names such as intelligent systems, virtual assistants (VAs), CA, and chatbots, are deployed across fields like education, fashion, and health, significantly influencing user experiences. In Western settings, extensive research has been conducted on diverse users of VAs, revealing that users expect these agents to exhibit intelligence, human-like behaviour, and the ability to code-switch during interactions [3,6,33,44,59].

However, the existing research predominantly focuses on literate, English-speaking users, overlooking the challenges faced by non-English-speaking, emergent users - a gap our study aims to address. Previous work has demonstrated the potential of conversational agents for low-literate or semi-literate users, particularly in non-WEIRD (Western, Educated, Industrialized, Rich, and Democratic) contexts [33,35,36,66]. Studies have shown that users in these populations prefer agents that communicate in local languages and provide contextual assistance. Yet, they often encounter difficulties in articulating their intent and experience frustrations with the agents' inability to understand code-mixed language [27,33].

Building on this body of work, our research investigates the suitability of ChatGPT as an information-seeking tool for non-English speaking, emergent users in India. By focusing on this demographic, our study contributes to a growing understanding of how conversational AI can be tailored to meet the needs of diverse user groups, providing insights that are critical for the design of more inclusive and accessible conversational agents.

2.3   ChatGPT

Among the various conversational agents, ChatGPT has emerged as a prominent tool due to its advanced natural language processing capabilities, positioning itself as an information-seeking tool [29] across diverse user groups. ChatGPT is often used for activities like machine translation, summarization, sentiment analysis, and general information seeking. However, research has shown that while ChatGPT performs well with high-resource languages, it consistently lags in low-resource languages, raising concerns about its effectiveness in non-English contexts [15,61].

Despite its conversational strengths, users have reported issues such as inaccuracies in speech-to-text conversion, difficulties in understanding gender-neutral pronouns, and the perpetuation of cultural biases [28]. These challenges are particularly relevant when considering the use of ChatGPT by non-English speaking, emergent users.

While existing studies have largely focused on the experiences of literate, English-speaking users, our research uniquely contributes to the field by examining ChatGPT's usability and language comprehension among non-English-speaking, emergent users in India. We aim to explore whether ChatGPT can effectively serve as an information-seeking tool for this demographic despite its known limitations in low-resource language contexts.

Given the documented challenges with speech recognition and culturally relevant content delivery, non-English speaking, emergent users might encounter significant barriers when interacting with ChatGPT. Our study investigates these specific usability issues, assessing how well ChatGPT meets the needs of this user group and providing insights that could inform future developments in conversational AI.

Understanding the limitations and potential of ChatGPT in non-English contexts is crucial for designing more inclusive AI tools. This study aims to address these issues by systematically evaluating the user experience of non-English speaking, emergent users with ChatGPT, offering insights that will contribute to the broader discourse on digital inclusivity and the design of conversational agents.

3   Methodology

This study aims to understand the suitability of ChatGPT as an information-seeking tool for emergent users, given the capabilities and expectations of emergent users. Specifically, our focus is on the UX offered by ChatGPT rather than on evaluating its technical performance on NLP (Natural Language Processing) tasks. We seek to explore whether a conversational agent, backed by advanced generative AI models like ChatGPT, can meet the expectations of users from an information-seeking tool.

We set the users a few tasks to be performed using ChatGPT and Google and asked the users to rate their experiences on a 5-point Likert Scale [5], with 1 being lowest and 5 being highest. We logged our observations of the user-interactions during and following the usage of the two platforms. The interviews were conducted in Telangana, Hyderabad, with the participants in their work-place without disturbing their work schedule or at their homes in the language they spoke. The interviews were conducted with the assistance of an HCI PhD candidate and an undergraduate computer science student who spoke the same languages as the participants. No monetary compensation was provided to the participants for participating in the study. The task list used for the survey is in Sect. 3.2.

3.1 Participants

The participants for the study were selected through convenience sampling. The study participants were selected from residents in and around the authors' university campus and are not related to the authors of the paper. All the participants regularly use smartphones in their daily lives and are familiar with using various applications like WhatsApp, Facebook and Google Maps. All the interviews were conducted during their free time, either at their homes or work-places. If the participant was in the workplace, permission was obtained from their supervisors to conduct the interview, but the supervisor did not influence the interview. We conducted the study with a total of 15 participants, ranging in age from 19 to 43, comprising nine men and six women. Among them, 4 participants spoke Hindi, while 11 were Telugu speakers. The participant pool includes unskilled labourers, students, and users holding bachelor's and master's degrees. Degree holders are valid participants in this study because, despite their qualifications, they are non-English speakers and cannot communicate fluently in English, matching with our profile of emergent users. While the participants had varying levels of education and proficiency with technology, this study is not concerned with assessing their technical skills. Instead, it is designed to investigate whether ChatGPT, as an information-seeking tool, can fulfil users' expectations, which might have been shaped by pre-existing mental models of information systems. The participants' demographic details are described in Table 1.

3.2 Procedure

In order to answer the research question, we conducted a mixed-method study with the participants. The interviews were conducted with the assistance of an HCI PhD candidate and an undergraduate computer science student who spoke the same languages as the participants. Before conducting the study, we obtained the participants' consent to log their interactions with the platforms and record their opinions. We also informed them that the data would be used only for research and that the anonymity of the participants would be preserved. Each interaction lasted for about 30 to 40 min. For the study, we designed tasks in five different categories. These categories were selected based on the emergent users'

Table 1. Demographic details of the participants

Participants	Language	Age	Education	Occupation	Gender
P1	Telugu	20	Class 12	Worker in a shop	Male
P2	Telugu	23	Class 10	Worker in a shop	Male
P3	Telugu	41	Class 5	Hostel Care Taker	Female
P4	Telugu	31	Class 12	Hostel Care Taker	Female
P5	Hindi	43	Master's Degree	Mess in-charge	Female
P6	Hindi	19	Class 7	Mess worker	Male
P7	Hindi	30	Class 8	Mess worker	Male
P8	Hindi	26	Class 10	Worker in a shop	Male
P9	Telugu	30	Class 12	Security Guard	Female
P10	Telugu	41	Bachelor's degree	Shop owner	Male
P11	Telugu	28	Bachelor's degree	Tailor	Female
P12	Telugu	19	ITI	Laundry worker	Male
P13	Telugu	22	Bachelor's degree	Student/Part-time worker in shop	Female
P14	Telugu	24	Diploma	Electrician	Male
P15	Telugu	28	Diploma	Plumber	Male

smartphone usage patterns documented by other researchers [31,41] and the tasks on which the platforms are evaluated is based on tasks set for evaluation of ChatGPT and GenAI systems by other researchers [30,45,69]. The five categories are listed next:

1. Entertainment/Leisure
2. Bank, Payments or utility related
3. Navigating popular app or website
4. Information Seeking task: with this category, users can perform information-seeking tasks
   (a) Example: How to write a letter asking for permission to leave early from your job.
5. Queries with short answers in a word or a line.
   (a) Example: Who is the winner of the show x (any show)?

Participants were encouraged to ask questions to the platforms within the above mentioned categories. Examples of the questions that could be asked or tasks to be performed by the participants are listed below.

1. Entertainment/Leisure
   (a) How to cook x (any specific dish)?
   (b) Search for a place. (Tourism)
   (c) Search for a specific music or video.
2. Bank/payment/utility Related:

(a) How to open a bank account?
(b) How to know your electricity bill online?
(c) How to book tickets online? Or buying medicines or groceries
(d) How to pay bills online?
(e) How to withdraw money from one's PF account (Provident Fund)?
3. Navigation
   (a) How to install and log in to Netflix/JIO Cinema/Zee5 or any other application?
4. Information Queries
   (a) How to write a letter to ask permission to avail leave from work.
5. Queries with short answers
   (a) Who is the main actor of the movie x (any movie)?
   (b) Who is the chief minister of a state?
   (c) What is the distance between x and y (any two places)? Or, how long will it take to travel from x to y?
   (d) Who won Big Boss season 2?
   (e) What is the capital of country x (any country)?

We provided the participants with an Android phone, which had the Chat-GPT[2,3](freely available in Play Store) and the Google Search apps preinstalled. We also demonstrated how to use these applications to perform the tasks. All the participants used the same phone to perform the task. After demonstrating how to use the platforms, we asked the participants if they understood how to perform the task. They would proceed only if they confirmed they had no confusion and could perform the task independently. Participants would ask questions in their first language (language they are most comfortable in) to both Google and ChatGPT3.5 in the five categories. Participants can choose the order of the questions that they would like to ask the platform. Participants first queried the Google platform, as it is the most familiar platform to them, and then they queried ChatGPT. The participants were asked to use the voice-input feature of the platforms for ease of use.

To capture the ease of use and understanding of the language by each of the platforms, we used a Likert scale. Each participant rated each of the platforms for ease of use and language understanding on a 5-point Likert scale for each of the categories listed above (a total of 20 Likert Scales were recorded by each participant. For each category, the participants had to rate each platform for ease of use and language understanding), with 1 indicating low satisfaction and 5 indicating high satisfaction. The rating was verbally communicated to the interviewers and recorded in a notebook for later tabulation. The rating on language understanding is important because when users interact with a language-based platform like ChatGPT, they develop a mental model or a conceptual framework of how well the platform comprehends and responds to their language input. This mental model includes their beliefs, expectations, and

---

[2] ChatGPT3.5 was used for conducting the study because it is available for free.
[3] https://play.google.com/store/apps/details?id=com.openai.chatgpt.

understanding of how accurately the platform interprets their prompts and provides relevant responses [52]. Therefore, the user's perception of how well the platform understands their language is a fundamental component of their overall understanding and experience with the platform. In addition, the researcher qualitatively logged observations from the user interaction when the participants were using the platforms. The observation logs were grouped into themes and are presented in Sect. 4.1.

3.3 Ethical Guardrails

Our university does not have a formal ethics board for human subjects research. We practice self-regulation in our research along the guidelines by Dearden et al. [18]. We informed the participants of the purpose of the study and that all information collected will be kept anonymous. No monetary compensation was provided to the participants for participating in the study.

3.4 Google and ChatGPT3.5

Google and ChatGPT3.5 represent two distinct yet complementary approaches to information retrieval and interaction. We have chosen Google as the information retrieval tool for comparison as the users are familiar with Google, and currently, that is the de-facto information-seeking tool. Google, a ubiquitous tool, leverages vast datasets and sophisticated algorithms to deliver relevant information quickly and efficiently. Users input keywords or phrases either through voice or text, and Google's search engine provides information required by the user in image, text and video format.

On the other hand, ChatGPT offers a more interactive and conversational experience. Users can engage in natural language conversations with ChatGPT, asking questions, seeking advice, or generating text based on prompts. ChatGPT utilizes machine learning techniques to understand and respond to user queries, drawing upon its training data to generate contextually relevant and coherent responses.

While Google Search excels in quickly retrieving information from the web, ChatGPT excels in its ability to engage users in more nuanced and personalized interactions. Together, these tools represent powerful assets in navigating and accessing information in the digital age, catering to diverse needs and preferences in information retrieval and interaction.

These platforms are chosen for the study as both Google and ChatGPT are used as information retrieval systems that assist users through natural language processing but differ in the way they are implemented.

4   Findings

We conducted quantitative analysis on the Likert scale ratings and qualitative analysis on the user observation logs. In this section, we present our findings from the analysis.

4.1   Qualitative Analysis

In this section, we report the observations made through the logging of the user interactions and share anecdotes from the participants about the interactions. Along with collecting quantitative data through the Likert scales, we documented user perceptions of each application, as detailed in this section.

Voice Input Interface and Interaction Timing. The voice-input interfaces for Google and ChatGPT3.5 is depicted in Fig. 1. Users encountered challenges in identifying the microphone icon to ask questions within the ChatGPT application because it is represented by a headset (Fig. 1), despite being shown during the demonstration how to ask questions and which button to use. This ambiguity confused users regarding how to initiate the voice input. On the Google interface, the voice-input feature is indicated using a microphone symbol that has become a standard part of Android keyboards and messaging platforms like WhatsApp. The users were familiar with the microphone symbol used in the Google interface but not the headset symbol in the ChatGPT interface.

Another source of confusion for the users regarding ChatGPT was the uncertainty about when to interact with the application. The application takes time to load, and once it does, it displays a small microphone icon at the bottom of the screen, indicating it is listening, but the users failed to notice this despite this being explained during the demonstration (Fig. 2). Consequently, users often asked questions at the wrong times when the application was not in the listening mode. This issue was evident in the ChatGPT interface, where users struggled to discern the appropriate moment for interaction due to the ambiguous representation of the microphone icon and a delay in the indication of when the application was listening.

Application Responsiveness. Despite both applications being on the same phone and operated using the same cellular network, users perceived ChatGPT as slower than Google because the ChatGPT application takes some time to be ready to listen to queries, whereas Google allows users to ask questions immediately after clicking the microphone icon.

Code Mixed Language. Users consistently encountered difficulty formulating questions entirely in their language, often struggling with the phrasing across different languages. This has also been documented by other researchers [12,33, 41]. A user, while thinking out loud while querying about a location, said:

"What is a 'place' called in Telugu, bro?" (P1)

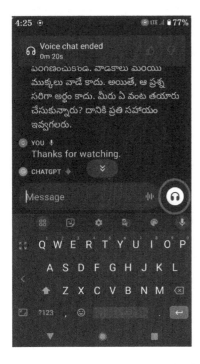 

Fig. 1. Input design for ChatGPT (left) and Google (right). The graphical buttons to activate the voice input feature are circled in red. (Color figure online)

Change in the Language of Response. Another consequential problem the users faced was that ChatGPT could not understand code-switching which users preferred while asking questions. Code-switching or code-mixing is the practice of switching between two or more languages [26]. In such scenarios, ChatGPT would switch to some other language abruptly, causing frustration to the users because users have to ask the question again and inform ChatGPT to answer in their language of choice despite already setting the language to their language of choice. During an interaction where a user enquired about a cooking recipe in Telugu, we observed that ChatGPT immediately switched the language to Hindi. Despite the question being posed in Telugu, ChatGPT responded in Hindi as the word *"Prepare"* ("thayyari" in Telugu and "tayyar" or "tayyari" in Hindi) has the same phonetic sound in Hindi and Telugu. The users did not face this issue of language switching while using the Google platform.

Accent of the Response. Some of the users had problems comprehending the response given by ChatGPT in the non-English language. This is more pronounced with users asking questions in the Telugu language. They felt that ChatGPT speaks the Telugu language with an English accent. One participant shared while talking about the language output by ChatGPT:

Fig. 2. Voice-input Interfaces of ChatGPT (left) and Google Search (right)

"It's like a crazy person. It's not clear and feels like English people are speaking in Telugu" (P11)

This observation aligns with the observation made by researchers Porcheron et al. and Pyae et al. [55,58].

Some of the participants, when told to ask questions in the entertainment/leisure category, queried about the songs in non-English language. ChatGPT would provide information about songs, like the music director or persons who have acted in the song, while Google provided the video of the songs. Participants with higher education[4] felt both were correct, while less educated participants felt it was providing wrong answers. So, the response by ChatGPT does not meet the expectations of the users shaped by pre-existing mental models. This led to a low rating for ChatGPT in the Entertainment category. A user said:

"Google directly gave the songs, but ChatGPT gave more information about songs, which is also good." (P15)

Needs Context Information. ChatGPT relies on contextual information to provide accurate responses to user queries, resulting in improved answers.

---

[4] Degree holders but non-English speakers.

Despite users recognizing this need for additional context, they often refrained from supplying it or asking follow-up questions, as they obtained satisfactory results with Google in their initial search. Consequently, users found it unnecessary to rephrase their queries. Some users required assistance in formulating queries to elicit accurate responses from ChatGPT. They perceived ChatGPT's insistence on specific details as a drawback, contrasting with Google's ability to provide immediate answers without such detailed prompts, a pattern observed across various search scenarios. One participant, who encountered ChatGPT's persistent questioning when inquiring about the syllabus and online ticket booking services, shared:

"It asks too many questions."(P13)

Another participant shared:

"We need to ask everything specifically to ChatGPT. If you ask clearly, then only will it answer "(P1)

This need to ask the questions specifically with a lot of context information in the query is not compliant with users' expectations and information-seeking behaviour.

An important observation is that users, being familiar with the context of their questions, presumed that ChatGPT also possessed this context and formulated their queries accordingly without clearly specifying the context. During an interaction, a participant (P13) wanted to know the syllabus for the second-year MBA programme. Google provided the answers in one hit, but ChatGPT kept on asking about the specific topic in the syllabus to respond more clearly. In this scenario, the participant got frustrated. The user presumed that ChatGPT would list all the topics. When it did not, the participant stopped asking follow-up questions.

Some of the highly educated users could easily form a mental model of the application using which they said that ChatGPT needed questions to be phrased with specific needs while Google would answer the queries with just the keywords. While this is an improvement, some less educated users felt frustrated with this realization, feeling that ChatGPT could not provide answers solely based on keywords, similar to Google's approach.

Answer Presentation Style. Users also noted a significant difference in the way Google and ChatGPT present answers: Google offers multiple options, whereas ChatGPT remains fixed on a single response.

Both applications allow the users to either type or say the queries they have. Google provides solutions in text and reads the text that it presents as answers to the questions, while ChatGPT verbally responds to the questions but does not show the text on its interface. Users would have to navigate back to read the answers. Some participants with higher education felt that if ChatGPT could show the answers that it is providing, it would be beneficial. But upon pointing out that this option is also available, the users were quick to point out that either you can read or hear but not together.

"We would concentrate more if we watch. We have less interest in listening. We will get the message in the text later. If the application shows text while it is telling it would be helpful." (P11)

Limitation in Addressing Current Events and Hallucination. Sometimes, when users ask questions for which ChatGPT might not know the answer or which are beyond its capacity, such as asking for the name of a state's chief minister, it may generate incorrect answers. This behaviour of ChatGPT can lead to further frustration among users. This behaviour of a GenAI platform is referred to as hallucination [37].

ChatGPT3.5 failed to give updated answers on current events as it was trained on data up to 2021. The ChatGPT3.5 version utilized for the survey did not have Retrieval Augmented Generation (RAG) capabilities [53]. RAG is the process of optimizing the output by referencing a knowledge base or database outside of its training data [49]. Consequently, users perceived it as incapable of addressing questions related to current events, leading to lower ratings for ChatGPT when questions about current events were asked.

4.2 Quantitative Analysis

A total of 15 users have evaluated the two platforms for their ease of use and language understanding by the platforms. In this section, we present the trends in the ratings provided by the participants. While the sample size in our study is too small to undertake deep statistical analysis, the data in this section can provide researchers and designers with trends which might be useful for designing platforms for emerging users.

A visual representation of the average of the user ratings across the different categories is depicted in Fig. 3.

Overall trends observed across all the categories:

1. Ease of Use of ChatGPT and Google: On average, the participants rated Chat-GPT 2.06 points lower than Google. On average, this rating for ChatGPT remains consistent across different genders, ages, languages, and education levels. Similarly, there is no variability in the ratings for Google across all sub-factors related to ease of use.
2. Language understandability by ChatGPT and Google: We observed a similar trend in ratings for language understandability as we did for ease of use. On average, the participants rated ChatGPT's language understanding 2.as34 points lower than Google's. As noted in the Sect. 4.1, some users found Chat-GPT's accent difficult to understand.

In summary, across all categories - entertainment/leisure, bank-related queries, navigation, information queries, and queries with short answers- irrespective of age and educational background, users consistently rated ChatGPT

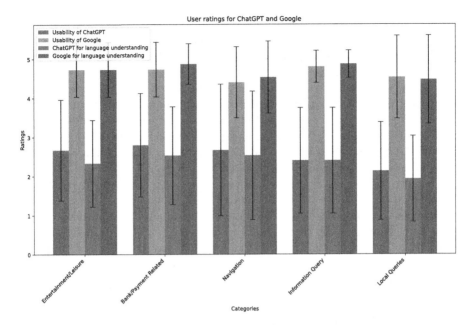

Fig. 3. Distribution of average user ratings for ease of use and language understanding of ChatGPT and Google. Sample size (n = 15).

lower than Google in terms of both ease of use and language understanding[5]. Specifically, users found ChatGPT less intuitive and its language comprehension less effective. This trend was evident across all task categories, highlighting a significant preference for Google. Users felt that Google was more user-friendly and better at accurately interpreting and responding to their language inputs in practical applications.

5   Discussion

Our study extends the existing understanding of the use of conversation agents based on Large Language Models among non-English speakers. We discussed users' experiences of using ChatGPT and Google. Based on the users' experiences, we propose some design recommendations for designing voice-based conversational AI systems for non-English speakers.

5.1   Accent Used by ChatGPT for Non-English Languages

Participants expressed strong opinions regarding ChatGPT's delivery of responses in an audio format in non-English languages, especially in Telugu. The

---

[5] The raw survey data is available at https://osf.io/c5qjd/?view_only=0d0b876 1f185467c847ef39e810b0dcf.

accent used by ChatGPT in Indian languages has evoked varied user reactions. While some appreciate its mechanical tone as relatable and engaging, others find it lacking in authenticity and fluency. Non-English speakers sometimes perceive it as unnatural, resembling speech from someone unfamiliar with the language. They found the "Telugu" language rendition lacking fluency, akin to someone unfamiliar with or learning the language. Much of the dialogue was unintelligible, requiring users to infer meaning from answer summaries. To address this, we suggest enhancing ChatGPT's accent and pronunciation in the Indian languages to make it sound more natural and fluent. Also, fluency can be further enhanced by including everyday words in the training corpus.

This inconsistency in linguistic accuracy poses a challenge for users seeking culturally appropriate and fluent interactions. Chivukula et al. [12], in their study of conversational agents in an Indian Context, observe that users expect the agent to converse with them like a known person. As a result, there's a need for refining ChatGPT's accent with Indian languages to better resonate with diverse linguistic and cultural contexts, ensuring smoother communication and user satisfaction.

5.2   Interaction Design

In the ChatGPT application, the headset symbol serves as a cue for oral interaction with the tool, which can be confusing and convey a different message. This ambiguity leads to uncertainty, especially after loading the application, making it difficult for users to discern if the application is prepared to respond to their queries. Aligning with the existing mental models, this interface design could better accommodate semi-literate or orally literate users. The confusion might also be arising because of a pre-existing mental model of the users where they are familiar with a microphone icon indicating voice-input.

Another significant challenge faced by users while using the ChatGPT application pertains to its language. Users often encounter a situation where the application inconsistently switches between languages during interactions, thereby hindering seamless communication. This inconsistency becomes particularly evident when users engage in code-switching, where ChatGPT fails to maintain linguistic continuity. For instance, even if the majority of the query is in a non-English language, if the query begins with an English word, ChatGPT responds exclusively in English. This language inconsistency not only disrupts the flow of communication but also complicates the user experience, highlighting the need for enhanced language handling capabilities within the application.

The ChatGPT application offers hybrid input options, allowing users to input text or use voice commands. While this is beneficial for users unfamiliar with typing in a non-English language, some participants preferred to read the responses, especially when the responses provided by ChatGPT were long. However, if they opt to read the response, they must interrupt the application's audio output to switch to reading mode. We suggest that ChatGPT provide text responses in the non-English language along with reading it aloud, facilitating easier comprehension, particularly for longer answers. This approach allows users to read and understand the content at their own pace, addressing the limitation of only being able to listen to audio responses once.

ChatGPT's tendency to prompt additional questions immediately after addressing a previous query can disrupt users' cognitive processes and go against the mental model of information systems like search engines. This rapid succession of prompts limits users' ability to fully digest and evaluate the solution provided, potentially impeding their comprehension and hindering their overall experience with the application.

This also questions the positioning of conversational systems as better models for information seeking, given several of the participants in this study struggled to articulate their queries in full sentences in a single language. Conversational systems would also be a barrier in information-seeking for reticent users who have difficulty making a conversation.

5.3 Digital Divide

ChatGPT has a very huge potential in catering to diverse user needs, spanning from aiding productivity to assisting various domains. This application has already proved its mettle and can change the dynamics of learning not just for literate users but also for oral literates or non-English speakers, as it can provide custom solutions to the various necessities or problems of people. Its adaptability and versatility suggest the potential for addressing a wide array of user requirements, irrespective of background or proficiency level. However, it also poses the risk of a widening the digital divide where advanced users, who can converse in high-resource languages like English, continue to take advantage of the technology, while semi-literate or non-English speakers would be left behind if we do not include the needs and expectations of the non-English speakers or the non-English languages thus creating the digital divide. In order to address the widening digital divide, it becomes important to be considerate of the needs of emergent and non-English speakers. This approach is really important because it helps everyone get fair access to technology.

6 Limitation

Our study is constrained by several limitations that warrant consideration. Firstly, the use of the free versions of the ChatGPT tool for participant interviews may have impacted the user experience and functionality due to potential restrictions or limitations inherent in these versions. Additionally, reliance on a cellular network for tool access may have introduced variability in performance and speed, potentially influencing participant perceptions and interactions. However, it is to be noted that most emergent users would use similar cellular connections to interact with the platforms and not pay for a premium ChatGPT experience.

Furthermore, the relatively small sample size of 15 participants limits the generalizability of our findings. With a limited number of participants, the representativeness of our sample may be compromised, leading to potential biases in our observations and conclusions. Moreover, our study focuses exclusively on two languages, thereby restricting the scope of language diversity considered in our analysis. As a result, the applicability of our findings to a broader linguistic context may be limited. Designers and researchers may use the results we present as initial trends in the usability of conversational generative AI platforms. Despite the limitations, the findings might be helpful for designers working towards developing conversational AI tools.

7   Conclusion

ChatGPT, with its capacity for hybrid input methods such as typing and speech, presents a unique opportunity to non-English speakers by facilitating effortless communication, learning and information seeking. To investigate this potential, we conducted a comparative study with 15 non-English language speakers utilizing GenAI tools like ChatGPT3.5 and an information retrieval platform, Google. The user rated the interactions on a 5-point Likert scale. We presented the findings from the user ratings and logs of user observations during interactions with the platforms. From the user observations, we noted the users did not like asking follow-up questions when the answer received was not satisfactory. It became apparent that users would engage more readily with applications offering content in a familiar language, facilitating greater user interaction and comprehension and complying with existing mental models. These findings underscore the importance of tailoring AI applications to meet the diverse linguistic and cultural needs and expectations of the users.

References

1. Ahuja, K., et al.: Mega: multilingual evaluation of generative AI. arXiv preprint arXiv:2303.12528 (2023)
2. Ahuja, S., et al.: Megaverse: benchmarking large language models across languages, modalities, models and tasks. arXiv preprint arXiv:2311.07463 (2023)
3. Ammari, T., Kaye, J., Tsai, J.Y., Bentley, F.: Music, search, and IoT: how people (really) use voice assistants. ACM Trans. Comput.-Hum. Interact. (TOCHI) 26(3), 1–28 (2019)
4. Balkrishan, D., Joshi, A., Rajendran, C., Nizam, N., Parab, C., Devkar, S.: Making and breaking the user-usage model: Whatsapp adoption amongst emergent users in India. In: Proceedings of the 8th Indian Conference on Human-Computer Interaction, pp. 52–63 (2016)
5. Batterton, K.A., Hale, K.N.: The likert scale what it is and how to use it. Phalanx 50(2), 32–39 (2017)
6. Bentley, F., Luvogt, C., Silverman, M., Wirasinghe, R., White, B., Lottridge, D.: Understanding the long-term use of smart speaker assistants. Proc. ACM Interact. Mob. Wearable Ubiquitous Technol. 2(3), 1–24 (2018)
7. Chakraborty, D., Ahmad, M.S., Seth, A.: Findings from a civil society mediated and technology assisted grievance redressal model in rural India. In: Proceedings of the Ninth International Conference on Information and Communication Technologies and Development, ICTD 2017. ACM, New York (2017)

8. Chakraborty, D., Seth, A.: Building citizen engagement into the implementation of welfare schemes in rural India. In: Proceedings of the Seventh International Conference on Information and Communication Technologies and Development, ICTD 2015, pp. 22:1–22:10. ACM, New York (2015). https://doi.org/10.1145/2737856.2738027. http://doi.acm.org/10.1145/2737856.2738027

9. Chandel, P., Doke, P.: A comparative study of voice and graphical user interfaces with respect to literacy levels. In: Proceedings of the 3rd ACM Symposium on Computing for Development, pp. 1–2 (2013)

10. Chatman, E.A.: Life in a small world: applicability of gratification theory to information-seeking behavior. J. Am. Soc. Inf. Sci. **42**(6), 438–449 (1991)

11. Chatterjee, A.: Art in an age of artificial intelligence. Front. Psychol. **13**, 1024449 (2022)

12. Chopra, S., Chivukula, S.: My phone assistant should know i am an Indian: influencing factors for adoption of assistive agents. In: Proceedings of the 19th International Conference on Human-Computer Interaction with Mobile Devices and Services, pp. 1–8 (2017)

13. Chung, W.: 2 - web searching and browsing: a multilingual perspective. In: Advances in Computers: Improving the Web, Advances in Computers, vol. 78, pp. 41–69. Elsevier (2010). https://doi.org/10.1016/S0065-2458(10)78002-5. https://www.sciencedirect.com/science/article/pii/S0065245810780025

14. Cohen, P.R., Oviatt, S.L.: The role of voice input for human-machine communication. Proc. Natl. Acad. Sci. **92**(22), 9921–9927 (1995)

15. Costa-jussà, M.R., et al.: No language left behind: scaling human-centered machine translation. arXiv preprint arXiv:2207.04672 (2022)

16. Cuendet, S., Medhi, I., Bali, K., Cutrell, E.: Videokheti: making video content accessible to low-literate and novice users. In: Proceedings of the SIGCHI Conference on Human Factors in Computing Systems, pp. 2833–2842 (2013)

17. Day, G.S.: The capabilities of market-driven organizations. J. Mark. **58**(4), 37–52 (1994)

18. Dearden, A., Kleine, D.: Minimum ethical standards for ICTD/ICT4D research (2018)

19. Dervin, B., Naumer, C.M.: Sense-making. Encyclopedia Commun. Theory **2**, 876–880 (2009)

20. Deshbandhu, A., Sahni, S.: Repurposing a whatsapp group: how a fantasy cricket group transformed into a site of care and support during India's second wave of covid-19. Mobile Media Commun. **11**(2), 271–293 (2023)

21. Dhaygude, M., Chakraborty, D.: Rethinking design of digital platforms for emergent users: findings from a study with rural Indian farmers. In: Proceedings of the 11th Indian Conference on Human-Computer Interaction, pp. 62–69 (2020)

22. Dhaygude, M.S., Lapsiya, N.D., Chakraborty, D.: There is no app for that: manifestations of the digital divides during covid-19 school closures in India. Proc. ACM Hum.-Comput. Interact. **6**(CSCW2), 1–26 (2022)

23. Flores-Vivar, J.M., García-Peñalvo, F.J.: Reflections on the ethics, potential, and challenges of artificial intelligence in the framework of quality education (SDG4). Comunicar **31**(74), 37–47 (2023)

24. Følstad, A., Brandtzaeg, P.B., Feltwell, T., Law, E.L., Tscheligi, M., Luger, E.A.: Sig: chatbots for social good. In: Extended Abstracts of the 2018 CHI Conference on Human Factors in Computing Systems, pp. 1–4 (2018)

25. García-Peñalvo, F., et al.: Koopaml: a graphical platform for building machine learning pipelines adapted to health professionals (2023)

26. Gardner-Chloros, P.: Code-Switching. Cambridge University Press, Cambridge (2009)

27. Garg, R., Cui, H., Kapadia, Y.: "Learn, use, and (intermittently) abandon": exploring the practices of early smart speaker adopters in urban India. Proc. ACM Hum.-Comput. Interact. **5**(CSCW2), 1–28 (2021)

28. Ghosh, S., Caliskan, A.: Chatgpt perpetuates gender bias in machine translation and ignores non-gendered pronouns: findings across Bengali and five other low-resource languages. In: Proceedings of the 2023 AAAI/ACM Conference on AI, Ethics, and Society, pp. 901–912 (2023)

29. Grant, N.: Google calls in help from larry page and sergey brin for A.I. fight (2023). https://www.nytimes.com/2023/01/20/technology/google-chatgpt-artificial-intelligence.html

30. Gundawar, A., Verma, M., Guan, L., Valmeekam, K., Bhambri, S., Kambhampati, S.: Robust planning with LLM-modulo framework: case study in travel planning. arXiv preprint arXiv:2405.20625 (2024)

31. Gupta, M., Mehta, D., Punj, A., Thies, I.M.: Sophistication with limitation: understanding smartphone usage by emergent users in India. In: ACM SIGCAS/SIGCHI Conference on Computing and Sustainable Societies (COMPASS), pp. 386–400 (2022)

32. Haleem, A., Javaid, M., Singh, R.P.: An era of chatgpt as a significant futuristic support tool: a study on features, abilities, and challenges. BenchCouncil Trans. Benchmarks Stand. Eval. **2**(4), 100089 (2022)

33. Harrington, C.N., Garg, R., Woodward, A., Williams, D.: "It's kind of like code-switching": black older adults' experiences with a voice assistant for health information seeking. In: Proceedings of the 2022 CHI Conference on Human Factors in Computing Systems, pp. 1–15 (2022)

34. Hwang, S.I., et al.: Is chatgpt a "fire of prometheus" for non-native english-speaking researchers in academic writing? Korean J. Radiol. **24**(10), 952 (2023)

35. Jain, M., Kota, R., Kumar, P., Patel, S.N.: Convey: exploring the use of a context view for chatbots. In: Proceedings of the 2018 CHI Conference on Human Factors in Computing Systems, pp. 1–6 (2018)

36. Jain, M., Kumar, P., Bhansali, I., Liao, Q.V., Truong, K., Patel, S.: Farmchat: a conversational agent to answer farmer queries. Proc. ACM Interact. Mob. Wearable Ubiquitous Technol. **2**(4), 1–22 (2018)

37. Ji, Z., et al.: Survey of hallucination in natural language generation. ACM Comput. Surv. **55**(12), 1–38 (2023)

38. Joshi, A., et al.: Supporting treatment of people living with HIV/AIDS in resource limited settings with IVRs. In: Proceedings of the SIGCHI Conference on Human Factors in Computing Systems, pp. 1595–1604 (2014)

39. Kasneci, E., et al.: Chatgpt for good? On opportunities and challenges of large language models for education. Learn. Individ. Differ. **103**, 102274 (2023)

40. Kazakos, K., et al.: A real-time IVR platform for community radio. In: Proceedings of the 2016 CHI Conference on Human Factors in Computing Systems, pp. 343–354 (2016)

41. Kendall, L., Chaudhuri, B., Bhalla, A.: Understanding technology as situated practice: everyday use of voice user interfaces among diverse groups of users in urban India. Inf. Syst. Front. **22**, 585–605 (2020)

42. Khosravi, H., et al.: Explainable artificial intelligence in education. Comput. Educ. Artif. Intell. **3**, 100074 (2022)

43. Kodagoda, N., Wong, W., Kahan, N.: Identifying information seeking behaviours of low and high literacy users: combined cognitive task analysis. In: 9th Bi-annual International Conference on Naturalistic Decision Making (NDM9). BCS Learning & Development (2009)
44. Kowalski, J., et al.: Older adults and voice interaction: a pilot study with google home. In: Extended Abstracts of the 2019 CHI Conference on Human Factors in Computing Systems, pp. 1–6 (2019)
45. Li, Y., Yang, N., Wang, L., Wei, F., Li, W.: Generative retrieval for conversational question answering. Inf. Process. Manag. **60**(5), 103475 (2023)
46. MacKenzie, D., Wajcman, J.: The Social Shaping of Technology. Open University Press (1999)
47. Malthouse, E.: Confirmation bias and vaccine-related beliefs in the time of covid-19. J. Public Health **45**(2), 523–528 (2023)
48. Manatsa, P.: An analysis of the impact of implementing a new interactive voice response system (IVR) on client experience in the Canadian banking industry (2019)
49. Martineau, K.: What is retrieval-augmented generation? (2023). https://research.ibm.com/blog/retrieval-augmented-generation-RAG
50. Medhi, I., Patnaik, S., Brunskill, E., Gautama, S.N., Thies, W., Toyama, K.: Designing mobile interfaces for novice and low-literacy users. ACM Trans. Comput.-Hum. Interact. (TOCHI) **18**(1), 1–28 (2011)
51. Medhi, I., Sagar, A., Toyama, K.: Text-free user interfaces for illiterate and semi-literate users. In: 2006 International Conference on Information and Communication Technologies and Development, pp. 72–82. IEEE (2006)
52. Norman, D.A.: Some observations on mental models. In: Mental Models, pp. 15–22. Psychology Press (2014)
53. Pambou, J.: A simple guide to retrieval augmented generation language models? (2024). https://www.smashingmagazine.com/2024/01/guide-retrieval-augmented-generation-language-models/
54. Patel, N., Agarwal, S., Rajput, N., Nanavati, A., Dave, P., Parikh, T.S.: A comparative study of speech and dialed input voice interfaces in rural India. In: Proceedings of the SIGCHI Conference on Human Factors in Computing Systems, pp. 51–54 (2009)
55. Porcheron, M., Fischer, J.E., Sharples, S.: "Do animals have accents?" talking with agents in multi-party conversation. In: Proceedings of the 2017 ACM Conference on Computer Supported Cooperative Work and Social Computing, pp. 207–219 (2017)
56. Prasad, A., Blagsvedt, S., Pochiraju, T., Medhi Thies, I.: Dara: a chatbot to help Indian artists and designers discover international opportunities. In: Proceedings of the 2019 on Creativity and Cognition, pp. 626–632. Association for Computing Machinery (2019)
57. Purington, A., Taft, J.G., Sannon, S., Bazarova, N.N., Taylor, S.H.: "Alexa is my new bff" social roles, user satisfaction, and personification of the amazon echo. In: Proceedings of the 2017 CHI Conference Extended Abstracts on Human Factors in Computing Systems, pp. 2853–2859 (2017)
58. Pyae, A., Joelsson, T.N.: Investigating the usability and user experiences of voice user interface: a case of google home smart speaker. In: Proceedings of the 20th International Conference on Human-Computer Interaction with Mobile Devices and Services Adjunct, pp. 127–131 (2018)

59. Reicherts, L., Rogers, Y., Capra, L., Wood, E., Duong, T.D., Sebire, N.: It's good to talk: a comparison of using voice versus screen-based interactions for agent-assisted tasks. ACM Trans. Comput.-Hum. Interact. **29**(3), 1–41 (2022)

60. Robinson, M.A.: An empirical analysis of engineers' information behaviors. J. Am. Soc. Inform. Sci. Technol. **61**(4), 640–658 (2010)

61. Robinson, N.R., Ogayo, P., Mortensen, D.R., Neubig, G.: Chatgpt MT: competitive for high-(but not low-) resource languages. arXiv preprint arXiv:2309.07423 (2023)

62. Shah, H., Sengupta, A.: Designing mobile based computational support for low-literate community health workers. Int. J. Hum. Comput. Stud. **115**, 1–8 (2018)

63. Srinivasan, V., et al.: Airavat: an automated system to increase transparency and accountability in social welfare schemes in India. In: Proceedings of the Sixth International Conference on Information and Communications Technologies and Development: Notes - Volume 2, ICTD 2013, pp. 151–154. ACM, New York (2013). https://doi.org/10.1145/2517899.2517937. http://doi.acm.org/10.1145/2517899.2517937

64. Srivastava, A., Kapania, S., Tuli, A., Singh, P.: Actionable UI design guidelines for smartphone applications inclusive of low-literate users. Proc. ACM Hum.-Comput. Interact. **5**(CSCW1), 1–30 (2021)

65. Stieglitz, S., Hofeditz, L., Brünker, F., Ehnis, C., Mirbabaie, M., Ross, B.: Design principles for conversational agents to support emergency management agencies. Int. J. Inf. Manage. **63**, 102469 (2022)

66. Medhi Thies, I., Menon, N., Magapu, S., Subramony, M., O'Neill, J.: How do you want your chatbot? An exploratory wizard-of-oz study with young, urban Indians. In: Bernhaupt, R., Dalvi, G., Joshi, A., Balkrishan, D.K., O'Neill, J., Winckler, M. (eds.) INTERACT 2017. LNCS, vol. 10513, pp. 441–459. Springer, Cham (2017). https://doi.org/10.1007/978-3-319-67744-6_28

67. Thies, I.M., et al.: User interface design for low-literate and novice users: past, present and future. Found. Trends® Hum.-Comput. Interact. **8**(1), 1–72 (2015)

68. Vaccaro, K., Agarwalla, T., Shivakumar, S., Kumar, R.: Designing the future of personal fashion. In: Proceedings of the 2018 CHI Conference on Human Factors in Computing Systems, pp. 1–11 (2018)

69. Venkataramanan, R., et al.: Cook-gen: robust generative modeling of cooking actions from recipes. In: 2023 IEEE International Conference on Systems, Man, and Cybernetics (SMC), pp. 981–986. IEEE (2023)

70. Zipf, G.K.: Human behavior and the principle of least effort: an introduction to human ecology. Ravenio Books (2016)

Using Graph Analysis for Evaluating Usability of Software-Based Keyboard for Password Creation

Manish Shukla$^{(\boxtimes)}$ ⓘ, Sreecharan Bojja ⓘ, Gokul Jayakrishnan ⓘ,
Vijayanand Banahatti ⓘ, and Sachin Lodha ⓘ

TCS Research, Pune, India
{mani.shukla,b.sreecharan,gokul.cj,vijayanand.banahatti,
sachin.lodha}@tcs.com

Abstract. A virtual keyboard is a software component that replicates the functionality of a physical keyboard, allowing users to input characters without physical keys. Virtual keyboards are commonly used in scenarios where a physical keyboard is unavailable or impractical due to constraints such as security considerations. From a security perspective, virtual keyboards help mitigate keylogger data sniffing and shoulder-surfing attacks. Consequently, many web applications, especially those related to banking and finance, use virtual keyboards for password entry. In this work, we propose a graph-based usability analysis of virtual keyboards. We convert the input key sequence into a graph and then apply relevant graph-based metrics to identify usability issues. To assess the effectiveness of this approach, we conducted a lab study with 30 participants. Preliminary results indicate that a user's discomfort and confusion while creating a password directly affect the properties of the graph.

Keywords: Graph Analysis · Virtual Keyboard · Usability · Password

1 Introduction

There are multiple ways to authenticate a human user, for example, text-based passwords, fingerprints, one-time passwords, facial recognition, and behavioral biometrics. Each of these methods has its advantages in certain environments and scenarios. However, text-based password remains the most common means of authenticating a human user, especially on web. This is due to the fact that it provides a good trade-off between the implementation effort, ease of management, ease of use, and security [1]. Despite its proliferation, the text-based password is often considered easier to attack than the latest authentication technologies due to its brevity [41] and poor password hygiene. Further, shoulder surfing, the commoditization of cyberattacks due to the availability of malware as a service [11], and the introduction of large language models (LLM) [34] have substantially contributed to credential stealing. In a recent data breach report by Verizon [21], poorly picked and protected passwords continues to be one of

N. Rangaswamy et al. (Eds.): IndiaHCI 2024, CCIS 2337, pp. 215–239, 2025.
https://doi.org/10.1007/978-3-031-80829-6_10

the major sources of breaches in 2023. Past research has looked into various ways of safeguarding from credential sniffing, for example, by fabricating passwords [2], using privileged limited accounts [20], using hybrid authentication, which combines text-based passwords with image-based passwords [14], and using a virtual keyboard [40].

Virtual keyboards are relatively more secure than physical keyboards as they mitigate the risk of hardware keyloggers, can easily support dynamic key layouts to confuse shoulder-surfing attackers [32], and are easy to integrate with continuous biometric authentication [13]. Due to these reasons, virtual keyboards are prevalent on web applications where extra security is required, for example, e-banking, insurance portals [36,43], etc. Our rationale for selecting the banking and insurance sectors as focal points of our study stems from a directive by the Reserve Bank of India (RBI), which mandates that financial institutions must provide a virtual keyboard for customers to create and enter passwords for accessing NetBanking services [37]. This is primarily done to protect the customer's credentials from being compromised by key-logger software installed on untrusted or shared computers. The application of a virtual keyboards for safeguarding customer credentials is also prevalent in other geographies [4,10,42].

For a user moving from a physical keyboard to a virtual keyboard is not intuitive, especially when they have to use it for entering important data like passwords. Even a small amount of change in character placement and its size affects the overall usability of the keyboard [52]. A similar statement was made by Ann-Marie Horcher [19], who proposed a new virtual keyboard design for mobile devices in her work. From a security perspective, prior work has studied the various aspects of the usability of a virtual keyboard for password-related tasks. For example, Schaub et al. [40] studied user experience variations when users have to use a virtual keyboard on a small-scale display for password creation and their susceptibility to shoulder surfing attacks. Melicher et al. [30] conducted a between-subjects online study with 2,709 participants. Their findings indicated that entering passwords using the virtual keyboard on a mobile device is significantly slower, more error-prone, and more frustrating compared to other password input methods (e.g., pattern lock, biometrics etc.). Yang et al. [51] studied the effect of text entry method on password security and showed significant effect of text entry methods on the amount of lowercase letters per password. Chang et al. [7] observed that increase in button width or height, and location of the button on a mobile-based virtual keyboard reduces the task completion time and error rate. Most past research has primarily focused on the usability of virtual keyboards on mobile devices. However, factors such as screen type, screen size and position of the virtual keyboard play crucial roles and significantly affect user performance, especially as age increases [55,56]. Additionally, password complexity tends to decrease with age, regardless of gender [23].

Most work related to the usability analysis of virtual keyboards begins by recruiting participants to use the system, either under moderated or unmoderated conditions. The experiments are preceded and followed by surveys and questionnaires to capture basic demographic details of the participants and their feedback of the system under evaluation. Finally, they employ various statistical methods to analyze data and draw meaningful conclusions about usability and user experience, for example, descriptive statistics (mean, median, mode, standard deviation) [26,51,55,56], inferential statistics (T-Tests, ANOVA, Chi-Square Test) [7,23,26,30,40,51,52,55,56], correlation analysis (Pearson's correlation coefficient, Spearman's rank correlation) [23], regression analysis (linear, logistic) [7,30], surveys [19,28,51] etc.

These statistical methods focus on quantifying and testing hypotheses about usability data. They provide a means to analyze data distributions, differences between groups, and relationships between variables. However, they are less effective at understanding user interactions and behaviors. Additionally, they also lack in visualizing and analyzing the structure and dynamics of user tasks and their navigation patterns, which is important to identify specific usability bottlenecks and inefficiencies by examining the flow of user interactions and targeted improvements in design. For instance, Ziefle et al. [56] used graph-based analysis to automatically evaluate the difficulty of solving tasks within a hypertext structure. Similarly, Chiou et al. [8] employed graphs, known as Keyboard Focus Flow Graphs (KFFG), to automatically detect navigation-based web accessibility barriers for keyboard users.

In this paper, we propose using graph analysis to evaluate the usability of virtual keyboards for password entry tasks. This approach is particularly relevant in the context of organizations that enforce strict password composition policies, which impose constraints such as update periods, length and character class requirements, and restrictions on reusing old passwords and common patterns. Research has shown that these policies often lead users to adopt coping strategies, such as incrementally modifying their passwords to meet the requirements [16,17]. The challenges users face under these policies-including the frequent need to make corrections and modifications can be effectively visualized and analyzed through sequence graphs. These graphs represent the entire sequence of characters entered by a user, along with any corrections or modifications made during the typing process.

Our approach is quantitative, focusing on analyzing graph properties to uncover relationships between usability and these identified properties. The rationale for using graph analysis is as follows: ① Graph-based usability analysis provides a comprehensive view of user interactions by visualizing the relationships and patterns between various elements of the virtual keyboard. ② Unlike static methods, graph-based analysis can dynamically capture and represent complex interactions and sequences of actions, offering deeper insights into user behavior and difficulties, such as the use of special symbols and a tendency toward lowercase letters. ③ Graph analysis helps identify specific usability bottlenecks and inefficiencies by examining the flow of user interactions, allowing for targeted improvements in design. Using the sequence graph, we try to answer the following research questions:

- **RQ1.** How do a user's discomfort, confusion, and interaction patterns affect the usability of virtual keyboards as reflected in the graph structure? We will

Explore how specific usability issues like difficulty in locating keys, awkward hand movements, or cognitive load are mirrored in the graph's structural properties.

- **RQ2.** How does the nature of the password creation task, including task-requirement and recall time gap, influence user experience and the corresponding graph structure? We investigate how different aspects of the task (e.g., password creation, short- and long-term password recall) impact user behavior and their experience, and how these are reflected in graph metrics.

- **RQ3.** Is there a correlation between usability metrics (e.g., task completion time, error rates, user confusion) and graph characteristics such as the number of edges, cycles, and graph density? We will try to understand how user experience factors correlate with structural elements in the graph.

While both, **RQ2** and **RQ3**, address the link between usability and graph metrics, the first statement connects task-specific factors (validation errors, navigation, and time pressure) to user experience and graph metrics, and the second statement correlates general usability metrics (like completion time, error rates, user confusion) with the graph's structural elements.

The rest of the paper is organized as follows. Section 2 presents a brief survey of the related work. We describe our data collection and analysis methodology in Sects. 4 and 3. We discuss the participant demographic details, result and observations in Sect. 5. Section 6 discusses the limitations of our study. We discuss the effectiveness of our work, mapping to the research questions, and future research problems in Sect. 7. Finally, we conclude in Sect. 8.

2   Related Work

After a thorough search, we found only a few research papers on applying graph analysis to the usability study of on-device numeric keyboards. While keystroke analysis for continuous biometric authentication is a well-studied topic [5,6,9,24,31], it is typically considered a non-intrusive verification scheme that authenticates a user based on their keystroke behavior. Any deviation from this normal behavior is flagged for further scrutiny. Some prior methods involve character sequence analysis, but these approaches are used to build user behavior models rather than for usability analysis.

Thimbleby et al. [45] demonstrated that it is possible to analyze the usability of a device using Markov models. They introduced the concept of a "knowledge/usability graph", which captures the impact of user knowledge on their perception of usability and potential biases resulting from prior knowledge. However, their approach was statistical, focusing on identifying possible user behaviors and only considering forward steps to achieve the goal.

In a later work, Harold Thimbleby [44] proposed "action graphs", which explicitly use user actions as arcs in a graph derived from the system specification. In this model, user actions represent the entire sequence of actions needed to reach a particular state; for example, "having performed action P, the user performs Q". This system can be used to evaluate the performance of an interactive system by applying user performance metrics. Thimbleby demonstrated the applicability of his solution to smaller keyboards used for system control. One key observation from his work was that optimal task time and keystroke counts are correlated, which aligns with our observations. However, Thimbleby considered the keyboard layout as irrelevant, his work focused on small keyboards for control devices, and his method for graph creation differs from our proposed approach.

Jochen Rick [38] investigated the influence of keyboard layout on stroke-based text entry. His study examined a four-stroke sequence to understand the effects of distance and angle on different segments of the sequence. The focus of Rick's work was more on performance than on the usability of the keyboard layout. For studying the usability of mobile applications, Balagtas et al. [3] employed graph-based analysis. Interaction graphs were created based on users' activities on mobile application screens. They used the total number of steps and the time taken to complete a task as measures of learnability, efficiency, and memorability of the system. Ziefle et al. [56] also used graph-based analysis to automatically evaluate the level of difficulty for solving a given task while navigating through a hypertext structure. Similarly, Chiou et al. [8] used graphs, referred to as Keyboard Focus Flow Graphs (KFFGs), to automatically detect navigation-based web accessibility barriers for keyboard users.

Our proposed analysis method is similar to the approaches described by Balagtas et al. [3] and Chiou et al. [8], but there are significant differences in the graph structure and graph creation strategy. For instance, our graph has a bounded state in terms of the number of nodes (vertices), whereas their graphs have nodes that represent individual user-interface controls on each screen, which vary depending on the application's coverage and context. Additionally, their analyses do not account for back-steps (backtracking) as a measure to evaluate usability, which limits their ability to capture user confusion when performing tasks.

3   Graph Analysis for Identifying Usability Issues

In this section, we will provide a brief overview of graph analysis and its application to usability analysis.

3.1   Introduction to Graph Analysis

Graph analysis is the study of graphs, which are mathematical structures used to model pairwise relationships between objects. In graph analysis, you examine the properties, patterns, and structures of graphs to gain insights into the relationships and dynamics represented by the graph. A graph G is a triple consisting of vertex set $V(G)$ and edge set $E(G)$ and a relation that associates with each edge two vertices called its endpoint [39,50]. The vertices u and v are said to be neighbors if they are the endpoints of an edge $e \in E$. Here, G represents an undirected graph as the edges do not have a direction, meaning that the connection between any two vertices is bidirectional [49]. This implies that if there is an edge between vertex u and vertex v, it can be traversed in both directions: from u to v and from v to u. A directed graph is a type of graph in which the edges have a direction. This means that each edge connects a specific starting vertex to a specific ending vertex, indicating a one-way relationship between them. In a graph G with vertices A, B and C, if the endpoints of an edge is same then that edge is called a loop (i.e. A $\rightarrow$ A), whereas, a cycle is a path in a graph that starts and ends at the same vertex, with all other vertices in the path being distinct, that is, if there are edges A $\rightarrow$ B, B $\rightarrow$ C, C $\rightarrow$ A, then A $\rightarrow$ B $\rightarrow$ C $\rightarrow$ A forms a cycle. Here, path is a sequence of vertices connected by edges.

Graph analysis is useful for understanding relationships by identifying how vertices are connected, detecting clusters or communities, and understanding the flow of information or resources. Various centrality measures are used to identify the most important or central nodes within a network (graph). Additionally, detecting patterns in networks can help identify specific subgraphs (e.g., cliques, trees), motifs (e.g., triangles, k-cores), or recurring structures (e.g., communities, paths, cycles) that reveal significant information about the data. For example, in social networks, detecting communities or influential subgroups can help in understanding social dynamics, while in biological networks, identifying motifs can reveal the functional roles of genes or proteins [54]. Furthermore, graph-based analysis can improve processes such as network design, routing, evaluation of interactive systems, and resource allocation.

```
p:6.092||BackSpace:1.578||CapsOn:0.275||P:0.879||CapsOff:0.75||h:0.4
47||l:0.333||k:0.208||BackSpace:5.163||k:4.226||$:11.684||BackSpace:
2.054||@:0.904||BackSpace:1.458||$:1.215||&:3.463||2:25.6||0:0.195||
I:11.114||BackSpace:1.401||!:1.183||Submit-Success||
```

Fig. 1. An example key-press sequence for final password Phlk$&20!

For better understanding, let us examine the key-press sequence shown in Fig. 1 to introduce the key graph concepts. Each key press is comprised of two components: the pressed character and the time taken to press that key (relative to the previous key press or the start of the experiment). We use : as the delimiter to separate the character from the time, and || as the delimiter to separate individual key presses. The final password string is Phlk$&20!, and the corresponding password structure is ULLLSSNNS, which is obtained by replacing each character of the password with its respective character-class. This structure-based approach helps in reducing the number of transition states (i.e., vertices), thereby decreasing the overall analysis complexity [48].

The key-press sequence shown in Fig. 1 can be represented as a directed graph, where the edges depict the temporal or causal relationships between key presses. This representation allows us to model and analyze the exact sequence of key presses, which is crucial for understanding the input flow or reconstructing

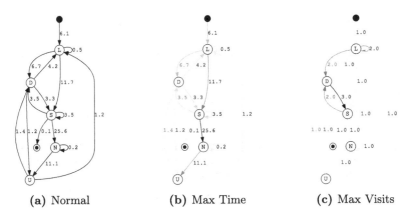

(a) Normal   (b) Max Time   (c) Max Visits

Fig. 2. Graphs generated from the key-press sequence of Fig. 1. In Fig. 2b and 2c, we color the edges of the directed graph using hues of grey based on normalized time and visits. The dark edge color indicate more frequently traversed than the light colored edge. In Fig. 2a and Fig. 2b, the edge label indicate the total time spent (in seconds) on that edge, whereas in Fig. 2c, the edge label shows the total number of time that edge was visited.

the input sequence. For instance, the final password in the key-press sequence shown in Fig. 1 was created in approximately 110 s. However, the most active paths, in terms of time and frequency of visits, are not immediately apparent. By representing the sequence as a directed graph (Fig. 2a) and coloring the edges based on normalized time and visit counts, these active paths become more visible (see Figs. 2b and 2c).

In the following sub-section, we will discuss various graph-based analysis techniques for the usability evaluation of a virtual keyboard in password entry tasks. Although our study focuses on a virtual keyboard, the proposed method is applicable to any data input mechanism with bounded states and known transitions.

3.2 Data Analysis

We capture virtual key press events to create a sequence graph for analyzing participants' behavior. For this analysis, let $G = (V, E, A)$ represent the directed sequence graph of the interaction, where V is the set of vertices consisting of click events, E is the set of edges between them, and A is the set of attributes associated with the vertices and edges. For QWERTY keyboard users, the total number of potential vertices is 94 (26 lowercase characters, 26 uppercase characters, 10 numbers, and 32 symbol keys). We reduced the number of vertices to six by extending the approach of Weir et al. [48]. Specifically, we replaced individual keys with their respective character classes (U' for uppercase, L' for lowercase, N' for numbers, and S' for symbols). Additionally, we included two more vertices for deletion (D') and feedback error (E'). This reduction in the number of vertices facilitates clearer visualization, reduces computation, and helps preserve end-user privacy, without affecting the outcome of the analysis.

For analyzing the usability of the virtual keyboard for password entry, we utilized the following metrics:

- VoteRank - It is a centrality measure that indicates the importance or influence of a vertex within a graph. VoteRank employs a voting scheme to compute the ranking of nodes. Initially, all nodes vote for their in-neighbors, and iteratively, the node with the highest number of votes is selected. In subsequent iterations, the voting power of the out-neighbors of the selected node is reduced [53]. The output of this algorithm is a list of nodes ranked by decreasing influence. If a deletion node (D) ranks in the top four, it suggests that the user has made a relatively high number of errors and corrections. In addition to VoteRank, other centrality measures can be utilized. For example, an out-degree centrality measure for the deletion (D) node indicates a user's choice of character class when they encounter feedback for a password validation error.
- Graph density - It refers to the ratio of the number of edges present in the graph to the maximum number of edges possible in a graph of the same size. Mathematically, the density (d) of a directed graph with n vertices and m edges is defined as:

$$d = \frac{m}{n * (n - 1)} \tag{1}$$

High density indicates that many vertices are connected to each other with directed edges and suggests a complex network structure where the user is consistently moving between different states. Whereas a low-density graph indicates a linear transition and most likely the use of simple dictionary words.
- Cycles - A cycle is a sequence of vertices and edges that forms a closed loop, where each edge has a direction. Formally, a cycle in a directed graph is represented as $(v_1, v_2, \ldots, v_k, v_1)$, where $(v_1, \ldots, v_k) \in V$ and there is a directed edge between $(v_i, v_{i+1}) \in E$ with $1 \le i \le k - 1$ and a directed edge from v_k to v_1. A graph with a large number of cycles suggests interconnectedness within the network. For virtual keyboard usability for password entry, the cycles can be interpreted as follows:
  - Cycles with one node - It represents the predominance of one character class, for example, using lowercase words. If the node is a deletion node (D), then it shows a major update in the password due to policy constraints.
  - Cycles with multiple nodes - It either represents a transition between different character classes to comply with the password policy. Whereas, cycles with D and E nodes suggest that the user is incrementally changing and submitting the password until the changed password complies with the policy.
- Transition Analysis - This process involves calculating transitions between nodes in a given sequence graph. Additionally, we use the time spent pressing each key as a factor to estimate the total time spent on a given edge $(u, v) \in E$.

This approach helps in extracting meaningful patterns (e.g., pattern reuse, common word usage) and identifying frequent sub-sequences. We also use the time taken to move from one key state to another as the edge weight. For complex tasks such as password entry, longer transition times can indicate a user's discomfort, confusion, or difficulty in reaching certain key combinations.

4 Experiment Methodology

4.1 Participant Recruitment

Figure 3 shows the different phases of our experiment. For the recruitment of participants for our lab study, we broadcasted an email within our organization, asking for their voluntary participation during a self-registration period of five days. All participants had a minimum education of bachelor's in engineering/technology, although it was not mandatory condition for registration. Participants were required to have some basic familiarity with internet browsers, navigating and accessing web-application, and the requirement of password for accessing the web-applications. These requirements ensure that participants are not complete novices and have the necessary skills to interact with the web application and the virtual-keyboard being studied. This helps to prevent issues arising from lack of basic technical knowledge, which could skew the results or complicate the analysis of usability issues. This allows the study to better isolate and assess specific usability aspects of the virtual keyboard rather than issues related to participants' basic technology skills.

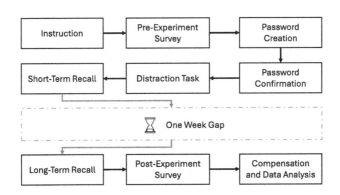

Fig. 3. Different phases in our experimental setup.

We received 36 responses from the employees of the organization. After removing the abandoning participation, the total count came down to 30 participants. We sent an email to all the respondents with details and the intention of our study, the data that we will capture for analysis, and the retention period of the data. Despite the email, the participants were explicitly instructed not to use their existing passwords. Finally, the email asked them to confirm their willingness to participate and provide their consent for analyzing their captured data.

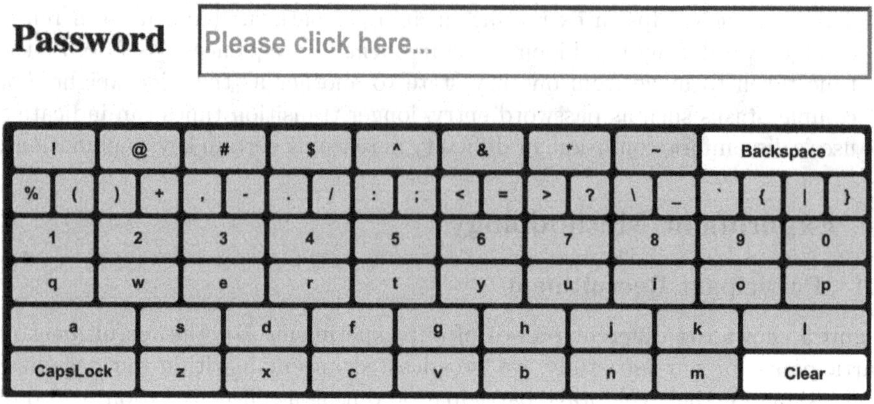

Password | Please click here...

Fig. 4. The virtual-keyboard implemented for the hypothetical bank application.

The compensation for participation was also clearly mentioned in the recruitment email. We paid participants USD 2 for completing the surveys, password creation, and long-term recall activity. Our analysis includes only participants who have completed all the parts.

4.2 Surveys

In the pre-experiment survey, we collected data on the number of passwords handled by the users on a regular basis. We gathered data related to any previous challenges encountered while creating passwords using a virtual keyboard. Along with that, we also collected basic demographic information about each participant, as well as their name and email address for contacting them and sending the compensation for participating in the experiments. The demography data that we captured consists of their gender, age bracket, highest education level, and self-assessment of basic cybersecurity concepts. In the post-experiment survey, we collected their overall rating of the virtual keyboard and any feedback on the virtual keyboard in plain text. We did not capture any data that could possibly lead to privacy concerns, for example, regional backgrounds, exact age, nature of accounts with passwords, frequency of access etc.

4.3 Experiment Setup

We created a web-based login screen for a hypothetical bank application and asked participants to create a password according to the fictional bank's password composition policy. The QWERTY virtual keyboard (Fig. 4) used for password entry (both creation and recall) did not include any special assistance features, and validation errors were shown only after the user submitted the password for processing on the server. Server-side processing was intentionally employed to simulate real-world conditions and observe the impact of such delays on users' password creation behavior. Participants were expected to use the virtual keyboard with a mouse, as is typical for setting passwords on desktop or laptop computers.

In the study, participants were first asked to create a password, then confirm it, and finally recall the password using the same keyboard. After successfully setting a compliant password, participants were given a distraction task to ensure that the password was not currently stored in their working memory. Following this task, they were asked to re-enter the password they had created. This setup allowed us to measure recall efficiency after a delay. If participants were unable to recall their password after five attempts, it was revealed to them in clear text. They were then instructed not to write down the password and were scheduled to return for a long-term recall experiment one week later.

Regarding the colors used on the keyboard, we selected those with high contrast and high luminance contrast, as these factors have been shown to improve legibility [25]. Luminance contrast refers to the difference in brightness between the foreground and the background [27, 46].

4.4   Distraction Task

We introduced a distraction activity after the password confirmation page. A distraction task helps divert the attention of participants for a brief period before the short-term recall stage [29]. This is shown to be useful in assessing the memorability of the created password [22]. As the NIST guidelines suggest, provide textual content for a 6th to 8th grade literacy level [15]; therefore, the distraction task consisted of two-digit addition and subtraction problems. The distraction task is generated at runtime to prevent participants from memorizing the result and sharing it with other participants. Password memorability refers to how easily and reliably a user can recall a password when needed.

5   Demographic Details, Result and Observation

This paper sets out to understand the applicability of sequence graph analysis for analyzing the usability of virtual keyboards for password entry tasks. We analyzed the responses received from 30 participants. Specifically, we looked to answer the research questions discussed earlier (Sect. 1). Among the 30 participants, 56.7% identified as male and 43.3% as female. Almost two-thirds of the participants reported an above-average understanding of cybersecurity concepts. Around 50% of the participants faced some issues while creating a password for an account using a virtual keyboard. Three-fourths of them reported having less than 20 accounts that require password authentication. Two-thirds of the participants were between the ages of 21 and 30, whereas 25% were between 31 and 40. More than half of the participants selected their qualification as post-graduation or above. More than three-fourths of the participants preferred to switch back to a physical keyboard. Acclimatization issues and a lack of muscle memory were two outstanding pieces of feedback given against the use of a virtual keyboard.

5.1   Prerequisites Color Usage and Nomenclature

Color Usage. In this study, we used Seaborn's "colorblind" color palette[1] in boxplots to ensure the plots are accessible to individuals with color vision deficiencies. This palette includes three distinct colors designed to be distinguishable from each other even for those with vision deficiencies. By adhering to this palette, we aim to provide visualizations that are both informative and inclusive. Following is the description of each color:

- ■ Used for ① password `creation` task in Fig. 7, and ② number of `cycles` in Fig. 9.
- ■ Used for ① `short-term` password recall task in Fig. 6, and ② number of `edges` in Fig. 9.
- ■ Used for ① `long-term` password recall task in Fig. 6, and ② number of `delete` operations in Fig. 9.

Nomenclature. The nomenclature used in the various sequence graphs presented in this paper are discussed below. The vertices in the sequence graph either represent the type of key-press or a special state (`start` and `end` of the experiment). The various vertex types used in Fig. 2, Fig. 5, Fig. 7 and Fig. 8 are described below:

1. Ⓤ - Uppercase character in the password. Value ranges from A–Z.
2. Ⓛ - Lowercase character in the password. Value ranges from a–z.
3. Ⓝ - Number used in the password. Value ranges from 0–9.
4. Ⓢ - A "special symbol" refers to any character that is not a letter or digit.
5. Ⓓ - Represents a `delete` operation.
6. Ⓔ - Represents a password `validation error` from the server.
7. ● - Represents `start` of the experiment.
8. ◉ - Represents `end` of the experiment.

Similarly, an edge describes the relationship between any two vertices, which could be same in case of loops (Sect. 3.1). Depending on the scenario, we have used different edge labels to accurately describe, analyze, and communicate the structure of the graph. The color of the edge label represents the following scenario:

- a ■ color label text represents a delete operation.
- a ■ color label text represents a new character class insertion after a delete or a validation error.
- a ■ label text represents a validation error.
- a ■ label text represents an edge between expected character-classes.

We color the edges of the directed graph using shades of grey based on normalized time or number of visits. Darker edge colors indicate that the edge is either traversed more frequently or has more time spent on it compared to lighter-colored edges.

---

[1] https://seaborn.pydata.org/tutorial/color_palettes.html.

Table 1. The graph attributes for a selected participant. The density of short-term is a bit higher than long-term density as short-term has one less node. The **true** for vote means presence of D or E in top 4 nodes.

	density	votes	cycles	nodes	edges	errors	deletes
create	0.48	true	9	7	20	0	5
short-term recall	0.33	false	0	6	10	0	0
long-term recall	0.29	false	0	7	12	0	1

5.2 Effect of Task on Sequence Graph

In our lab experiment, we have asked users to first create a password for a fictional bank and then recall that password after a short and long break. Here, a short break is the amount of time required by a participant to solve the distraction task, which consists of the sum of two randomly generated numbers of three digits. Such complexity is desirable because it increases variability and tends to tax the participant's attention and immediate memory [12]. It increases a participant's chance of forgetting the password and helps test the memorability of the set password. The long break was set to be seven days after the password creation experiment.

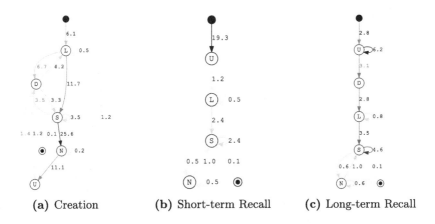

(a) Creation (b) Short-term Recall (c) Long-term Recall

Fig. 5. Effect of task on sequence graph for a selected participant. The edge label represents the total time spent (in seconds) on that edge.

Table 1 and Fig. 5 shows the interaction of a selected participant with the virtual keyboard. The edge label consists of two parts: ① the total amount of time spent on that particular edge, and ② the number of times that edge was visited. The sequence graph in Fig. 5a is more dense than the other two graphs, as the user tried to create a memorable, but policy-compliant password. As it can be observed that there are multiple edits and backtracking due to password validation error. The user effort is evident from the amount of time spent on the initial edges between D→L and L→D, that is, either deleting a character or inserting a lowercase character, which results in cycle in the graph. A similar behavior (higher edge time) can be seen for the following edges: L→S, S→N, and N→U (Fig. 2b). As mentioned in prior work [40], we also observed that it takes longer to type a special character on virtual keyboards with full QWERTY layout.

For short-term recall (Fig. 5b), no corrections were made, so the graph primarily consists of basic character classes. In contrast, Fig. 5c shows a single correction made during long-term recall (U→D); otherwise, all other edge attributes remain unchanged. This correction was attributed to a typo by the participant, as evidenced by the linear structure of the graph. Similar findings were reported in previous research on the usability of virtual keyboards for password entry across various stages of experimentation [40].

Overall, participants reported unusually high times for a small number of visits, attributing this to confusion in decision-making or infrequent use of the mouse pointer as an input method. Despite using the standard QWERTY keyboard layout, the mouse-pointer input mechanism and the virtual keyboard's positioning made navigation challenging for new and infrequent users. Figure 2c also illustrates users' bias towards certain character classes (L and S). Usability issues, such as difficulty locating keys, awkward hand movements, and cognitive load, are reflected in the graph's structural properties, addressing the research question **RQ1**.

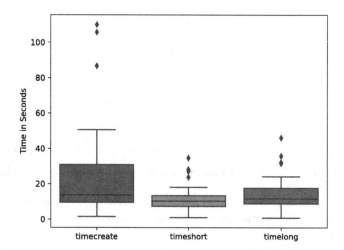

Fig. 6. Comparing the total time taken by all participants for password creation (`timecreate`), short-term recall (`timeshort`), and long-term recall (`timelong`).

The relationship between the usability of a virtual keyboard and the assigned task is also evident in Fig. 6. The median time taken for password creation is longer than the median time taken for short-term and long-term recall. The length of the box in the figure indicates greater variability for the password creation task. The spread for long-term recall is slightly higher than that for short-term recall, primarily due to the additional time needed to recall the password after a one-week gap. This can be attributed to: ① the purpose for which the password was created and the inherent value it protects [18], and ② the frequency of usage of the input device, which helps in forming muscle memory [47].

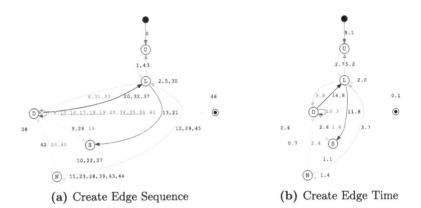

(a) Create Edge Sequence   (b) Create Edge Time

Fig. 7. For a selected participant Fig. 7a shows **sequence** of edge traversal, whereas Fig. 7b shows the amount of **time** spent on each edge.

There were a few outliers in all three stages. Their times were higher than those of other participants due to either attempting to create a compliant but memorable password or a complex password that was harder to recall. The tendency of users to create either memorable (and compliant) passwords or complex (but strong) passwords also impacts individual tasks. For instance, memorable and compliant passwords often require more edits due to validation errors, as shown in Fig. 7. In contrast, complex passwords tend to take longer to recall after a long gap, as evidenced by the substantial time taken and multiple submission errors. This is illustrated by the repeated visits to vertex E in Fig. 8. Furthermore, Fig. 8b shows 72 delete operations, indicating user frustration from repeatedly failing to recall the correct password and submitting incorrect ones consecutively. This issue is linked to infrequent use of the virtual keyboard during password creation. These observations suggest that various aspects of the task-such as password creation and both short- and long-term password recall-impact user behavior and overall experience. This is reflected in the sequence graph and addresses the research question **RQ2**.

5.3   Relationship Between Graph Attributes and Usability

We found that when participants use the delete key more than twice, it typically indicates that they are encountering issues due to password validation errors.

The incremental updates to their passwords are making them less memorable. This memorability issue was identified by comparing the graphs of both recall steps. In these situations, users often either restart from scratch or remove a significant portion of the entered password.

Figure 7 illustrates the password creation behavior of such users. The delete key usage during steps (6–8), (15–19), and (34–36) indicates the removal of a substantial portion of the password, while steps (24, 25) and (40, 41) show minor incremental updates. Overall, frequent use of the delete key increases the number of cycles and edges, leading to higher graph density.

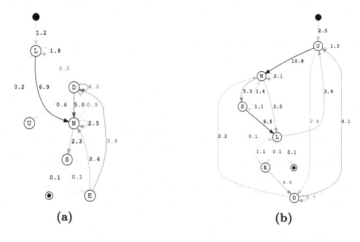

(a)   (b)

Fig. 8. The effect of error feedback on the usage of "delete" (D) as a corrective measure by two different participants for long-term recall.

In Fig. 7a, the graph shows 11 cycles and 47 edges due to extensive delete key use (18 times), resulting in a graph density of 1.12, approximately 133% higher than the maximum graph density reported in Table 1. For the same participant, Fig. 7b depicts the amount of time spent on each node and the frequency with which each edge is visited. There are three key observations:

1. The maximum cumulative time is for in-and-out edges from delete node (approximately 36 s). The participant attributed this to use of a pointing device for password creation.
2. Second largest edge time is for edges going to symbol node, which is in accordance with previous work [40].
3. We observed higher edge time for D→L and L→D for multiple users. This is evident from Fig. 7b and Fig. 5a. Past work has also highlighted the dominance of lowercase over other character classes, but unfortunately none of them mentioned any correlation between delete operation and lowercase characters to compare our observation.

Table 2. Graph attributes of the long-recall sequence graphs of Fig. 8.

	Density	Cycles	Edges	Delete Operations
Fig. 8a	1.0	7	56	21
Fig. 8b	2.21	13	124	72

A similar behavior was observed during the long-term recall phase; however, the increase in the complexity of the sequence graphs is primarily due to failures in recalling the set password within the allowed number of attempts. Figure 8 shows the sequence graphs from the long-term recall experiment for two different users. In Fig. 8a, it can be seen that users either make minor changes to the password before resubmitting (E→N, N→S, S→E), or perform major updates before resubmission (E→D, D→D, D→N or D→U). In contrast, Fig. 8b shows that the participant first attempted an incremental change (E→L) and, upon encountering an error, completely removed the entire string and started from scratch (E→D, D→D, D→N or D→U). The density, number of transitions, and cycles increase due to the higher use of the delete key than usual. Table 2 displays various graph attributes for two different users who experienced difficulties recalling their passwords.

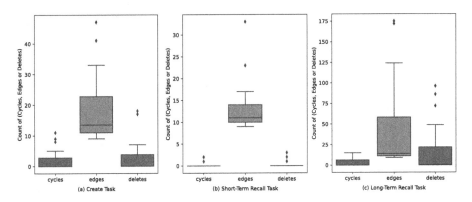

Fig. 9. Effect of number of edges on the various graph based metrics. The Y-axis scale is different for all three plots.

The number of edges in a sequence graph has a direct impact on density, cycles, transitions, and delete operations (VoteRank). The edges themselves depend on the nature of the task; that is, complicated and confusing tasks will have a higher number of edges (e.g., password creation) than simpler tasks (e.g., short-term recall). Another contributing factor to the higher edge count is the memorability of the password, which is influenced by the incentive associated with it. In our experiment, we did not explicitly mention any incentive for the memorability of the password. The participants were expected to just finish both stages (creation and long-term recall). However, in a recent study, Nicholson et al. [33] have shown that associating a small financial incentive with password creation helps with the security and memorability of the password. Due to this, some of the participants failed to recall their respective passwords and eventually ended up correcting their input string multiple times. In post-survey feedback, they attributed this to a change in password input mechanism, which is the same as the finding of Schaub et al. [40] and a lack of incentive for remembering it. Figure 9 shows the effect of these two factors on the number of cycles, edges, and delete operations. It can be observed that for all three scenarios (create, short-term recall, and long-term recall), the data is positively skewed for all three metrics (edges, cycles, and deletes). The median number of edges for all three scenarios is between 12 and 14. The higher variability in deletes for the create scenario is due to validation feedback, whereas the variability in deletes for long-term recall is due to some users forgetting their passwords.

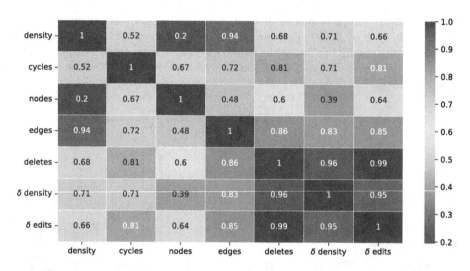

Fig. 10. Correlation between different graph based metrics. The attribute δ **density** refers to the difference in the graph densities of password **creation** graphs and **short-term** recall graphs. The δ **edits** is graph edit distance between the password **creation** graphs and **short-term** recall graphs, that is, number of edits needed to convert one graph to other.

Finally, in Fig. 10, we present the correlation matrix for different graph attributes and the metrics discussed earlier. It can be observed that density, number of delete operations, and edge count are highly correlated. Although the correlation between cycles and edges is moderate. This could be due to the fact that sequence graphs are relatively small in size, and we traverse the graph as per the direction of the edge between vertices, which may not result in cycles. Further, if the graph itself is dense, then the addition of edges might not have a more noticeable effect as the cycles may already be prevalent. From the usability perspective of a virtual keyboard, cycles with specific nodes ('E' and 'D') are more important than the rest of the nodes (character classes) as they convey the error and correction behavior of the user. This demonstrates a correlation between usability metrics (e.g., cumulative and granular-level task time, error rates, user confusion) and graph characteristics such as the number of edges, cycles, VoteRank, and graph density, thereby validating our research question **RQ3**.

6   Limitation

In our experiments, the population is not representative of all groups, and future research could broaden the population (for example, students versus professionals, teenagers versus old people, different educational backgrounds, etc.). Since we have not incentivized successful long-term recall, there were issues due to the memorability of the created passwords. Also, our study has a skewed distribution of different age groups and education of the participants. This was not deliberate, as we kept the recruitment window open for all employees working in our research lab for a period of five days. We speculate that it is due to the short recruitment time window and channel of communication used for recruitment (e-mail in this case). Furthermore, we did not collect any data that could raise privacy concerns, such as regional background, specific age, account details including passwords, or account access frequency. While such data might have offered insights into their impact on factors affecting the usability of the virtual keyboard for password creation and the overall study, we chose to exclude it to protect participant privacy. Despite these limitations, our preliminary results seem encouraging, as some of our observations agree with recent work in the area of human factors in computing systems.

7   Discussion, Design Suggestions and Open Problems

In this paper, we propose a graph-based method for augmenting the statistical analysis of usability in a virtual keyboard for password entry tasks. The intuition behind using graphs is that users often encounter validation errors while creating passwords, leading them to either iteratively modify the entered string or correct it in one attempt to achieve compliance. This back-and-forth behavior generates a sequence of characters that can be represented as a sequence graph. Our method aims to complement traditional statistical analysis by capturing user interactions and analyzing them for potential issues, thereby providing a more comprehensive understanding of usability challenges.

For confusion and complex behaviors, the resultant graph tends to exhibit more edges, higher edge weights (representing the time to transition between nodes), cycles, and increased density. Even in cases of simpler behaviors, where the sequence graph is nearly linear, the large edge weights highlight the challenges associated with using a mouse pointer as an input device. This addresses **RQ1**, which investigates how user discomfort (or confusion) affects the graph structure. Additionally, it provides insights into **RQ3**, concerning the correlation between the number of edges, cycles, and graph density (as detailed in Sect. 5.3). We also explored **RQ2** in Sect. 5.2, where we examined how the nature of the task influences the graph structure.

To evaluate the effectiveness of our method, we conducted a lab study focusing on password creation, short-term recall, and long-term recall. A key finding of our research is that virtual keyboard usability varies depending on the task. For password creation, nearly all participants required more time compared to short-term recall. This task impacted the number of edges, cycles in the graph, transitions, time needed for transitions, and overall graph density. Additionally, some participants attributed the complexity of their sequence graph to the switch from a physical keyboard to a virtual keyboard. Based on the findings of Nicholson et al. [33], we hypothesize that this complexity may be due to a lack of muscle memory when using a virtual keyboard.

We presented a specific scenario where the proposed graph-based analysis could be utilized. While this technique can be applied to other use cases, such as training a graph neural network (GNN) to detect anomalous user login sessions given sufficient labeled samples, it also has broader applications. For example, we can analyze unique paths through the graph to identify user-specific habits, preferences, or areas where they might struggle with keyboard use. This analysis could inform the tailoring of the keyboard layout according to users' behaviors.

During data analysis, we observed that the majority of users tend to follow a predetermined pattern of using U(1), L(2-4), N(1-2), and S(1-2), where the capital letters represent character classes and the numbers indicate the typical number of characters used from each class. This behavior is vulnerable to probabilistic guessing attacks, suggesting that a proactive, dynamic layout could be implemented to mitigate such risks.

7.1   Design Suggestions

Based on our findings, we propose the following changes to virtual keyboards meant for password related tasks:

1. Position of symbols and numbers - As shown in Fig. 4, the symbols and numbers are positioned adjacent to each other. This arrangement may bias users into selecting a number immediately after pressing a symbol key, or vice versa. This behavior ($N{\to}S$ or $S{\to}N$) is evident in all the graphs (Fig. 5a, Fig. 7a, Fig. 8a and Fig. 8b). Previous research indicates that such predictable behaviors can lead to weaker passwords. We hypothesize that repositioning these two character classes could help users make better decisions and enhance password strength.

2. Curated list of symbols - Past research has shown that users exhibit a bias towards certain symbols when creating passwords (e.g., !, @ and #) [41]. We conjecture that this bias arises because these symbols are easy to type and are among the first three symbols on standard QWERTY keyboards, making them convenient choices for users aiming to create passwords that are strong,

manageable, and compliant with password policies. We propose that instead of displaying standard QWERTY symbols, the virtual keyboard should shuffle the symbols and present a limited set. Our hypothesis is that this approach would enhance password strength (by encouraging the use of less frequently used symbols) and reduce cognitive load (by presenting fewer symbols). A similar approach was taken by Pathak et al. [35], who analyzed the structure of passwords against predefined heuristics and nudged users to improve their passwords.

3. Provide in-place validation - Some participants noted that server-side password validation can be time-consuming, which adds to user frustration. We propose implementing basic validations on the client side, such as checking password length, character class usage, the top 10,000 blacklisted passwords (small list from performance perspective), and common sequences and repetitions. If a password passes these client-side tests, a more extensive validation can be performed on the server side. This approach would help reduce user frustration and encourage the creation of stronger passwords by avoiding poor password practices.

4. Visual categorization - The various character classes (uppercase, lowercase, numbers, and symbols) can be separated into different sections or visually distinguished using different background colors. This approach would facilitate easier navigation between these character classes for users.

5. Standardization - Different banks use varying visualizations of the virtual keyboard. As discussed earlier, factors such as size, location, and font significantly affect the usability of the virtual keyboard. Therefore, we hope that a regulatory body will step in to standardize virtual keyboards for password-related tasks.

7.2   Future Work

There are several open research problems we aim to explore in the future. As discussed in previous work, users often create passwords based on the perceived value of the information they are protecting. Additionally, password creation behavior observed in lab settings may not accurately reflect users' real-world behaviors. To address these issues, we plan to deploy a browser add-on to study users' actual password creation behavior in a longitudinal study.

Furthermore, to address the trust issues associated with data collected in lab studies, we are interested in investigating whether the "Bayesian Truth Serum" can serve as an effective mechanism. This approach has been shown to enhance the accuracy of surveys and polls in scenarios where participants might misrepresent their responses.

From an analytical perspective, Graph Neural Networks (GNNs) offer potential for studying the password creation process. For example, GNNs could be used to predict the onset of confusion or discomfort, allowing for dynamic corrective measures. Additionally, the design recommendations suggested in Sect. 7.1 could be explored as independent research problems.

8   Conclusion

Virtual keyboards may resemble traditional keyboards, but when used for tasks that require significant cognitive effort, we observed a decline in user performance. Our experiments were conducted on a large screen with a computer mouse as the navigation device, which introduced additional delays in the edge weights. While we were unable to fully address this issue, we believe there is potential for improvement. Additionally, we plan to extend this study to include a more comprehensive password composition policy and virtual keyboards with dynamic key placement layouts. Although further research is needed to establish graph-based methods for usability analysis, our proposed metrics have demonstrated useful properties and can effectively assess issues with software-based character input interfaces.

References

1. Abdrabou, Y., et al.: "your eyes tell you have used this password before": identifying password reuse from gaze and keystroke dynamics. In: CHI Conference on Human Factors in Computing Systems, pp. 1–16 (2022)
2. Adhikary, N., Shrivastava, R., Kumar, A., Verma, S.K., Bag, M., Singh, V.: Battering keyloggers and screen recording software by fabricating passwords. Int. J. Comput. Netw. Inf. Secur. 4(5), 13 (2012)
3. Balagtas-Fernandez, F., Hussmann, H.: A methodology and framework to simplify usability analysis of mobile applications. In: 2009 IEEE/ACM International Conference on Automated Software Engineering, pp. 520–524. IEEE (2009)
4. Bani-Hani, A., Majdalweieh, M., AlShamsi, A.: Online authentication methods used in banks and attacks against these methods. Procedia Comput. Sci. **151**, 1052–1059 (2019)
5. Bergadano, F., Gunetti, D., Picardi, C.: User authentication through keystroke dynamics. ACM Trans. Inf. Syst. Secur. (TISSEC) **5**(4), 367–397 (2002)
6. Bhana, B., Flowerday, S.: Passphrase and keystroke dynamics authentication: usable security. Comput. Secur. **96**, 101925 (2020)
7. Chang, J., Jung, K.: Effects of button width, height, and location on a soft keyboard: task completion time, error rate, and satisfaction in two-thumb text entry on smartphone. IEEE Access **7**, 69848–69857 (2019)
8. Chiou, P.T., Alotaibi, A.S., Halfond, W.G.: Bagel: an approach to automatically detect navigation-based web accessibility barriers for keyboard users. In: Proceedings of the 2023 CHI Conference on Human Factors in Computing Systems, pp. 1–17 (2023)
9. Crawford, H., Ahmadzadeh, E.: Authentication on the go: assessing the effect of movement on mobile device keystroke dynamics. In: Thirteenth Symposium on Usable Privacy and Security (SOUPS 2017), pp. 163–173 (2017)
10. Credit Europe Bank: Online Banking Safety Measures (2024). https://www.crediteuropebank.com/about-us/online-banking-services/online-banking-safety-measures/. Accessed 23 Aug 2024
11. Davidson, R.: The fight against malware as a service. Netw. Secur. **2021**(8), 7–11 (2021)

12. Engle, R.W., Kane, M.J.: Executive attention, working memory capacity, and a two-factor theory of cognitive control. Psychol. Learn. Motiv. **44**, 145–200 (2004)
13. Feng, T., Zhao, X., Carbunar, B., Shi, W.: Continuous mobile authentication using virtual key typing biometrics. In: 2013 12th IEEE International Conference on Trust, Security and Privacy in Computing and Communications, pp. 1547–1552. IEEE (2013)
14. Gopali, S., Sharma, P., Khethavath, P.K., Pal, D.: HyPA: a hybrid password-based authentication mechanism. In: Arai, K. (ed.) FICC 2021. AISC, vol. 1363, pp. 651–665. Springer, Cham (2021). https://doi.org/10.1007/978-3-030-73100-7_47
15. Grassi, P.A., et al.: NIST Special Publication 800-63B - Digital Identity Guidelines (2022). https://doi.org/10.6028/NIST.SP.800-63b. Accessed 30 Aug 2022
16. Habib, H., et al.: Password creation in the presence of blacklists. In: Proceedings of USEC, p. 50 (2017)
17. Habib, H., et al.: User behaviors and attitudes under password expiration policies. In: Fourteenth Symposium on Usable Privacy and Security (SOUPS 2018), pp. 13–30 (2018)
18. Haque, S.T., Wright, M., Scielzo, S.: A study of user password strategy for multiple accounts. In: Proceedings of the Third ACM Conference on Data and Application Security and Privacy, pp. 173–176 (2013)
19. Horcher, A.M.: One size does not fit mobile: designing usable security input on mobile devices. In: Proceedings of SOUPS, p. 5 (2018)
20. Hung, C.W., Hsu, F.H., Chen, S.J., Hwang, Y.L., Tso, C.K., Hsu, L.P.: Defend a system against keyloggers with a privilege-limited account. Appl. Mech. Mater. **284**, 3385–3389 (2013)
21. Hylender, C.D., Langlois, P., Pinto, A., Widup, S.: Data Breach Investigations Report (2023). https://www.verizon.com/business/resources/T657/reports/2023-data-breach-investigations-report-dbir.pdf. Accessed 31 Ded 2023
22. Jayakrishnan, G.C., et al.: Passworld: a serious game to promote password awareness and diversity in an enterprise. In: Sixteenth Symposium on Usable Privacy and Security (SOUPS 2020), pp. 1–18 (2020)
23. Juozapavičius, A., Brilingaitė, A., Bukauskas, L., Lugo, R.G.: Age and gender impact on password hygiene. Appl. Sci. **12**(2), 894 (2022)
24. Kim, J., Kang, P.: Freely typed keystroke dynamics-based user authentication for mobile devices based on heterogeneous features. Pattern Recogn. **108**, 107556 (2020)
25. Knoblauch, K., Arditi, A., Szlyk, J.: Effects of chromatic and luminance contrast on reading. JOSA A **8**(2), 428–439 (1991)
26. Költringer, T., Grechenig, T.: Comparing the immediate usability of graffiti 2 and virtual keyboard. In: CHI'04 Extended Abstracts on Human Factors in Computing Systems, pp. 1175–1178 (2004)
27. Legge, G.E., Parish, D.H., Luebker, A., Wurm, L.H.: Psychophysics of reading. XI. Comparing color contrast and luminance contrast. JOSA A **7**(10), 2002–2010 (1990)
28. Ling, Z., et al.: Privacy enhancing keyboard: design, implementation, and usability testing. Wirel. Commun. Mob. Comput. **2017**(1), 3928261 (2017)
29. Liu, Y., Fu, X.: How does distraction task influence the interaction of working memory and long-term memory? In: Harris, D. (ed.) EPCE 2007. LNCS (LNAI), vol. 4562, pp. 366–374. Springer, Heidelberg (2007). https://doi.org/10.1007/978-3-540-73331-7_40

30. Melicher, W., et al.: Usability and security of text passwords on mobile devices. In: Proceedings of the 2016 CHI Conference on Human Factors in Computing Systems, pp. 527–539 (2016)
31. Messerman, A., Mustafić, T., Camtepe, S.A., Albayrak, S.: Continuous and non-intrusive identity verification in real-time environments based on free-text keystroke dynamics. In: 2011 International Joint Conference on Biometrics (IJCB), pp. 1–8. IEEE (2011)
32. Nand, P., Singh, P.K., Aneja, J., Dhingra, Y.: Prevention of shoulder surfing attack using randomized square matrix virtual keyboard. In: 2015 International Conference on Advances in Computer Engineering and Applications, pp. 916–920. IEEE (2015)
33. Nicholson, J., Vlachokyriakos, V., Coventry, L., Briggs, P., Olivier, P.: Simple nudges for better password creation. In: Proceedings of the 32nd International BCS Human Computer Interaction Conference, vol. 32, pp. 1–12 (2018)
34. Pa Pa, Y.M., Tanizaki, S., Kou, T., Van Eeten, M., Yoshioka, K., Matsumoto, T.: An attacker's dream? exploring the capabilities of chatgpt for developing malware. In: Proceedings of the 16th Cyber Security Experimentation and Test Workshop, pp. 10–18 (2023)
35. Pathak, R., et al.: Design and evaluation of a password diversifier tool. In: Indian Conference on Human-Computer Interaction, pp. 51–74. Springer, Heidelberg (2023). https://doi.org/10.1007/978-981-97-4335-3_3
36. Rajarajan, S., Maheswari, K., Hemapriya, R., Sriharilakshmi, S.: Shoulder surfing resistant virtual keyboard for internet banking. World Appl. Sci. J. **31**(7), 1297–1304 (2014)
37. Reserve Bank of India: Internet Banking - Security Features (2024). https://www.rbi.org.in/hindi1/Upload/content/PDFs/C229260416_2.pdf. Accessed 23 Aug 2024
38. Rick, J.: Performance optimizations of virtual keyboards for stroke-based text entry on a touch-based tabletop. In: Proceedings of the 23nd Annual ACM Symposium on User Interface Software and Technology, pp. 77–86 (2010)
39. Rosen, K.H., Krithivasan, K.: Discrete Mathematics and its Applications, vol. 6. McGraw-Hill, New York (1999)
40. Schaub, F., Deyhle, R., Weber, M.: Password entry usability and shoulder surfing susceptibility on different smartphone platforms. In: Proceedings of the 11th International Conference on Mobile and Ubiquitous Multimedia, pp. 1–10 (2012)
41. Shay, R., et al.: Encountering stronger password requirements: user attitudes and behaviors. In: Proceedings of the Sixth Symposium on Usable Privacy and Security, pp. 1–20 (2010)
42. Subsorn, P., Limwiriyakul, S.: An investigation of internet banking security of selected licensed banks in Vietnam. Walailak J. Sci. Technol. (WJST) **13**(6), 411–432 (2016)
43. Tan, D.S., Keyani, P., Czerwinski, M.: Spy-resistant keyboard: more secure password entry on public touch screen displays. In: Proceedings of the 17th Australia conference on Computer-Human Interaction: Citizens Online: Considerations for Today and the Future, pp. 1–10 (2005)
44. Thimbleby, H.: Action graphs and user performance analysis. Int. J. Hum. Comput. Stud. **71**(3), 276–302 (2013)
45. Thimbleby, H., Cairns, P., Jones, M.: Usability analysis with Markov models. ACM Trans. Comput.-Hum. Interact. (TOCHI) **8**(2), 99–132 (2001)

46. Troiano, L., Birtolo, C., Cirillo, G.: Interactive genetic algorithm for choosing suitable colors in user interface. In: Proceedings of Learning and Intelligent Optimization, LION3, pp. 14–18 (2009)
47. Van Koningsbruggen, R., Hengeveld, B., Alexander, J.: Understanding the design space of embodied passwords based on muscle memory. In: Proceedings of the 2021 CHI Conference on Human Factors in Computing Systems, pp. 1–13 (2021)
48. Weir, M., Aggarwal, S., De Medeiros, B., Glodek, B.: Password cracking using probabilistic context-free grammars. In: 2009 30th IEEE Symposium on Security and Privacy, pp. 391–405. IEEE (2009)
49. West, D.B.: Introduction to graph theory (2001)
50. Wilson, R.J.: Introduction to Graph Theory. Pearson Education India (1979)
51. Yang, Y., Lindqvist, J., Oulasvirta, A.: Text entry method affects password security. In: The LASER Workshop: Learning from Authoritative Security Experiment Results (LASER 2014) (2014)
52. Zhai, S., Hunter, M., Smith, B.A.: Performance optimization of virtual keyboards. Hum.-Comput. Interact. **17**(2–3), 229–269 (2002)
53. Zhang, J.X., Chen, D.B., Dong, Q., Zhao, Z.D.: Identifying a set of influential spreaders in complex networks. Sci. Rep. **6**(1), 27823 (2016)
54. Zhang, S., Jin, G., Zhang, X.S., Chen, L.: Discovering functions and revealing mechanisms at molecular level from biological networks. Proteomics **7**(16), 2856–2869 (2007)
55. Zhou, Z., Zhou, J.: Small screen-big information challenge for older adults: a study on visual momentum and gesture navigation. Behav. Inf. Technol. **42**(6), 744–757 (2023)
56. Ziefle, M., Schroeder, U., Strenk, J., Michel, T.: How younger and older adults master the usage of hyperlinks in small screen devices. In: Proceedings of the SIGCHI Conference on Human Factors in Computing Systems, pp. 307–316 (2007)

Spatial Audio Training for Visually Impaired Users Navigation in VR: An Analytical Approach

Gaurish Garg$^{(\boxtimes)}$ and Shimmila Bhowmick

Indian Institute of Technology, Jodhpur, Rajasthan 342030, India
gaurish_garg@outlook.com

Abstract. Vision impairment is four times more prevalent in developing countries like India as compared to high-income areas and impacts the psychological development of a person in many ways. This paper explores training methods for partially visually impaired individuals (PVIs) using Virtual Reality (VR) technology. The study discusses the development of a VR game in a school environment aimed at improving spatial audio perception among partially visually impaired users. We conducted a user study that addresses a significant gap in educational and training tools for PVIs. This study found that the users could locate the sound source within 15 dB sound attenuation, with the best result locating within 6 dB sound attenuation falling within the radius of 22 cm from the sound source, suggesting potential in training. The findings suggest the potential efficiency of VR-based training in enhancing spatial perception skills in the partially visually impaired, as the results are concurrent with those in real-world settings.

Keywords: Partially Visually Impaired · Mild Glaucoma · Navigation · Training · Virtual Reality · Human Sound Perception · Spatial Audio

1 Introduction

Globally, at least 2.2 billion people have near or distant vision impairment. The prevalence of vision impairment in low and middle-income regions (Asia Pacific, sub-Saharan Africa, etc.) is four times higher than in high-income areas. In this regard, school-age children in developing countries (like India) with partial vision impairment can experience lower levels of educational achievement, impact quality of life among adult populations, experience lower rates of employment and higher rates of depression and anxiety [1, 2]. At the same time, throughout the world, about 8 million people either suffer or are likely to suffer from macular degeneration, while similar estimates amount to 7.7. Million for glaucoma [1, 2].

The motivation for creating a VR game instead of analogue games was that the primary motive of the study was to develop a framework for the partially visually impaired (PVI) and statistically analyse how VR-based training on spatial audio can enhance spatial processing capabilities. This framework allowed us to directly collect data on the exact direction of the player from the sound source, attenuation values, and absorption coefficients, which would have posed logistics challenges in Analogue games.

As an emerging technology, VR has established the foundation for exploring virtual worlds using VR headsets. Typically, standard VR headsets like Meta Quest or Apple Vision Pro, being expensive, are not easily accessible to users in most developing countries, limiting the scope of VR expansion [3, 4]. In this regard, Google Cardboard offers an economical solution that leverages the capabilities of smartphones, hence making it a base for further research as VR provides a unique platform for simulations due to its ability to create an immersive and interactive environment by avoiding logistical challenges that would have occurred in the real world enhancing precise data collection.

The entirely visually impaired (EVIs), i.e., people who are blind, on average, can discriminate the direction of auditory motion on a horizontal plane with an accuracy of 85–90%, as mentioned by Sabourin et al. (2022) in [5]. However, the spatial hearing perception of the partially visually impaired (PVI) is somewhat less. While there are assistive devices for navigation for the visually impaired, these have yet to be widely accepted by the partially visually impaired, i.e. whose vision impairments are not that bad but still make life a challenge for them. Thus, there has been some research that proposes training through simulations of the natural world in Extended Reality (XR) for the visually impaired, as reported by Elgendy (2019) and Guerreiro et al. (2020) that can help PVIs memorise short routes. [6, 7].

The existing scenario of PVIs has established an opportunity that this paper tries to address. First, we need to analyse the spatial hearing capabilities of the partially visually impaired, especially those with mild to moderate glaucoma or macular degeneration. Secondly, we need to train the users to use spatial audio cues. Thus, a data collection framework is required to fulfil these goals. We focus on developing this framework and initial testing for this study. Therefore, for this purpose, we created a Virtual Reality (VR) game that was based on locomotion and sound localization in which the users are required to locate the source of sound by perception of sound direction from spatial audio rendering and perception of volume changes in the environment from distance-based attenuation of sound while viewing the virtual scene from the perspective of PVI, with the data being simultaneously recorded in an online database, a part of which was analysed. The analysis of this data produced results that concurred with the real world, thus making it an effective solution for the training of the partially visually impaired. However, it has a hardware limitation in that it works properly only on devices that support Dolby Atmos for surround sound or explicitly spatial audio rendering from device speakers.

This paper is organised into various sections. Section 2 provides a comprehensive summary of the existing literature, and Sect. 3 focuses on the design and development of the methodology and evaluation procedure for the proposed framework. After this, we present the evaluation studies in Sect. 4 and their results with analysis in Sect. 5. At the end of the paper, we conclude with our findings and discuss possible expansions of this work in Sect. 6.

2 Analysis of Existing Studies

2.1 Assistive Devices for the Visually Impaired

Much research has been conducted on people with visual impairments to help them navigate their environment using smart canes. One such concept is mentioned by Ivanov (2010) [8], which uses special hardware like ultrasonic sensors and object recognition coupled with RFID technology. A study was conducted by Sivakumar et al. (2019) with 413 patients at a low-vision clinic, Aravind Eye Care, Madurai, in Tamil Nadu, India, and their data was collected over the years until 2019. Their study observed that 53% of the PVI users, especially those in the low to mild spectrum of visual impairment, have not acquainted themselves with Low Vision Assistive Products (LVAPs). It was primarily due to its bulkiness and psychological factors, such as social pressure and pity, that arise with these devices, especially in developing countries like India [9].

Despite consistent efforts by the government and doctors to acquaint PVIs with LVAPs, it is less likely to help in the long run when the visual impairment conditions for these people vary due to different biological factors across humans, for which strengthening other sensory perceptions is required along with training users in VR to adapt to the LVAPs. The positional accuracy of people who are blind for object detection with the use of LVAPs is generally 22 cm based on navigation systems for the visually impaired proposed by Ran et al. (2004) and Plikynas et al. (2020) [8, 10, 11]. However, no user demographic has been mentioned in their studies for the positional accuracy of 22 cm; instead, it has been calculated from the error rate of the differential GPS sensors, ultrasonic sensors, and Open-Source Gateway Initiative software bundle on data for their "Hardware" solution to "Indoor Navigation" for the "Visually Impaired", collected over the years.

Despite advancements in assistive devices, there has been less research on training users with mild to moderate visual impairments like mild glaucoma, in which the periphery of the user's visual field is partially blocked, as discussed by Hu et al. (2014), which is also known as tunnel vision in moderate glaucoma, or macular degeneration in which the central visual field is partially blocked [12]. These visual impairments currently have no cure; however, treatment can delay their progression and living with these visual impairments throughout life is a challenge. Other visual impairments that still pose a risk of blindness are cataracts and progressive myopia. Still, these have surgical cures like phacoemulsification for cataracts and symptomatic cures for myopia using LASIK, Contoura Vision, SILK, etc.

2.2 Spatial Audio for the Partially Visually Impaired

Human hearing can perceive the two main traits of sound: frequency using loudness and pitch and timbre and spatial position of the sound source, as mentioned by Xie [13]. Spatial sound deals with the physical (mechanical properties of sound) and physiology (perception of sound) of hearing. Just like the visual field, human sound perception also has a sound field when the human comes near the sound source, as shown in Fig. 1 where Ω is the solid angle for the 3D sound field, and d_s is the distance from the sound source to the centre of the head.

The sound waves from the sound source travel through the air as pressure changes as a pressure function $p(d_s, t)$. The pressure function in the frequency domain at either ear (denoted by P_L or P_R) is proportional to the HRTF (Head Related Transfer function denoted by H_L or H_R) in the frequency domain multiplied by the Pressure function in the frequency domain at the centre of the head (denoted by P_C) as shown in Eq. 1 and Eq. 2. The pressure function in the frequency domain is obtained by taking the Fourier transform of the pressure function in the time domain.

$$P_L = H_L * P_C \tag{1}$$

$$P_R = H_R * P_C \tag{2}$$

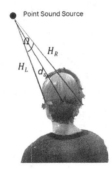

Fig. 1. The sound field from a point sound source forms a conical section with an apex angle Ω as the user reaches near the sound field, with the sound Intensity depending on the HRTFs *HL* and *HR*

However, VR environments might not capture certain variations in how each human perceives spatial sound through Head Related Transfer Functions (HRTFs). Simulation of HRTFs in software considers the audio cues such as Interaural Time Difference (ITD), Inter-aural Level Difference (ILD) and spectral cues. The spatial sound rendering mentioned by Xie (2016) refers to multiple speakers or channels like one, two, or five, etc., in the real world. [13]. However, for modern-day mobile phones, spatial sound is realised by Dolby Atmos, which implicitly is based on acoustic cues like ITD, ILD and HRTF, recognising the principle of binaural reproduction. ITD is the difference in the time the sound pressure changes take to reach both ears. At the same time, ILD is the difference in the sound intensity at both ears, as mentioned by Schissler et al. (2016), while also considering the sound attenuation factor as in [14].

$$Attenuation = \frac{1}{1 + d_s^2} \tag{3}$$

Both papers have highlighted the importance of auditory fidelity in virtual reality via spatial audio, making VR the right choice for training users, especially those who are partially visually impaired, to spatial audio cues and improving the accuracy of spatial audio localisation. Once the concept of HRTFs is established, it is now required to consider variations and uncertainties in the data where Inoue et al. (2005) proposed that the uncertainties due to HRTFs are about 5 dB independent of the solid angle formed with the user's head [15].

2.3 Locomotion Interaction in VR

To effectively utilise VR technology, interaction with the VR environment is necessary. Mine (1995) discussed several interaction techniques, which include but are not limited to 6 Degrees of Freedom (DOF) tracking devices like hand-tracking controllers or traditional button-based XBOX-like gamepads [16, 17]. Other tracking types include head tracking and gaze interaction (both available in all HMDs). The 6 DOF movements include a combination of three kinds of translations, like Surge, Sway and Heave and three types of rotations, like Yaw, Pitch and Roll, as shown in Fig. 2.

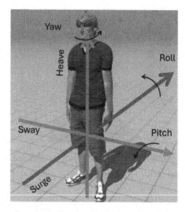

Fig. 2. The 6-DOF movement involves three translational and three rotational movements. Yaw, Pitch and Roll define the rotations around the Y, Z, and X axes, while Heave, Sway and Surge define translations along these axes.

3 Methodology and Evaluation Procedure

3.1 Overview

To develop an efficient framework for effectively training partially visually impaired (PVI), this paper leverages the spatial capabilities of sound in the real world, as discussed in detail in Sect. 2, which can be simulated in virtual environments in modern phone-based HMDs (Head Mounted Displays) like Google Cardboard or standalone HMDs like Meta Quest 2 [3, 18].

This framework was realised using a VR experiment in which the participants wear the Google Cardboard mounted with a Dolby-enabled or explicit spatial audio rendering enabled phone to navigate through a virtual reality environment from the perspective of the visually impaired like glaucoma or macular degeneration in which a sound was playing at a particular position in the virtual environment. The participants were to stop when no more loudness of sound could be perceived.

By simulating a virtual school environment, specific parameters like room dimensions, material properties, default pitch and loudness, etc., can be tuned precisely while simultaneously allowing the participants to navigate the environment virtually. This analysis was possible on modern-day mobile devices with the evolution of Dolby Atmos for surround sound. However, spatial audio settings in VR games impact the spatial audio accuracy determined using this technology.

3.2 Design of the VE and Configuration

The Playing Environment (Virtual School Building). The VR game referred to in Sect. 1 leverages the spatial audio technology discussed in Sect. 2 and was implemented with the help of Unity Game Engine's Inbuilt Audio Engine and Steam Audio Spatializer and a virtual school environment downloaded from Unity Asset Store. [19–21]. The environment was modified for spatial audio by adding physics-based 3D colliders to the building, objects, and certain materials in the steam library like marble, bricks, plaster, etc. Some of the materials possess sound absorption properties, as discussed by S. S. Houda (2009), which can be measured by pressure changes and distance-based attenuation as the sound absorption by the materials reduces the energy of sound waves. [22]. The building model is shown in Fig. 3, where the room on the left at the end of the corridor from the front door contains the audio source; let's call it a demonstration room.

The mapping of materials is mainly aligned with standard settings in semi-urban and urban schools, as shown in Table 1. Though sound absorption per material could not be recorded due to Unity Game Engine's limitations, sound absorption for different frequency ranges like Low, Mid and High could be recorded with Steam Audio Spatializer Plugin. The sound absorption coefficient is a decimal value between 0 and 1, and an absorption coefficient of 0.4 would mean 40% of the sound has been absorbed.

Fig. 3. The school building model consisted of different rooms through which the users had to navigate to locate the sound source.

Table 1. Materials Simulated in Virtual Environment

Object	Material
Walls	Bricks and Plaster
Tables and Chairs	Wood
Almirahs and Lockers	Metal
Grills	Metal
Chalkboards	Glass
Projector Screens	Ceramic
Floor	Tiles

The Player. The player in VR is a character controller formed by a capsule collider of width 0.5 m and height 1.25 m. The head height is roughly one-eighth of the body height while the head width is nearly two-thirds of the head height, as discussed by Piva et al. (2006), which makes the width of the player's head roughly 10 cm while the head height is 15.625 cm [9]. The distance between the sound source and the user's head's centre, i.e. ds, can be calculated as shown in Fig. 4 and Fig. 5, which considers the height of the head's centre and the height of the sound source, which was 0.67 m from the floor in the virtual world. Since this VR implementation did not consider the crouching of the users, it has been assumed that some of the users crouch to half of their body height while finding sound sources, and data for analysis can be augmented considering both scenarios, which ultimately allows us to consider the positional accuracy in the X-Z plane only.

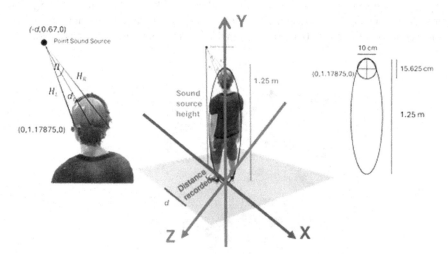

Fig. 4. Calculations for computing the distance from the sound source to the centre of the user's head by considering the user's height and approximate body proportions. All values in this figure are in metres.

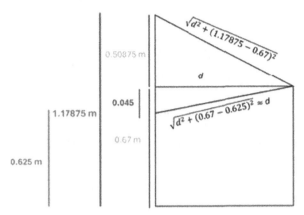

Fig. 5. The calculations showed that the distance from the sound source to the centre of the user's head, considering the user's height and approximate body proportions, is approximately equal to the distance measured without considering body proportions. Here, half the body height (0.625 m) has been considered based on the assumption of crouching for comparison between this height and the height of the sound source (0.67 m). However, there is also no significant difference if the centre of the head is also compared to the height of the sound source, except for the uncertainties of 5 dB, as mentioned in Sect. 2. All values in this figure are in metres.

Sound Properties and Rendering. Sound Properties Setup for Spatial Audio Rendering involves the two main components of audio spatialisation, one of which includes spatial post effects, and the other is a spatial blend.

For the spatial blend, the spatialise variable of the Unity Engine's Audio Source component must be set to true. This option is available only when an external audio spatialisation plugin, like the Steam Audio plugin, etc., is configured in the project. For the 3D sound settings, the spatial blend was set to 1, the maximum spatial blend for spatial audio.

The volume roll-off was set to logarithmic as it is in the real world, wherein distance attenuation and occlusion factors were set to physics-based rendering. Since spatial audio depends on various parameters such as HRTFs, attenuation, sound absorption, etc., along with Doppler level, which is based on the difference between the frequency at which sound waves leave a source and that at which they reach an observer, caused by the relative motion of the observer and the wave source, specific parameters corresponding to these settings were initially randomised for some users using C# script in Unity. These parameters include minimum roll-off distance, maximum roll-off distance, occlusion radius, doppler level and reflection mix level.

To account for reflections and reverberations, each room in the virtual school building is designated an audio reverb zone using predefined reverb presets to account for reverberations.

3.3   Methodology for Data Analysis and Result Estimation

The logarithmic volume Rolloff, used in the real world, where volume Rolloff refers to how the listener perceives sound intensity at a distance from the sound source, is one of the main deciding factors for spatial audio localisation. However, Unity does not provide any method to get the actual Volume y (normalised between 0 to 1) that the user hears at a particular distance x from the audio source. For this, the points provided by the Unity graph were manually observed, as shown in Table 2, and algebraic analysis of these points was performed using the concept of geometric progressions.

Table 2. Data from the volume roll-off graph

S. No	Distance (m)	Volume (fraction after roll-off)
1	1	0.5
2	2	0.25
3	4	0.125
4	8	0.063
5	16	0.031
6	32	0.016
7	64	0.008
8	128	0.004
9	256	0.002
10	512	0.001

At every such discrete point, as in Table 2, the distance was approximately doubled while the volume was approximately halved. This was found by writing the volume and distance as a function of a parametric variable, t, as both variables formed a Geometric Progression. This parametric variable t was eliminated by using the tth term of these geometric progressions, and the final equation came out as shown in Eq. 4 for a minimum distance of 0.5 and a maximum distance of 1000. Further equations are discussed in Subsect. 4.4 of Sect. 4.

$$y = 2^{-(\log_2 x + 1)} \tag{4}$$

4 Evaluation Study

4.1 Study Setup and Apparatus

Virtual Environment and Simulations. The VE was a school environment with various physics properties, as mentioned in Sect. 3. The participants were required to navigate the VR game from the perspective of the visually impaired, and the rendering of the VR game is shown in Fig. 6. The visual impairment simulations were developed based on image filter methods, as discussed by Zhang and Codinhoto (2020) [23]. These methods have been shown to closely approximate real-world visual impairment scenarios, ensuring high accuracy in our simulation. By adhering to this well-established framework, we ensured that the visual impairment simulations in our study were credible and reflective of actual conditions, thereby enhancing the validity of our findings. This approach also enables us to precisely control the simulation of different levels of visual impairment, allowing for an analysis of how varying degrees of visual impairment impact an individual's spatial processing capabilities.

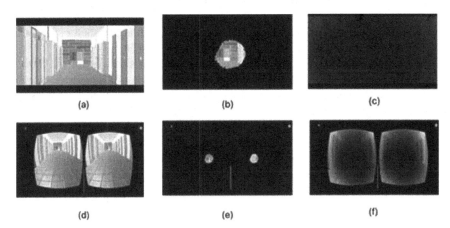

Fig. 6. (a). View from healthy sighted. (b). View from the perspective of glaucoma impairment. (c). View from the perspective of Macular Degeneration. (d). Rendered Stereoscopic view from healthy sighted. (e). Rendered Stereoscopic view from the perspective of glaucoma impairment. (f). Rendered Stereoscopic view from the perspective of Macular Degeneration.

Device Limitations. It is to be noted that spatial audio works only on devices that support Dolby Atmos and spatial sound, with higher accuracies reported in devices that allow explicit setting of spatial sound, as Dolby Atmos deals with surround sound while spatial sound explicitly considers HRTFs. To check whether the device supports surround sound or even explicitly spatial audio, one needs to search for "Dolby Atmos" or "Spatial Sound" in the device settings. Most smartphones allow spatialisation on device speaker mode only, and the spatialisation for earphones/headphones depends on their hardware.

Devices and Locomotion Controls. We used a phone-based HMD, and a controller for locomotion was required. In this case, a physical button-based controller, a wireless

USB device like a conventional keyboard or XBOX-like gamepad that can be used with mobile devices via On-the-go USBs (OTGs), was used. However, it also depends on the choice of HMDs, as some cardboard-based HMDs don't support OTG, while others do. Thus, a simple VR Box that supported OTG was used instead of popular phone-based HMDs for this research. The controls were based on physical button-based devices and implicit head tracking. The controls are mentioned herein.

Mode for Left Hand/Right Hand Movement. Activate the Left Thumbstick or WASD for movement by pressing the """ on the keyboard or the Left Trigger button on the Gamepad and the Right Thumbstick or Arrow keys for speed or vice versa by pressing "1" on the keyboard or right trigger button on the gamepad.

Reporting Collision. Report collision on the left side by pressing the left shoulder button on the gamepad or pressing the "bumped" F key, and report collision on the Right side by the right shoulder button on the gamepad or pressing the "bumped" J key on the keyboard. Typically, in conventional keyboards, the F and J keys are bumped; thus, these were used to report collisions in VR, as the real world is not visible in VR.

Controlling Movement and Speed. The left thumbstick or WASD is used for movement, and the right thumbstick or arrow keys are used for speed or vice versa, depending on the trigger button pressed. If the right trigger button or "1" key was pressed on the start, the right thumbstick was used for movement and the left thumbstick for speed. The rotation was controlled by looking around, as mentioned further.

Rotation. The players need to rotate their head/body, which is recorded by the phone's gyroscope and the VR scene is rotated accordingly. In contrast, in PC games, the rotation is done by the right thumbstick on gamepads or a conventional mouse. In this case, since rotation is implicit with head tracking, the right thumbstick was used to modify the speed if the user had activated the left thumbstick movement by pressing the left trigger button, and the use of a mouse is ruled out in VR.

Controlling Movement and Speed. The user could signal the target location, i.e. where he feels no more loudness can be perceived, by pressing Left Control or Numpad Enter on the keyboard or pressing both thumbstick buttons simultaneously on the gamepad.

4.2 Task and Participants

Task. The experiment used the same mobile device and phone-based HMD at 100% device speaker volume for all trials. This approach allowed for uniform data collection, ensuring that differences were attributed to the variables under study rather than inconsistencies in audio delivery. This VR experience of spatial audio was a VR game potentially targeting school students of classes 7th to 10th. The users were first asked to find the source of sound by navigating through the VR environment, wherein an invisible sound source is playing Punjabi folk music, which is kept in the demonstration room (the room towards the left at the end of the corridor as mentioned in Sect. 3) of the virtual school building. The users must stop when they feel they have reached the sound source when they can hear the maximum possible sound intensity or loudness, and no more loudness can be perceived. Additionally, the use of speakers replicated the real world better than earphones/headphones, as real-world sounds are mostly heard with naked ears, i.e. without earphones/headphones. Earphones/headphones will create a sense of consciousness of something over the ears, which might impact the data collection.

Participants. 35 sighted students, some suffering from moderate myopia, participated in the study across various rural schools in the district of Barnala in Punjab state, India. Several filters simulating visual impairments like glaucoma or macular degeneration were applied in the VR world to get a rough data estimate, as mentioned in Subsect. 4.2. However, some students who wear spectacles, i.e. have myopia, reported more difficulties than healthy students when a visual impairment like glaucoma or macular degeneration was overlayed in their VR game. The study was conducted between participants where different participants experienced different simulations, eliminating bias and ensuring valid comparisons.

Regarding the choice of sighted participants, our initial focus on non-PVIs was a strategic decision to detect anomalies and explore how VR could train PVIs to spatial audio cues. As detailed in Sect. 1, where entirely visually impaired individuals (EVIs) exhibit superior spatial processing capabilities, PVIs generally have somewhat lower capabilities, which still need to be precisely quantified. By starting with non-PVIs, our study's primary objective was to develop a controlled and fine-tuned framework to theoretically and statistically analyse how VR-based training could enhance spatial audio processing for PVIs. This method strengthens the reliability and applicability of our findings, ensuring the system is robust and effective before applying it to the PVI population (Fig. 7).

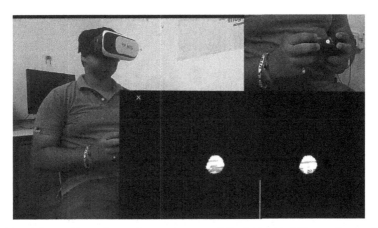

Fig. 7. A participant trying to locate the sound source while playing the VR game from a glaucoma perspective

4.3 Data Handling

Data Collection. The data thus recorded is uploaded to a single CSV file in a MongoDB online database through HTTP web requests as the participant is playing the VR game, and this data can be used for further analysis.

Data Format. The data included various parameters such as Userid (UID), Visual Impairment Simulated (SVI), Target or Collision (Type), Collision or Target Direction

(DIR), Indicated Direction (ID), Distance from Source (Dist.), Player Forward Direction, Reference Frame for Actual, Player Position, Sound Position, Volume, Doppler Level, Pitch, Roll-off Mode, Maximum Influence Distance, Minimum Influence Distance, Steam Audio Occlusion Radius, Steam Audio Reflections Mix, Reverb Low, Reverb Mid, Reverb High, Attenuation, Absorption Low, Absorption Mid, Absorption High, Player Velocity, etc. A snippet of data thus obtained is shown in Table 3.

4.4 Method for Analysis

The accuracy of spatial sound perception will be determined from the perspective of volume Rolloff fraction and loudness in Decibels and Intensity levels. For the loudness in Decibels, we use the Sound Pressure Level equation. For the relation between distance from the sound source at the target position and Intensity changes, we use the Power Equation. It is to be noted that the Power of a sound source remains the same, and only the intensity changes with distance. The equations used for these calculations are shown in Eq. 5 to Eq. 10, while the calculations are shown in Sect. 5.

$$Sound \ Intensity \ in \ Decibels = (10 \ decibels) \times \log_{10}\left(\frac{Sound \ Intensity}{Reference \ Intensity}\right) \quad (5)$$

$$Power = Intensity \times Area \quad (6)$$

$$I = \frac{P}{A} \quad (7)$$

$$A = k \times d^2 \quad (8)$$

$$P = I \times k \times d^2 \quad (9)$$

$$d^2 = \frac{P}{I \times k} \quad (10)$$

$$d = \sqrt{\frac{P}{I \times k}} \quad (11)$$

5   Results and Analysis

5.1   Data Collected and Basic Observations

A snippet of collected data is shown in Table 3. The data consisted of various parameters, as mentioned in Subsect. 4.3 of Sect. 4. For this study, we considered the recorded distance from the target source for accuracy estimation for the recording type as "Target", i.e. the distance at which no more loudness could be perceived. From the data, it was observed that the nearest distance to the sound source was reported to be 23.6 cm when the game was played with the perspective of healthy sighted, i.e. no visual impairment filters were overlayed, followed by nearly 28.5 cm when the game was played with the perspective of glaucoma-based visual impairment, and almost 41 cm for macular-degeneration-based visual impairment. The graphical representation of these observations is shown in Fig. 8 and Fig. 9. However, it can be observed that the best nearest distance was within 0.5 m from the sound source, which is analysed further in Subsect. 5.2

Table 3. Snippets of Data Obtained for fields User-id (UID), Visual Impairment Simulated (SVI), Target or Collision (Type), Collision or Target Direction (DIR), Distance from Source (Dist.). Here, the distance for the type "Target" represents the distance from the source where that particular user experienced maximum loudness.

UID	SVI	Type	Normalised DIR (m)	Distance (m)
985	glaucoma	Movement	$(0.47, -0.01, -0.88)$	21.2453
985	glaucoma	Collision	$(-0.25, -0.12, 0.01)$	0.2775
985	glaucoma	Collision	$(-0.25, -0.16, 0.00)$	0.2985
985	glaucoma	Collision	$(-0.25, -0.16, 0.00)$	0.2985
150861	healthy	Target	$(-0.57, 0.00, 0.07)$	0.573998
157920	healthy	Target	$(0.21, 0.00, 0.11)$	0.236109
119708	glaucoma	Target	$(0.13, 0.00, -0.26)$	0.285128
5614	healthy	Target	$(-0.34, 0.01, -0.23)$	0.4105339

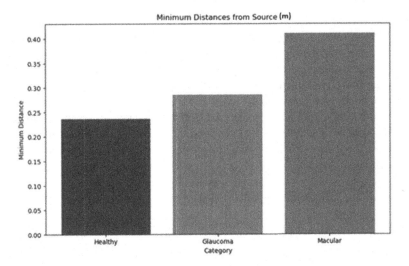

Fig. 8. Comparison of nearest distance for all three simulations- The Best Nearest Distance for positional accuracy was for healthy sighted, reported to be nearly 22 cm. Here, the distance represents the distance from the source where that particular user experienced maximum loudness.

3D Plot of Trajectory

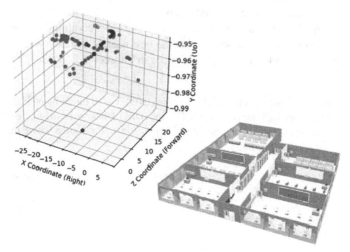

Fig. 9. The values on the axes represent the actual coordinates of the virtual space in metres. The trajectory of the users with the highest positional accuracy from the healthy-sighted perspective (blue), glaucoma perspective (green) and macular degeneration perspective (red), with minimum deviation in healthy-sighted and maximum deviation in macular degeneration. Green dots are less visible as their trajectory closely aligns with the healthy-sighted, and it is evident from the results that the difference in their nearest distance is only 5 cm.

5.2 Calculations and Accuracy Estimation

From Table 2 and Eq. (4), it can be observed that 1 m from the sound source results in 50% perceived volume, and 2 m would result in 25% perceived volume. Considering this logic, a 0.5 m distance would hint at 100% perceived volume, meaning we need to analyse at a smaller scale from this point. For this, we consider the uncertainties of 5 dB and the Just Noticeable Difference (JND) of human hearing, which is 1 dB and the reference intensity of human hearing as 10^{-12} W/m^2.

To get the intensity in W/m^2, we played the audio file and observed its loudness on the loudness meter. The loudness at 0.1 m from the source was 88.9 dB. Since we know the distance, the loudness level, and the reference intensity, we can put these values in Eq. 5, as shown in Eq. 12.

$$88.9 \text{ dB} = (10 \text{ dB}) \times \log_{10}\left(\frac{Sound\ Intensity}{10^{-12}W/m^2}\right) \tag{12}$$

$$SoundIntensity = 10^{8.89} \times 10^{-12} = 7.76 \times 10^{-4} \text{ W/m}^2 \tag{13}$$

For a sound source, the power P doesn't change with distance, as power is the property of the sound source. From Eq. 9, we can get the power from this intensity as a constant k times this intensity times the square of 0.1, as shown in Eq. 14. We utilise this power to calculate the distance for 1 dB and 5 dB sound attenuation and also get loudness attenuation at 0.5 m and 0.22 m.

$$P = I \times k \times d^2 = 7.76 \times 10^{-4} \times k \times 0.1^2 = 7.76 \times 10^{-6} \times kW \tag{14}$$

We first calculate the distance at 1 dB sound attenuation. For this, we consider the dB level to be 87.9 dB, which is one less than the original; using the calculations mentioned in Eqs. 5, 12 and 13, we get the sound intensity as 6.16×10^{-4} W/m^2. By utilising this value in Eq. 11, we can get the distance as 0.11 m.

$$SoundIntensity = 10^{8.79} \times 10^{-12} = 6.16 \times 10^{-4} \text{ W/m}^2 \tag{15}$$

$$\text{d} = \sqrt{\frac{P}{I \times k}} = \sqrt{\frac{7.76 \times 10^{-6} \times k}{6.16 \times 10^{-4} \times k}} = 0.11 \text{ m} \tag{16}$$

We can get the distance for sound attenuation of 5 dB with the same calculations. The sound intensity at 83.9 dB is 2.45×10^{-4} W/m^2. Thus, the corresponding distance is 0.17 m from the sound source for an attenuation of 5 dB.

We also need to get the loudness at a 0.5 m distance to get an idea of sound attenuation at this distance. For this, we perform elementary operations on the equations shown in Eq. (17), which comes out to be 3.104×10. The loudness level at this point can be calculated from Eq. (5), as shown in Eq. (18), which is 74.9 dB, i.e. 14.9 dB less than the source intensity. Similarly, we can calculate for 0.22 m, 0.28 m, and 0.4 m, as mentioned in Table 4.

$$d^2 = \frac{P}{I \times k} \Rightarrow I = \frac{P}{d^2 \times k} \Rightarrow I = \frac{7.76 \times 10^{-6} \times k}{0.5^2 \times k} = 3.104 \times 10^{-5} \text{ W/m}^2 \tag{17}$$

$$\text{Sound Intensity (dB)} = (10 \text{ decibels}) \times \log_{10}\left(\frac{3.104 \times 10^{-5} W/m^2}{10^{-12} W/m^2}\right) = 74.9 \text{dB} \tag{18}$$

5.3 Accuracy Estimation and Discussions

We can observe from Table 4 that at any distance closer than 0.51 m, which is just 0.01 m more than the minimum distance in Table 1, the loudness attention was nearly 14.2 dB, though accuracy by volume Rolloff was more than 98%. Based on these observations, if a person reported the sound source at 23 cm, then the person had a high accuracy of more than 98% based on volume roll-off and 91% accuracy based on loudness attenuation of 7.1 dB. These calculations prompt us to consider the human perception of hearing, which can provide insights into how accurately loudness is perceived with distance. However, no such literature supports the volume roll-off for distances closer than 0.5 m; it can be analysed by converting it into decibels, meaning certain zero errors must be considered for proper assessment. The absolute magnitudes might differ from the real world, but the relative change still can be mapped to the real world.

The JND of human hearing for loudness is defined as 1 dB in existing literature on psychophysics and psychoacoustics. However, it varies across humans, and the uncertainties of 5 dB for HRTF are due to spatial audio rendering. By considering this perceptual difference, we can ignore attenuation of 6 dB, i.e. the perception of sound due to spatial audio rendering with HRTF is nearly the same at 88.9 dB and 82.9 dB. From the

Table 4. Sound attenuation at different distances. Here, the distance represents the distance from the source where the user experienced maximum loudness.

Nearest Distance (m)	Sound Intensity (W/m2)	Loudness Value (dB)	Loudness Attenuation (dB)	Loudness Accuracy (%)	Volume-based Accuracy (%)
0.1	7.76×10^{-4}	88.9	Reference	Reference	Reference
0.11	6.16×10^{-4}	87.9	1	98.87	>98
0.17	2.45×10^{-4}	83.9	5	94	>98
0.23	1.47×10^{-4}	81.7	7.2	91	>98
0.28	9.9×10^{-5}	80	8.9	89	>98
0.41	4.6×10^{-5}	76.6	12.3	86	>98
0.5	3.104×10^{-5}	74.9	14	84	>98
0.51	3×10^{-5}	74.7	14.2	74.8	98

observations for the nearest distance, spatial audio is potentially practical in indoor navigation, especially for memorising short routes. These findings highlight the precision of our methods for relevant data collection and statistical analysis, reinforcing the study's contribution to understanding VR's potential for enhancing the spatial audio processing capabilities of PVIs.

6   Conclusion and Future Work

In this paper, we explored the concept of spatial audio that can train the partially visually impaired (PVI) to spatial audio cues. We explored how VR can help collect data for performing theoretical and psychophysical statistical analysis through an experiment described in Sect. 4 and Sect. 5, thus providing a starting point for training PVIs to spatial audio cues. We analysed the collected data theoretically using psychophysical statistics and mathematical equations, concluding that the distance at which the maximum loudness was perceived does not significantly attenuate sound, indicating its potential effectiveness. Thus, the insights gained from our study contribute to the—growing body of knowledge in the field of Human-Computer Interaction. This study contributes to the broader HCI community by providing empirical evidence on the effectiveness of VR-based training for PVI users. It underscores the importance of designing accessible and inclusive interfaces that cater to the needs of users with special abilities. The findings from this study can inform the design of more effective VR-based assistive tools that rely on spatial audio for navigation and interaction. This research serves as a starting point for further investigation into using VR and spatial audio in training PVI users. It opens new avenues for exploring how immersive environments can be optimised for accessibility and how these environments can contribute to our theoretical understanding of spatial audio perception in PVI users.

The study was performed on school children by converting the idea to a VR game in which the participants had to locate the source of sound while seeing the virtual environment from the perspective of the PVIs. This study addresses a significant gap in educational and training tools for PVIs, especially in developing countries like India, leveraging modern technology to improve their spatial awareness and potentially enhance their quality of life. Based on the observations and analysis, this study concludes that the data collection framework using a VR game, when configured with optimal settings, is a reliable way to develop further technology to train the PVIs, as the results are consistent with the natural world studies. The obtained accuracy matches the existing studies with an error margin of $\pm$ 5–10 dB and the JND of human hearing. The results can be validated at par with the real world through an ongoing project by performing the study with partially visually impaired users and training them in VR to use spatial audio cues.

In future work, we plan to expand the study to include a more extensive and more diverse group of PVI participants and conduct longitudinal studies to evaluate the long-term impact of VR-based training. We also aim to refine the VR training modules by incorporating more complex, real-world scenarios to enhance the sensory experience. Additionally, this framework can be extended to various platforms like Oculus VR alone as per requirement with Google Cardboard, Windows PC, Android, Web-VR, etc., by modifying the current experimental setup to education-based reward-based games that align with the Education Policies of developing countries like New National Education Policy (NEP) that highlight the use of XR in classroom settings leveraging the spatial capabilities of modern day devices by not just limiting to mobile devices, as even PC games can sometimes give a semi-VR experience. Moreover, optimising the environment for headphones would also allow the detection of potential hearing damage in PVI kids by predicting their threshold when they can't hear more loudness of sound using certain loudness and distance equations, as discussed in Sect. 5.

References

1. Blindness and vision impairment. https://www.who.int/news-room/fact-sheets/detail/blindn ess-and-visual-impairment
2. GBD 2019 Blindness and Vision Impairment Collaborators, Vision Loss Expert Group of the Global Burden of Disease Study: Causes of Blindness and Vision Impairment in 2020 and Trends Over 30 years, and prevalence of avoidable blindness in relation to VISION 2020: the right to sight: an analysis for the global burden of disease study. The Lancet Global Health. 9, e144–e160 (2021). https://doi.org/10.1016/S2214-109X(20)30489-7
3. Meta Quest 2. https://www.meta.com/quest/products/quest-2/
4. Apple Vision Pro. https://www.apple.com/apple-vision-pro/
5. Sabourin, C., Merrikhi, Y., Lomber, S.: Do blind people hear better? Trends in Cognitive Sciences. 26 (2022). https://doi.org/10.1016/j.tics.2022.08.016
6. Elgendy, M., Herperger, M., Guzsvinecz, T., Sik-Lányi, C.: Indoor navigation for people with visual impairment using augmented reality markers. Presented at the October (2019). https:// doi.org/10.1109/CogInfoCom47531.2019.9089960

7. Guerreiro, J., Sato, D., Ahmetovic, D., Ohn-Bar, E., Kitani, K.M., Asakawa, C.: Virtual navigation for blind people: Transferring route knowledge to the real-World. Int. J. Hum. Comput. Stud. **135**, 102369 (2020). https://doi.org/10.1016/j.ijhcs.2019.102369

8. Ivanov, R.: Indoor navigation system for visually impaired. In: Proceedings of the 11th International Conference on Computer Systems and Technologies and Workshop for PhD Students in Computing on International Conference on Computer Systems and Technologies, pp. 143–149. Association for Computing Machinery, New York, NY, USA (2010). https://doi.org/10.1145/1839379.1839405

9. Piva, S., Comes, L., Asadi, M., Regazzoni, C.: Grouped-people splitting based on face detection and body proportion constraints. Presented at the November (2006). https://doi.org/10.1109/AVSS.2006.56

10. Ran, L., Helal, S., Moore, S.: Drishti: an integrated indoor/outdoor blind navigation system and service. In: Second IEEE Annual Conference on Pervasive Computing and Communications, 2004. Proceedings of the, pp. 23–30 (2004). https://doi.org/10.1109/PERCOM.2004.1276842

11. Plikynas, D., Žvironas, A., Budrionis, A., Gudauskis, M.: Indoor navigation systems for visually impaired persons: mapping the features of existing technologies to user needs. Sensors. **20**, 636 (2020). https://doi.org/10.3390/s20030636

12. Hu, C.X., et al.: What do patients with glaucoma see? Visual symptoms reported by patients with glaucoma. Am. J. Med. Sci. **348**, 403–409 (2014). https://doi.org/10.1097/MAJ.0000000000000319

13. Xie, B.: Spatial sound—history, principle, progress and challenge. Chin. J. Electron. **29**, 397 (2020). https://doi.org/10.1049/cje.2020.02.016

14. Schissler, C., Nicholls, A., Mehra, R.: Efficient HRTF-based spatial audio for area and volumetric sources. IEEE Trans. Visual Comput. Graphics **22**, 1356–1366 (2016)

15. Inoue, N., Kimura, T., Nishino, T., Itou, K., Takeda, K.: Evaluation of HRTFs estimated using physical features. Acoust. Sci. Technol. **26**, 453–455 (2005). https://doi.org/10.1250/ast.26.453

16. Mine, M.: Virtual environment interaction techniques (1995)

17. Xbox Official Site: consoles, games and community I Xbox, https://www.xbox.com/, Accessed 24 Aug 2024

18. Google Cardboard. https://arvr.google.com/cardboard/

19. Unity. https://unity.com/

20. Steam audio. https://valvesoftware.github.io/steam-audio/downloads.html

21. School assets - unity asset store. https://assetstore.unity.com/packages/3d/

22. Houda, S.S.: Factors influencing acoustic performance of sound absorptive materials. Presented at the (2009)

23. Zhang, Y., Codinhoto, R.: Developing a visually impaired older people Virtual Reality (VR) simulator to apply VR in the aged living design workflow. In: 2020 24th International Conference Information Visualisation (IV), pp. 226–235. IEEE (2020)

Culturally Relevant Novel Interaction Methods for Immersive Video Streaming Experience in Virtual Reality

Himanshu Raj⬡, Samia⁽⊠⁾⬡, Juben Basumatary⬡, and Shimmila Bhowmick⬡

School of Design, Indian Institute of Technology (IIT), Jodhpur, Rajasthan, India
{m231dx004,m231dx011,m231dx006,shimmilabhowmick}@iitj.ac.in

Abstract. Virtual Reality (VR) technology has emerged as a transformative medium for immersive experiences, particularly within the entertainment sector. However, challenges persist in terms of accessibility and user interaction, hindering widespread adoption. This paper addresses these challenges by exploring and developing natural, intuitive, and culturally relevant hand gestures tailored for VR video streaming applications, focusing on YouTube VR. Drawing upon existing literature and user feedback, we identified the need for more intuitive interaction methods, particularly for volume control and pause-play functions. Through our user study, we proposed 9 unique hand gestures. Results from user studies indicate that these gestures have cultural relevance, with participants finding them easy to use and accessible, even for users with hand-shivering health issues. This research contributes to enhancing the user experience in YouTube VR and informs the development of more intuitive interaction methods for VR applications, ultimately fostering broader acceptance and engagement in the VR space.

Keywords: VR video streaming · HCI · Interaction methods · Cultural context · Usability · User experience · Hand gestures · Meta Quest 3

1 Introduction

Virtual reality (VR) technology has emerged as a powerful tool for creating immersive experiences, enabling users to immerse themselves in virtual worlds and interact with their surroundings. It is a groundbreaking platform with the potential to revolutionize the entertainment sector and redefine how users engage with digital content. Within the entertainment industry, VR has been embraced as a medium for delivering experiences across diverse domains, including gaming, narrative experiences, and media consumption. Platforms such as YouTube VR and Netflix VR have capitalized on this trend, allowing users to consume videos, movies, and TV shows within fully immersive virtual environments.

H. Raj and Samia—Contributed equally.

N. Rangaswamy et al. (Eds.): IndiaHCI 2024, CCIS 2337, pp. 259–272, 2025.
https://doi.org/10.1007/978-3-031-80829-6_12

Despite the advancements made in VR technology, challenges persist in terms of accessibility and user interaction. Navigating through conventional input methods, such as controllers and keyboards, may prove complex, cumbersome, and unintuitive [1, 3], particularly for users who are new to VR. Selecting small or closely spaced items, such as video thumbnails or control buttons, can be difficult using current VR controllers. This lack of precision can result in repeated attempts to perform simple actions, diminishing the overall user experience and potentially causing physical discomfort. This issue holds significant relevance, especially in the entertainment sector, where immersive experiences are increasingly becoming the norm. When input methods do not align well with the VR environment, it can cause users to feel disoriented and negatively impact the overall experience. Improper or inconsistent input interactions can contribute to user disorientation and motion sickness. While YouTube VR offers unparalleled immersion and engagement, navigating and interacting within the platform presents some challenges, particularly regarding input interaction. The current reliance on traditional (2D) input methods limits accessibility and hinders the widespread adoption of YouTube VR [6, 8]. Recognizing this need, we explored and developed natural interaction methods tailored for VR video streaming applications, specifically YouTube VR, to enhance user experience and foster broader acceptance and engagement.

In this paper, we present our study to extract natural and intuitive gestures, particularly within the context of VR video streaming applications like YouTube VR. We aim to address existing challenges in user interaction within VR environments by exploring innovative approaches to gesture-based controls. Leveraging insights from existing literature on VR technology, interaction methods, and user experience design, we embarked on an iterative process of prototype development and user testing. Through this process, we aimed to understand user challenges, preferences, and needs in navigating and interacting within VR environments, with a specific emphasis on controlling volume and pause-play functions. By identifying gaps and opportunities in current VR interfaces, we aimed to develop intuitive, culturally relevant gesture-based interaction methods that enhance user experience and accessibility in VR video streaming applications. Our research contributes to advancing the discourse on VR interaction design and offers valuable insights into the development of more intuitive and user-friendly VR interfaces.

The rest of this paper is organized as follows. Section 2 provides a comprehensive summary of the existing selection techniques. In Sect. 3 we provide a background to the study. Section 4 contains the details of the experimentation and the study procedure. We discuss the results in Sect. 5 and conclude the paper in Sect. 6.

2 Literature Review

Psycholinguistic literature has established how speakers from all cultural and linguistic backgrounds use gestures [25], while gesture communication emerges in young children even before the development of language [26]. Even more, gestures are so deeply interwoven with our thought processes that blind people gesture as they speak just as much as sighted individuals do, even when they know their listener is also blind [27]. These previous works show that there exists a form of innate gesture knowledge in the individual based on various factors, which represents a strong motivation to pursue the development of intuitive gesture methods in virtual reality.

Intuitiveness in VR is crucial, as traditional input methods like controllers and keyboards, along with many hand gestures, may be challenging for users if they are unrealistic or hard to perform. Researchers have explored alternative input methods, such as hand gestures, voice commands, and gaze-based interactions, to address this challenge. However, there should be a match between virtual and real-world (YouTube on mobile) interactions for video streaming applications like YouTube VR. Studies indicate that hand gestures offer a more natural and intuitive interaction in virtual environments, enhancing immersion and engagement [9].

Gesture-based interactions have been extensively studied in the field of VR user experience design, with researchers investigating the effectiveness and usability of different gesture recognition systems. Mapping the hand gestures with real-world actions greatly influences the experience of the users within the virtual environment (VE). Ideally, gestures should be easy to memorize and perform. Users prefer gestures that mimic real-world actions, such as pointing, rather than new and unrealistic gestures. Visual feedback confirming successful gesture recognition enhances usability and user engagement. In addition to hand gestures, audio input options, such as voice commands, have been explored as accessible interaction methods in VR applications. Studies have shown that combining gestures and voice has received positive feedback in terms of user experience, indicating a promising direction for such interactive methods [4]. This can also improve task completion times and reduce user frustration compared to traditional input methods.

The effectiveness of interaction methods significantly impacts the immersive experience in VR and their ability to transport users into virtual environments. VR as a technology is designed to be immersive and support full-body, lifelike (or 'natural') interactions. As a result of this, studies reveal users treat the environment as a fully supported real-world space. The cultural impact of these behaviors cannot be overlooked. The expectation of natural interaction is not merely a technological requirement but also shaped by cultural experiences and the user's familiarity with real-world analogs. For instance, users from cultures with prevalent touch-based interaction in real life may expect similar ease and fluidity in virtual environments. This kind of natural interaction makes users feel natural and harmonious in the process of interacting with computers, thus lowering the threshold of human-computer interaction. Interaction is the application of the skills and experiences we learn when interacting with entities in our daily environment to the virtual environment created by the computer. Users can interact with objects in the virtual world as if they were communicating in the real world without any special learning [13]. For example, we see users seeking to walk long distances, use untracked body parts (such as kicking whilst boxing), and lean on virtual-only objects. These actions all fall outside of the design of the VR experience but could be considered 'expected' behaviors [2]. So, intuitive interaction methods can enhance presence in the virtual environment, leading to greater immersion and engagement.

Furthermore, research has shown that various contexts (like culture) play a role in the design and reception of VR interactions. Users have different gesture preferences [14–16] and variability exists in gesture articulation as well [17–21]. For instance, Rekik et al. [18, 19] showed that users vary their multi-touch gestures in terms of number of fingers and the way hands move in parallel or sequence. Also, gesture production in public spaces depends on location and audience [22, 23], and the social acceptance of gestures is influenced by culture, time, and interaction type [24].

By combining intuitive gestures, simple interactions, and audio input options, YouTube VR can create more compelling and accessible experiences for users, regardless of their level of experience or physical abilities. We have studied how user-centric design approaches can assist in the development of intuitive interaction methods for VR applications. Additionally, it's worth noting that there are no papers addressing cultural references related to gestures in VR environments. This gap highlights an opportunity for our research to explore how cultural differences might influence the effectiveness and interpretation of gestures in virtual reality settings.

3   Evaluation Study

This evaluation study aims to investigate the most natural and intuitive set of hand gestures for YouTube applications in virtual reality.

3.1   Study Background

To propose hand gestures that enhance the user experience in YouTube VR on Meta Quest 3, we followed a multi-step process. First, we conducted a pilot study with 30 participants, all graduate students with prior VR experience. We asked participants to use various VR applications, including gaming, training and simulation, social VR, meeting rooms, and video streaming apps like Netflix and YouTube, specifically on Meta Quest 3. This allowed us to gain insights into current VR technology and the challenges users face in interacting with virtual environments.

Next, we carried out extensive experimentation by having participants watch a mix of 2D and 3D videos on YouTube VR using Meta Quest 3. Participants collectively watched around 10–11 h of video, with each individual viewing approximately 20 min. To ensure comfort, participants used a revolving office chair, which was beneficial for 3D video streaming. We observed that shorter-duration videos were preferred to reduce fatigue, and the heaviness associated with prolonged headset use. However, we noted arm fatigue, particularly during longer videos, due to repetitive hand or controller-based interactions in VR. Common actions such as pausing, playing, changing the volume, and browsing videos required frequent hand movements, which were cumbersome and tiring.

Despite the availability of hand gestures like *point and pinch, pinch and scroll, and palm pinch* during hand tracking mode on Meta Quest 3, navigating YouTube was a time-consuming process as these gestures were not very familiar to the user. We researched common video interactions on YouTube and other streaming apps based on user feedback. Volume control and pause-play functions were identified as crucial, with 22 of 30 participants agreeing. We aimed to develop more natural hand gestures for volume control and pause-play functions in YouTube VR based on these insights.

4 User Evaluation Study

4.1 Design of the Virtual Environment

We developed the virtual environment using Unity3D software, which enabled us to design 3D assets and create an environment like the existing YouTube VR setup. Unity's Meta SDK all-in-one Interaction Toolkit was integrated to facilitate VR interactions. We configured the necessary Unity settings for VR experiences and used basic coding to import and play videos, aiming to replicate the user experience found in current YouTube VR systems. The environment features 2K resolution video playback, providing users with a clearer and more immersive visual experience. It was designed as an open space, with the main projection zone set 10 feet away from the user and a screen size of 10.5 x 6 feet, like the 16:9 aspect ratio commonly used in VR video content.

After developing these prototypes, we conducted user testing in the created virtual environment, which resembled the YouTube VR interface. A 4:15 min clip from National Geographic titled 'India from Above' in 2K resolution was selected to enhance immersion and engage participants. Key improvements included optimizing the scene for better rendering performance and ensuring seamless interactions by reducing latency in hand-tracking and controller-based inputs. We used a conventional 2D video to focus on gesture effectiveness within a mass-consumption media application that can be easily translated to VR, isolating the impact of gestures on the user experience. Additionally, most YouTube content, including documentaries and short-form media, remains in 2D formats, which is why optimizing user interactions for these experiences was prioritized. This allowed for a targeted analysis applicable to other VR applications, with plans for future research on 360-degree video experiences.

The 4:15-min video balanced engagement and avoided cognitive fatigue, ensuring sufficient data collection without overwhelming participants. We aimed to prevent user discomfort while ensuring enough time for interaction testing and collecting meaningful data. In 2020, Afify [28] showed that the performance of students who learned through short 6-min videos achieved better results in immediate cognitive achievement and post-cognitive achievement which is the retention of learning effects in the long

Fig. 1. The VE used for the study. The video showcased 'India from Above' by National Geographic in VR.

term. The selected National Geographic clip was specifically chosen for its visual richness and steady camera movements, which allowed participants to focus on the interaction techniques without experiencing motion sickness often associated with fast-paced or unsteady footage. It provided an immersive experience, essential for evaluating VR interactions (Fig. 1).

4.2 Experimental Setup and Apparatus

The study utilized the Oculus Quest 3 HMD device. The visual stimuli were presented through the Oculus Quest 3, offering a resolution of 4k per eye and a diagonal FOV of 265.52°. For this setup, the Oculus Quest was connected to a computer with an i7 processor, integrated graphics 5500, 16 GB RAM, and running Microsoft Windows 10, via the Oculus Link cable. A video camera was positioned diagonally to the participant to capture visual data for further analysis. Figure 2 shows the experimental setup used for the study.

Fig. 2. A participant performing the gestures for pausing the video. A video camera placed diagonally to the participant captured visual data for further analysis.

4.3 Task

During the study, participants were tasked with performing volume control gestures, to increase and decrease volume, while immersed in watching the video. Additionally, they were prompted to execute play and pause gestures while being fully engaged in the video content. Participants were encouraged to perform these gestures intuitively, without deliberate thought about whether the gesture would be effective or appropriate. This approach aimed to assess the naturalness and effectiveness of the proposed gestures within the immersive VR environment.

4.4 Participants

The study involved 30 non-paid participants (16 males, 14 females), aged 18–33 (Mean = 28.76, SD = 5.61). All participants were graduate students specializing in XR design with prior experience using HMD-VR platforms (e.g., Oculus Quest 2 and HTC Vive). They had completed VR-related courses in the previous semester, ensuring familiarity with VR technology and advanced equipment. The target group was chosen based on their comfort with transforming digital usage into a VR experience and their exposure to VR for at least 8 months.

4.5 Study Procedure

The study was conducted in a laboratory environment. Before the task, a moderator verbally introduced the study to each participant. Participants were shown the VE before they performed the task. This allowed the participants to think before they proposed any gesture. To minimize pre-exposure biases and confusion we familiarized participants with the VR setup so they could give subjective comparisons and feedback in gestures.

Participants were then asked to perform up to 2 gestures of their choice that they thought would be the most natural and intuitive. They were then shown a 4:15-min video from National Geographic titled 'India from Above'. Participants were prompted to perform a gesture at the 1:40 min mark during the video. They were asked to increase and decrease the volume by coming up with a natural and intuitive gesture. Similarly, the participants were prompted at the 3:28 min mark to perform another gesture to pause and play the video. Once the participants performed the body gestures, they informed the moderator. The beginning, end, and trajectory of the gesture were carefully noted and confirmed with the participant to maintain the accuracy of the performed gesture considering a Wizard of Oz setup and to ensure accurate data collection. Participants were asked to explain the choice of a particular gesture. We also encouraged participants to talk and think aloud while performing the task to understand the motivation behind performing a specific gesture. The study was video recorded, with each session lasting approximately 15 min, totaling 7.5 h. Prior consent was obtained from each participant.

5 Results

In total, 30 participants contributed to 60 gestures, out of which 51 gestures (including the frequency of the gestures being performed) were found to be existing gestures and were performed by multiple participants. These included *pinch with ray casting, tap using 4 fingers, tap using 2 fingers, sliding the palm left and right, ray casting with the index finger, pinch with the middle finger, sliding with one finger, sliding with the thumb, moving the arm up and down, waving with one hand, and point gesture*. Some of these gestures were inspired by WIMP (Windows, Icons, Menus, Pointer) interfaces, making them familiar and easy to recall. Users *pinch with ray casting* to adjust the volume from a distance, pinching to select and drag a virtual volume slider for precise control. For quick muting or unmuting, users rely on the *tap using four fingers* gesture, which acts as a convenient shortcut for major audio adjustments. To control playback, they use the *tap using two fingers* gesture to toggle play and pause, a simple and natural action for starting or stopping media.

For dynamic volume control, users perform the *sliding the palm left and right* gesture, swiping to increase or decrease the volume, much like swiping a volume slider on a touchscreen. With *ray casting using the index finger*, users point at and select media controls like volume and playback buttons, emulating the familiar act of pointing in the physical world. When using the *pinch with the middle finger* gesture, users mute the sound or toggle play/pause, differentiating this from the more commonly used pinch action.

The *one finger sliding gesture* is used for smooth volume adjustment, like touch gestures on mobile devices, while thumb sliding allows for quicker changes in playback settings, such as scrolling through media or adjusting volume with broader thumb motions. The larger motion of moving the arm up and down lets users adjust volume incrementally, with an upward movement increasing and a downward movement decreasing sound. Finally, the waving with one hand gesture is employed to activate or deactivate playback, acting as a play/pause toggle, while the *point* gesture is used to directly select and control media settings like volume and playback with precision and ease. The index finger is usually preferred to create a *pointing* gesture. We also use a *pointing forward gesture* to point at something in real-world scenarios. Similarly, in virtual environments, *pointing gestures* can be used to point at an object like we use a mouse pointer [11]. One participant said, *"This feels similar to a mouse click and is easy to remember."* This finding is in line with [29, 30] in which traditional WIMP interfaces inspired the gestures collected for a VR shopping application and scientific molecular visualization applications.

Nine gestures were identified as unique, with various inspirations and associations noted. The gestures are *palm-facing outward, fingertips of all hands together, palm up and down, making a fist and releasing, clapping, two-finger vertical swipe, rotating a knob* using an index finger and thumb *pinch and release, and palm tap* gesture. The *palm-facing outward gesture* to stop the video is an intuitive and easily recognizable gesture performed. This gesture also resembles the *Abhaya Mudra* in the Indian context which signifies giving blessings. A participant said, *"I performed this gesture as I just watched the priest giving a blessing in the video. This gesture also felt very accurate and intuitive to stop the video."* The gesture involves simple hand movements, making it ergonomic and easy to perform. It does not require extensive physical effort, reducing the potential for fatigue during extended use in VR environments (Fig. 3).

One of the gestures is to *touch the fingertips of all hands together*. This gesture also symbolizes coming to a point of focus or concentration, intuitively aligning with the idea of pausing. This gesture also resembles the *Hakina Mudra* associated with focus in Indian culture. This gesture can be comfortably performed without much effort, reducing the potential for fatigue.

The *palm up and down gesture* by putting the thumb under the palm to increase/decrease volume intuitively correlates with increasing or decreasing volume levels. Raising a hand or palm also signifies offering or attention, while lowering it signifies confirmation or completion. This gesture is also fitting for interactions that require attention, selection, and confirmation. The motion is natural, avoiding abrupt or complex movements that might disrupt the immersive experience [7].

Another gesture for volume control resembled *rotating a knob* using an index finger and thumb increasing the space within the index finger and thumb while rotating. The participant used the thumb and index finger to mimic the motion of rotating a physical

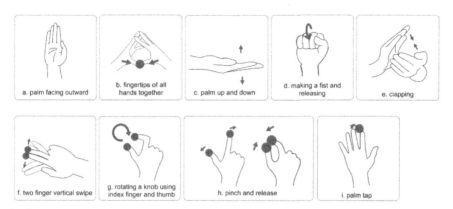

Fig. 3. *(a) palm facing outward (b) fingertips of all hands together (c) palm up and down (d) making a fist and releasing (e) clapping (f) two finger vertical swipe (g) rotating a knob using index finger and thumb (h) pinch and release (i) palm tap.*

knob. The participant said, *"This is similar to using old radio devices"*. The starting point of the gesture is a pinch which also resembles 'little' as a gesture in some cultures. This gesture leverages familiar physical actions, ensuring immediate user understanding and ease of use. It provides users with precise and natural control over volume settings [5].

Similarly, the gesture for volume control, particularly using *two fingers for a vertical swipe (wave gesture)*, feels very comfortable and easy to use and at the same time, it is intuitive to perform, suggesting a connection between the gesture and users' real-life experiences, as discussed in the study by [11] where in-air gestures can be an input modality for touchless user interfaces, which allow users to operate the interface like interacting with real-world objects. Touchless user interfaces with in-air gesture controls (e.g., *tapping, sliding, and dragging*) could further reduce the gulf of execution between the user and digital information. It can also reduce problems such as fat fingers or occlusion caused by restricted touch space.

Another unique gesture was the *clapping* gesture. Participants found the gesture intriguing, noting its engagement of both hands for task execution. However, they acknowledged the potential challenge of requiring both hands simultaneously. Nonetheless, they appreciated the concept of integrating sound and gesture to initiate and halt video playback, indicating a positive reception towards multimodal interaction approaches.

Another unique gesture for the pause and play function was *making a fist and releasing (with one hand)*. It can be easily executed and requires minimal arm movement, reducing fatigue during longer videos. Fist and open hand gestures are also rooted in everyday actions and social signals. For example, making a fist can indicate a pause in conversation or activity, while an open hand can signal continuation or permission to proceed. A participant responded, *"I wanted the person in the video to stop speaking so I made the fist gesture to stop the video"* [10].

Similarly, the adoption of the *pinch and release* gesture was aimed at simplifying task execution by eliminating the necessity for precise pointing. By affixing a pointer to the fingers, users could initiate actions from any point without the need for pinpoint accuracy.

This design modification significantly eased task completion for users, enhancing their overall experience with the system.

The *palm tap gesture* is a quick and natural way to control media playback. Users simply tap their palm with one or more fingers to toggle between playing and pausing. This gesture replicates the action of pressing a physical button, making it intuitive for users to interact with media controls. Since it requires minimal movement, the *palm tap gesture* is efficient and reduces the need for more complex interactions, providing a seamless way to manage playback in immersive environments. A participant commented, *"this gesture feels really natural as tapping my palm to play or pause feels like I'm pressing an actual button, and it's easy to remember without breaking immersion."*

6 Discussion

Overall, the study underscores the significance of aligning gestures with users' mental models and task relevance in VR interaction design. The study highlights that most gestures favored by participants aligned closely with their task expectations, reinforcing the importance of intuitive design in VR environments. For example, the *swipe* gesture could be extended to be used for switching tabs or videos in a web browser [11]. This preference stems from the widespread use of swipe gestures in touch interfaces, where a quick horizontal swipe typically translates to moving between pages, tabs, or items. For volume control, participants preferred straightforward *pointing* gestures over more complex multitask gestures, finding them easier to perform and more congruent with their mental models. Conversely, for functions like play and pause, participants preferred familiar gestures that are culturally relevant and that matched their intuitive expectations, highlighting the value of leveraging existing user knowledge in interface design. For instance, the *Abhaya Mudra* and *Hakini Mudra* gesture, where the palm is held outward to signal "stop," was favored for pausing videos. These gestures are deeply rooted in cultural practices, making them easily recognizable and intuitive.

Most participants found the hand gestures easy and intuitive to use, emphasizing the preference for gestures that align with their mental models or task objectives. This preference was particularly evident in volume control, where participants favored gestures directly correlating with the desired action, such as simple pointing motions. In contrast, for play and pause functions, participants preferred gestures that were already familiar to them, reflecting the significance of leveraging users' existing knowledge and expectations in interface design.

The study also identified a high repetition rate of familiar gestures, including *"pinch with ray casting"* and *"sliding the palm left and right,"* reinforcing their alignment with users' mental models and the ease of their integration into VR systems. Unique gestures like making a fist and releasing for pause/play and the adoption of pinch and release gestures further demonstrate the potential to simplify user interactions and improve overall system usability.

Gestures that felt both natural and simple to perform received particularly favorable responses from participants, such as the *two-finger vertical swipe* and the *clapping gesture*, indicating their engagement with multimodal interaction approaches. These insights underscore the value of intuitive, culturally relevant gestures in creating immersive and user-friendly VR experiences.

One of the key findings of our study was the strong cultural underpinnings of the gestures identified by participants. For example, the "palm-facing outward" gesture, which was intuitively used to stop the video, resonates with the Indian gesture "*Abhaya Mudra,*" a cultural symbol of giving blessings. Similarly, the "fingertips of all hands together" gesture, associated with pausing, aligns with the "*Hakini Mudra,*" symbolizing concentration and focus. These culturally rooted gestures were not explicitly taught to participants, yet they emerged naturally during the study, highlighting their deep-seated intuitiveness across cultural backgrounds.

The cultural relevance of these gestures reflects the participants' subconscious alignment with familiar cultural practices. In this study, we focus on the Indian cultural context rather than any demographic group and are not aiming to explore the diversity within Indian culture. This finding underscores the importance of considering cultural context in designing intuitive VR interactions. Our study emphasized cultural aspects in gesture design, acknowledging cultural differences in interpretation. While broader perspectives could enhance inclusivity, the idea is to use cultural references to create better hand gestures, not to limit cultural gestures' use to corresponding user backgrounds. One thing to note is that the participants did not know about culturally linked gestures to capture unbiased reactions, ensuring cross-cultural intuitiveness.

The findings from this study have significant implications for VR interaction design, particularly in the context of video streaming applications. By aligning gestures with users' cultural practices and mental models, we can create more intuitive and engaging VR experiences. This approach not only enhances usability but also fosters greater immersion, as users can interact with the virtual environment in ways that feel natural and familiar to them.

Overall, these findings contribute to the ongoing discourse on VR interaction design and its impact on entertainment experiences. By prioritizing intuitive interaction methods and aligning gestures with users' mental models, designers can enhance usability and accessibility in VR environments, ultimately improving the overall user experience.

7 Conclusions

In this paper, we identified and developed natural and intuitive gestures tailored for virtual reality (VR) interactions, particularly within the context of VR video streaming applications like YouTube VR. We proposed 9 natural and intuitive unique gestures. The main contribution of this work is the identification of natural and culturally relevant gestures for VR video streaming, which need to be sufficiently investigated in an HMD-VR context. The study substantiates the efficacy of culturally relevant novel hand gestures as a primary interaction modality for VR video streaming applications. The overwhelmingly positive user feedback and swift adaptability to this approach underscores its potential to redefine accessibility and user experience standards within the VR domain. By leveraging intuitive interaction methods, such as hand gestures, we anticipate a paradigm shift in VR interaction design, paving the way for a more inclusive and immersive virtual reality ecosystem. By leveraging intuitive interaction methods, such as hand gestures, we anticipate a paradigm shift in VR interaction design, paving the way for a more inclusive and immersive virtual reality ecosystem. These conclusions not only validate our research objectives but also present actionable insights for designers and scholars alike, charting a course toward a more user-centric future in VR technology. As part of future work, we intend to further validate and refine our insights.

Our future work will focus on conducting comprehensive user studies with larger and more diverse participants, as well as incorporating objective metrics like task completion times to rigorously assess gesture effectiveness. We also plan to address accessibility concerns, particularly for users with hand-shivering conditions, to ensure that our VR interfaces are inclusive and usable by a wider audience. Expanding the sample size and demographic diversity will allow us to capture a broader range of cultural perspectives, further validating the cultural relevance and intuitiveness of the identified gestures.

The practical implementation of these gestures in VR systems will require careful consideration of technical viability, hardware compatibility, and scalability. While the identified gestures show promise, their integration into commercial VR platforms like YouTube VR will necessitate further testing and refinement. Issues such as latency, gesture recognition accuracy, and the physical demands of performing certain gestures must be addressed to ensure a seamless user experience.

Author Contribution Statement. Himanshu Raj and Samia equally contributed to the conception and design of the study. (Raj led the experimental setup and performed data collection, while Samia focused on data analysis and experimental design. All authors contributed to the development of the virtual environment and the integration of gesture-based interactions. Shimmila Bhowmick supervised the whole project. All authors discussed the results, refined the analysis, and contributed to the final manuscript.)

References

1. Berkman, M.I., Akan, E.: Presence and immersion in virtual reality. In: Lee, N. (eds.) Encyclopedia of Computer Graphics and Games, pp 1–10. Springer, Cham. (2019). https://doi.org/10.1007/978-3-319-08234-9_162-1
2. Dao, E., Muresan, A., Hornbæk, K., Knibbe, J.: Bad breakdowns, useful seams, and face slapping: analysis of VR fails on YouTube. In: CHI 2021: Proceedings of the 2021 CHI Conference on Human Factors in Computing Systems, Article No. 526, pp. 1–14. ACM, Yokohama, Japan (2021). https://doi.org/10.1145/3411764.3445435
3. Dudley, J., Yin, L., Garaj, V., Kristensson, P.: Inclusive Immersion: a review of efforts to improve accessibility in virtual reality, augmented reality and the metaverse. Virtual Reality **27**, 2989–3020 (2023). https://doi.org/10.1007/s10055-023-00850-8
4. Fang, K., Wang, J.: Interactive design with gesture and voice recognition in virtual teaching environments. IEEE Access **12**, 4213–4224 (2024). https://doi.org/10.1109/ACCESS.2023.3348846
5. Feick, M., Zenner, A., Ariza, O., Tang, A., Biyikli, C., Krüger, A.: Turn-it-up: rendering resistance for knobs in virtual reality through undetectable pseudo-haptics. In: UIST 2023: Proceedings of the 36th Annual ACM Symposium on User Interface Software and Technology, pp. 1–10. ACM, San Francisco, CA, USA (2023). https://doi.org/10.1145/3586183.3606787
6. Khan, R., Azam, F., Ahmed, S., Anwar, W., Chughtai, R., Farid, A.: Comparative analysis of interaction techniques in virtual reality. In: IEEE 23rd International Multitopic Conference (INMIC), pp. 1–6. IEEE, Bahawalpur, Pakistan (2020). https://doi.org/10.1109/INMIC50486.2020.9318194

7. Khundam, C.: First person movement control with palm normal and hand gesture interaction in virtual reality. In: 12th International Joint Conference on Computer Science and Software Engineering (JCSSE), pp. 325–330. IEEE, Songkhla, Thailand (2015). https://doi.org/10.1109/JCSSE.2015.7219818

8. Mäkelä, V., et al.: What are others looking at? Exploring 360° videos on HMDs with visual cues about other viewers. In: ACM International Conference on Interactive Experiences for TV and Online Video (TVX 2019), pp. 1–12. ACM, Salford (Manchester), United Kingdom (2010). https://doi.org/10.1145/3317697.3323351

9. Monteiro, P., Coelho, H., Gonçalves, G., Melo, M., Bessa, M.: Exploring the user experience of hands-free VR interaction methods during a Fitts' task. Comput. Graph. **117**, 1–12 (2023). https://doi.org/10.1016/j.cag.2023.10.005

10. Pei, S., Chen, A., Lee, J., Zhang, Y., Hand interfaces: using hands to imitate Objects in AR/VR for expressive interactions. In: Proceedings of the 2022 CHI Conference on Human Factors in Computing Systems, pp. 1–16. ACM, New Orleans, LA, USA (2022)

11. Shanthakumar, V., Peng, C., Hansberger, J., Cao, L., Meacham, S., Blakeley, V.: Design and evaluation of a hand gesture recognition approach for real-time interactions. Multimedia Tools Appl. **79**, 17707–17730 (2020). https://doi.org/10.1007/s11042-019-08520-1

12. YAN 1 2, Y., YI 1 2, X., YU 1 2 3 4, C., SHI 1 2 3 4, Y.: Gesture-based target acquisition in virtual and augmented reality. Virt. Real. Intell. Hardware **1**(3), 276–289 (2019). https://doi.org/10.3724/SP.J.2096-5796.2019.0007

13. Chang, C.-Y., Sung, H.-Y., Guo, J.-L., Chang, B.-Y., Kuo, F.-R.: Effects of spherical video-based virtual reality on nursing students' learning performance in childbirth education training. Interact. Learn. Environ. **30**, 400–416 (2019). https://doi.org/10.1080/10494820.2019.1661854

14. Vatavu, R.D., Zaiti, I.A.: Leap gestures for TV: insights from an elicitation study. In: Proceedings of the 2014 ACM international conference on interactive experiences for TV and online video, TVX'14. ACM, New York, pp 131–138 (2014) https://doi.org/10.1145/2602299.2602316

15. Vatavu, R.D., Wobbrock, J.O.: Formalizing agreement analysis for elicitation studies: new measures, significance test, and toolkit. In: Proceedings of the 33rd annual ACM conference on human factors in computing systems, CHI 2015, ACM, New York, pp 1325–1334 (2015). https://doi.org/10.1145/2702123.2702223

16. Wobbrock, J.O., Morris, M.R., Wilson, A.D.: User-defined gestures for surface computing. In: Proceedings of the SIGCHI Conference on Human Factors in Computing Systems, CHI 2009, ACM, New York, pp 1083–1092 (2009). https://doi.org/10.1145/1518701.1518866

17. Anthony, L., Vatavu, R.D., Wobbrock, J.O.: Understanding the consistency of users' pen and finger stroke gesture articulation. In: Proceedings of graphics interface 2013, GI'13. Canadian Information Processing Society, Toronto, pp 87–94 (2013). http://dl.acm.org/citation.cfm?id=2532129.2532145

18. Rekik, Y., Grisoni, L., Roussel, N.: Towards many gestures to one command: a user study for tabletops. In: Proceedings of the 14th IFIP TC 13 international conference on human–computer interaction, INTERACT 2013, Springer, Berlin, pp 246–263. (2013). https://doi.org/10.1007/978-3-642-40480-1_16

19. Rekik Y., Vatavu, R.D., Grisoni, L.: Match-up and conquer: a two-step technique for recognizing unconstrained bimanual and multi-finger touch input. In: Proceedings of the 2014 International Working Conference on Advanced Visual Interfaces, AVI 2014. ACM, New York, pp 201–208 (2014). https://doi.org/10.1145/2598153.2598167

20. Tu, H., Ren, X., Zhai, S.: A comparative evaluation of finger and pen stroke gestures. In: Proceedings of the SIGCHI conference on human factors in computing systems, CHI'12. ACM, New York, pp 1287–1296. (2012) https://doi.org/10.1145/2207676.2208584

21. Tu, H., Ren, X., Zhai, S.: Differences and similarities between finger and pen stroke gestures on stationary and mobile devices. ACM Trans Comput. Hum. Interact. **22**(5), 22:1–22:39 (2015). https://doi.org/10.1145/2797138

22. Rico, J., Brewster, S.: Gestures all around us: user differences in social acceptability perceptions of gesture-based interfaces. In: Proceedings of the 11th International Conference on Human–Computer Interaction with Mobile Devices and Services, MobileHCI 2009, ACM, New York, pp. 64:1–64:2 (2009). https://doi.org/10.1145/1613858.1613936

23. Rico, J., Brewster, S.: Usable gestures for mobile interfaces: evaluating social acceptability. In: Proceedings of the SIGCHI Conference on Human Factors in Computing Systems, CHI 2010, ACM, New York, pp. 887–896 (2010). https://doi.org/10.1145/1753326.1753458

24. Montero, C.S., Alexander, J., Marshall, M.T., Subramanian, S.: Would you do that? understanding social acceptance of gestural interfaces. In: Proceedings of the 12th International Conference on Human–Computer Interaction with Mobile Devices and services, MobileHCI 2010, ACM, New York, pp. 275–278 (2010). https://doi.org/10.1145/1851600.1851647

25. Feyereisen, P., De, Lannoy.: Gestures and speech: psychological investigations. Cambridge University Press, New York (1991). https://books.google.co.in/books?id=VL2YyP7qN8sC&lpg=PP15&ots=_zy5tY9mPT&lr&pg=PP11#v=onepage&q&f=false

26. Goodwyn, S., Acredolo, L., Brown, C.: Impact of symbolic gesturing on early language development. J. Nonverbal Behav. 81–103 (2000). https://doi.org/10.1023/A:1006653828895

27. Iverson, J.M., Goldin-Meadow, S.: Why people gesture when they speak. Nature (1998). https://doi.org/10.1038/24300

28. Afıfy, M.K.: Effect of interactive video length within e-learning environments on cognitive load, cognitive achievement and retention of learning. J. Educ. Tech. Res. Dev. **21**(4), 68–89 (2020). https://dergipark.org.tr/en/pub/tojde/issue/57047/803360

29. Wu, H., Yu, W., Jiali, Q., Jiayi, L., Xiaolong, Z.: User-defined gesture interaction for immersive VR shopping applications. Behav. Inf. Technol. **38**, 726–741 (2019). https://doi.org/10.1080/0144929X.2018.1552313

30. Bhowmick, S., Pratul, K., Keyur, S.: A gesture elicitation study for selection of nail size objects in a dense and occluded dense HMD-VR.In: Proceedings of the 11th Indian Conference on Human-Computer Interaction, pp. 12–23 (2020). https://doi.org/10.1145/3429290.3429292

Lessons from Skill Development Programs - Livelihood College of Dhamtari

Arnab Paul Choudhury[1]([⊠])(iD) and Nihal Patel[2](iD)

[1] Viksit Labs Foundation, Silchar, Assam, India
arnabpchoudhury@viksitlabs.in,arnabpc.oshin94@gmail.com,
https://www.viksitlabs.in
[2] Indian Institute of Technology Guwahati, Guwahati, Assam, India

Abstract. Skill training is crucial for enabling dignified livelihood opportunities. In India, various schemes and initiatives aim to provide skill training in different domains, with ICT and digital technologies playing a vital role. However, there is limited research on understanding on-ground capacities & constraints and the use of digital tools in these programs. In this study, we look into the mobilization, counseling, and training stages of the 5-stage skill development process that also includes placement and tracking, adopted in Dhamtari's Livelihood College in Chhattisgarh, India, and other programs nationwide. Through the immersion/crystallization approach and mixed-method analysis including GIS mapping, video analysis of CCTV streams, quantitative analysis, and unstructured conversations with administrators, trainers, mobilizers, counselors, and nearby industry personnel for over a year, we identified three major challenges. A lack of inclusive and gendered access to skilling; a tedious manual counseling process with insufficient support staff; and inconsistent trainee attendance alongside sub-standard utilization of digital assets. Finally, we discuss, ways to improve access to skill training by leveraging Vocational Training Partners (VTPs), ways to improve the utilization of existing digital assets, and considerations for improving the counseling process. We conclude by summarizing that skill development programs currently lack institutional elements that enable effective information exchange between stakeholders, thereby creating information bottlenecks that result in inefficiencies, hindering the service delivery. In sum, our study informs the HCI and ICTD literature on the on-ground challenges and constraints faced by stakeholders and the role of technology in supporting such initiatives.

Keywords: Human Computer Interaction · Skill Development · Education · HCI for Social Good · Empirical studies in HCI

1 Introduction

The impact of COVID-19, the Russia-Ukraine war, and AI technology disruption have significantly influenced global health, geopolitical dynamics, and economic

This work was done while the author was at the Indian Institute of Management Kozhikode, Mahatma Gandhi National Fellowship.

trends, resulting in varied outcomes for labor markets worldwide [27]. Notably, low- and lower-middle-income countries continue to experience heightened unemployment rates, particularly among individuals with basic education and women [28,72]. Concurrently, real wages are declining due to an ongoing cost-of-living crisis, and changing worker expectations, such as a desire for better work-life balance, job security, career growth opportunities, and a healthy work environment, have emerged as prominent global issues, including in India [18,30,40,46]. India boasts the youngest workforce globally, with a median age of 28, and 68% of its population in the working age group (15–64) now has a demographic dividend [24,52]. This demographic advantage historically fueled economic growth, translating into a larger workforce, rapid urbanization, and industrialization, attracting investments in infrastructure and human capital development leading to increased economic productivity, a rise of the middle class, and a greater purchasing power [33,35]. However, making effective use of this demographic dividend requires a robust Skill Development process that can adapt to people from diverse socio-economic backgrounds across the country [32]. The situation is especially dire for blue-collar jobs, which are often less adaptable to disruptions, underscoring the need for targeted efforts to minimize shocks for workers in this section of jobs [51]. In response, the Government of India has launched several Skill Development initiatives to enable effective skilling in various trades with a goal to provide meaningful, dignified livelihood and effectively utilize India's demographic dividend for its continued growth. In particular, the Government of Chhattisgarh has initiated the "Livelihood College" program which aims to impart training in vocational courses and upskill youth from low and middle-income backgrounds in all districts of the state [64]. Prior literature surrounding skill development, ICT and HCI largely focuses on the perspectives of the beneficiaries and the design & development of tools and technologies to support their skilling. However, very little is known about the challenges faced by the authorities and stakeholders in such skill training centers and their interactions with technology. Hence in this study, we explore the challenges faced by stakeholders of a livelihood college in *mobilization, counseling, and training* stages of the 5-stage skill development process adopted in the Livelihood Colleges, which also includes *placement and tracking.*We followed the "immersion/crystallization" approach to conducting a year-long study involving stakeholders of a Livelihood College such as trainers, administrators, mobilizers, counselors, and also nearby industry personnel, through unstructured conversations, participant observation, GIS mapping, quantitative and video analysis to understand,

RQ1: *What are the challenges and bottlenecks in the implementation of the 5-stage process in the skill development programs adopted by the state of Chhattisgarh through Livelihood College and throughout India under national schemes?*

RQ2: *How are digital tools implemented, and utilized in Livelihood Colleges and other skill development programs in India?*

The qualitative inputs revealed a lack of inclusive mobilization and gendered access to skill training, challenges with the overall counseling procedure, limited human resources, and inconsistent trainee attendance/presence in classrooms. The qualitative inputs' on lack of inclusivity and challenges in counseling, were further investigated and triangulated quantitatively using data on home addresses, gender of the trainees, GIS mapping of the before mentioned, and analysis of publicly available data on district demographics. Finally, the inputs on inconsistent trainee attendance/presence were tested by comparing the biometric attendance data with video analysis of CCTV streams using a Yolov5 object-detection model which shows discrepancies in the implementation of biometric attendance collection. Following these findings, we discuss reasons for the lack of trainee representation from different parts of the districts and ways to improve access to skilling, how to improve the utilization of existing digital assets, and considerations on improving counseling procedure. The learnings from this study can be utilized not just within the state of Chhattisgarh but throughout the country in various other skill development initiatives. In sum, this work makes the following contributions to HCI and ICTD literature focusing on the design and implementation of skill development programs in India:

a) We performed a year-long qualitative study that provides insights into the challenges faced in the mobilization, counseling, and training process of the Livelihood College skill development program.
b) We performed video analysis, quantitative analysis, and GIS mapping to investigate and triangulate the qualitative inputs received from stakeholders at the Livelihood College.
c) We identified challenges concerning access to skill development, counseling procedures, limited and sub-optimal use of digital assets, and inadequate attendance/presence of trainees in the skill development programs.
d) We discuss the role of ICT and digital technologies in improving access to skill training; improving utilization and implementation of digital assets and highlighting considerations on improving the counseling process of skill development programs in India using technology interventions.
e) We conclude by summarizing that the livelihood college initiative and skill development programs in general currently lack institutional elements that allow for robust communication exchange between stakeholders leading to inefficiencies, and sub-standard service delivery.

2   Background and Related Work

2.1   Current Skill Ecosystem in India

The Skill India initiative was launched by the government in 2015 to train Indians using a result-oriented framework for industry-related jobs [61]. The primary objective was to train the youth to secure a better livelihood through a convergence of the overall skilling ecosystem by strengthening institutional mechanisms at both national and state levels, building quality trainers and assessors, establishing robust monitoring & evaluation systems, and providing access to skill training opportunities. This umbrella initiative incorporates various schemes and programs, encompassing the journey from education to skill acquisition and ultimately securing a sustainable livelihood. It integrates multiple elements, such as short-term training, employment fairs (rozgar melas), recognition of prior learning, special projects, and guidelines for monitoring and placement, all within a unified platform [62]. The institutional mechanism to implement this mission consists Governing council at the apex level, a Steering Committee, and a Mission Directorate (along with an Executive Committee) as the executive arm of the Mission supported by the National Skill Development Agency (NSDA), National Skill Development Corporation (NSDC), and the Directorate General of Training (DGT) all of which lie under the Ministry of Skill Development and Entrepreneurship. At the State level, States are encouraged to create State Skill Development Missions (SSDM) along the lines of National Skill Development Missions with a Steering Committee and Mission Directorate [29].

2.2   Initiatives by the Government of Chhattisgarh

Similarly, the Chhattisgarh government has passed the Chhattisgarh Right of Youth to Skill Development Act 2013 to secure the right to opportunities for skill development to every person between the age of 15 and 45 years residing in Chhattisgarh, in any vocation of choice consistent with eligibility and aptitude [15,47]. Contemporaneously, the "Livelihood College" initiative was piloted in the Dantewada district-a region affected by tribal and Naxal violence since 2011, and has been replicated in 28 districts by 2023 [64]. These colleges focus on two main areas: emerging market trends like hospitality and industrial stitching, etc., and local skill deficits in trades such as plumbing, electrical work, solar panel installation, mobile repair, and many more. Further, the livelihood colleges are required to ensure training facilities, lab equipment, training regularity, monitor & evaluation through CCTV, prevent unethical practices by the administration, and verify trainer qualifications through Training of Trainers (ToT) Certification [43,45]. The Skill development process undertaken by different arms of the Government usually adopts some common practices [44,63]. The 5 major steps that are generally adopted are detailed below:

- **Mobilization:** In this initial stage, mobilizers visit gram panchayats - a unit of local self-governance - to identify potential beneficiaries. Diverse methods, such as door-to-door mobilization, panchayat-level engagement, and local newspaper advertisements, are employed to raise awareness among youth and pique their interest.
- **Counseling:** In the Counseling stage, appointed counselors guide potential trainees on the schemes and the benefits of skill certification. The mobilizers and counselors are responsible for site selection accommodating a minimum of 30 candidates per session and ensuring accessibility and comfort. After counseling, batches of up to 30 trainees per trade/course are formed, and skill training commences.
- **Training:** The Training phase involves providing skill training in various trades chosen by the candidates. The training duration is four hours per

day, and biometric attendance is collected to monitor attendance. Candidates also participate in a minimum seven-day on-the-job training coordinated by the Livelihood College with potential employers. This experience is further followed by theoretical training, preparing candidates for deployment in the market.

- **Placement:** Finally, the training institute takes the initiative to organize job fairs upon the successful completion of the course primarily for courses where employment opportunities are sought. Trainees can also secure loans from banks to start their ventures by presenting their certificates where they are assisted in business planning and obtaining bank approvals.
- **Tracking:** During this phase, the livelihood college administration monitors the placed trainees for a duration of 12 months supporting them through homesickness or harassment and assessing their employment status.

2.3   Impact and Effectiveness of Skill Development

Studies have also been conducted to understand the effectiveness of skill development programs in India. Studies show that in addition to increasing the economic status of trainees, it brings about apathy toward migration [25]. Skill training has also been found to improve job performance, productivity, and promote self-employment among unemployed youth [1,60]. A perception study in Karnataka found that training had medium effectiveness although trainees perceived that it helped them improve their knowledge and skills [39]. However, some studies also show that training does enhance job market prospects however other labor market forces, like caste-based discriminations, undo the positive effects [14]. One study that examines factors that facilitate and hinder women's enrolment in skill development programs found that women who joined and completed courses could better cope with domestic economic challenges [59]. Studies also find that training semi-literate youth from disadvantaged rural backgrounds does improve "soft skills" but then places them in undesirable low-paid urban services leading them to quit in a few weeks and return home in search of other job opportunities [73].

Many more such studies have also been conducted that assess and examine the impact of such training programs which bring out the nuances in the outcomes, although most agree that training does lead to positive outcomes in knowledge and skill gain [2,50,56,67,69].

2.4   Skill Development and HCI

Prior literature surrounding skill development, vocational training, livelihood, labor, and HCI in India has primarily examined how digital technologies impact vocational workers. Work done to examine the perceptions and practices of vocational workers on automation found that technicians were unaware of the growth of automation but upon learning about it they expressed that they felt excluded by current technological platforms [68]. Another study that examined the experiences of workers on digital labor platforms acknowledges the evolving conditions surrounding skill-building among platform workers and highlights the need to support worker-centered skill-building [37]. Studies have also been conducted to design, develop, and evaluate technologies to support skilling using Augmented reality, and haptic simulation to make skilling more accessible [3,5]. One study that details the design and measures efficacy of Technical Vocational Education and Training among low-literate rural users found that users perform better with ICT interventions [57]. Earlier studies also attempted to design and deploy computerized vocational training courses on mobile-learning platforms delivered using automobile units [6]. Some studies also focus on the need to update the skills of the gig economy amidst trends such as working from home, AI-enabled automation and the role of industry and government policies in supporting gig workers and employees prepare for the future of work [11,12]. Scholars have also designed applications to support migrant workers during the COVID-19 pandemic search for jobs and develop skills through videos and interactions through video [23]. A study that looks into the PMKVY trainee perspectives concludes that even though skill training can provide opportunities for youth from working-class backgrounds, it is considered a last resort for trainees with poor academic records and is associated with lower esteem [49].

Although multiple such studies exist in literature that hope to understand the perspectives of the beneficiaries and develop technologies to support their skilling, very little is known about the challenges and constraints the stakeholders such as trainers, administrators, counselors, and mobilizers face in implementing skill training programs and how technologies are used in supporting their work.

2.5 Digitalization of Skill Development Programs in India

The Government of India (GoI) has given a lot of thrust to digitalizing India on all fronts. Starting from mid-1990s, the GoI started multiple e-governance projects to provide citizen-centric services. This was further improved upon by the national level e-governance program called National e-Governance Plan (NeGP) initiated in the year 2006 [20]. Finally, in the year 2015, the GoI launched the Digital India Mission which acted as an umbrella initiative for supporting multiple government schemes including the PMKVY which is part of the Skill India Mission and Livelihood College initiative [21]. The New Education Policy, of 2020 also highlights the need for integrating ICT and other digital tools in classrooms and calls for more interactive teaching [42,77]. Along similar lines, the livelihood college initiative also utilizes ICT technologies such as geo-tagging venues for counseling, biometric attendance, and CCTV installations for appropriate monitoring and evaluation [44,45,63].

Although existing policies highlight the need to decrease the digital divide and utilize ICT to increase the efficacy of skill development and educational programs, very little is documented on how digital tools are implemented on the ground and the challenges & concerns surrounding them from real-life implementations in skill development programs. Additionally, little to no work documents the service delivery of the Livelihood College initiative in Chhattisgarh, along with the impact and use of digital tools to augment the 5-stage process. Keeping in mind that a similar 5-stage process is adopted not just in the state of Chhattisgarh but also in the National level Skill Development programs in India, it becomes imperative to investigate how effective is the 5-step process and what more needs to be done to effectively deliver such skill development programs in different parts of the country. The learnings from this study can be used to identify key areas that need further improvement in service delivery and bring forth better outcomes for the beneficiaries. To fill this critical gap, we indulged in site immersion at a representative Livelihood College and performed a mixed-methods analysis to draw our findings.

3   Methodology

As a part of the Chhattisgarh Right of Youth to Skill Development Act, the State Authority, CSSDA is mandated to conduct Research and Development in collaboration with various bodies to improve upon the service delivery of the skill development process [15]. Hence, this work was done under due recognition and consent of the Office of the District Skill Development Authority as well as assent of the stakeholders and the authors were provided physical access to the facility & data regarding various aspects of the Livelihood College during the study. We followed the "immersion/crystallization" approach that guided our year-long study. The process was iterative involving multiple stages of data gathering and analysis while remaining reflexive throughout the process [17].

3.1   Geographical Area

This study focussed on the Dhamtari district of Chhattisgarh, India. Dhamtari district is situated in the lower central part, fertile plains of Chhattisgarh region. Dhamtari, Nagri, and Kurud are included as Tehsils, and Dhamtari, Nagri, Kurud, and Magarlod are included as the district blocks. The district has a total population of 7,99,781 of which 6,62,443 are in its rural areas spread throughout 370 Gram Panchayats (GPs) - a unit of local self-governance, which are further combined to form 4 blocks namely Dhamtari, Kurud, Magarlod, and Nagri each containing 94, 108, 66, and 102 Gram Panchayats respectively [19]. Demographically, Dhamtari has a mixed population and the district is also home to sizeable tribal groups who account for 25.96% of the district's population [34]. The district is also endowed with natural wealth in abundance with Mahanadi as the principal river and diversity in flora and fauna majorly in the Nagri region.

3.2   Data

In our study, we performed a mixed-methods analysis involving qualitative & quantitative analysis along with GIS mapping, CCTV video, and biometric data analysis. Table 1 lists the type of data and their source that have been utilized in this study for analysis.

Table 1. Data description.

Data	Source
Unstructured Conversations	Primary
CCTV data	Primary
Biometric attendance	Primary (system generated)
trainee details	Secondary (from Livelihood College)
Physical Map of Dhamtari	Secondary (Publicly available - Govt. of Chhattisgarh)
District demographics	Secondary (Publicly available - Govt. of Chhattisgarh)

3.3   Qualitative Analysis

We started the study by gathering information through unstructured conversations primarily with the administrators, employees (clerks, mobilizers, counselors), trainers, and local industry personnel & businesses. The details of the participants are mentioned in Table 2. The administrators, employees (clerks, mobilizers, and counselors), and trainers were responsible for the proper functioning of the Livelihood College. They were also the first point of contact for the authors in the Livelihood college hence their perspectives formed the initial outlook on the college's functioning. Following this we also engaged with local industry personnel and businesses who are often the primary employers of the trainees who graduate from the Livelihood College. One of the authors in the study was physically present at the Livelihood College throughout the entire duration of the study to investigate and further improve the service delivery and functioning of the College. This physical on-ground interaction lasted for more than a year. The author had the assent, privilege, and free access to interact with the people in the Livelihood College. This prolonged exposure and interaction with the various stakeholders along with passive observations gave us a firm grasp on the current capacities of the program implementation as well as the constraints. Given the year-long study with unstructured conversations, the questions evolved over time. Some high-level questions aligned to our RQs that guided our interactions are added to Appendix A. However, the conversations were conducted largely to identify the bottlenecks in the 5-step process undertaken by skill development programs in India. These conversations allowed us to collect qualitative data that enabled us to identify and filter out some major challenges that needed further investigation.

3.4   Quantitative Analysis and GIS Mapping

Following the unstructured conversations, data on the trainee's attendance and their backgrounds were collected from the database of the Livelihood College. For this study, the latest data available at the time were for the year 2019–2020 where 670 trainees received training. The Financial year 2019–20 was the last year during which such data was collected as the activities of the college were disrupted since

Table 2. Participant Details.

Participant profession	Number	Gender
Administrators	2	All male
Clerks	6	All male
Trainers	3	All male
Trainers who also worked as mobilizers	3	All male
Counselors who also worked as mobilizers	1	Female
Mobilizers	1	Female
Business person (retail shop owner, rice mill owner, etc.)	More than 10	All male

2020 due to COVID-19. This data primarily included the trainee's name, their home address, the Gram Panchayat to which they belonged, district block, age, sex, and many more. This trainee data was first anonymized and de-identified to maintain the privacy of each trainee. Following this, the data was further filtered to remove information on those trainees who did not provide their place of residence or the Gram Panchayat to which they belonged. This resulted in 81 trainees' data being filtered out while the remaining 589 were then visualized into a histogram as can be seen in Fig. 1. Each bar in Fig. 1 shows the number of Gram Panchayats (y-axis) that contributed n-number of trainees (x-axis).

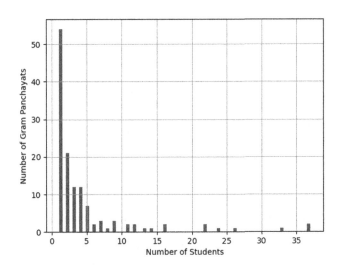

Fig. 1. Histogram showing number Gram Panchayats i.e., GPs (y-axis) contributing n-number of students/trainees (x-axis), (this excludes 81 trainees who were from cities/towns)

It was later found that the 81 trainees were not from villages but were from towns/cities and hence the information on their Gram Panchayat was empty.

We also found that out of the 81, more than 70 were from the district head-quarters of Dhamtari, the rest were from the major towns of the other three blocks. Finally, we manually collected latitude and longitude values for each of the trainee address locations using Google Earth Pro software and utilized ArcMap software to create a GIS map which can be seen in Fig. 2. The GIS map shows the spatial distribution of trainees along with the number of trainees studying in the Livelihood College from that particular location using graduated symbols. Finally, we also compare the information on the spatial distribution of trainees with the physical map of Dhamtari provided by the Government of Chhattisgarh that contains information on the location of Gram Panchayat's and settlements, forest map, lithology map, and groundwater prospects as can be seen in Fig. 3 [41]. Additionally, we also compared the publicly available data from the Government of Chhattisgarh's official website on the district's demographics with the data from the livelihood college which can be seen in Table 3 [13].

Table 3. Statistics on a block level

	Dhamtari	Kurud	Magarlod	Nagri
Total number of GPs	94	108	66	102
Number of GPs represented	32	42	29	32
% of GPs represented from block	34%	39%	44%	31%
Total Population of GPs	183373	197723	115150	166197
Average number person/GP	1950.78	1830.77	1744.70	1629.38
Number of trainees (GP only)	133	169	172	115
% of total trainees (GP only)	23%	29%	29%	20%
Number of trainees (GP+city/town)	207	170	175	118
% of total trainees (GP+city/town)	31%	25%	26%	18%
Male-to-female ratio (GP only)	0.40	0.47	1.61	1.02
Male-to-female ratio (GP+city/town)	0.52	0.48	1.62	1.07

3.5   Attendance Analysis Using CCTV and Biometric Data

The CCTV cameras installed at the Livelihood College were also analyzed by taking snapshots at an interval of 10 min every working day for 1 month from 09:00 am to 01:00 pm which are the usual working hours for our targeted courses i.e., Electrical and Retail. During the time of this study, the livelihood college had 4 running courses namely, Electrical, Retail, Computer hardware and software, and Sewing. However, upon inspection, it was found that the CCTV placement of all the courses except electrical and retail had some errors i.e. either the entire class was not visible, or the angles were incorrect. It was also noted that

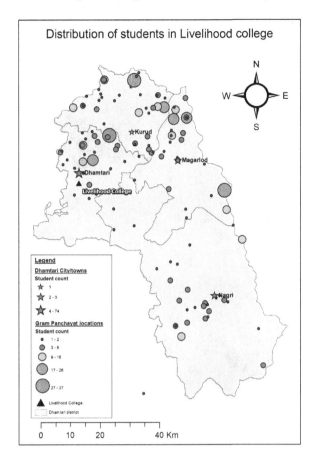

Fig. 2. Map showing the spatial distribution of students/trainees from different Gram Panchayat in Dhamtari

the CCTVs are usually unutilized assets and were seldom used for any productive purposes. In two of the CCTV cameras, the video feed was obstructed by spider webs and we had to manually clean them before attempting to utilize the video data. As a result, we performed video analysis only on Electrical and Retail courses. Since direct access to the video streams was not readily available through the CCTV application, we used the Bluestacks emulator to run the CCTV application on a desktop. A python script was written which would then take images at every 10-minute interval starting from 9:00 am to 01:00 pm. Consecutive courses were mapped onto the same screen and hence the images were further cropped to get the final set of images. In total 25 images were captured per day for each course and the same was repeated for 18 working days in the month. Finally, this resulted in a total of 900 images, 450 for each course. Along with taking the snapshots, the date and time at which they were captured were retained in their filenames in snake casing so as to ensure data integrity.

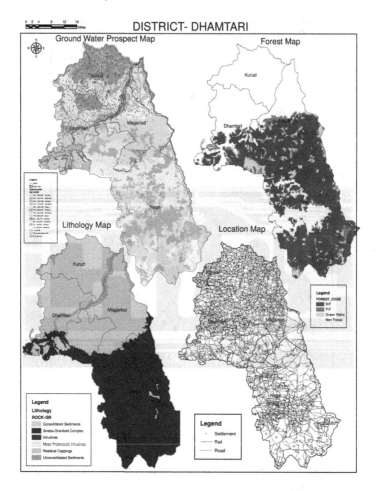

Fig. 3. Physical Map of Dhamtari district [41]

Person detection was then performed using an open-source Object detection model, YOLOv5 with the pre-trained model checkpoint "yolov5x6u.pt" with the default parameters and threshold values. We used this pre-trained checkpoint as during this study it had one of the highest Mean Average Precision 50–95 (mAP50-95) values of 56.8% among all known real-time object detection models [79]. The entire process of prediction and inference from the images was conducted on a Google Colab notebook. To further ensure that the model results were not erroneous, we randomly selected a subset of images from the 900 and manually checked for the correctness of the outputs which in most cases resulted in a correct count or at most had an error count of 1 or 2 in a handful of cases due to trainees overlapping each other while moving around to get inside or move out of the class which is not the usual practice during training sessions as trainees are expected to sit separately in their appropriate places which ensures

Fig. 4. Representative image for person detection in class

no overlaps in the video feed. A reference image of a particular course is shown in Fig. 4 however the faces of individual trainees have been blacked out manually to retain their privacy. The predicted outputs from each snapshot were then collated together to generate time series data showing the number of trainees present in the classroom throughout the day. The same method was applied for all the other working days and both the courses respectively to create master data for the two courses with days as column headers and time as index with numbers in each cell indicating the trainee count at a particular date and time. Upon analyzing this table, we could identify some NULL values in cells which resulted from images that had blank screens primarily due to network issues. All such NULL values were removed and were filled by linearly interpolation. In addition, for the retail course, the lab had two dummy models placed within the premises of the class which were used as part of the training. The YOLOv5 model consistently identified these two dummies as persons, hence we corrected this error by negating 2 from all the predictions. Once the data was cleaned, a median count of trainees present at any given time was calculated for these 18 days. Median was used as a measure so as to limit the impact of outliers in the data. This was repeated for both courses respectively. The resulting median value time series is interpreted as the trend of trainees present in the classrooms at any given time during that month. Finally, the time series for each course was visualized using a line graph as can be seen in Fig. 5 and Fig. 6. We also utilized the biometric data used by the trainees in the Livelihood College to register their attendance. Biometric data was available for 15 days as opposed to the 18 that was generated using the Yolov5 object detection model. Hence, only, 15 days of pairwise data was used for comparison between Biometric data and the output from the object detection model. The trainees typically register their attendance twice using the biometric attendance system using their fingerprints when they first reach the Livelihood College and when they move out. Since the biometric data generates a single value for each day representing the number of trainees present in class, we took the maximum number of trainees present at any given time found using Yolo to compare with the biometric data. The bar chart comparing the two can be seen in Fig. 7 and Fig. 8.

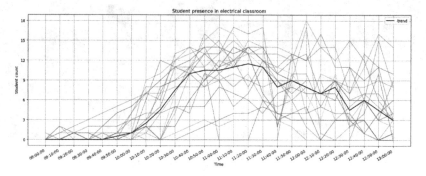

Fig. 5. Student/trainee presence in electrical classrooms, x-axis: time, y-axis: trainee count

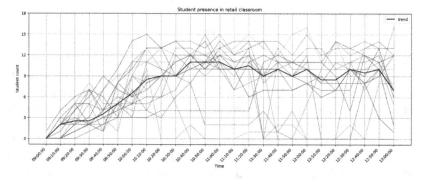

Fig. 6. Student/trainee presence in retail classrooms, x-axis: time, y-axis: trainee count

3.6 Positionality and Reflexivity

Our goal is to improve skill training service delivery such that it is inclusive, relevant, high-quality, and effective in generating meaningful livelihoods for beneficiaries. All authors are of Indian origin having experience working with low-middle-income and marginalized groups. One author, fluent in Chhattisgarhi, interacted with the participants and beneficiaries for over a year. While our

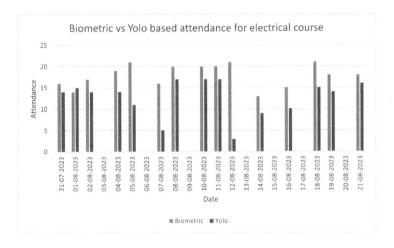

Fig. 7. Biometric vs Yolo-based attendance for electrical course

study participants aren't necessarily marginalized and we didn't exert significant influence or power, we acknowledge our privileged access to information, remain mindful of our assumptions & biases, and strive for reflexivity throughout the research process centering the needs of the beneficiaries and participants.

4 Findings

Our analysis revealed multiple challenges and constraints faced in the service delivery of the skill development program. In the below section, we highlight our major findings:

4.1 Lack of Inclusive Mobilization

An initial mapping of a limited number of trainee data revealed some level of selective recruitment based on geography, in the livelihood college. Upon questioning the mobilizers and counselors on the same, they reported how limited resources disincentivized them to reach out to far-flung areas of the districts. In particular, they mentioned how reaching out to far-flung areas would not reap any benefits as there was no operational accommodation facility for housing trainees from these areas. They also raised concerns about the lack of better transportation and arrangements for reaching out to trainees from hard-to-reach interior regions of the district who could not travel to the livelihood college daily from their houses. This was further investigated using the data available on trainees' backgrounds for the year 2019–2020 which had information on the geographical location of the Gram Panchayats and communities to which they belong. The analysis showed that only 130 Gram panchayats are receiving the benefits of the courses being imparted at the Livelihood College out of the total

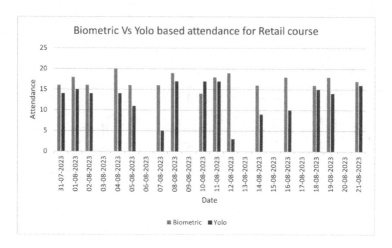

Fig. 8. Biometric vs Yolo-based attendance for retail course

370 Gram Panchayats in Dhamtari leaving the remaining 240 Gram Panchayats completely untouched. Even among those 130 Gram Panchayats, Fig. 1 shows that only a few Gram Panchayats are contributing a substantial number of trainees. Most Gram Panchayats only have 1–4 trainee representatives. Similarly, from Fig. 2 we can see that most of the trainees are clustered around the major cities and towns of the district with the highest representation from the upper regions of the Dhamtari and Kurud blocks. Looking at Table 1, it becomes clear that in almost all blocks the percentage of Gram Panchayats being represented is less than 50% in all with Nagri being the least at 31%. If we consider the number of trainees from Gram Panchayats of different blocks we do not see a stark difference in representation though Kurud and Magarlod contribute slightly higher number of trainees. However, when we consider the numbers along with the city of Dhamtari and other major district towns we see that Nagri contributes 18% of the total trainees which is almost half of Dhamtari contributing 31%. Taking a look into the male-to-female ratio, we find that in the blocks of Kurud and Dhamtari, females seem to be attending the classes in more numbers as compared to trainees from Magarlod where males are more in number.

4.2   Tedious Counseling Procedure

The counselors and mobilizers also reported that the current counseling process was manual, time-consuming, and did not guarantee a substantial turnover rate of trainees, which also contributed to the final selection process being less inclusive. They mentioned that the current counseling process is a multi-stage process where first, the counselors and mobilizers reach out to selected villages and mobilize prospective trainees to educate them about the livelihood college. Here, they are supported by organizations called Vocational Training Partners (VTPs), agencies that support the Livelihood College in reaching out to trainees from hard-to-reach areas. VTPs also conduct training but with highly limited capacity as they are heavily resource-constrained. The mobilizers take support from these VTPs who have social capital in the region, arrange for the venue, and mobilize candidates for the awareness programs. Next, the candidates are invited to the livelihood college where they are provided in-depth information about the benefits of the course. In reality, most of the candidates do not turn up at the livelihood college, and only a fraction visit. Following this, even among the candidates who visit the Livelihood College, only a few decide to join. In most cases, the number of candidates who show interest is less than 30, which is the suggested number of trainees required to start a course. On rare occasions, when there are more than 30 candidates, the counselor has the freedom to select the ones who show the most promise and withhold the rest for the next batch based on their subjective analysis. The counselors and mobilizers noted that these hurdles primarily arise as it is challenging to ascertain the right fitment of a particular trainee in a course, identify the comprehension levels, and interests of trainees, and provide appropriate personalized guidance. Rather, at present they have to counsel people in masses at one go during the physical village visits or when some trainees visit the livelihood college in mass, neither of which allows them to understand the constraints of the trainees or provide individualized feedback which might encourage or motivate them to join the training.

Limited Human Resources Impacting Trainers. A major reason for the counseling procedure being tedious was the lack of required human resources. The livelihood college primarily requires the following of human resources for its functioning, administrators, clerks, counselors, mobilizers, and trainers. From our conversations with the trainers, it became evident that the ranks of the mobilizers, counselors, and clerks were not fulfilled appropriately and very often there were vacant positions. This essentially meant that the trainers had to tend to the extra work and perform mobilization, and counseling for the trainees, thereby putting a lot of burden on them and reducing their capacity to perform their actual job roles and responsibilities which included sorting course structures, making lesson plans, evaluating trainees answer sheets, and many more. Upon asking the stakeholders, what might be the reasons for the continual vacant positions, they unanimously agreed that the job remuneration and career growth were not lucrative enough for someone to engage in the position for a longer term.

4.3 Inadequate Trainee Presence in Classrooms

A few of the stakeholders also reported absenteeism in classes despite registering attendance using biometric data. We looked at the biometric attendance data and found that using this data we could not conclude that trainees remain absent from classes as they were just point values in a day. Hence to investigate this, we analyzed the CCTV streams. As can be seen from Fig. 5 and Fig. 6, most trainees arrive late at classes indicating that the classes are not starting as per the schedule and the time spent in classrooms by a majority of the trainees is almost half the actual allotted time for instructions. The situation in the retail course is perhaps slightly better where once the trainees are inside the classes they maintain their presence throughout the entire duration however for the electrical course it seems trainees not only arrive late but also leave early which is indicated by the declining trend in classroom presence from around 12:00 pm. Taking a look at Fig. 5 and Fig. 6 makes it clear that the maximum number of trainees who attend the classes also seems to be capped well below the total strength of the trainees found present through the Biometric data. On some days, the biometric data and the Yolo detected data are nearly close indicating that trainees do ensure to register their biometric attendance even if they arrive late and move out early. However, we also found a few days where the Yolo models detected very little presence as compared to the biometric data, and the difference is quite stark.

Method of Registering Biometric Attendance. A few of the stakeholders we spoke to mentioned various reasons ranging from lack of interest to trainees from low-income backgrounds requiring to support their family business during college hours and many more as reasons for the inadequate trainee attendance and presence. Following this, we enquired the stakeholders about the biometric attendance registration procedure in depth. They reported that trainees utilize their Aadhar information - an individual identification number acknowledged by the Government of India as proof of address and identity, to provide biometric attendance using fingerprints every working day [71]. The system registers attendance as present for the day only if a trainee has punched in their information twice during the 24-hour cycle. Additionally, the system also captures the timestamp during which the two punches were made. However, the duration between the two punches is not taken into consideration for attendance registration. Hence, a trainee spending 4 h in the class may show the same attendance as someone who has hardly spent an hour or none at all.

Utilization of CCTV. While attempting to analyze the CCTV streams, it was noticed that many of the CCTVs were not placed at the correct angles meaning that the entire class was not visible from the camera. In addition, some also had cobwebs blocking the video feed which indicated that the video was not being utilized for any practical purposes or served any utility for the day-to-day operations of the livelihood college though one key reason for the installation of the CCTV was to ensure proper monitoring and evaluation.

5   Discussions

Drawing on the findings, we now discuss their implications and possible ways to mitigate challenges in the below sections:

5.1 Improving Access to Skill Training

One of the key findings was that mobilizers and counselors were not motivated to reach out to certain villages and Gram Panchayats because they were aware that they couldn't provide residential accommodation to trainees from such farm-flung areas. If we look at the distribution of trainees in Fig. 2, and the physical maps in Fig. 3, we can see more clearly how the upper regions of the district which are relatively more urbanized and well-connected owing to their proximity to the state capital of Raipur, contribute more trainees as compared to the lower and forested regions which are more rural and the transportation system is not as developed. Similarly, we also find that more females are being trained from the upper blocks which might be because they could travel back and forth every day as opposed to female trainees from the blocks of Magarlod and Nagri where a female trainee may have to rent houses adding in a cost factor. Additionally, existing social norms and gender roles concerning women in rural India would not make it easy for them to rent a house and stay independently, away from their homes [9,10]. A major concern however is that the regions that are empty in Fig. 2 are typically Naxal-affected forest areas as can be seen in Fig. 3, with a significant population of people from marginalized groups who should have been among the beneficiaries of such a program. Although the counselors and mobilizers did not exhibit any bias against marginalized groups during our conversations, we did notice a subtle indifference arising from their current constraints, and the inability to make any strides in this direction is a cause for major concern.

To address this concern, one effective approach could be to enhance the role of Vocational Training Providers (VTPs). Recognizing that operationalizing residential accommodations or improving transportation infrastructure - both of which demand significant political commitment and bureaucratic support-might take considerable time, a more immediate solution lies in improving the capacities of the VTPs which are physically in close proximity to the different villages. Currently, VTPs are not capable of imparting such training, and arranging physical resources for each individual VTP may be cost-intensive, instead it may be prudent to effectively use ICT tools and advances in low-cost AR/VR technologies to provide trainees with similar experiences that they may receive in the Livelihood College [4,16,68].

5.2 Improving Utilization of Digital Assets

One of the key observations made during the course of the study was that the digital assets in place were either not utilized properly or were completely left unused. Even though policies mandate the implementation of digital technologies to ensure better service delivery, how these technologies are implemented and utilized is largely left to be decided ad-hoc. For e.g.: the way the attendance is registered from the biometric devices has multiple scopes of errors. At present, even if a trainee punches in twice consecutively within a short period of time even after class hours, attendance is considered to be accepted. It might be so that a person has classes from 09:00 am to 01:00 pm but they arrive at 12:30 pm, punch in twice, and leave the premises. We also find evidence of such practices when we compare the results of the Yolo-based attendance with the biometric attendance. It is essential to ensure that the attendance captured correctly reflects the presence of trainees in the class as all policy-related decisions are taken by authorities considering such data and a wrong understanding of the on-ground situation would lead to no improvement in the process. For e.g., to a policymaker/administrator who may have little information on the day-to-day activities of the college, looking at the current biometric data would give a false impression that trainees are attending classes without any hiccups when the reality is far from this. This also raises questions as to why the trainees may be bunking classes or not attending the entire duration. There may be a multitude of answers to this and the best source of this information is perhaps the trainees themselves who were not part of this study. However, questions such as these can only be raised and investigated only when technologies are implemented appropriately and with due care. Following this, we also noted that many of the CCTV cameras had improper camera angles and some had cobwebs obstructing the video feed indicating that the video was not being utilized for any monitoring or evaluation purposes. An easy solution to biometric attendance is to consider the timestamp when the trainees punch in twice, this should provide enough information to understand if a trainee truly has attended classes. In addition, if the video feed is analyzed using an offline object detection model using systems that are already present and capable of checking for the presence of trainees, this information can further augment the biometric attendance data. Finally, the video data can also be used for various other purposes such as identifying the concentration and stress levels of trainees which can then be used to provide personalized support [38,65,74]. However, one must also take note that such solutions preserve the privacy of the trainees and don't have any adverse impact on trainees [54,78].

Need for Retrofit, Offline, Edge Solutions. One way to increase the utilization of these assets is through low-cost retrofit solutions rather than those that need fundamental changes either on the technology stack or from a management perspective. For example, at the Livelihood College, some level of video analysis could be provided by the application running the CCTV, however, this feature was not made an explicit requirement in policy and hence was not subscribed as this was a paid service. Also, making such intricate changes in policy would be a tedious and lengthy process requiring approvals on multiple levels of the government hierarchy. Rather, the flexibility to make implementation decisions on the ground given to the administrators should be utilized to implement retrofit solutions that do not tamper with the existing infrastructure or require lengthy approvals either due to monetary or management reasons. E.g., in our case, the stakeholders in the livelihood college did not have direct access to the raw video stream or were unaware of how to access it. Hence, we utilized a retrofit method to do the video analysis which was much more feasible to implement on the ground with limited resources than having to gain access to the live video data. In addition, livelihood colleges are usually located in small towns & cities and have to deal with resource constraints including lack of a high bandwidth or stable internet connectivity. In such a situation, depending on cloud services is not an ideal solution, rather making use of edge-based solutions on moderate to low-compute devices such as mobile/smartphones, laptops, and desktops may be a better alternative.

5.3   Considerations on Improving Counseling Procedure

One key challenge mentioned by the participants was the tedious and manual nature of the counseling procedure that primarily involves identifying the right fitment of trainees, comprehension levels, and interests and finally advising trainees on a career path. The major reason is a lack of adequate human resources to reach out to the beneficiaries and provide individualized feedback. Here too, the VTPs may play a critical role in reaching out to the beneficiaries given their physical proximity and on-ground presence. However, it would not be wise to assume that the VTPs would be capable of providing counseling to the beneficiaries appropriately, rather, they may act as points of contact at which people can receive counseling through video conferencing on ubiquitous platforms like WhatsApp, Zoom, MS Teams, Gmeet, etc., from expert counselors. Though some studies show that online career counseling intervention increases trainees' level of career development, existing interventions largely focus on service providers and augmenting their conventional practices with little attention to the beneficiaries [7,8,53]. In addition, there are also concerns relating to privacy, internet access, interface design, counselor's skill, client's willingness, the platform of choice, and many more which need to be appropriately addressed for such intervention to have good effect [55,58]. One of the participants also mentioned the possible use of AI/ML techniques for mitigating challenges in the counseling process. Multiple methods have been explored where AI and ML can be used for providing career counseling some of which include using a chatbot to conduct the Holland test (RIASEC test) and big 5 test for identifying personality followed by suggesting job opportunities [22], utilizing social media messaging applications [66], to AI-powered career counseling for trainees graduating higher secondary school [26,75] and many more [31,36]. However, very little work has been done to identify the efficacy and impact of utilizing algorithmic systems for career counseling on vocational training especially for low-literate, low-income, and marginalized communities in the global south and India. In addition, though such technologies may prove useful, they must be dealt with caution as prior research suggests that blindly applying AI/ML technologies may cause more harm as most AI models are still black boxes and prone to failure. Prior work shows that persons with limited digital and low literacy might have incorrect perceptions of the fact-fulness of these models which may result in users blindly trusting these models often assuming that the machine's expertise outweighed their own [48]. A study also demonstrates that it may not be fully possible to address bias issues like gender in AI recommendations without addressing the bias in humans [76]. Despite these concerns, acknowledging the fact that the task of counseling at present is tedious, time-consuming, and detrimental to beneficiaries, it may be prudent to design and implement explainable, rule-based, non-probabilistic systems whose underlying processes are well-understood. Additionally, for probabilistic and black box systems, the trainees should have clear disclaimers on the potential errors, preferably through a human moderator/counselor/trainer to highlight its capabilities, limitations, and flaws to give them a fair understanding of their options and make an informed decision. More importantly, irrespective of what kind of systems are designed they must be rigorously tested before deployment to avoid any potential harms.

The learnings and findings from this study are not just limited to the Livelihood College at Dhamtari but are relevant to the rest of the Livelihood colleges in Chhattisgarh and shed light on the myriad of challenges that are faced while implementing Skill Development programs throughout the country. With multiple skill development schemes being launched at the state as well as National levels, it is pertinent to ensure that these programs are inclusive, high-quality, result-oriented, and one that can generate meaningful livelihoods for their beneficiaries. Even though this study sheds light on the challenges being faced in the first 3-steps of mobilization, counseling, and training stages in the Skill Development programs by the college authorities, it is still hard to ascertain what may be the actual reasons for some of the identified challenges such as the lack of trainees presence in the classrooms. Additionally, seeking information on the quality of training, and placement, and tracking from the college authorities may not provide an actual representation of reality as they may be inherently biased to respond positively. Hence, the entire picture can be further clarified from inputs from the beneficiaries of the Livelihood College who are in a better position to share a realistic view of the outcomes from training, placement, and tracking stages of the skill development programs. Finally, many of the tech-oriented solutions discussed need further in-vivo testing before they can be deployed on scale and we encourage future empirical research including controlled trials, longitudinal, interventional studies, and other methods to explore causal relationships while adhering to ethical standards and test, refine/refute such ideas.

In summary, our findings suggest that skill development program implementation still faces a myriad of on-ground challenges that are not necessarily reflected at the policy-making or bureaucratic level highlighting inefficiencies, bottlenecks, and delays in information transmission. Drawing on amplification theory, we affirm that technology cannot be a substitute for institutional capacity and human intent [70]. While we did not find significant evidence that would bring the intent of the stakeholders we interacted with into question, the findings on lack of inclusive mobilization, a resource-constrained counseling process, sub-optimal use of digital assets, and the inadequate presence of trainees in classrooms, indicate missing institutional elements that can enable a seamless, efficient information exchange and prompt decision-making in current skill development programs. Technology here may be used as an enabler to support service delivery, however, establishing robust two-way communication channels among all stakeholders would go a long way in delivering better outcomes.

6   Conclusion

This study looks into the service delivery of the Skill Development Program under Govt of Chhattisgrah's Livelihood College. By following the immersion/crystallization approach, we engaged in unstructured conversations and participant observations with administrators, trainers, mobilizers, and counselors of the Livelihood College of Dhamtari district along with nearby industry personnel, over one year. We also performed quantitative analysis and GIS mapping to further triangulate the qualitative inputs. Addressing **RQ1** on identifying challenges and bottlenecks in the implementation of the 5-stage process, first, we find a lack of inclusive mobilization, especially for rural inhabitants and gendered access to skill training arising from un-operational accommodation facilities and a lack of access to transportation services for trainees from far-flung regions of the district. Second, a tedious counseling process owing to its time-consuming and manual nature. Additionally, the lack of adequate support staff burdens the trainers with responsibilities that impact both the counseling as well as training activities. Third, we also find that there is inadequate trainee attendance/presence in the classrooms indicating that trainees may not be receiving a prescribed amount of training, thereby damaging their prospects. With regards to **RQ2** on how digital tools are implemented, we found sub-optimal implementation, and utilization of digital assets like biometric attendance, and CCTV installations. Following the findings, we discuss prospective methods to improve access to skill training by empowering the Vocational Training Partners (VTPs) using the latest developments in digital technologies. We also discuss and recommend ways to improve the implementation and utilization of existing digital assets like biometric attendance and CCTV. Lastly, we discuss key considerations while designing, deploying, and implementing solutions for improving the counseling process. We conclude by summarizing that skill development programs in India in particular the Livelihood College lack institution elements that allow for robust 2-way communication between stakeholders often resulting in inefficiencies and sub-standard service delivery. By addressing these issues, the program stands a higher chance of enhancing trainee engagement, ensuring more inclusive and effective skill training, and ultimately leading to better outcomes for the beneficiaries.

7   Limitations

The authors acknowledge some limitations of this study. The current study looks into the challenges in implementing skill development programs from the perspectives of the administration, employees, and trainers of the Livelihood College. However, the views of an important stakeholder, i.e. the trainees who are the beneficiaries of the program were not represented in this study as their involvement in the implementation of the mobilization and counseling, and partly in the training process was minimal. Future work should look into understanding the perspectives of the trainees, their wants, needs, concerns, and constraints which is essential in delivering better outcomes. Additionally, our study only looks into the challenges faced at only one Livelihood College, and one may raise an argument that the findings from this work may not represent the rest of the livelihood college. On this point, we argue that the livelihood Colleges throughout the state of Chhattisgarh function under similar capacities and constraints, and the challenges identified are not particular to the district of Dhamtari. Our interactions with the college administrators and employees also confirmed the same. Having said this, we also acknowledge the limited sample size and it would surely have been beneficial if inputs could have been gathered from a set of Livelihood colleges from different districts allowing one to make a relative comparison of their performances. While our work takes the first step in this direction, we encourage more such empirical work taking into consideration different stakeholders across various districts to ensure that the intended beneficiaries of such programs are not left behind.

Acknowledgments. We thank our participants who graciously shared their insights, and experiences, and made this work possible. We also extend our thanks to the Mahatma Gandhi National Fellowship and the Office of District Skill Development Authority, Dhamtari, Chhattisgarh, India for supporting this work. Our heartfelt thanks to Professor Anirudha Joshi, Professor, IDC, IIT Bombay, for shepherding the paper and Professor Aditya Vashistha, Assistant Professor, Cornell University, for guiding us throughout the process. Finally, we thank the reviewers for their thoughtful comments and feedback on the paper.

A   Appendix A: Questionnaire

- Questions on background and motivation:

- What kind of prior experience did you have in skill training?
- What motivated you to join the Livelihood College?

- Awareness and mobilization:

- How do you make people aware of the facilities at the Livelihood College?
- How do you reach out to interior parts of the district?
- What happens in the counseling stage?
- What kind of support do you receive in mobilization? Who helps you in the process?
- What kind of challenges do you face in mobilizing and creating awareness?
- Why do you think trainees turn up in fewer numbers?

– Training:

- What kind of challenge do you face in training?
- Resource availability:
- What kind of resources do you utilize to train the trainees?
- Did you ever face resource shortages? If yes, what kind?

– Digital tool use:

- What are the steps involved in registering attendance using the Biometric system?
- How do you utilize the CCTV cameras?

– Business persons

- Do you think the trainees from the Livelihood college are well trained? If No, what more is required? If Yes, can you explain how they add value to your enterprise?
- Is the training in line with on-the-job requirements? What more can be added?

References

1. Agrawal, M., Singh, C., Thakur, K.: Demographic dividend: skill development evidence in India. Available at SSRN 3590719 (2020)
2. Agrawal, M., Thakur, K.: Impact of pradhan mantri kaushal vikas yojana on the productivity of youth in gwalior region, India. Int. J. Recent Technol. Eng. (IJRTE) **8**(4), 801 (2019)
3. Agrawal, R., Pillai, J.S.: Augmented reality application in vocational education: a case of welding training. In: Companion Proceedings of the 2020 Conference on Interactive Surfaces and Spaces, ISS 2020, pp. 23–27. Association for Computing Machinery, New York (2020). https://doi.org/10.1145/3380867.3426199
4. Ahuja, K., Harrison, C., Goel, M., Xiao, R.: Mecap: whole-body digitization for low-cost VR/AR headsets. In: Proceedings of the 32nd Annual ACM Symposium on User Interface Software and Technology, UIST 2019, pp. 453–462. Association for Computing Machinery, New York (2019). https://doi.org/10.1145/3332165.3347889
5. Akshay, N., et al.: Design and evaluation of a haptic simulator for vocational skill training and assessment. In: IECON 2013 - 39th Annual Conference of the IEEE Industrial Electronics Society, pp. 6108–6113 (2013). https://doi.org/10.1109/IECON.2013.6700139
6. Akshay, N., Sreeram, K., Anand, A., Venkataraman, R., Bhavani, R.R.: Move: mobile vocational education for rural India. In: 2012 IEEE International Conference on Technology Enhanced Education (ICTEE), pp. 1–5 (2012). https://doi.org/10.1109/ICTEE.2012.6208644
7. Amos, P.M., Bedu-Addo, P.K.A., Antwi, T.: Experiences of online counseling among undergraduates in some ghanaian universities. SAGE Open **10**(3), 2158244020941844 (2020)

8. Amritesh, Chandra Misra, S., Chatterjee, J.: Emerging scenario of online counseling services in India: a case of e-government intervention. Transforming Gov. People Process Policy **8**(4), 569–596 (2014). https://doi.org/10.1108/TG-10-2013-0040

9. Anukriti, S., Herrera-Almanza, C., Pathak, P.K., Karra, M.: Curse of the mummy-ji: the influence of mothers-in-law on women in India†. Am. J. Agr. Econ. **102**(5), 1328–1351 (2020). https://doi.org/10.1111/ajae.12114

10. Balachandran, A., Desai, S.: Transportation, employment and gender norms: evidence from Indian cities. Reg. Sci. Policy Pract. 100060 (2024). https://doi.org/10.1016/j.rspp.2024.100060

11. Balakrishnan, J.: Building capabilities for future of work in the gig economy. NHRD Netw. J. **15**(1), 56–70 (2022)

12. Behera, B., Gaur, M.: Skill training for the success of the gig economy. J. Pharm. Negative Results **13**, 2835–2840 (2022). https://doi.org/10.47750/pnr.2022.13.S05.429

13. Block & panchayat | Dhamtari district | India. https://dhamtari.gov.in/en/about-district/administrative-setup/block/. Accessed 14 May 2024

14. Chakravorty, B., Bedi, A.S.: Skills training and employment outcomes in rural Bihar. Indian J. Labour Econ. **62**, 173–199 (2019)

15. Chhattisgarh right of youth to skill development act, 2013 no. 17 of 2013 date 26.04.2013. https://www.indiacode.nic.in/bitstream/123456789/12618/1/chhattisgarh_right_of_youth_to_skill_development_act%2c_2013_no._17_of_2013_date_26.04.2013.pdf. Accessed 12 May 2024

16. Chiang, F.K., Shang, X., Qiao, L.: Augmented reality in vocational training: a systematic review of research and applications. Comput. Hum. Behav. **129**, 107125 (2022). https://doi.org/10.1016/j.chb.2021.107125

17. Crabtree, B.F., Miller, W.L.: Doing Qualitative Research. Sage Publications (2023)

18. Das, A., Usami, Y.: Downturn in wages in rural India. Rev. Agrarian Stud. **13**(2), 4–28 (2023). https://ideas.repec.org/a/fas/journl/v13y2023i2p4-28.html

19. Dhamtari district | land of sacred pond | India. https://dhamtari.gov.in/. Accessed 11 Mar 2024

20. Digital India: Introduction. https://www.digitalindia.gov.in/introduction/. Accessed 26 May 2024

21. Digital India week: Digital locker, mygov.in, and other projects that were unveiled | technology news - the Indian express. https://indianexpress.com/article/technology/tech-news-technology/projects-and-policies-launched-at-digital-india-week/. Accessed 27 May 2024

22. D'Silva, G., Jani, M., Jadhav, V., Bhoir, A., Amin, P.: Career counselling chatbot using cognitive science and artificial intelligence. In: Vasudevan, H., Michalas, A., Shekokar, N., Narvekar, M. (eds.) Advanced Computing Technologies and Applications. AIS, pp. 1–9. Springer, Singapore (2020). https://doi.org/10.1007/978-981-15-3242-9_1

23. Dugar, S., Mitra, A., Nandi, S., Adhikary, B., Paul, S., Manusuriya, M.: Interaction design for the next billion users. In: Stephanidis, C., et al. (eds.) HCII 2021. LNCS, vol. 13094, pp. 16–23. Springer, Cham (2021). https://doi.org/10.1007/978-3-030-90238-4_2

24. Ghosh, M.D.: Youth can be a clear advantage for India- the hindu. https://www.thehindu.com/opinion/lead/youth-can-be-a-clear-advantage-for-india/article30897179.ece. Accessed 11 Mar 2024

25. Ghosh, P., Goel, G., Bhongade, A.: Skilling the Indian youth: a state-level analysis. Benchmarking Int. J. **29**(10), 3379–3395 (2022)

26. Ghuge, M., Kamble, T., Mandrawliya, A., Kumari, A., Raikwar, V.: Envisioning tomorrow: AI powered career counseling. In: 2023 3rd International Conference on Innovative Mechanisms for Industry Applications (ICIMIA), pp. 377–383 (2023). https://doi.org/10.1109/ICIMIA60377.2023.10426016

27. Global labour market to deteriorate further as Ukraine conflict and other crises continue | international labour organization. https://www.ilo.org/resource/news/global-labour-market-deteriorate-further-ukraine-conflict-and-other-crises-0. Accessed 26 Aug 2024

28. GoI-MOSPI: Periodic labor force survey, nsso, July 2022 - June 2023. https://mospi.gov.in/sites/default/files/publication_reports/AR_PLFS_2022_23N.pdf?download=1. Accessed 12 May 2024

29. GoI-MSDE: National skill development mission. https://www.msde.gov.in/sites/default/files/2019-09/National%20Skill%20Development%20Mission.pdf. Accessed 11 Mar 2024

30. Gourinchas, P.O.: Global economy on track but not yet out of the woods. https://www.imf.org/en/Blogs/Articles/2023/07/25/global-economy-on-track-but-not-yet-out-of-the-woods. Accessed 26 Aug 2024

31. Guleria, P., Sood, M.: Explainable AI and machine learning: performance evaluation and explainability of classifiers on educational data mining inspired career counseling | education and information technologies. Educ. Inf. Technol. **28**, 1081–1116 (2023). https://doi.org/10.1007/s10639-022-11221-2

32. Hayes, A., Setyonaluri, D.: Taking advantage of the demographic dividend in indonesia. A Brief Introduction to Theory and Practice (2015)

33. Hosan, S., Karmaker, S.C., Rahman, M.M., Chapman, A.J., Saha, B.B.: Dynamic links among the demographic dividend, digitalization, energy intensity and sustainable economic growth: empirical evidence from emerging economies. J. Clean. Prod. **330**, 129858 (2022)

34. India - census of India 2011 - Chhattisgarh - series 23 - part xii a - district census handbook, Dhamtari. https://censusindia.gov.in/nada/index.php/catalog/334. Accessed 11 Mar 2024

35. Jafrin, N., Mahi, M., Masud, M.M., Ghosh, D.: Demographic dividend and economic growth in emerging economies: fresh evidence from the saarc countries. Int. J. Soc. Econ. **48**(8), 1159–1174 (2021)

36. Joshi, K., Goel, A.K., Kumar, T.: Online career counsellor system based on artificial intelligence: an approach. In: 2020 7th International Conference on Smart Structures and Systems (ICSSS), pp. 1–4 (2020). https://doi.org/10.1109/ICSSS49621.2020.9202024

37. Kim, P., Sawyer, S.: Many futures of work and skill: Heterogeneity in skill building experiences on digital labor platforms. In: Proceedings of the 2nd Annual Meeting of the Symposium on Human-Computer Interaction for Work. CHIWORK 2023. Association for Computing Machinery, New York (2023). https://doi.org/10.1145/3596671.3597655

38. Krishnnan, N., Ahmed, S., Ganta, T., Jeyakumar, G.: A video analytics based solution for detecting the attention level of the students in class rooms. In: 2020 10th International Conference on Cloud Computing, Data Science & Engineering (Confluence), pp. 498–501 (2020). https://doi.org/10.1109/Confluence47617.2020.9057967

39. Kumar, G., Nain, M., Singh, R., Kumbhare, N., Parsad, R., Kumar, S.: Training effectiveness of skill development training programmes among the aspirational districts of Karnataka. Indian J. Extension Educ. **57**(4), 67–70 (2021). https://doi.org/10.48165/IJEE.2021.57415

40. Kunal, K., Coelho, P., Pooja, S.: Employer attractiveness: generation z employment expectations in India. CARDIOMETRY (2022). https://api.semanticscholar.org/CorpusID:252243610

41. Map of district | Dhamtari district | India. https://dhamtari.gov.in/en/about-district/map-of-district/. Accessed 01 June 2024

42. MHRD, G.o.I.: New Education Policy (2020). https://www.education.gov.in/sites/upload_files/mhrd/files/NEP_Final_English.pdf. Accessed 01 June 2024

43. MSDE: Monitoring guidelines pmkvy 3.0. https://msde.gov.in/sites/default/files/2021-04/Monitoring%20Guidelines_PMKVY%203.0.pdf. Accessed 11 Mar 2024

44. MSDE: Pmkvy guideline report_(06-01-2021)_v5. https://www.msde.gov.in/sites/default/files/2021-01/PMKVY%20Guideline%20report_(06-01-2021)_V5.pdf. Accessed 11 Mar 2024

45. National Skill Development Corporation, Ministry of Skill Development & Entrepreneurship, G.o.I.: Pmkvy (2015). https://www.mofpi.gov.in/sites/default/files/PMKVY.pdf. Accessed 10 June 2024

46. Ngoc, T.N., Dung, M.V., Rowley, C., Bach, M.P.: Generation z job seekers' expectations and their job pursuit intention: evidence from transition and emerging economy. Int. J. Eng. Bus. Manag. **14**, 18479790221112548 (2022). https://doi.org/10.1177/18479790221112548

47. NSDC: District wise skill gap study for the state of Chhattisgarh. https://skillsip.nsdcindia.org/sites/default/files/kps-document/chattisgarh-district-skill-gap-study-final-report_18thJune.pdf. Accessed 11 Mar 2024

48. Okolo, C.T., Kamath, S., Dell, N., Vashistha, A.: "It cannot do all of my work": community health worker perceptions of AI-enabled mobile health applications in rural India. In: Proceedings of the 2021 CHI Conference on Human Factors in Computing Systems. CHI 2021. Association for Computing Machinery, New York (2021). https://doi.org/10.1145/3411764.3445420

49. Behera, P., Singh, M., Tarai, S.: Short-term vocational courses as a career-building program for the youth in Chhattisgarh, India. Child Youth Serv. 1–24 (2024). https://doi.org/10.1080/0145935X.2024.2340551

50. Pandey, A., Gupta, N., Pandey, A., Singh, S.: Impact of vocational training on value addition in knowledge and adoption of rural women. Indian J. Extension Educ. **53**(3), 36–39 (2017). https://acspublisher.com/journals/index.php/ijee/article/view/4977

51. Pathak, D.: Technology could disrupt the blue-collar workforce worldwide | world economic forum (2023). https://www.weforum.org/agenda/2023/04/growth-summit-2023-technology-is-about-to-disrupt-the-blue-collar-workforce-in-emerging-markets/. Accessed 26 Aug 2024

52. Population ages 15-64 (% of total population) - India | data. https://data.worldbank.org/indicator/SP.POP.1564.TO.ZS?locations=IN. Accessed 12 May 2024

53. Pordelan, N., Sadeghi, A., Abedi, M.R., Kaedi, M.: How online career counseling changes career development: a life design paradigm. Educ. Inf. Technol. **23**(6), 2655–2672 (2018)

54. Preuveneers, D., Garofalo, G., Joosen, W.: Cloud and edge based data analytics for privacy-preserving multi-modal engagement monitoring in the classroom. Inf. Syst. Front. **23**(1), 151–164 (2021)

55. Purwaningrum, R.: Online ingarianti and purwaningrum's integrative career counseling model: An analysis of implementation. In: Proceedings of the 5th International Conference on Learning Innovation and Quality Education. ICLIQE 2021.

Association for Computing Machinery, New York (2022). https://doi.org/10.1145/3516875.3516986

56. Roy, A., Das, B., Chandra, G., Das, A.K., Raman, R.: Knowledge and skill development of Bihar farmers on inland fisheries management: a terminal evaluation. Indian J. Fish. **65**(2), 119–123 (2018)

57. Sachith, K.P., Gopal, A., Muir, A., Bhavani, R.R.: Contextualizing ICT based vocational education for rural communities: addressing ethnographic issues and assessing design principles. In: Bernhaupt, R., Dalvi, G., Joshi, A., Balkrishan, D.K., O'Neill, J., Winckler, M. (eds.) INTERACT 2017. LNCS, vol. 10514, pp. 3–12. Springer, Cham (2017). https://doi.org/10.1007/978-3-319-67684-5_1

58. Sampson, J.P., Kettunen, J., Vuorinen, R.: The role of practitioners in helping persons make effective use of information and communication technology in career interventions. Int. J. Educ. Vocat. Guidance **20**(1), 191–208 (2020)

59. Sheshadri, S., Pradeep, A., Chandran, M.: Towards gender inclusive skill development in rural India: factors that inhibit and facilitate skill women's enrolment in vocational training. Environ.-Behav. Proc. J. **6**(SI4), 239–243 (2021). https://doi.org/10.21834/ebpj.v6iSI4.3032. https://ebpj.e-iph.co.uk/index.php/EBProceedings/article/view/3032

60. Sinha, S.: Impact analysis of skill development on the performance of small tea growers of Assam. Pacific Bus. Rev. (Int.) **14**(7), 97–108 (2022)

61. Skill India, strengthening new India, goi-msde. https://www.skilldevelopment.gov.in/sites/default/files/2020-01/English-ebook.pdf. Accessed 11 Mar 2024

62. Skill India, digital platform, skill India digital platform launched to bring skilling initiatives under single umbrella, et government. https://government.economictimes.indiatimes.com/news/education/skill-india-digital-platform-launched-to-bring-skilling-initiatives-under-a-single-umbrella/103648139. Accessed 12 May 2024

63. Skill-saathi-guidelines. https://www.skilldevelopment.gov.in/sites/default/files/2019-12/Skill-Saathi-Guidelines.pdf. Accessed 11 Mar 2024

64. State project livelihood college society-home page. https://splcs.cg.nic.in/. Accessed 11 Mar 2024

65. Su, M.C., Cheng, C.T., Chang, M.C., Hsieh, Y.Z.: A video analytic in-class student concentration monitoring system. IEEE Trans. Consum. Electron. **67**(4), 294–304 (2021). https://doi.org/10.1109/TCE.2021.3126877

66. Suresh, N., Mukabe, N., Hashiyana, V., Limbo, A., Hauwanga, A.: Career counseling chatbot on facebook messenger using AI. In: Proceedings of the International Conference on Data Science, Machine Learning and Artificial Intelligence, DSM-LAI 2021, pp. 65–73. Association for Computing Machinery, New York (2022). https://doi.org/10.1145/3484824.3484875

67. Swain, R.B., Varghese, A.: The impact of skill development and human capital training on self help groups. Working Paper 2009:11, Uppsala University, Department of Economics, Uppsala (2009). https://hdl.handle.net/10419/82586. urn:nbn:se:uu:diva-106712

68. Thakkar, D., Kumar, N., Sambasivan, N.: Towards an AI-powered future that works for vocational workers. In: Proceedings of the 2020 CHI Conference on Human Factors in Computing Systems, CHI 2020, pp. 1–13. Association for Computing Machinery, New York (2020). https://doi.org/10.1145/3313831.3376674

69. Tiwari, P., Malati, N.: Employability skill evaluation among vocational education students in India. J. Tech. Educ. Train. **12**(1) (2020). https://publisher.uthm.edu.my/ojs/index.php/JTET/article/view/4873

70. Toyama, K.: Technology as amplifier in international development. In: Proceedings of the 2011 IConference, iConference 2011, pp. 75–82. Association for Computing Machinery, New York (2011). https://doi.org/10.1145/1940761.1940772

71. UIDAI: What is aadhaar? - unique identification authority of India | government of India. https://uidai.gov.in/en/16-english-uk/aapka-aadhaar/14-what-is-aadhaar.html. Accessed 09 June 2024

72. Unemployment rate in India (2008 to 2024): Current rate, historical trends and more- forbes India. https://www.forbesindia.com/article/explainers/unemployment-rate-in-india/87441/1. Accessed 12 May 2024

73. Upadhya, C., RoyChowdhury, S.: Crafting new service workers: skill training, migration and employment in Bengaluru, India. Third World Q. **45**(4), 753–770 (2024). https://doi.org/10.1080/01436597.2022.2077184

74. Veer, N.D., Momin, B.F.: An automated attendance system using video surveillance camera. In: 2016 IEEE International Conference on Recent Trends in Electronics, Information & Communication Technology (RTEICT), pp. 1731–1735 (2016). https://doi.org/10.1109/RTEICT.2016.7808130

75. Vignesh, S., Shivani Priyanka, C., Shree Manju, H., Mythili, K.: An intelligent career guidance system using machine learning. In: 2021 7th International Conference on Advanced Computing and Communication Systems (ICACCS), vol. 1, pp. 987–990 (2021). https://doi.org/10.1109/ICACCS51430.2021.9441978

76. Wang, C., et al.: Do humans prefer debiased AI algorithms? A case study in career recommendation. In: Proceedings of the 27th International Conference on Intelligent User Interfaces, IUI 2022, pp. 134–147. Association for Computing Machinery, New York (2022). https://doi.org/10.1145/3490099.3511108

77. Waoo, D.A.A., Waoo, D.A.A.: The new educational policy in India: towards a digital future. Journal La Edusci **2**(6), 30–34 (2022). https://doi.org/10.37899/journallaedusci.v2i6.558

78. Wu, H., Lu, Z., Zhang, J.: A privacy-preserving student status monitoring system. Complex Intell. Syst. **9**(1), 597–608 (2023)

79. Yolov5 - ultralytics yolo docs. https://docs.ultralytics.com/models/yolov5/#performance-metrics. Accessed 01 June 2024

AllerGuard: An Innovative mHealth Solution for Food Allergy Management in India

Harshit Agarwal[1], Nilanjana Sarma[1], Rohit Samanta[1], Siddharth Gulati[2], and Wricha Mishra[1(✉)]

[1] MIT Institute of Design, MIT-ADT University, Loni Kalbhor, India
wricha@indiahci.org
[2] University of Manchester, Manchester, UK

Abstract. Food allergy is a growing concern in India, and there is a need for innovative solutions to help individuals manage their conditions effectively. This study presents the development of AllerGuard, a user-centered mobile health intervention designed to empower food-allergic individuals in India. The development process involved contextual inquiries, surveys, and interviews with healthcare professionals and food-allergic individuals. The proposed system integrates a mobile application and a wearable device, offering features such as symptom tracking, meal logging, and pollen trigger alerts, all informed by the Health Belief Model. Additionally, AllerGuard provides seamless access to emergency medical services and fosters a supportive community platform, grounded in the principles of Social Cognitive Theory. By leveraging mobile technology, wearable devices, and behavior change theories, AllerGuard aims to enhance the quality of life for food-allergic individuals in India. This study serves as a basis for creating comparable mHealth initiatives targeting chronic conditions in resource-limited settings.

Keywords: AllerGuard · mHealth · Food allergy management · User-centered design · India

1 Introduction

Food Allergy, an immune disorder, is a growing public health concern in India, with a significant increase in prevalence over the past few decades. According to Alex Gazzola, the writer of the book "Living with Food Allergies," India's massive population of over a billion individuals could potentially face a significant food allergy crisis. Estimates indicate that up to 3 percent of the Indian population may already suffer from food allergies, with the majority of affected individuals being under 40 years old. Gazzola further states that food allergies in India result in approximately 30,000 emergency treatments and between 100 to 200 fatalities annually [18]. Additionally, it is estimated that up to 3 million Indians may have

N. Rangaswamy et al. (Eds.): IndiaHCI 2024, CCIS 2337, pp. 303–325, 2025.
https://doi.org/10.1007/978-3-031-80829-6_14

a peanut allergy alone. Allergies affect individuals' quality of life and impose a significant financial strain on the healthcare system [21].

Managing food allergies in India presents unique challenges due to factors such as limited access to specialized care, lack of awareness, and diverse environmental triggers across the country [36]. In this context, mobile health (mHealth) applications and wearables offer a promising solution by providing individuals with accessible, affordable, and personalized tools for allergy management [44]. With the widespread adoption of smartphones and internet connectivity in India, mobile health (mHealth) applications present an opportunity to address the challenges in allergy care and empower individuals with allergies to actively manage their conditions [30]. Wearable computing technology has also emerged as a promising instance for enabling personalized and patient-centric healthcare delivery through a distributed information-sharing model [4].

However, existing mHealth solutions predominantly focus on allergen detection and anaphylaxis management, with limited research on wearable biosensors for continuous monitoring and real-time detection of allergic reactions. The current research seeks to bridge this existing knowledge gap by developing a novel tool, AllerGuard, for food allergy management in India. The objectives of this study are twofold:

1. To improve the safety and quality of life for individuals with food allergies through continuous monitoring and real-time alerts.
2. To provide healthcare professionals with a tool for diagnosing and managing food allergies, facilitating timely intervention and improved patient outcomes.

The significance of this study lies in its potential to address the unique challenges of food allergy management in India while contributing valuable insights to the expanding research on mHealth interventions within the Indian context. By providing insights into the design and development of AllerGuard, this research can inform the development of culturally relevant and accessible mHealth tools for food allergy management in India. Furthermore, the findings from this study may guide healthcare professionals in integrating mHealth solutions into the existing healthcare infrastructure to improve food allergy care and patient outcomes.

2   Literature Review

According to the National Institute of Allergy and Infectious Diseases (NIAID) in the U.S., a food allergy is an adverse physiological response triggered by a specific immunological reaction that consistently manifests upon exposure to a particular food source [42]. The prevalence of food allergies in India has been increasing steadily, highlighting the need for effective management strategies and treatment options [18]. Currently, the primary approach to managing food allergies involves allergen avoidance, education, and the use of epinephrine in case of severe reactions [19,34]. However, this approach can significantly impact affected individuals' and their families' quality of life [13].

Failure to properly identify and avoid allergens can lead to severe allergic reactions, including life-threatening anaphylaxis, which often necessitates emergency medical intervention and hospitalization. Moreover, the psychosocial impact of food allergies can be profound, with individuals and families experiencing anxiety, social isolation, and a diminished quality of life due to the constant vigilance required to avoid allergen exposure [10]. Effective management strategies and proper education on allergen avoidance are crucial to mitigating these detrimental effects and reducing the overall burden on healthcare systems and individuals [28, 34].

The integration of technology into food allergy management strategies has become increasingly pivotal in mitigating the risks and burdens associated with this condition. Technological solutions, such as mobile applications and wearable devices, offer a multitude of advantages in empowering individuals with food allergies and their caregivers [2–4]. Among these advancements, wearable technology is particularly noteworthy due to its potential for continuous and real-time health monitoring [4]. By offering a proactive approach to managing food allergies, specifically those triggered by known allergens like food proteins, wearable devices can significantly enhance the detection and prevention of allergic reactions.

2.1 Application-Based Interventions Globally

With the growing smartphone market, interventions delivered through applications have entered the healthcare domain due to their accessibility to health information. The worldwide market for mobile health applications has experienced immense growth and is anticipated to continue thriving [29]. Mobile health applications range from basic apps to advanced technologies like voice messaging, SMS text messaging, multimedia messaging service, Bluetooth, and more, possessing the potential to revolutionize global health services, particularly in low- and middle-income nations such as India [26]. The growing adoption of mobile health applications is apparent in patient communication, monitoring, and education initiatives within medical services and public health practices.

Numerous mHealth apps have been developed globally to help individuals effectively manage their food allergies in various contexts. For instance, 'Allergybot,' a chatbot software, assists allergy-prone young individuals by providing information on restaurant accommodations [22]. Another tool is a food allergy situational awareness-driven framework that offers users details about dishes containing allergenic ingredients and associated proteins [38]. The 'Personal Mobile Restaurant' system matches user preferences with suitable restaurants, considering factors such as societal traditions, faith-based practices, allergen categories, medical issues, and food preferences [11]. Additionally, the NutFree app allows users to assess how well restaurants are informed about nut allergies and their adherence to best practices [16].

Additional interventions include the use of Universal Food Allergy Numbers on food products and menu cards, which consumers can scan with their smartphones to verify if a product is safe for consumption [15]. A menu selection system tailored to individuals' dietary conditions helps ensure a safe dietary life [23], while food diary software aids children in managing non-IgE adverse food reactions [20]. Some tools are designed for early allergy diagnosis [43] and anaphylaxis management, offering guidance on using adrenaline auto-injectors (AAIs) and providing personalized lists of known reaction triggers, current medications, and emergency contacts [5]. A self-care app for adolescents with nut allergies allows users to record allergy details and share them with friends and family via a QR code [12]. However, in India, there is a notable lack of interventions focused on the detection of food allergies, and the effectiveness of mHealth applications remains a crucial factor in their success.

2.2 Wearable Innovations in Food Allergy Monitoring and Management

Wearable computing technology has emerged as a promising instance for enabling personalized and patient-centric healthcare delivery through a distributed information-sharing model [4]. Researchers have comprehensively studied wearable devices' applications in outpatient monitoring, utilizing biosensors to offer continuous and real-time vital sign tracking [2]. While wearable technologies have been explored for a diverse array of health disorders [2], their potential in the context of food allergies remains largely unexplored. In the context of food allergens, a patent has been filed for a food allergen detection method employing molecularly imprinted polymers [7] and another patent is being used for the development of a device that would detect common food allergens [1]. Additionally, a "smart" case for epinephrine autoinjectors linked to the user's smartphone has been proposed to improve anaphylaxis management and decrease patients' anxiety.

2.3 Impact of mHealth Applications Across Health Sectors in India: A User-Centered Approach

The effectiveness of mHealth applications has been proven over time in India. For example, during the ReMiND project, there was a significant increase in Iron-folic acid intake, spotting issues, self-reporting, and seeking care during/after pregnancy [26], as well as cost savings [33]. Similarly, the ImTECHNO app, used in Primary Health Centers (PHCs) and supported by Accredited Social Health Activists (ASHAs), led to improved reach and higher standards of care for mothers, newborns, and children compared to those who did not use the app [32]. The mMitra voice-based application positively influenced infant birth weight by delivering tailored mobile voice messages to expectant mothers [35]. Additionally, text messaging interventions have proven effective in improving diabetes-related health behaviors [37], while mHealth applications have provided culturally tailored educational resources to enhance hypertension health literacy among nurses and healthcare professionals [17]. SMS-based oral health education has also been shown to improve oral health outcomes [24].

The successful implementation of mHealth solutions for food allergy management relies heavily on the principles of user-centered design, which emphasizes active participation from end-users. By prioritizing the needs, preferences, and behaviors of the target users, mHealth interventions are more likely to be functional, relevant, and emotionally resonant with users. Incorporating user-centered design throughout the development process maximizes the impact and usability of these interventions, fosters behavior change, and promotes sustained engagement. The World Health Organization (WHO) advocates for integrating user-centered design into the lifecycle of mHealth interventions to ensure effective outcomes [14]. This approach not only enhances adoption and adherence but also ensures long-term engagement, making the solutions more effective in managing food allergies and reducing the risk of potentially life-threatening reactions. Furthermore, incorporating behavior change theories into mHealth interventions can amplify their effectiveness by addressing the psychological and social factors that influence health-related behaviors.

2.4   Application of Behavior Change Theories in mHealth Interventions

Behavior change theory is a set of theories explaining and structuring factors influencing health behavior. It's widely used in studies on behavior change or health promotion interventions [9]. Key theories include the Health Belief Model (HBM) and the Social Cognitive Theory (SCT). The HBM model suggests a higher probability of healthy behavior adoption when people recognize the health problem's seriousness, and perceived benefits, consider barriers/costs manageable, and get influenced by self-efficacy beliefs and cues to action [25]. Conversely, the SCT proposes that observing others enables learning, with behavior shaped by personal and environmental factors and their action depends on outcome expectancy and self-efficacy [6]. The application of behavior change theories has been instrumental in designing mobile health interventions like improving medication adherence among stroke patients using social support and providing behavior feedback based on the SCT and the HBM [27], providing reminders and motivational messages following HBM [31], offering tailored counseling calls, SMS, and readiness for behavior change at five sequential stages based on HBM [40], and using automated SMS based on HBM to improve medication adherence [41].

In the present study, insights from behavior change theories, specifically the Health Belief Model (HBM) and Social Cognitive Theory (SCT), are incorporated into the design and development of AllerGuard, a novel mHealth intervention for food allergy management in India. By integrating these theoretical frameworks, we aim to create a solution that not only provides technological support but also addresses the psychological and social factors influencing the adoption and sustained use of the intervention by individuals with food allergies.

3   Methodology

3.1   Design Process

Our methodology employed a user-centric design approach to develop the final concept of the AllerGuard app and a wearable integrated with it. This approach facilitated us with a concrete foundation and understanding of the topic and supported us with strong ideations and concepts. The whole process is structured into three distinct phases: research, define, and ideate.

Phase I: Research. A comprehensive secondary research and contextual inquiries [39] were conducted to analyze and gather information about the causes, symptoms, and types of food allergies prevalent in India. The secondary research involved extensive desk research, referring to relevant websites and journals to establish a foundational understanding of the topic. To expand upon the insights gained from the secondary research, we conducted contextual inquiries to validate and deepen our understanding. We carried out a survey and semi-structured interviews with healthcare professionals and food-allergic individuals.

Interview with Healthcare Professionals. Semi-structured interviews were conducted with 4 healthcare professionals: one general physician, two paramedic doctors, and one critical care specialist. Two researchers were associated with conducting the interviews, while the third researcher ensured comprehensive data capture through audio recording and note-taking for further analysis. A total of 20 questions were prepared, which were mostly covered along with other follow-up questions. The main objective was to understand the current healthcare practices, ongoing research, and innovations in India, as well as diagnosis and testing procedures concerning food allergy management and treatment (Fig. 1).

Food Allergy Survey. An online survey was conducted in Pune, Maharashtra, India to assess awareness and prevalence of food allergies within the target population which includes people with diverse dietary habits including vegetarians, non-vegetarians, and seafood consumers. The survey questionnaire was created using Google Forms, and the responses were saved in Google Sheets for analysis. To encourage participation, a QR code was generated, redirecting participants to the Google form. This process was implemented to capture unbiased and genuine responses. The questionnaire consisted of 8 questions, structured to understand participants' awareness regarding food allergies, previous medical history, and treatment procedures.

Interview with Food-Allergic Participants. Semi-structured interviews were held with 4 participants. The procedure for conducting the interview was similar to the protocol implemented for interviewing the health care professionals. A predefined interview guide consisting of approximately 23 questions for the interview served as the foundation for the discussion. Starting with gathering information

Fig. 1. Healthcare professional interviews on food allergy management practices in India.

about their daily activities and eating habits, gradually the interview proceeded towards gathering responses related to their health conditions, symptoms, treatment, and previous medical history concerning their allergic condition.

Phase II: Define. After conducting the contextual inquiry, we developed different contextual models, such as flow models and sequence models. The flow model is a structured representation that includes the location where communication happens, the artifacts used for communication, and breakdowns that negatively impact the work [8]. We created two flow models attached in the appendix: one from the perspective of healthcare practices in India for individuals with food allergies, and another from the perspective of an individual's activities and precautions to manage their allergies and symptoms.

Based on the flow models, we structured the sequence models, which are low-level representations of the step-by-step information on how a task is performed. They include the intent behind the action, the trigger that leads the user to take the action, and the breakdowns that create problems [8]. Two sequence models were created: one for the steps followed by a food-allergic person encountering a food allergy for the first time, and another for the steps followed by the allergic person in emergency conditions when exposed to an allergen.

After capturing all the gaps and breakdowns from the contextual models, affinity mapping was used to categorize different gaps. We prioritized them using a critical vs. feasibility matrix to identify which problems to address. All researchers rated the highly critical and highly feasible problems based on their knowledge of the topic, time constraints, and creativity. Two major problems were identified:

1. Most allergic patients are unable to record their eating history after the first allergic encounter
2. Difficulty in detecting early signs of food allergies.

Following the prioritization process, a competitive analysis was conducted for 6 food allergy apps, websites, or services. The main objective was to understand the purpose, strengths, weaknesses, and strategies employed by these organizations for their products.[1]

Phase III: Ideate. Following the identification of various user needs and challenges during the define phase, we arrived at our main problem statement: How could people manage their dietary habits or detect their food allergic condition upon the occurrence of allergic symptoms? A total of eight unique design solutions were generated to address the identified needs, out of which two ideas were selected. These shortlisted concepts were then merged to create a novel solution: a mobile application integrated with a wearable device (Fig. 2).

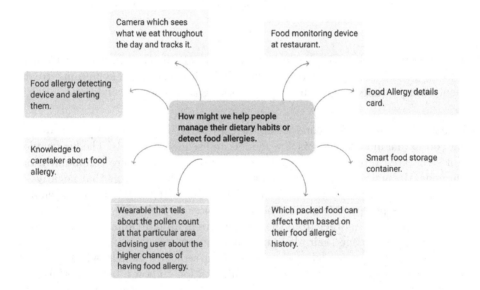

Fig. 2. Different ideations for the problem statement

4   Results

4.1   Interview with Healthcare Professionals

Thematic analysis of interviews with healthcare professionals revealed several key themes regarding food allergies in India:

---

[1] Due to space constraints, contextual model and competitive analysis is made available open source at https://osf.io/nm5q2/.

1. Prevalence: Food allergies, particularly among college students and working professionals who frequently relocate, are becoming more prevalent. Environmental changes, dietary habits, and lifestyle factors associated with relocation contribute to this rising trend.
2. Common Allergens: Healthcare professionals reported that shellfish, dairy products, and tree nuts are among the most common food allergens encountered in India.
3. Challenges in Management: Significant obstacles to effective food allergy management in India include limited public awareness, difficulties identifying allergens, inadequate testing infrastructure, limited access to and high costs of treatments, and poor patient adherence to follow-up visits.
4. Impact: Food allergies have a substantial impact on individuals, encompassing physical symptoms, emotional challenges, and diminished quality of life. Complications such as anaphylaxis underscore the importance of proper management strategies.
5. Reported Symptoms: Common symptoms experienced by food-allergic patients include itching, abdominal pain, diarrhea, swelling, respiratory difficulties, nausea, and vomiting. Symptom onset and severity vary among individuals.
6. Psychological Effects: In addition to physiological symptoms, food allergies can have significant psychological impacts, including anxiety and fear of reactions.

4.2 Food Allergy Survey

Participants independently completed a self-administered survey comprising seven questions. The survey conducted in Pune, Maharashtra, India, gathered a total of 17 responses, with 8 female (47.06%) and 7 male (41.18%) participants. Among them, only 4 individuals had food allergy conditions, representing a diverse range of dietary habits, including vegetarian, non-vegetarian, and seafood consumption. The key findings of the survey are as follows:

1. A high proportion of participants (88.2%) were aware of food allergies.
2. 23.5% of the respondents had food allergies.
3. 50% of the participants had undergone a food allergy test.
4. Common food allergens reported were shellfish, cow milk, mushrooms, and kiwi.
5. People with food allergies sought advice and treatment from various sources, including allergists or immunologists, primary care physicians, and self-management.
6. 50% of the participants recognized their food allergic condition in childhood, 25% in adolescence, and 25% in adulthood.

4.3 Interview with Food-Allergic Participants

Four interviews were conducted with food-allergic participants, consisting of 23 questions ranging from demographics to specific questions related to their allergic conditions. The participants included 2 males (50%) and 2 females (50%), with 3 participants aged 18–30 years and one aged 44–60 years. The key insights from the interviews are:

1. Variation in Onset and Trigger of Food Allergy: From the interviews, we could see the diverse nature of food allergy onset. One of the participants' interviews highlighted the possibility of late-onset allergies emerging in adulthood, while others recognized food allergic conditions in their childhood. This emphasizes the need for continued careful observation throughout life and the importance of considering food allergies as a potential trigger for reactions, even among older individuals.

2. Genetic Influence: While instances from some of the participants suggest that food allergies can arise without any family connection, other cases with family members having similar food allergies suggest a genetic influence on food allergy.

3. Self-Diagnosis and Necessity of Expert Guidance: One of the participants self-diagnosed quite a lot of times when he encountered allergic reactions through trial and error. This emphasizes that the individual might lack awareness about food allergies and the importance of consulting a doctor for a proper diagnosis of food allergies. This may lead to future sudden exposure to potential allergens causing severe reactions and missed chances of required treatment and guidance from experts. Similarly, another participant's initial dependency on home remedies gives the idea of the importance of seeking professional help when encountering an allergic reaction. An early diagnosis by a healthcare professional would help in detecting the right allergen for further treatment, in turn improving quality of life

4. Impact on Daily Life and Social Engagements: Participants' social circle including co-workers and friends who lacked awareness about food allergies faced challenges in social settings. Other participants whose friends and family were aware of allergies facilitated a supportive environment. This signifies the importance and need for open communication and awareness about one's food allergic condition and food allergy in general.

5. Approaches to Food Allergy Management: The most common approach that participants follow to manage food allergy is avoiding the allergen. But in case of emergency, the patient is taken to the hospital for emergency treatment which is the suppression of severe allergic symptoms. One participant's habit of asking about food ingredients before sharing or consuming meals demonstrates a proactive step towards avoiding food allergic reactions from allergen exposure.

4.4   Contextual Model

The user study provided valuable insights that informed the development of contextual models, specifically the flow model and sequence model, which were instrumental in analyzing the healthcare processes related to food allergy management and the challenges faced by individuals in managing their conditions. The analysis of these models revealed several key breakpoints.

1. Inability to Recognize Early Symptoms: Patients often struggle to identify early signs of an allergic reaction, which can lead to delayed treatment and potentially severe, life-threatening consequences.
2. Lack of Region-Specific Prevalence Data: The absence of comprehensive data on food allergy prevalence in different regions of India hinders the development of targeted interventions and resource allocation.
3. Limited Availability of Allergen Detection Tests: The scarcity of allergen detection tests adapted to the Indian context complicates the diagnostic process, potentially resulting in unnecessary dietary restrictions and reduced quality of life.
4. Insufficient Training and Educational Resources: Inadequate training and educational materials for caregivers and parents can impede the early recognition and management of food allergies in children.
5. Confusion Regarding Appropriate Medical Professionals: Patients often experience uncertainty about which medical specialists to consult for food allergy diagnosis and treatment, leading to delayed care and sub-optimal management.
6. Low Patient Follow-up After Emergency Treatment: Inadequate follow-up after emergency treatment for allergic reactions can hinder accurate allergen identification and the development of personalized management plans.
7. Potential Cross-Contamination Risks at Home: Improper food preparation practices in the home environment can increase the risk of cross-contamination and accidental allergen exposure.
8. Limited Awareness of Ingredients in Various Settings: Insufficient information about ingredients in restaurants, cafeterias, and store-bought meals can heighten the risk of unintentional allergen exposure for individuals with food allergies.
9. Challenges in Identifying Allergens After Mild Reactions: Difficulty in pinpointing the specific allergen responsible for mild reactions can lead to future risks and uncertainty in managing the condition.

4.5 Final Problem Identification

Based on these analyses conducted during the define phase, two primary problems were identified regarding the needs and pain points of individuals with food allergies:

1. Challenges in Detecting Early Signs of Food Allergy: Recognizing early symptoms of food allergies, especially those related to common allergens such as nuts, shellfish, and dairy, can be difficult for patients. The proposed solution focuses on monitoring and detecting these reactions through wearable technology and mHealth applications, which are designed to track physiological responses and symptoms in real-time. While the solution does not rely on an external database for identifying specific allergens, it leverages user-reported data and patterns detected by the wearable devices to alert users of potential allergic reactions, facilitating timely intervention and management.

2. Difficulty in Recording Eating History After The First Allergic Encounter: Patients often struggle to maintain an accurate record of their food intake and symptoms following an initial allergic reaction, which can impede the identification of triggering allergens and the development of appropriate management strategies.

By addressing these key issues, healthcare providers and researchers can work towards developing targeted interventions and support systems to enhance the diagnosis, management, and quality of life of individuals with food allergies in India.

5   Proposed Solution: AllerGuard

To address the challenges faced by individuals with food allergies, we propose a comprehensive management system aimed at improving their well-being through real-time monitoring, enhanced safety measures, self-management support, and a strong community network. The solution integrates a mobile application with a wearable device, creating a seamless connection that allows for efficient data exchange and communication. This integration enables both components to work in parallel, helping users track allergic reactions and take appropriate actions promptly (Figs. 3 and 4).

User Persona (Allergic Individual)

Pranav Menon

Age: 24   **Occupation:** Currently pursuing M.Des   **Location:** Pune

Pranav is an adventurous individual who enjoys exploring new places and activities. However, due to past experiences of allergic reactions, particularly to shellfish like prawns, he now exercises caution when trying new foods. He prefers sticking to familiar foods whose ingredients he knows to avoid any potential allergic triggers. Pranav is sociable and enjoys engaging in conversations, sharing his thoughts and ideas with others.

"I wish there was a simple solution to manage my food allergies"

Needs
1. To identify and avoid allergens in food to prevent allergic reactions.
2. To keep a record of food intake for allergy management.
3. Access to emergency resources and guidelines for handling allergic reactions.
4. Reliable information on food allergies and treatments.

Goals
1. Identify safe food options to prevent allergic reactions.
2. Explore new and unique dishes during his travels.
3. Prompt access to medical assistance in case of allergic reactions.
4. Stay informed about advancements in food allergy treatments.
5. Challenges:

Patient Behaviour
1. Relies on regular medications to alleviate symptoms.
2. Engages in improper food eating habits.
3. Seeks consultation when the condition becomes serious.
4. Tends to avoid post-treatment checkups.

Challenges
1. Limited ability to try new foods due to fear of allergic reactions.
2. Difficulty in tracking daily food consumption.
3. Lack of awareness about potential allergens in certain foods.
4. Limited availability of effective medical treatments for allergies.

Technology Usage
1. Uses Google Maps to locate nearby clinics or hospitals during emergencies.
2. Searches for symptoms online to understand his condition.
3. Communicates with doctors or loved ones through WhatsApp or chat for consultation.

Fig. 3. User Personas - Depicting the needs, goals, and challenges of an allergic individual.

User Persona (Doctor)

"I wish there was a simple solution to manage my food allergies and enjoy my meals without stress."

Dr. Amit, Allergy Specialist

Age: 35   **Occupation:** Doctor (Allergy Specialist)   **Location:** Pune

Amit specializes in diagnosing and treating allergies, including food allergies. Dr. Amit emphasizes the importance of thorough patient assessments and personalized treatment plans. He often encounters challenges in identifying allergens and lacks comprehensive testing options. Despite limited medical solutions, Dr. Amit remains dedicated to providing support and guidance to his patients, aiming to reduce allergic reactions and improve their quality of life.

Needs
1. Track patients' food history to detect allergens.
2. Keep updated on new medical guidelines and remedies.
3. Quick access to emergency resources for allergic reactions.
4. Maintain records of patients for medical history.

Goals
1. Recognize possible food allergens.
2. Reduce allergic reactions in patients.
3. Warn patients about allergens to prevent recurrence.
4. Provide timely medication to alleviate allergic conditions.

Patient Behaviour
1. Patients engage in improper eating habits, which can worsen allergic reactions.
2. Post-treatment checkups are not consistently followed by patients.
3. Medical assistance is sought only when the allergic condition becomes severe.
4. Proactive allergy management is lacking among patients.

Challenges
1. Difficulty in detecting allergens at an early stage.
2. Lack of proper records for food allergic patients.
3. Limited appearances of food allergic conditions, making management challenging.
4. Lack of effective medical treatment to suppress allergies.

Technology Usage
1. Uses testing kits or machines for allergy testing.
2. Utilizes consultation platforms to provide patient guidance.
3. Stays updated on research findings and medical progress through the internet.
4. Provides consultations to patients via WhatsApp or chat facilities.

Fig. 4. User Personas - Depicting the needs, goals, and challenges of an allergy specialist doctor.

5.1   Key Functionalities of the App

The interface provides users with real-time information about their vital symptoms, including itching, blood pressure, heart rate, swelling, and respiratory status.

1. Food Allergy Symptom Tracking and Alerts (Fig. 5a): The application allows users to log their symptoms and receive real-time alerts when physiological markers indicate a potential allergic reaction.
2. Meal Logging with Reminders (Fig. 5b): Users can record their dietary intake and receive reminders to promote adherence to allergen avoidance and maintain a comprehensive food diary.
3. Pollen Allergen Trigger Alerts Based on the Health Belief Model (HBM) (Fig. 5a): The application integrates local pollen data and provides personalized alerts to users when pollen counts are high, encouraging them to take preventive measures. The HBM is employed to reinforce the perceived severity and susceptibility to allergic reactions and to promote self-efficacy in managing the condition.
4. Emergency Medical Service Access: In the event of a severe allergic reaction, the application facilitates quick access to emergency medical services, ensuring timely intervention and treatment.
5. Community Platform Grounded in Social Cognitive Theory (SCT) principles (Fig. 5c): Enables users to connect with others who have similar experiences, share knowledge, and provide mutual support. The platform leverages SCT principles to promote observational learning, social support, and self-efficacy in managing food allergies.

The following screenshots illustrate how these features are integrated into the user interface to provide a comprehensive and user-friendly experience for managing food allergies.

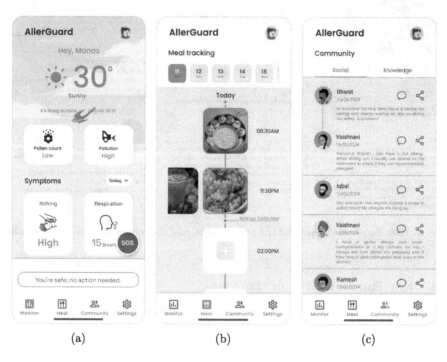

Fig. 5. App Screens - Showcasing key features of the AllerGuard app, including (a) symptom tracking, (b) meal tracking, and (c) the community platform for user interaction.

5.2   Key Functionalities of the Wearable Device

The wearable device (Fig. 6), designed as a ring, complements the mobile application by providing real-time monitoring and alerts. Its key functionalities include:

1. Two-Light Strip Indicator: The ring features a two-light strip indicator that activates and blinks when physiological markers are detected by sensors built into the ring (Fig. 7) with distinct light colors representing different levels of severity. Red light for a highly severe reaction, orange light for a mild allergic reaction. This color-coded system aims to provide users with rapid, easily interpretable information about their current allergic status and potential exposure risks.
2. Auditory Alarm for Severe Reactions: The ring emits a distinct beep sound along with a red light, alerting the user and those nearby to the urgency of the situation.

3. SOS Button with Emergency Alerts: When pressed and held for three seconds, transmits an emergency alert to pre-designated emergency contacts. The alert includes the user's real-time location data, facilitating swift assistance during medical emergencies.
4. Proactive Allergen Detection Alerts: A purple light indication when potential allergens are detected in the environment, such as during periods of high pollen count. These alerts enable users to take preventive measures and minimize the risk of exposure.

Fig. 6. Wearable ring for real-time monitoring and allergy management.

5.3 AllerGuard System Workflow

When the user receives a notification to log their meal, they upload a photo through the app, providing details such as the name and ingredients. Fifteen minutes later, if the user experiences symptoms like itching and rashes, the wearable device, synced with the AllerGuard app, alerts them through lights and sounds. Simultaneously, the app sends a notification to their phone, prompting them to take action or use the SOS feature. The user selects "Take Action" to assess their condition, review vital health metrics, and receive an allergy alert. They then identify their symptoms as "mild itching and rashes." The app offers management steps, but when the discomfort persists, the user activates the "Call Ambulance" feature, which also sends their current location to emergency services. After the emergency has been handled, the user returns to the meal tracking page to identify the possible allergen for future prevention (Figs. 8 and 9).

Symptom	Parameter being tracked	Possible Sensor	Tracking Method	Type of Data Recorded
Itching	Muscle movement (When the skin is scratched, it generates frequency signals that travel from the fingers throughout the hand.)	"Scratching" produces frequency above 200Hz while non scratching activities produces frequency less than 200Hz. Accelerometer could track these signals and help in recording the itching behavior's.	The accelerometer could be placed near the fingers as its the best positions where the frequency recorded would be high.	Includes the frequency rate that could be noted depending on the time interval.
Swelling Of Body Parts	Skin conductivity (When a person is stressed or experiences a strong emotional response, the sweat glands in the skin become more active. This can lead to an increase in skin conductivity)	'Skin conductance sensors' or 'galvanic skin response sensors'. These sensors are designed to measure the electrical conductance of the skin, which changes with sweat gland activity and emotional responses.	Skin conductance sensors typically consist of two electrodes that are placed on the surface of the skin. One electrode is positively charged, and the other is negatively charged. These electrodes measure the electrical conductance of the skin between them.	Includes continuous or real-time measurements of galvanic skin response (GSR). Measured in microsiemens (μS) or ohms (Ω)
Rapid Heart Rate	Heart Rate (Allergic reactions can widen blood vessels, causing low blood pressure. To maintain vital organ blood flow, the heart beats faster.)	Photoplethysmography (PPG) Sensor. PPG is a non-invasive optical technique that measures changes in blood volume by illuminating the skin with light	When the person's heart beats, more blood is pumped through the finger, causing variations in the amount of light absorbed by the PPG sensor. These variations are used to calculate your heart rate.	Real time heart rate data, measuring the number of heartbeats per minute (beats per minute or BPM).
Dizziness	Blood Pressure (Allergic reactions can lead to a drop in blood pressure (anaphylaxis). Blood vessels get dilated (widen), causing a decrease in blood pressure.	Photoplethysmography (PPG) Sensor. PPG is a non-invasive optical technique that measures changes in blood volume by illuminating the skin with light	PPG sensor measures changes in blood volume by emitting light into the skin, and the amount of light absorbed by blood vessels is detected. Changes in the light absorption patterns help derive blood pressure measurements.	Continuous blood pressure data, including systolic and diastolic readings, allowing for the monitoring of fluctuations related to dizziness and low blood pressure.
Shortness Of Breath	Pulse Rate and Blood Oxygen Saturation (SpO2) Blood oxygen saturation may drop during severe allergic reactions due to compromised breathing, making these vital signs essential to monitor during allergies.	PPG sensors can monitor pulse rate and SpO2, which are crucial for assessing respiratory health and detecting shortness of breath. These sensors utilize the changes in blood volume to measure these parameters.	The PPG sensor emits and detects light as it penetrates the skin. By analyzing the variations in light absorption caused by blood flow, it can calculate the user's pulse rate and SpO2 levels in real-time.	The PPG sensor records data on pulse rate (in beats per minute) and SpO2 levels (measured as a percentage)

Fig. 7. Wearable ring with integrated indicators and sensors.

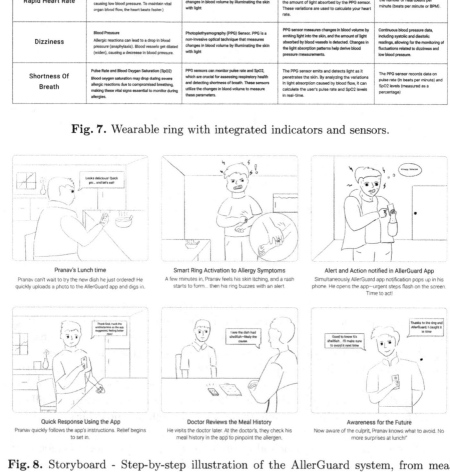

Fig. 8. Storyboard - Step-by-step illustration of the AllerGuard system, from meal logging to symptom detection and response.

(a) Notification   (b) Click picture   (c) Add details   (d) Allergy alert

(e) Continue   (f) Mild reaction   (g) Wait for 15 min   (h) Click next

(i) Still symptoms?   (j) Emergency   (k) Meal Tracking   (l) Profile

Fig. 9. Mild allergic symptoms app flow

6   Discussion

The proposed integration of a wearable device with the Allerguard application presents a promising opportunity for the effective tracking and management of food allergies. The system's continuous monitoring capabilities and real-time alerts empower users to proactively manage their allergic conditions. The wearable device, equipped with immediate visual and auditory alerts, provides users with timely information regarding potential allergic reactions, enabling rapid intervention. This swift response is particularly crucial in managing and tracking allergic reactions, as it can be life-saving in cases of severe anaphylaxis.

In addition to real-time monitoring, the Allerguard application offers integrated meal logging and reminder functionalities, which facilitate consistent and detailed record-keeping of dietary intake. This systematic approach aids in the identification of potential allergen exposures, leading to enhanced overall dietary control and management. Furthermore, the incorporation of pollen trigger alerts, based on HBM, strengthens user awareness and encourages preventive actions, thereby reducing the risk of environmental allergen exposure. The HBM posits that individuals tend to adopt health-promoting behaviors when they see a threat to their health and believe that the benefits of acting outweigh the obstacles [25].

The Allerguard system also prioritizes user safety by providing immediate access to emergency medical services and an SOS button that transmits real-time location data. During emergencies, the rapid transmission of alerts and location information facilitates swift medical intervention, potentially reducing the morbidity and mortality associated with severe allergic reactions. Moreover, the application's community platform, grounded in the Social Cognitive Theory (SCT) principles, provides a supportive space for users to exchange experiences, seek advice, and offer aid to others facing similar health conditions. Observational learning, social backing, and self-belief are highlighted by SCT as pivotal for health behavior promotion [6]. By fostering a sense of community and enabling the exchange of knowledge and experiences, the Allerguard system contributes to increased awareness and improved management practices for individuals with food allergies.

6.1   Limitations and Future Work

Acknowledging the limitations of the current study is essential as it provides valuable directions for future research. Firstly, the usability of the Allerguard system has not been evaluated in this study. Future research should focus on conducting comprehensive usability testing to assess the system's user-friendliness, acceptability, and effectiveness in real-world settings. Secondly, the restricted sample size in the present study could impact the generalizability of the results. Future studies should strive to recruit larger, more diverse samples to provide more robust insights and ensure better representativeness of the target population.

Lastly, the current study did not involve long-term evaluations. To fully understand the impact of the Allerguard system on patient outcomes, healthcare utilization, and overall quality of life, future research should conduct longitudinal studies. These studies should assess the system's effectiveness over an extended period, taking into account factors such as adherence, user satisfaction, and the incidence of allergic reactions. Additionally, future studies should explore the potential integration of the Allerguard system with existing healthcare infrastructures and its cost-effectiveness in the Indian context

By addressing these limitations and expanding the scope of future research, we can gain a deeper insight into the Allerguard system's potential to revolutionize food allergy management in India and beyond.

7   Conclusion

In this study, we suggest Allerguard which represents an innovative approach to the management of food allergies in India, addressing the unique challenges faced by food-allergic individuals in this context. By integrating a wearable device, mobile technology, and theory-driven design principles, the app offers a comprehensive and user-centric solution that empowers users to proactively manage their conditions and improve their quality of life.

The app's key features, including real-time monitoring and alerts, meal logging and reminders, pollen trigger alerts based on the Health Belief Model, emergency medical service access, and a supportive community platform grounded in the Social Cognitive Theory, work together to provide a holistic approach to food allergy management. By facilitating rapid intervention, promoting consistent record-keeping, reinforcing preventive behaviors, and fostering a sense of community, the Allerguard app has the potential to significantly improve the lives of food-allergic individuals in India.

Moreover, the app's potential to reduce the strain on the healthcare system by preventing severe allergic reactions and decreasing healthcare utilization highlights its broader public health implications. The Allerguard app serves as a model for the development of similar mHealth interventions targeting chronic conditions in resource-limited settings.

Future research should focus on evaluating the app's usability, effectiveness, and long-term impact on patient outcomes and healthcare utilization in the Indian context. By addressing the limitations of the current study and expanding the scope of future investigations, we can gain a more comprehensive understanding of the Allerguard app's potential to revolutionize food allergy management in India and beyond.

In conclusion, the Allerguard app represents a significant step forward in the management of food allergies in India, offering a user-centric, technology-driven solution that prioritizes patient needs and well-being. With further research and refinement, this innovation holds promise to transform the landscape of food allergy management and act as a model for creating comparable interventions in other chronic disease contexts.

A   Appendix

The questionnaire used for the interview has publicly been made available online: https://osf.io/nm5q2/.

References

1. Allergy Amulet. https://www.allergyamulet.com. Accessed 01 Aug 2024
2. Ajami, S., Teimouri, F.: Features and application of wearable biosensors in medical care. J. Res. Med. Sci. **20**(12), 1208 (2015). https://doi.org/10.4103/1735-1995. 172991. https://journals.lww.com/10.4103/1735-1995.172991
3. Alvarez-Perea, A., et al.: Impact of "eHealth" in allergic diseases and allergic patients. J. Investig. Allergol. Clin. Immunol. **29**(2), 94–102 (2019). https://doi. org/10.18176/jiaci.0354. http://www.jiaci.org/summary/vol29-issue2-num1763
4. Amft, O.: How wearable computing is shaping digital health. IEEE Pervasive Comput. **17**(1), 92–98 (2018). https://doi.org/10.1109/MPRV.2018.011591067. https://ieeexplore.ieee.org/document/8317990/
5. Anderson, J.K., Wallace, L.M.: Applying the behavioural intervention technologies model to the development of a smartphone application (app) supporting young peoples' adherence to anaphylaxis action plan. BMJ Innovations **1**(2), 67–73 (2015). https://doi.org/10.1136/bmjinnov-2014-000016. https://innovations.bmj. com/lookup/doi/10.1136/bmjinnov-2014-000016
6. Bandura, A.: Social Cognitive Theory: An Agentic Perspective (2000)
7. Barnes, A., BelBruno, J.: (54) Food Allergen Detection Methods and System is Using Molecularly Imprinted Polymers
8. Blechner, M., et al.: Using Contextual Design to Identify Potential Innovations for Problem based Learning (2003)
9. Cho, Y.M., Lee, S., Islam, S.M.S., Kim, S.Y.: Theories applied to m-health interventions for behavior change in low- and middle-income countries: a systematic review. Telemed. e-Health **24**(10), 727–741 (2018). https://doi.org/10.1089/tmj. 2017.0249. https://www.liebertpub.com/doi/10.1089/tmj.2017.0249
10. Cummings, A.J., Knibb, R.C., King, R.M., Lucas, J.S.: The psychosocial impact of food allergy and food hypersensitivity in children, adolescents and their families: a review. Allergy **65**(8), 933–945 (2010). https://doi.org/10.1111/j.1398-9995.2010. 02342.x. https://onlinelibrary.wiley.com/doi/10.1111/j.1398-9995.2010.02342.x
11. Daraghmi, E.Y., Yuan, S.M.: PMR: personalized mobile restaurant system. In: 2013 5th International Conference on Computer Science and Information Technology, pp. 275–282. IEEE, Amman, Jordan (2013). https://doi.org/10.1109/CSIT. 2013.6588792. http://ieeexplore.ieee.org/document/6588792/
12. Davidson, N., et al.: Supporting self-care of adolescents with nut allergy through video and mobile educational tools. In: Proceedings of the 2017 CHI Conference on Human Factors in Computing Systems, pp. 1078–1092. ACM, Denver Colorado USA (2017). https://doi.org/10.1145/3025453.3025680. https://dl.acm.org/doi/10.1145/3025453.3025680
13. Davis, C.M., Kelso, J.M.: Food allergy management. Immunol. Allergy Clin. North Am. **38**(1), 53–64 (2018). https://doi.org/10.1016/j.iac.2017.09.005. https://linkinghub.elsevier.com/retrieve/pii/S0889856117301005

14. Farao, J., Malila, B., Conrad, N., Mutsvangwa, T., Rangaka, M.X., Douglas, T.S.: A user-centred design framework for mHealth. PLoS ONE **15**(8), e0237910 (2020). https://doi.org/10.1371/journal.pone.0237910. https://dx.plos.org/10.1371/journal.pone.0237910

15. Frey, R.M., Ryder, B., Fuchs, K., Ilic, A.: Universal food allergy number. In: Proceedings of the 6th International Conference on the Internet of Things, pp. 157–158. ACM, Stuttgart Germany (2016). https://doi.org/10.1145/2991561.2998462. https://dl.acm.org/doi/10.1145/2991561.2998462

16. Garbett, A., Comber, R., Jenkins, E., Olivier, P.: App movement: a platform for community commissioning of mobile applications. In: Proceedings of the 2016 CHI Conference on Human Factors in Computing Systems, pp. 26–37. ACM, San Jose California USA (2016). https://doi.org/10.1145/2858036.2858094. https://dl.acm.org/doi/10.1145/2858036.2858094

17. Garner, S., et al.: Effectiveness of an mHealth application to improve hypertension health literacy in India. Int. Nurs. Rev. **67**(4), 476–483 (2020). https://doi.org/10.1111/inr.12616. https://onlinelibrary.wiley.com/doi/10.1111/inr.12616

18. Gazzola, A.: Living with Food Allergies. B. Jain Publishers Pvt, Limited (2010)

19. Gupta, R.S., et al.: Prevalence and severity of food allergies among US adults. JAMA Netw. Open **2**(1), e185630 (2019). https://doi.org/10.1001/jamanetworkopen.2018.5630. http://jamanetworkopen.jamanetwork.com/article.aspx

20. Henricksen, K., Viller, S.: Design of software to support families with food-allergic and food-intolerant children. In: Proceedings of the 24th Australian Computer-Human Interaction Conference, pp. 194–203. ACM, Melbourne Australia (2012). https://doi.org/10.1145/2414536.2414571. https://dl.acm.org/doi/10.1145/2414536.2414571

21. Hossny, E., et al.: Challenges of managing food allergy in the developing world. World Allergy Organ. J. **12**(11), 100089 (2019). https://doi.org/10.1016/j.waojou.2019.100089. https://linkinghub.elsevier.com/retrieve/pii/S1939455119312451

22. Hsu, P.P.T., Zhao, J., Liao, K., Liu, T., Wang, C.: AllergyBot: a chatbot technology intervention for young adults with food allergies dining out. In: Proceedings of the 2017 CHI Conference Extended Abstracts on Human Factors in Computing Systems, pp. 74–79. ACM, Denver Colorado USA (2017). https://doi.org/10.1145/3027063.3049270. https://dl.acm.org/doi/10.1145/3027063.3049270

23. Iizuka, K., Okawada, T., Matsuyama, K., Kurihashi, S., Iizuka, Y.: Food menu selection support system: considering constraint conditions for safe dietary life

24. Jadhav, H.C., et al.: Effect of reinforcement of oral health education message through short messaging service in mobile phones: a quasi-experimental trial. Int. J. Telemed. Appl. **2016**, 1–7 (2016). https://doi.org/10.1155/2016/7293516. http://www.hindawi.com/journals/ijta/2016/7293516/

25. Janz, N.K., Becker, M.H.: The health belief model: a decade later. Health Educ. Q. **11**(1), 1–47 (1984). https://doi.org/10.1177/109019818401100101. http://journals.sagepub.com/doi/10.1177/109019818401100101

26. Joshi, V., Joshi, N.K., Bhardwaj, P., Singh, K., Ojha, D., Jain, Y.K.: The health impact of mHealth interventions in India: systematic review and meta-analysis. Online J. Public Health Inform. **15**, e50927 (2023). https://doi.org/10.2196/50927. https://ojphi.jmir.org/2023/1/e50927

27. Kamal, A.K., et al.: A randomized controlled behavioral intervention trial to improve medication adherence in adult stroke patients with prescription tailored Short Messaging Service (SMS)-SMS4Stroke study. BMC Neurol.

15(1), 212 (2015). https://doi.org/10.1186/s12883-015-0471-5. https://bmcneurol. biomedcentral.com/articles/10.1186/s12883-015-0471-5

28. Kurowski, K., Boxer, R.W.: Food allergies: detection and management. Am. Family Physician 77(12), 1678–1686 (2008)

29. Lee, J., et al.: Effectiveness of an application-based neck exercise as a pain management tool for office workers with chronic neck pain and functional disability: a pilot randomized trial. Eur. J. Integr. Med. 12, 87–92 (2017). https:// doi.org/10.1016/j.eujim.2017.04.012. https://linkinghub.elsevier.com/retrieve/pii/ S1876382017300987

30. Mandracchia, F., Llauradó, E., Tarro, L., Valls, R.M., Solà, R.: Mobile phone apps for food allergies or intolerances in app stores: systematic search and quality assessment using the mobile app rating scale (MARS). JMIR Mhealth Uhealth 8(9), e18339 (2020). https://doi.org/10.2196/18339. http://mhealth.jmir.org/2020/9/ e18339/

31. Mbuagbaw, L., et al.: The Cameroon mobile phone SMS (CAMPS) trial: a randomized trial of text messaging versus usual care for adherence to antiretroviral therapy. PLoS ONE 7(12), e46909 (2012). https://doi.org/10.1371/journal.pone. 0046909. https://dx.plos.org/10.1371/journal.pone.0046909

32. Modi, D., et al.: mHealth intervention "ImTeCHO" to improve delivery of maternal, neonatal, and child care services-a cluster-randomized trial in tribal areas of Gujarat. India. PLoS Med. 16(10), e1002939 (2019). https://doi.org/10.1371/ journal.pmed.1002939. https://dx.plos.org/10.1371/journal.pmed.1002939

33. Modi, D., et al.: Costing and cost-effectiveness of a mobile health intervention (ImTeCHO) in improving infant mortality in tribal areas of Gujarat, India: cluster randomized controlled trial. JMIR Mhealth Uhealth 8(10), e17066 (2020). https:// doi.org/10.2196/17066. https://mhealth.jmir.org/2020/10/e17066

34. Muraro, A., et al.: EAACI food allergy and anaphylaxis guidelines: diagnosis and management of food allergy. Allergy 69(8), 1008–1025 (2014). https://doi.org/10. 1111/all.12429. https://onlinelibrary.wiley.com/doi/10.1111/all.12429

35. Murthy, N., et al.: The impact of an mHealth voice message service (mMitra) on infant care knowledge, and practices among low-income women in India: findings from a pseudo-randomized controlled trial. Matern. Child Health J. 23(12), 1658–1669 (2019). https://doi.org/10.1007/s10995-019-02805-5. http:// link.springer.com/10.1007/s10995-019-02805-5

36. Peters, R.L., Mavoa, S., Koplin, J.J.: An overview of environmental risk factors for food allergy. Int. J. Environ. Res. Public Health 19(2), 722 (2022). https://doi. org/10.3390/ijerph19020722. https://www.mdpi.com/1660-4601/19/2/722

37. Pfammatter, A., et al.: mHealth intervention to improve diabetes risk behaviors in India: a prospective, parallel group cohort study. J. Med. Internet Res. 18(8), e207 (2016). https://doi.org/10.2196/jmir.5712. http://www.jmir.org/2016/8/e207/

38. Quevedo, N.M.D.M., Da Costa, C.A., Righi, R.D.R., Rigo, S.J.: A food allergy risk detection model based on situation awareness. J. Appl. Comput. Res. 5(1), 32–43 (2016). https://doi.org/10.4013/jacr.2016.51.03. http://revistas.unisinos.br/index. php/jacr/article/view/10109

39. Raven, M.E., Flanders, A.: Using contextual inquiry to learn about your audiences. ACM SIGDOC Asterisk J. Comput. Doc. 20(1), 1–13 (1996). https://doi.org/10. 1145/227614.227615. https://dl.acm.org/doi/10.1145/227614.227615

40. Rubinstein, A., et al.: Effectiveness of an mHealth intervention to improve the cardiometabolic profile of people with prehypertension in low-resource urban settings in Latin America: a randomised controlled trial. Lancet Diabetes

Endocrinol. **4**(1), 52–63 (2016). https://doi.org/10.1016/S2213-8587(15)00381-2. https://linkinghub.elsevier.com/retrieve/pii/S2213858715003812

41. Shariful Islam, S.M., Niessen, L.W., Ferrari, U., Ali, L., Seissler, J., Lechner, A.: Effects of mobile phone SMS to improve glycemic control among patients with type 2 diabetes in bangladesh: a prospective, parallel-group. Randomized controlled trial. Diabetes Care **38**(8), e112–e113 (2015). https://doi.org/10.2337/dc15-0505. https://diabetesjournals.org/care/article/38/8/e112/31586/Effects-of-Mobile-Phone-SMS-to-Improve-Glycemic

42. Sicherer, S.H., Sampson, H.A.: Food allergy: a review and update on epidemiology, pathogenesis, diagnosis, prevention, and management. J. Allergy Clin. Immunol. **141**(1), 41–58 (2018). https://doi.org/10.1016/j.jaci.2017.11.003. https://linkinghub.elsevier.com/retrieve/pii/S0091674917317943

43. Twomey, N., Temko, A., Hourihane, J.O., Marnane, W.P.: Allergy detection with statistical modelling of HRV-based non-reaction baseline features. In: Proceedings of the 4th International Symposium on Applied Sciences in Biomedical and Communication Technologies, pp. 1–5. ACM, Barcelona Spain (2011). https://doi.org/10.1145/2093698.2093832. https://dl.acm.org/doi/10.1145/2093698.2093832

44. Verhoeven, E., et al.: Digital tools in allergy and respiratory care. World Allergy Organ. J. **15**(7), 100661 (2022). https://doi.org/10.1016/j.waojou.2022.100661. https://linkinghub.elsevier.com/retrieve/pii/S1939455122000370

Visual Feedback Interface for Audio Communication Over Lossy and High Delay Networks

Heinsamding Thou$^{(\boxtimes)}$ ⓘ, Bhaskaran Raman ⓘ, Manish Kumar ⓘ,
and Ajith Pasuvula ⓘ

Indian Institute of Technology Bombay,Mumbai, India
{heinsamding,br,ajith}@cse.iitb.ac.in, 22m2110@iitb.ac.in

Abstract. In an audio communication via VoIP (Voice over Internet Protocol) over a network with high delay and/or loss, participants can step-over each other and have a poor user experience. This paper presents a novel approach to mitigate step-overs during audio call and hence enhance user experience in audio communications, particularly in scenarios characterized by high network delays and/or loss. The proposed solution involves the integration of dynamic visual feedback into the user interface (UI). Through the use of dynamic animations displayed on the user's screen, real-time updates regarding the reception status of the transmitted audio, at the intended recipient are provided. This innovative method aims to enhance the user experience during audio communication sessions under adverse network conditions. We employed a combination of qualitative and quantitative methods to validate our hypothesis, which aimed to reduce step-overs during audio calls with high delay, ultimately enhancing the user experience. The results were positive, with participants reporting improved experiences when animation was enabled where the average rating of the Mean Opinion Score (MOS), which ranges from 1 to 5 (with 1 indicating the lowest and 5 indicating the highest satisfaction), increased from 2.6 to 3.7. And we also observed a significant reduction of approximately 35% in step-overs when the animation was enabled ("animation on") as compared to when it was disabled ("animation off").

Keywords: HCI · VoIP · Animation · VCA · high delay · lossy network · User experience · User study · Pilot study

1 Introduction

Numerous Video Conferencing Applications (VCA) such as Microsoft Teams, Zoom, and Google Meet facilitate audio communication. While these platforms have demonstrated commendable performance, they generally lack or inadequately provide user feedback on their screens. Microsoft Teams has made attempts to furnish users with certain metrics [18] like Round Trip Time (RTT),

© The Author(s), under exclusive license to Springer Nature Switzerland AG 2025
N. Rangaswamy et al. (Eds.): IndiaHCI 2024, CCIS 2337, pp. 326–343, 2025.
https://doi.org/10.1007/978-3-031-80829-6_15

Received Packet Loss, Teams Send Limit, and Teams Received Limit. Similar to Teams, Zoom offers a "Call Quality" indicator [19] within the call window, displaying real-time network metrics like packet loss, jitter, and latency. Meet doesn't directly display detailed network metrics during calls. However, users can access basic information like connection strength and bandwidth usage through the settings menu. Webex provides real-time network metrics [20] like bandwidth usage, latency, and jitter within the call window. This information is available for both individual users and meeting hosts. Skype displays basic connection status indicators like "Excellent," "Good," or "Poor" during calls. Clicking on this indicator reveals limited information like average latency and packet loss. However, a major issue lies in the complexity of interpreting these statistics, even for individuals with technical proficiency, let alone the general population.

Consider a scenario during a voice call where there is a noticeable delay in your voice reaching the other person, causing interruptions and overlaps in the conversation, where the two speakers step-over each other. In such a situation, individuals often resort to manually coordinating their speech by inserting pauses or providing cues to ensure a smoother conversation. What if cues from the user's interface on the phone were automatically provided instead of relying on manual input?

In this work, we ask the question: Can the user experience be improved by providing suitable visual feedback on the user's phone screen?. In the [8] paper, the author suggests that incorporating visual elements can enhance people's understanding and improve their interpretation of information. We start with the observation that today, most VoIP conversations use a device with a rich screen, such as a smart-phone or a laptop. Can we use the screen to provide the visual feedback?

Our approach involves addressing this issue by automating the feedback process by providing visual animations on their screen. These animations serve as cues to help users time their speech, ultimately reducing interruptions and step-overs during the conversation. Considering these factors and the current landscape, our proposed design offers a compelling solution to enriching user experiences, especially when confronted with challenges arising from high network delay and/or packet loss.

Designing the animation posed its own set of challenges, particularly in ensuring user-friendliness and intuitive functionality because our approach aimed to visually represent the latency and audio loss through animations, distinguishing it from the conventional method of presenting such information solely through numerical values, as commonly observed in other mainstream video and audio conferencing applications. Our focus was on creating a design that would enhance the user experience, specifically for the speaker, by providing feedback on the status of their audio packets reaching the receiver. In our design we adopted a visual approach. We introduced a speaking icon to symbolize the speaker, from where the audio packets are generated, and a listening icon to indicate the receiver's reception status (see Fig. 2). Through appropriate representation of these packets, and their movement on the screen based on feedback from the receiver side, we intuitively convey the network quality in terms of delay and loss to the user.

We have implemented a prototype of our proposed UI, and have conducted a user-study on 40 users[1]. It yielded positive reviews regarding the user experience, and we achieved around 35% reduction in step-overs as well as improved average rating in user experience from 2.6 to 3.7 when the animation was enabled compared to when the animation was disabled. The qualitative feedback from the users suggests that we were able to address the challenge of intuitive UI design effectively.

In the following section, we provide a concise summary of the feedback mechanism used by popular VoIP tools (Sect. 2). The next section then delves into the architecture and interface design (Sect. 3) including the details of our implementation. We then provide insights into the methodology employed for the user study (Sect. 4), elaborate on the process of data collection and its evaluation. Moving forward, we engage in a discussion of the obtained results (Sect. 5). Lastly, the paper concludes with an exploration of the challenges encountered during the user study and the valuable lessons derived from these experiences (Sect. 6).

2   Feedback Mechanism in Popular VoIP Tools

Although the domain of Voice-over-IP is quite old, to our knowledge, most systems do not show any user feedback when network conditions are poor. Users are left to themselves in identifying the poor conditions, such as by saying "sorry, can you please repeat". Among the popular commercial tools as far as we are concerned, initially MS Teams was the first to provide network-related information [18] to the user. For audio, they have incorporated metrics such as sent packets, Round Trip time (RTT), received jitter, received packets, received packet loss, and more. Similarly, other widely-used video and audio conferencing applications have begun offering network information to users. For instance, Webex provides metrics such as bandwidth usage, latency, and jitter [20], while Zoom offers data on packet loss, jitter, and latency [19]. Although Google Meet does not directly present detailed network metrics during calls, users can access basic information such as connection strength and bandwidth usage through the settings menu. Additionally, Skype displays basic connection status indicators like "Excellent," "Good," or "Poor" during calls. However, it is worth noting that while some of these metrics can be comprehended by individuals with technical expertise, they are not user-friendly and are not designed for the average user, making them of limited utility for the general audience. The feature in WhatsApp that displays "typing..." to the user is intuitive and provides the receiver with information that the other person is in the process of typing a message. This feature enhances the user experience. WhatsApp's implementation of this feature also served as motivation for our work. Our interface design for real time audio conversation is

---

[1] As the individuals participating in our experiment serve as evaluators rather than subjects, formal approval from the institute was not sought.

more challenging however as we need to convey complex network conditions to naive users.

3   System Architecture and UI Design

3.1   The System Architecture of Our Proposed System

The architecture comprises three key components: the speaker, the server, and the receiver (as depicted in Fig. 1). It is worth emphasizing that our current focus is on audio communication between two users, with plans to expand to multiple users in the future.

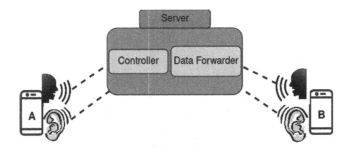

Fig. 1. System Architecture

The server itself is divided into two distinct segments: the Controller and the Data Forwarder. The primary role of the controller is to manage data validation when a client (in this context, referring to both the speaker and the receiver) submits a request to create or join a meeting room. The primary function of the data forwarder is to relay the audio data from the speaker to the receiver. It also relays important feedback information regarding network performance as seen by one party to the other. As depicted in Fig. 1, both Client A and B assume the roles of speaker and listener. However, it is crucial to emphasize that the visual feedback provided is with respect to the speaker's actions. That is, the UI seen by client-A is relevant to A's role as speaker in the conversation, while the UI seen by client-B is relevant to B's role as speaker in the conversation.

3.2   Visual Feedback: The Design

Our primary intuition is to provide the speaker with a visual representation of the time it takes for audio Fackets to reach the receiver, essentially indicating the delay incurred, as well as identifying any lost audio packets. We conjecture that conveying this information intuitively to the speaker will make the speaker adjust naturally, and avoid situations of over-stepping and subsequent frustration. Consequently, our design revolves around achieving this goal and this design relies on constant feedback from the receiver. In this subsection, we will primarily focus on discussing the design and functionality of the animation. Subsequently, in the next subsection, we will delve into the specific implementation details.

To achieve UI design, we incorporate the concept of acknowledgment, drawing inspiration from TCP (Transmission Control Protocol) [22]. This involves assigning a unique sequence number to each audio packet before it is transmitted. Consequently, when the receiver receives an audio packet, it can promptly generate and transmit the corresponding acknowledgment back to the sender. The UI screen design includes a rectangular container situated between a speaker icon

Fig. 2. Example of user interface with animation

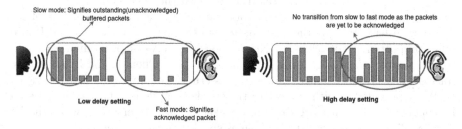

Fig. 3. Example of packet delay experienced by the speaker

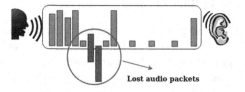

Fig. 4. Example of packet lost experienced by the speaker

and a listener icon. Within the rectangular container, there is an animated representation of audio playback. This animation offers dual speed modes: a deliberate, unhurried pace characterized as "slow," and an accelerated pace denoted as "fast". Furthermore, the height of the animation is dynamically influenced by the intensity of the user's voice. As the user continues to speak, a rectangular bar (light blue in colour) representing each audio packet (each packet has a sequence number associated with it) is sequentially added to the rectangular container (see Fig. 2). These rectangular bars begin to move at a steady, slow pace toward the receiver's icon as it accumulates in the container. However, when the speaker's phone receives an acknowledgment (the receiver's phone generates acknowledgments for each received audio packet) from the receiver's phone, the animation promptly transitions into the faster mode. Following this transition, the animation concludes its visual trajectory, exiting the user's screen. This visually indicates to the speaking user, that those particular audio packets have been successfully received at the receiver. We intend that even a layperson user can interpret (correctly) that that section of the audio had been heard by the listener. This entire process, from the bar's initial addition to the user's screen to its departure towards the listener's icon after receiving acknowledgment, symbolizes the **delay** (see Fig. 3) experienced by the audio packet. Figure 3 provides examples illustrating both low delay and high delay scenarios. In the low delay scenario, the speaker will see only a few rectangular bars in the slow moving left part of the screen. Whereas in the high delay scenario the speaker will see a lot more blue bars queued up, yet to be heard by the listener. This approach ensures a streamlined and informative representation of audio transmission progress, enhancing the user's comprehension of network delay in the communication process. Regarding **lost** (see Fig. 4) audio packets, we have represented them using a red-colored bar in the UI. As these light blue bars are added to the user's screen while the user is speaking, the speaker's phone continually awaits acknowledgment, specifically the acknowledgment associated with the received audio packet's sequence number. For instance, if the sequence number "n" of the audio packet is added to the user's screen, it proceeds to move at a slow pace toward the listener's icon until it receives acknowledgment for "n". When the speaker's phone does receive the acknowledgment, denoted as "s", it calculates a value "m = s-3". This value "3" means that it allows up to 3 out-of-order packets similar to the context of TCP 3 duplicate acknowledgments [22] which allows up to 3 out-of-order packets. Subsequently, we compare whether n is less than or equal to m. If this condition holds true, the bar corresponding to sequence number "n" changes to a red color and promptly descends from the screen in a downward motion until it disappears. This serves as a visual indicator of lost sections of the audio. In a high loss scenario, we intend that with such visualization, even a naive user can interpret that large sections of the audio are dropped by the network and simply not being heard by the listener.

3.3   Implementation Details

With the above described visual depictions of network delay and loss behaviour, to the speaker, our conjecture is that the human speaker will naturally adjust their expectations - leading to minimized step overs in the conversation and overall enhanced user experience. We now describe the prototype implementation followed by our validation study of this conjecture. We have developed a prototype for the proposed UI design, along with the required server system. The primary intention behind building this prototype was to facilitate the user study. The designed prototype starts by sending create or join (as shown in Fig. 5) request of a meeting room to the controller using a TCP (Transmission Control Protocol) socket (see Fig. 6(a)), then the controller checks for the validation of the requested data. After conducting the necessary validation and confirming the authenticity of the request, the controller proceeds to forward (see Fig. 6(a)) the pertinent details, such as the Room ID to the data forwarder.

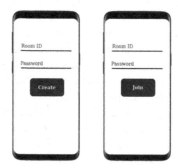

Fig. 5. Example of Creating/ Joining a meeting

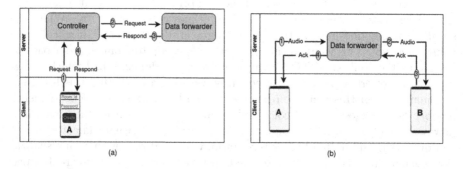

Fig. 6. Steps involve in creating/ joining room and audio communication

The Data Forwarder, on the other hand, is responsible for establishing two UDP (User Datagram Protocol) sockets-one for audio and another for acknowledgments-corresponding to the identified Room ID. These sockets are then sent back to the client via the controller as response, utilizing a TCP socket, as visualized in Fig. 6(a). The reason for routing the response through the controller is because there is no direct connection between the client and the Data Forwarder at this point. Such an approach also permits one or both clients to be behind NAT (Network Address Translation) routers - a very common scenario in today's networks. Upon receiving this response, the client also initiates the creation of two UDP ports-one for audio and one for acknowledgments. Subsequently, it expeditiously transmits a dummy message to the Data Forwarder, sending one to the audio socket from the audio socket of the client and another to the acknowledgment socket from the acknowledgement socket of the client. This action serves to record the IP address and port of the client for future use. A data structure within the Data Forwarder is utilized to maintain the collection of client IP addresses and corresponding ports for each meeting room.

After completing the aforementioned procedures, the actual communication commences. When the speaker begins speaking, the audio data initially travels to the Data Forwarder. Subsequently, the Data Forwarder forwards this audio data to the receiver (see Fig. 6(b)).

It is important to note that this communication occurs through UDP (User Datagram Protocol) sockets. To facilitate this, we employ RTP (Real-time Transport Protocol) over UDP [17]. The mechanism of acknowledgment is facilitated through the incorporation of a sequence number field within the Real-Time Protocol (RTP) header. RTP includes a sequence number within its header, which is attached to every audio packet before sending out. Upon receiving the audio, the receiver utilizes this sequence number to generate the appropriate acknowledgment for each packet and promptly transmits it back to the sender.

4   User Study

We conducted two user studies, each with 40 participants, to evaluate whether the animation displayed on the user's screen was helpful in identifying possible disruptions during a call. The first study had some shortcomings, which led to the design and execution of a second study to address these issues. Further details are discussed in the following subsection.

4.1   First Study: The Set-up and The Details

The objective of our study with 40 participants was to determine if they could identify disruptions in a conversation by observing the animation displayed on their mobile phone's user interface. To achieve this, we introduced a one-way delay and packet loss from the speaker to the receiver, making the conversation appear smooth except for the delayed responses. For our study, we utilized two Android smartphones: a Realme X running Android version 10 and a OnePlus Nord CE2 running Android version 13. We introduced a one-way delay of 2 s and a packet loss rate of 20% from the Realme X to the OnePlus Nord CE2 using Linux Network Traffic Control. To minimize any unforeseen delays or packet loss during the conversation, we opted to use institutional Wi-Fi instead of mobile internet.

For our study, we conducted two separate recordings of conversations between the same two researchers. In both recordings, one person acted as the speaker using the Realme X, while the other served as the receiver using the OnePlus Nord CE2. The speaker asked a series of structured questions, to which the receiver responded.

Both conversations were carried out in a quiet environment within the department to ensure no disturbances affected the recordings. The first conversation was conducted under normal conditions, without any network delays or packet loss, and lasted 33 s (Recording_1). In the second conversation, we introduced a one-way delay of 2 s and a packet loss rate of 20% from the speaker (Realme X) to the receiver (OnePlus Nord CE2), resulting in a recording duration of 43 s (Recording_2). The recording was conducted using the Realme X. The purpose of introducing a one-way delay was to ensure that participants in the user study did not perceive a disruption solely based on the audio conversation. Aside from the response delay, there were no significant differences between the two recordings.

4.2 First Study: The Process

We initiated our study by approaching random individuals in the hostel, first seeking their consent to participate in our user study. After obtaining consent, we provided a brief explanation of the user interface shown in Fig. 2, including the symbolism of the icons, the meaning of the audio bars, and their functionality, which took approximately 15 s.

We informed the participants that they would watch a recording of our conversation, after which they would be asked a question. To prevent any response bias, we randomized the order in which the recordings were shown. After showing each recording, we asked the participant, "Do you think/feel there was any disruption in the conversation? (Q_1)" The possible responses were Yes, No, or Maybe.

For those who answered "Yes," we followed up with, "How were you able to identify the disruption in the conversation? (Q_2)" This question was asked to determine if the feedback displayed on the user screen helped identify the disruption in the conversation. For participants who responded "Maybe," we asked, "What was the difficulty in identifying the disruption? (Q_3)" This additional feedback was sought to identify potential areas for improvement in our prototype.

4.3 First Study: Data Collection and Results

We conducted a user study with 40 participants from the institute, as this is a pilot study. Our aim is to expand the user study to a larger group and eventually deploy our prototype more broadly. Participants viewed two recordings, and their responses were collected accordingly.

For Recording 1 (R_1) with no delay or loss, 32 out of 40 participants did not perceive any disruption in the conversation. Of the remaining 8, 4 answered "Yes" to Question 1 (Q_1) and were subsequently asked Question 2 (Q_2). They indicated that they identified the disruption through both audio quality and animation. Another 4 participants who responded "Maybe" were asked Question 3 (Q_3) and mentioned that they could not understand the animation shown in the user interface.

For Recording 2 (R_2), which included a 2-s delay and 20% packet loss, 28 out of 40 participants identified disruptions. They were then asked Q_2. Of these, 22 from the 28 participants identified the disruption solely from the delayed responses in the audio, 5 from the 28 participants identified it through both audio and animation, and 1 from the 28 participants identified it through animation alone.

Among the remaining 12 participants, 1 answered "Maybe" to Q_1 for R_2 and, upon follow-up with Q_3, explained that they could not determine whether there was a disruption or if the receiver was deliberately pausing before responding. The other 11 participants did not perceive any disruption in R_2. Upon reviewing our data, we noted that these 11 participants had viewed R_2 before R_1. We suspect that their inability to identify the disruption in R_2 may be due to their lack of familiarity with a conversation without disruptions.

In Recording 1 (R_1), which had no disruptions, 4 participants incorrectly identified a disruption, likely due to background noise. However, 32 participants correctly perceived no disruption.

In Recording 2 (R_2), 28 participants correctly identified the disruption, but 22 did so without relying on the animation (visual feedback) on their screens. Only 6 participants found the animation helpful. This suggests that participants were unfamiliar with the new audio conferencing interface and had difficulty interpreting the animation, even when they paid attention to it.

The study revealed several shortcomings: participants were not directly involved in the conversation, and they were shown only a short recording. Additionally, the interface design was not adequately explained. To address these issues, we conducted another user study involving live conversations with participants and provided a demo video along with a detailed explanation of how the animation works.

4.4   Second Study: The Set-up

In our user study, we utilized two Android smartphones, specifically the Realme X (android version 10) and a OnePlus Nord ce2 (android version 13). We employed earphones to ensure optimal audio quality and minimize external noise interference. The audio transmission followed a path from the speaker to the server and then to the receiver. Our research focuses on investigating user experience in a specific context marked by significant delays. To simulate the delays users may encounter, we deliberately introduced a 1.5-second delay in the server system utilizing Linux Network Traffic Control. The delay was selected by experimenting to find the right amount that would disrupt the conversation slightly. In our study, we opted for an institutional Wi-Fi network instead of relying on standard mobile internet. This choice was made to minimize the presence of any unforeseen delays between the two phones. All this set-up (especially including the delay) was important as we wanted to simulate a delay just enough to hamper the user experience by making them step-over each other during conversation. The experiment was carried out within a controlled environment, comprising both a dedicated room where the participants were placed in different rooms and laboratory setting, aimed at mitigating potential external noise interference that could disrupt the integrity of the conducted conversations.

4.5   Second Study: The Process

The user study was conducted with the primary objective of assessing the impact of on-screen animations on mitigating conversational interruptions and thereby enhancing the overall user experience. The study was meticulously designed to encompass both qualitative and quantitative measurements. Prior to the conversation, all participants were presented with a brief demonstration video, illustrating the functioning of the animation. The methodology involved pairing two participants for each experimental session, with the presence of two researchers of this research project facilitating the setup process, which included the provision of necessary credentials such as an "id" and "password," as well as an explanation of the procedure of how the experiment will be carried out. We also ensured that participants were informed of the importance of equitable contribution from both individuals engaged in the conversation, emphasizing the significance of avoiding dominance by either party. This approach was adopted to facilitate the quantification of interruptions, or "step-overs," during the course of the conversation. To mitigate the challenge of participants experiencing difficulty engaging in spontaneous conversation during the experiment, we utilized a randomized shopping list of grocery items displayed on a computer screen. However, this approach inadvertently redirected participants' focus away from the phone screen and toward the shopping list on the computer screen, introducing a new issue. Subsequently, the two users engaged in a 2-minute conversation without the presence of the animation on their screens. This was followed by another 2-minute conversation session during which the animation was visible on the user's screen. Importantly, both conversations, both with and without the animation, were recorded on the user's device with their explicit consent. We chose to limit the conversation to a duration of 2 min because it was challenging for the participants to engage in continuous conversation for an extended period.

Post-conversation, user feedback was systematically collected through a structured questionnaire, the details of which are elaborated upon in a subsequent subsection.

4.6   Second Study: Data Collection and Analysis

In order to comprehensively evaluate our outcomes, we adopted a dual-pronged approach, incorporating both qualitative and quantitative methods. Our study encompassed a total of 40 participants.

For the qualitative aspect of our assessment, we devised a set of five structured questions to elicit detailed responses from the participants. It is important to observe that the questions were developed in alignment with the nature of the study, which, in this case, was a pilot study. These questions were instrumental in gauging their subjective experiences and insights. The questions encompassed various domains: the first two inquiries focused on satisfaction, here we employed the Mean Opinion Score (MOS), which is often referred to as a Likert scale [14]. This scale is commonly utilized for assessing opinions, with a range from 1, representing a negative rating, to 5, signifying an excellent rating [16]. The third addressed the user interface (UI), the fourth centered around improvement, and the final question was of a more general nature.

1. How was your experience without animation on a scale of 1 to 5?
2. How was your experience with animation on a scale of 1 to 5?
3. Any difficulties in understanding the interface of the application?
4. What improvements would you suggest for this application, or are there any features you would like to add?
5. Will you prefer animation for audio communication in the future? (In poor network as well as in a stable network)

In pursuit of quantitative assessment, we endeavored to quantify instances of conversational interruptions, specifically focusing on the occurrence of "stepping-over" during the course of conversations. it is noteworthy that we conducted two distinct conversations, one with the presence of the animation and one without. To accomplish this, we recorded the participants' screen during these conversations, diligently obtaining their consent for this purpose. Subsequently, we meticulously compared and analyzed the occurrences of "stepping-over" in both conversations to draw meaningful quantitative conclusions. It is crucial to emphasize that we are specifically focusing on addressing step-overs in conversations caused by delays, rather than those that occur when one person does not wait for the other to finish speaking and starts talking.

4.7   Second Study: The Outcome

We were able to include a total of 40 participants, all of whom were students from our institute. This was due to the pilot nature of the study, where ROSCOE's rule of thumb [1] states that "for experiment with tight controls, successful research may be conducted with samples as small as 10 to 20" and moreover there were time constraint as well. **MOS reduction:** Regarding the qualitative results, participants provided an average rating of 2.6 for their experience during a two-minute audio communication without the presence of animation. However, this rating significantly improved to an average of 3.7 as shown in Fig. 7 when animation was activated during the two-minute conversation. Additionally, the variability in Mean Opinion Score (MOS) decreased notably from 0.83 to 0.65 (see Fig. 7) with the activation of the animation feature. **Ease of understanding UI:** In response to a question related to the ease of understanding the interface, 7 out of the 40 participants reported difficulty in comprehending how the animation on the user's screen functioned while 2 of them initially encountered challenges in comprehending the animation, their understanding improved progressively as they went on with the conversation, as for the remaining 31 participants they encountered no challenges or difficulties. This is significant, as we spent very little time familiarizing users with the UI screen of our visualization design **Feedback on further improvements:** When participants were asked about potential improvements for the Android application, many suggested enhancing the user interface, which includes modifying how the user's audio is represented on the screen, like changing the design of the bar into rounded shapes, displaying text indicating that there is a delay or loss of audio, making the animation more user-friendly. Additionally, one participant recommended the inclusion of a loudspeaker button. Incorporating these suggestions are part of our future work. Given our emphasis on furnishing feedback to speakers regarding the status of their audio packets reaching the receiver, some participants proposed extending this feedback mechanism to encompass the receiver as well. This expansion, they posited, could potentially enhance communication efficacy by minimizing interruptions during conversations. **Overall participant preference for visual feedback:** The fifth question inquired about participants' preferences regarding incorporating animation in audio calls in the future. Out of the respondents, 25 participants expressed a strong preference for including animation in all calls. 9 participants indicated they would prefer animation only for important calls, 3 participants expressed the necessity for the inclusion of animations specifically tailored for instances of poor network conditions, while the remaining 3 participants stated they saw no need for animation during calls and believed they could manually adjust to any call delays (see Fig. 8). When asked about the reason, they specified that they found discomfort in looking at the phone screen while talking. For those who wanted the animation, they were able to synchronize themselves with the help of the audio status provided in the user's screen, hence the conversation was smoother. We also aimed to quantify the number of step-overs that occurred due to audio delay and assess whether the presence of animation had an impact on reducing these step-overs. As previously mentioned, we recorded the conversations of each participant with and without animation. And we found out that there were total of 72 step-overs during "animation off" and total of 47 step-overs during "animation on". Although minimal, there was variation of step-over behavior among a few individuals. For some individuals who has more step-overs during the conversation, the animation did not seem to help them much as their focus was not on the screen.

By comparing the instances of step-overs in the "animation off" and "animation on" conditions, we calculated the percentage difference. Our findings

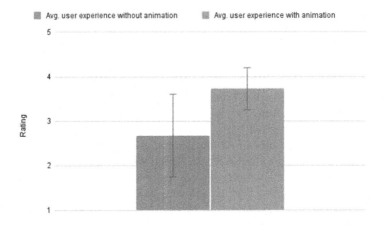

Fig. 7. Average rating of user experience with and without animation

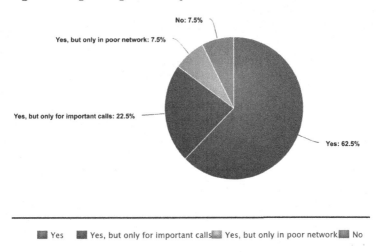

Fig. 8. User preference of using animation

revealed that there was an approximate **35% reduction** in step-overs when animation was enabled.

It is worth noting that this reduction occurred even though participants were not entirely familiarized with the animation, and many of them tend to avert their gaze from the phone's screen because they are not accustomed to it. Therefore, we anticipate that the reduction in step-overs could potentially be even greater if participants were given more time to become familiar with the animation. This could be explored in a future user study.

5 Challenges and Lesson Learnt

It proved challenging to encourage participants to engage in random conversations, particularly because finding suitable discussion topics between two strangers proved difficult. Additionally, participants were aware that their conversations were being recorded, which added to their hesitation. This behavior aligns with the findings from recent studies on digital dataveillance [13], which suggest that the awareness of being monitored can lead to a chilling effect on communication, causing self-censorship and reduced willingness to engage freely.

To address this issue, we initially attempted to introduce an element of randomness by generating a shopping list on the computer screen using a Python script. The idea was for one participant to convey the list to the other, introducing a conversational task. However, this approach had the unintended consequence of diverting their attention away from the phone's screen and towards the shopping list displayed on the computer's screen. In the end, our solution was to enlist participants who shared a pre-existing friendship. This approach effectively addressed the issue, leading to more seamless and natural conversations during the study.

Our primary aim for the 2-minute conversation was to simulate a high-delay network, leading to participants unintentionally talking over each other. However, we observed that for overlapping speech to occur more frequently, both participants needed to contribute to the conversation almost equally, which was not always the case. Sometimes, one participant dominated the conversation.

We also noted that it is a common tendency for people not to maintain constant eye contact with their phone screens during voice calls. This presented a challenge since our research relied on participants paying attention to the animations displayed on their screens during the call. This issue can be addressed by possibly exploring short vibrations on a smart phone? to convey a large delay? Or short beeps in audio? Studies like "Unveiling the Touch Revolution" [6] and "Good Vibrations" [7] shows that haptic feedback has been shown to enhance user engagement and responsiveness by providing tactile cues that capture attention even when visual focus is not constant.

In our evaluation, we required an uninterrupted continuous conversation between two individuals. However, it proved challenging for some of them to sustain a continuous conversation for an extended period without breaks.

The efficacy of a demonstration video was found to be limited, as some participants appeared to deviate from the primary focus of our work, despite its initial presentation. Consequently, they became engrossed in conversation, neglecting to refer back to the phone during their interactions.

Furthermore, we recognized that a few minutes of conversation were insufficient to make users comfortable with this new mode of audio communication, where looking at the screen is crucial. To obtain more valuable insights, we concluded that another user study would be necessary, allowing users to use the application over an extended period to become familiar with this novel approach to audio communication and provide meaningful feedback. We are greatly encouraged by the fact that even in our limited study, step overs reduced significantly and MOS improved from 2.6 to 3.7 with the use of our visual feedback.

6   Conclusion and Future Work

In VoIP (Voice over Internet Protocol) technology, the issue of participants talking over each other in high-delay or lossy network conditions can be frustrating and diminish the user experience. Therefore, our approach involves employing animations on the user's screen to convey information about audio packet delays and losses to the speaker. This is done with the expectation that the speaker will naturally adjust their communication, thereby reducing instances of talking over each other and ultimately enhancing the user experience.

The user study results are encouraging, with positive reviews about the user experience and approximately 35% reduction in step-overs achieved. However, there is still significant room for improvement in our work. We acknowledge the need to enhance the user interface, possibly revise the representation of audio in the user's interface and making them more intuitive. Despite these areas for improvement, the results were promising.

In our present study, we have exclusively simulated fixed delays, while losses were randomly determined by network conditions. Our future plans involve conducting experiments with variable delays and introducing loss alongside these delays.

We believe that user familiarity with the new method of audio communication, such as looking at the phone's screen during conversations, could further reduce the instances of step-overs. To explore this, we plan to allow users more time to familiarize themselves with the application, which we expect will yield even better results.

Looking ahead, we are also considering expanding our work to accommodate multi-user audio conference, as we continue to refine and develop our approach.

Acknowledgments. We would like to extend our heartfelt appreciation to all the participants who generously devoted their time and provided invaluable feedback during the user study. Their contributions were instrumental in the success of this endeavor. We would also like to express our gratitude to Akshay Patidar for his time and assistance in conducting the user study.

References

1. Hill, R.: What sample size is "enough" in internet survey research. Interpersonal Comput. Technol.: Electron. J. 21st Century **6**(3-4), 1–12 (1998)
2. Johanson, G.A., Brooks, G.P.: Initial scale development: sample size for pilot studies. Educ. Psychol. Measur. **70**(3), 394–400 (2010). https://doi.org/10.1177/0013164409355692
3. Viechtbauer, W., et al.: A simple formula for the calculation of sample size in pilot studies. J. Clin. Epidemiol. **68**(11), 1375–1379 (2015). https://doi.org/10.1016/j.jclinepi.2015.04.014

4. Sim, J., Saunders, B., Waterfield, J., Kingstone, T.: Can sample size in qualitative research be determined a priori? Int. J. Soc. Res. Methodol. **21**(5), 619–634 (2018). https://doi.org/10.1080/13645579.2018.1454643

5. Lakens, D.: Sample size justification. Collabra. Psychol. **8**(1), 33267 (2022). https://doi.org/10.1525/collabra.33267

6. He, L.: Unveiling the touch revolution: how haptic feedback elevates wearable device experiences. arXiv preprint arXiv:2307.16179 (2023). https://doi.org/10.48550/arXiv.2307.16179

7. Hadi, R., Valenzuela, A.: Good vibrations: consumer responses to technology-mediated haptic feedback. J. Consum. Res. **47**(2), 256–271 (2020)

8. Tversky, B., Morrison, J.B., Betrancourt, M.: Animation: can it facilitate? Int. J. Hum Comput Stud. **57**(4), 247–262 (2002). https://doi.org/10.1006/ijhc.2002.1017

9. Franconeri, S.L., Padilla, L.M., Shah, P., Zacks, J.M., Hullman, J.: The science of visual data communication: what works. Psychol. Sci. Publ. Interest **22**(3), 110–161 (2021). https://doi.org/10.1177/15291006211051956

10. Munzner, T.: Visualization Analysis and Design. CRC Press, Boca Raton (2014)

11. Head, V.: Designing Interface Animation: Improving the User Experience Through Animation. Rosenfeld Media, New York (2016)

12. Kim, D.H., Hoque, E., Agrawala, M.: Answering questions about charts and generating visual explanations. In: Proceedings of the 2020 CHI Conference on Human Factors in Computing Systems, pp. 1–13 (2020). https://doi.org/10.1145/3313831.3376467

13. Büchi, M., Festic, N., Latzer, M.: The chilling effects of digital dataveillance: a theoretical model and an empirical research agenda. In: Big Data & Society, vol. 9, no. 1, pp. 20539517211065368 (2022). https://doi.org/10.1177/20539517211065368

14. Lewis, J.R.: Psychometric properties of the mean opinion scale. In: Proceedings of HCI International 2001: Usability Evaluation and Interface Design, pp. 149–153 (2001)

15. Heimdahl, O.: How can thoughtful use of animations in mobile user interfaces increase user understanding and performance? In: Student Conference in Interaction Technology and Design, pp. 77

16. Streijl, R.C., Winkler, S., Hands, D.S.: Mean opinion score (MOS) revisited: methods and applications, limitations and alternatives. Multimedia Syst. **22**(2), 213–227 (2016). https://link.springer.com/article/10.1007/s00530-014-0446-1

17. Karapantazis, S., Pavlidou, F.-N.: VoIP: a comprehensive survey on a promising technology. Comput. Netw. **53**(12), 2050–2090 (2009). https://doi.org/10.1016/j.comnet.2009.03.010

18. Microsoft Corporation: Monitor call and meeting quality in Microsoft Teams. https://support.microsoft.com/en-gb/office/monitor-call-and-meeting-quality-in-microsoft-teams-7bb1747c-linebreakd91a-4fbb-84f6-ad3f48e73511. Accessed 10 Feb 2023 (2022)

19. Zoom Video Communications, Inc.: Network Connectivity Test and Call Quality Indicators in Zoom. https://support.zoom.com/hc/en/article?id=zm_kb&sysparm_article=KB0070504. Accessed 20 Jan 2024 (2024)

20. Cisco Systems, Inc.: Check the performance of your Webex meetings. https://help.webex.com/en-us/article/ns63yvy/Check-the-performance-of-your-Webex-meetings. Accessed 10 Jan 2024 (2023)

21. Audio-Video Transport Working Group, Schulzrinne, H., Casner, S., Frederick, R., Jacobson, V., et al.: RTP: a transport protocol for real-time applications. RFC 1889, RFC Editor (1996). https://www.rfc-editor.org/rfc/rfc3550
22. Allman, M., Paxson, V., Blanton, E.: TCP congestion control. RFC 5681, RFC Editor (2009). https://dl.acm.org/doi/abs/10.17487/RFC5681

Author Index

Printed in the United States
by Baker & Taylor Publisher Services

.